Direct
33.50
Sep 2 '80

READINGS
IN BUSINESS CYCLE
THEORY

AMS PRESS
NEW YORK

READINGS IN BUSINESS CYCLE THEORY

Selected by a Committee of
THE AMERICAN ECONOMIC ASSOCIATION

Philadelphia   Toronto
THE BLAKISTON COMPANY
1951

Wingate College Library

Library of Congress Cataloging in Publication Data

American Economic Association.
Readings in business cycle theory.

Reprint of the 1951 issue of the work published by
Blakiston Co., Philadelphia, which was issued as v. 2
of Blakiston series of republished articles on economics.
"Bibliography of the literature on business cycle
theory, by Harold M. Somers": p.
Includes index.
1. Business cycles—Addresses, essays, lectures.
I. Title.
HB3711.A426   1980   338.5'42'01   76-29403
ISBN 0-404-15330-5   Sep 2 '80

Reprinted from the edition of 1951, Philadelphia. Trim size
of the original has been slightly altered. [original trim size:
14.5 × 21.2 cm]. Text area remains the same.

MANUFACTURED
IN THE UNITED STATES OF AMERICA

To
The Memory of
DR. HORACE G. WHITE, JR.

Whose diligence, scholarship and enthusiasm were of invaluable help in starting this series of republished articles in economics.

The ship on which he sailed, on a government mission, was torpedoed in the North Atlantic in February, 1943.

PREFACE

The Blakiston Series of Republished Articles on Economics is designed to make accessible in its successive volumes the most useful periodical literature in the various fields of economic analysis and policy. By an agreement between The Blakiston Company and the American Economic Association, the Company, during an initial experimental term, will undertake the publication of an annual volume devoted to a subject chosen by a standing committee of the Association and edited by a special committee of experts on that subject. The favorable reception of the first volume in the series—Social Control of Industry—has encouraged the publishers to continue the venture without interruption despite technical and editorial difficulties entailed by the war.

Primarily the Series is oriented toward the tuition of senior and graduate university students; but there is also the hope that professional economists will find it a useful means of keeping abreast of developments in other fields than their own. Thus the Series may help to lessen the intellectual provincialism of specialists, which, it is said, threatens them with having nothing in common, not even an education. Furthermore, despite the aridity which economists seem to cherish, and despite their affectation of technical jargon and even of terminological monsters called up for the occasion, the intelligent layman will in general be able to find his way successfully through these collections to his lasting benefit, if not delight.

It should go without saying that the editorial committees desire not only to acquaint the reader with doctrines common to many or all of the scholars in the field, with the contentious issues, and with the more interesting idiosyncracies of certain writers, but also to do all this without bias in the selection of content.

These requirements imposed upon the editors of the present volume, under the chairmanship of Professor Gottfried Haberler, a singularly arduous task, since the subject matter includes, beside the technical analysis of cyclical variations, the expression of profound and sometimes violent differences in economic and social philosophy extending far beyond the sphere of the immediate subject.

The Series will be continued in a third collection of articles, edited by a committee of which Proffessor Bernard F. Haley is chairman, devoted to distribution theory, the national income, and the distributive shares. Suggestions regarding future volumes are welcome; they may be sent to Professor James Washington Bell, Secretary, American Economic Association, Evanston, Illinois.

HOWARD S. ELLIS.
Chairman, General Committee
on Republications.

WASHINGTON, D. C.
March, 1944.

CONTENTS

PREFACE vii
    By HOWARD S. ELLIS

INTRODUCTION xiii
    By GOTTFRIED HABERLER

PART I. OVER-ALL PICTURE OF THE BUSINESS CYCLE AND METHOD OF ANALYSIS

1. THE ANALYSIS OF ECONOMIC CHANGE 1
    By JOSEPH A. SCHUMPETER
    From *The Review of Economic Statistics*, 1935

2. THE LONG WAVES IN ECONOMIC LIFE 20
    By NIKOLAI D. KONDRATIEFF
    From *The Review of Economic Statistics*, 1935
    (First published in German, *Archiv für Sozialwissenschaft und Sozialpolitik*, 1926)

3. BUSINESS CYCLES 43
    By WESLEY C. MITCHELL
    From *Business Cycles and Unemployment*, National Bureau of Economic Research, 1923

4. ECONOMETRIC BUSINESS CYCLE RESEARCH 61
    By JAN TINBERGEN
    From *The Review of Economic Studies*, 1940

PART II. SAVING, INVESTMENT AND NATIONAL INCOME

5. SOME NOTES ON THE STOCKHOLM THEORY OF SAVING AND INVESTMENT 87
    By BERTIL OHLIN
    From *The Economic Journal*, 1937

6. THE OUTCOME OF THE SAVING-INVESTMENT DISCUSSION . 131
    By FRIEDRICH A. LUTZ
    From *The Quarterly Journal of Economics*, 1938

7. SAVING AND INVESTMENT: DEFINITIONS, ASSUMPTIONS, OBJECTIVES. 158
    By ABBA P. LERNER
    From *The Quarterly Journal of Economics*, 1939

8. THE RATE OF INTEREST AND THE OPTIMUM PROPENSITY TO CONSUME. 169
    By OSCAR LANGE
    From *Economica*, 1938

PART III. THE MULTIPLIER, ACCELERATION PRINCIPLE AND GOVERNMENT SPENDING

9. MR. KEYNES' THEORY OF THE "MULTIPLIER": A METHODOLOGICAL CRITICISM 193
    By GOTTFRIED HABERLER
    From *Zeitschrift für Nationalökonomie*, 1936

10. PERIOD ANALYSIS AND MULTIPLIER THEORY. 203
    By FRITZ MACHLUP
    From *The Quarterly Journal of Economics*, 1939

11. BUSINESS ACCELERATION AND THE LAW OF DEMAND: A TECHNICAL FACTOR IN ECONOMIC CYCLES. 235
    By JOHN M. CLARK
    From *The Journal of Political Economy*, 1917
    (Reprinted in *A Preface to Social Economics*, Farrar and Rinehart, 1936)

12. INTERACTIONS BETWEEN THE MULTIPLIER ANALYSIS AND THE PRINCIPLE OF ACCELERATION 261
    By PAUL A. SAMUELSON
    From *The Review of Economic Statistics*, 1939

13. DEFICIT SPENDING. 270
    by JOHN H. WILLIAMS
    From *The American Ecomomic Review, Supplement*, 1941

14. AN APPRAISAL OF THE WORKABILITY OF COMPENSATORY
    DEVICES 291
    By JOHN M. CLARK
    From *The American Economic Review, Supplement*, 1939

PART IV. MONETARY THEORY OF THE BUSINESS CYCLE

15. A SURVEY OF MODERN MONETARY CONTROVERSY . . . 311
    By DENNIS H. ROBERTSON
    From *The Manchester School*, 1938
    (Reprinted in *Essays in Monetary Theory*, P. S. King, 1940)

16. THE TRADE CYCLE 330
    By RALPH G. HAWTREY
    From *De Economist*, Rotterdam, 1926
    (Reprinted in *Trade and Credit*, Longmans, Green and Company, 1928)

17. PRICE EXPECTATIONS, MONETARY DISTURBANCES AND
    MALADJUSTMENTS 350
    By FRIEDRICH A. HAYEK
    From *Profits, Interest and Investment*, Routledge, 1939
    (First published in German, *Nationalökonomisk Tidsskrift*, Copenhagen, 1935)

PART V. UNDERCONSUMPTION THEORY AND SECULAR STAGNATION THESIS

18. ECONOMIC PROGRESS AND DECLINING POPULATION GROWTH 366
    By ALVIN H. HANSEN
    From *The American Economic Review*, 1939

19. GENERAL OVERPRODUCTION 385
    By HANS NEISSER
    From *The Journal of Political Economy*, 1934

20. MONETARY POLICY AND INVESTMENT 405
    By HOWARD S. ELLIS
    From *The American Economic Review, Supplement*, 1940

PART VI. SPECIAL COMMODITY CYCLES

21. THE COBWEB THEOREM 422
 By MORDECAI EZEKIEL
 From *The Quarterly Journal of Economics*, 1938

BIBLIOGRAPHY OF THE LITERATURE ON BUSINESS CYCLE THEORY 443
 By HAROLD M. SOMERS

INDEX TO BIBLIOGRAPHY 489

INTRODUCTION

The primary purpose of the present volume, as well as of the others in this series, is usefulness in teaching graduate and advanced undergraduate courses. Originality of articles is only a subsidiary consideration. The inclusion of chapters from books, which in some cases might have served better than articles in periodicals, would raise more cumbersome copyright questions and is not within the scope of the present series as delineated in the agreement between the publishers and the American Economic Association. The choice of articles for this volume was in some cases influenced by the fact that companion volumes are contemplated in related fields, such as Economic Theory and Money and Banking.

The members of the Selection Committee found it extremely difficult to decide what to include in the selection. They are under no illusion that they were able to do a perfect job. It is simply impossible to satisfy, within the allotted space, all legitimate demands and to comply with all wishes expressed by those interested in the field.

The procedure of making the selection was as follows: A comprehensive list of articles was sent to a small group of experts with the request to indicate their first and second choices. This ballot was, however, very inconclusive. Only a few articles were selected by more than one member of the group.

The items selected by at least one member of the first group were then combined in a second list. This list was again circulated among approximately the same group. The outcome was again discouraging because it revealed little agreement. The chairman of the Committee then drew up a list, which after numerous discussions and consultations with many experts in the field resulted in the selection here offered.

The following persons were kind enough to serve on the selection committee or to give generous advice: J. W. Angell, J. Bain, A. F.

Burns, H. S. Ellis, W. Fellner, G. N. Halm, A. H. Hansen, S. Kuznets, O. Lange, F. Lutz, F. Machlup, A. Marget, C. E. Puffer, A. P. Lerner, P. A. Samuelson, A. Smithies, J. A. Schumpeter, H. M. Somers, H. Staehle, W. Stolper, J. H. Williams. Many of them permitted the inspection of reading lists used in their business cycle courses.

. . . .

It was decided to limit the present book to business cycle *theory* and to present only a minimum of descriptive and statistical-methodological material. The reasons are lack of space and the hope that it will be possible to prepare a special volume on statistical methodology in the field of economics.

No articles in foreign language have been translated for the present volume, but some of the included articles, taken from American or English periodicals have originally appeared in foreign languages or have foreigners as authors. It will be observed that the group of authors represented in the present volume is quite cosmopolitan.

There is one serious gap which requires a word of justification. The name of Arthur Spiethoff is absent from our list. The reason is that his *chef-d'oeuvre*, the famous article "Krisen,"[1] which is a full-fledged descriptive and theoretical monograph on business cycles, will be published in an English translation as a separate book by the University of California. His earlier articles[2] are today only of historical value for the expert and his article "Overproduction"[3] does not give an adequate picture of his thinking.

The inclusion of Professor Schumpeter's little classic does not call for special explanation. Kondratieff's famous article is still the best material in article-form available in English on the long waves. The interested reader should, however, consult the instructive article "Kondratieff's Theory of Long Cycles" by

---

[1] *Handwörterbuch der Staatswissenschaften*, Vol. VI, Jena 1925, pages 8–91 (large quarto size).

[2] See Bibliography page 493.

[3] *Encyclopaedia of the Social Sciences*, Vol. XI, pages 513–517.

George Garvy[1] which contains a critical review of the extensive literature in Russian, by Kondratieff and other writers, on the subject of the long waves. Professor Mitchell's article is probably the best suited short exposition of his views on business cycles which underlies the well-known National Bureau technique of cycle analysis. No detailed, technical analysis of the latter has, however, been included, because such an article would take much space and belongs rather to a volume on economic-statistical methodology. Professor Tinbergen's admirable paper is short and it deals with the logic rather than the statistical technique of his approach. Therefore it was included. An alternative choice might have been Dr. Koopman's "Logic of Econometric Business Cycle Research."[2]

In every business cycle course it is found necessary to devote much time to the discussion of the relationships between saving, investment, consumption and national income, which play such a great role in many explanations of the cycle. To distinguish between definitional and causal relationships is not easy and the student should get a good feeling for this distinction. He also should become familiar with the logical pitfalls and the opportunities of terminological tangles and controversies provided by the existence of overlapping alternative definitions. For these reasons some space was allotted to a subject of which many scholars have become weary in recent years.

The last item in this group—Professor Lange's celebrated article—constitutes a transition to the next subject. The literature on the multiplier, acceleration principle and Government deficit spending is enormous as can be seen from the bibliography. It is hoped that the present selection will be found useful.

The monetary theories of the business cycle are no longer so much in vogue as they were ten years ago. Professor Robertson's admirable article, however, goes much beyond the purely monetary theories. The included contributions by Professors Hawtrey and

---

[1] *The Review of Economic Statistics*, November 1943, Vol. xxv, pages 203–220.
[2] *Journal of Political Economy*, Vol. IL, pages 157–181.

Hayek are probably the best short statements of their respective theories.

Professor Hansen's presidential address is still the best presentation in article-form of the secular stagnation thesis, the long-run version of the underconsumption theory. Professor Neisser's somewhat unconventional statement of the underconsumption theory has the great advantage that it discusses the Marxian and other older doctrines. These two papers and Professor Ellis' subtle criticism should give a fairly rounded picture of the subject.

Dr. Ezekiel's paper does not confine itself to the cobweb cycles, but contains also a brief discussion of other mechanisms used for the explanation of special commodity cycles. And all of these mechanisms find their place also in the explanation of the general business cycle.

It should be mentioned that some of the authors have been kind enough to make a number of revisions. A few articles have been shortened, others adorned with more footnotes.

· · · ·

The reprints of articles are followed by a very extensive bibliography, which was compiled by Professor H. M. Somers. It is hoped that the bibliography will be useful not only for teaching purposes, but also as a reference list for the expert. Because of the great number of items included, it was possible to use in the bibliography a much more detailed classification than in the collection of articles. The principles of the classification and the difficulties encountered are fully described by Dr. Somers' on page 443.

GOTTFRIED HABERLER.
Chairman, Selection Committee

1

THE ANALYSIS OF ECONOMIC CHANGE*
By Joseph A. Schumpeter‖

Ever since, in the sixties of the past century, Clement Juglar definitely established the existence of wave-like movements which pervade economic life within the institutional framework of capitalist society, the work of finding, linking-up, measuring relevant fact, has been steadily progressing. Although much hampered by needless controversy and inadequate technique, this work has yielded results which, it is believed, need only be properly coördinated and developed in order to enable economics to offer a substantially satisfactory and reasonably exhaustive picture of the phenomenon, and thus to make what would certainly be its most immediately practical contribution to human welfare. Coördination is particularly necessary of the historical, statistical and analytical modes of approach which are each of them thwarted by that reluctance to coöperation incident to the differences in training, tastes and horizons of individual workers. The purpose of this paper is to explain the main features of an analytic apparatus which may be of some use in marshaling the information we have and in framing programs for further research.

Outside Factors

If we survey, for instance, the course of economic events in England from the beginning of the French Wars in 1792, through the suspension of specie payments, the Peace of Amiens, the trade

---

* *The Review of Economic Statistics*, Volume XVII, Number 4, May 1935, pages 2–10. Reprinted by the courtesy of The Review of Economic Statistics and the author.
‖ Harvard University.

war with America, up to the crisis in 1809–1810, it becomes obvious that we could without any glaring absurdity account by political "disturbances" for all the fluctuations we observe in our material. Or if we follow the course of the world crisis through the spring of 1931, we may trace the breakdown of the distinct upward movement observable at the beginning of that year to a string of events arising out of the flutter caused by the reopening of the question of the union of Austria to Germany and the movements of short balances incident thereto.[1] Common sense immediately suggests that here we have discovered an obviously important source of economic fluctuations. From the ubiquity of such events it follows that practically every economic fluctuation must be a historic individual and cannot be made amenable to explanation but by minute historical analysis of the innumerable factors actually at work in each case. In other words, in order to understand business cycles we must first of all acquire what may be termed historical experience of the way in which economic life reacts to such disturbances, and this is one of the reasons why every conquest of past fact is of paramount practical importance, in some respects of greater importance than additions to our stock of contemporaneous fact which can increase our knowledge over time only by infinitesimal steps.

---

[1] If we further ask how it was that that particularly sensitive short-balance situation arose in Germany, we find, following events from 1924 to 1929, that the steadily increasing public expenditure, and the methods by which it was financed, amounted to taxing away what would otherwise have been an annual average increase of working capital of about one billion marks. If we deduct from the figure of foreign short-term indebtedness as it stood in 1930 not only the four billions of counterclaims of German banks on short capital account, and the four to five billions which simply were revolving credits financing Germany's foreign trade and which, therefore, were not dangerous, but also the, roughly, five to six billions, which could and would have been accumulated but for that fiscal policy, it is easily seen that the interest rate would have been lower and that that part of foreign short indebtedness, the proceeds of which replaced the formation of domestic working capital, would have been so small as to be no major factor in the situation. We are thus enabled to account for some of the darkest hues of the situation of 1931–1932 by what was not only on the surface, but also in a more fundamental sense, a political cause. Cf. the last two sentences of this section for a defense of this way of reasoning.

The statistical and analytical description of the various mechanisms of reaction (with a hope in our minds that we may ultimately get as far as to be able to measure the effects attributable to every such disturbance) seems thus to be the most urgent task before us It should be observed in passing that for various reasons any influence acting on the economic process is practically sure to produce not a single dent but a wave-like motion extending over a longer time than it takes to reach the next disturbance, as well as, if it impinges on a particular spot, a vibration throughout the whole system. Moreover, with adaptation proceeding almost always with a lag and very often with reference to the rate of change of prices rather than to their absolute magnitude, our attempts at exact description are more than likely to result in expressions admitting of periodic integrals.

This being so, the question arises whether there are any fluctuations at all which arise out of the behavior of business communities as such and would be observable even if the institutional and natural framework of society remained absolutely invariable. Although disturbance of the kind glanced at and reaction thereto may in individual cases be much more important, yet the presence or absence of a fluctuation *inherent* to the economic process in time is practically and scientifically the fundamental problem and the only one to be considered here. In order to make headway with it, we shall proceed as physical sciences do in those cases in which it is impossible actually to isolate a phenomenon by producing it in a laboratory: from our historic and everyday knowledge of economic behavior we shall construct a "model" of the economic process over time, see whether it is likely to work in a wave-like way, and compare the result with observed fact. Henceforth, therefore, we shall disregard not only wars, revolutions, natural catastrophes, institutional changes, but also changes in commercial policy, in banking and currency legislation and habits of payment, variations of crops as far as due to weather conditions or diseases, changes in gold production as far as due to chance discoveries, and so on. These we shall call *outside factors*. It will be seen that in some cases it is not easy to distinguish them from features of business behavior.

All we can do about this here is to recommend to the reader to hold tight to the common sense of the distinction and to consider that every business man knows quite well that he is doing one kind of thing when ordering a new machine and another kind of thing when lobbying for an increase of the import duty on his product. It will also be seen that many of the things we list as outside factors are, when considered on a higher plane and for a wider purpose, the direct outcome of the working of the capitalist machine and hence no independent agencies.[1] This is surely so but does not reduce the practical value of the distinction on our plane and for our purpose.

Cycles, Trends, Equilibria, Growth, Innovation

For shortness' sake, we assemble in this section a few necessary definitions and propositions, which are really quite simple, although we cannot help adding here and there somewhat pedantic formulations which are necessary in order to make our meaning perfectly precise to the specialist.

---

[1] Professor W. C. Mitchell, in his review of Professor L. Robbins' recent book (*Quarterly Journal of Economics*, May, 1935), objects to the latter's attributing part of the phenomena of the depression 1929–1934 to "politics." Sociologically, he is of course quite right not only for this case, but generally. The action, e.g., of Sir Robert Peel's administration in repealing the corn laws in 1846 undoubtedly arose out of, and is to be accounted for by the economic pattern of the time and place, itself created by the working of the *whole* social system, of which the capitalist mechanism was a part. But this is relevant only for *some* purposes, for instance, if we wish to *judge* the action of politicians. As far as this is done on predilections of the scientist for certain types of social institutions, it is certainly extra-scientific as well as extra-economic. We should, in this case, have to disagree with *both* the eminent authors mentioned, as they both of them display such predilections. The argument is, however, not relevant if the question is merely what of observable effects may have been due to the Peel policy: for an investigation of the course of English cycles in the 1840's that policy is as much of an outside factor as an earthquake would have been. For the sake of clearness it is essential to keep both standpoints strictly separate. The same reasoning applies, of course, to the distinction of an economic process and its institutional setting in general. The distinction is, in a sense, quite unrealistic. But if we do not make it, we shall never be able to say more than that everything depends upon everything.

Statistically, the term "cycle" means two things: first, that sequences of values of economic quantities in historic time (as distinguished from theoretic time) do not display monotonic increase or decrease, but (irregular) recurrence of either these values themselves or their first or their second time-derivatives; and secondly, that these "fluctuations" do not occur independently in every such time series, but always display either instantaneous or lagged association with each other.

Statistically, we mean by the word "trend" the fact that in many, although not in all, such time series it is possible to divide the whole interval covered by our material into sub-intervals such that the mean values of the time integrals over these sub-intervals are monotonically increasing or decreasing as we go along in time, or that they display recurrence only once.

If we study, say, the economic state of things in all countries in 1872 and behold the wild excesses of that boom, we shall have no difficulty in assigning very realistic meaning to the terms "want of balance" or "disequilibrium." Nor is it difficult, if we look at things one year after, to recognize that however much the then situation differed from that of 1872 it was similar to it in that it was about equally unbalanced. Again, if we analyze the course of events in, say, 1897, we may well sum up the result by speaking of a comparatively equilibrated state of things. This common sense distinction between comparatively balanced and comparatively unbalanced states of the economic system is of utmost importance for the description and measurement of cyclical phenomena. In order to bring out the exact skeleton of such observations we define: (Marshallian) *particular equilibrium* exists in an individual industry if this industry as a whole displays no tendency either to increase or decrease its output or to alter the combination of the productive factors it employs. *Aggregative equilibrium* exists if the sum total of receipts of business as a whole, expressed in current dollars, equals the sum total of costs similarly expressed and including as much profit as will induce everybody to keep on doing what he is actually doing. This kind of thing, which is compatible with plenty of disequilibrium as between industries and within industries, is the basic concept in Mr. Keynes' analysis of the monetary process. *General equilibrium* exists if every household and every firm in the domain under research is individually in a state of equilibrium in the sense of Léon Walras. It is only this last concept that matters for us. To give it statistical meaning, we must link it up with certain points on the graphs of our time series. These we call "normal points." As in reality such states can never be perfectly realized we can be concerned only with states which are nearer to, or farther from, them than other states. Hence we further define: *neighborhoods of equilibrium* are time intervals in which normal points occur in the graphs of our time series excepting those which in that interval are deflected by a definite and provable individual circumstance. (The word "neighborhood" is therefore not used here in its strict mathematical sense.) Discussion of the question how we are to locate these neighborhoods cannot be entered upon in this article.

By "growth" we mean changes in economic data which occur continuously in the sense that the increment or decrement per unit of time can be currently absorbed by the system without perceptible disturbance. Increase of population, resulting in an increase of the supply of labor of at most a few per cent per year (historically an increase of three per cent per year is already high), is the outstanding example. If the factors which enter into this category were the only ones at work, there would be obvious economic meaning to the concept of trend and to its determination by least squares or other methods resting on similar assumptions. In what follows we shall, however, not deal with the problems arising out of mere growth, nor with the very complicated questions of their relation to the other types of factors involved in economic change. In fact we shall, for clearness' sake, disregard it altogether, which, as in the case of outside factors, does not imply any view about its importance.

It stands to reason, finally, that outside factors and growth factors do not exhaust the list of the influences which produce and shape economic change. Obviously the face of the earth would look very different if people, besides having their economic life changed by natural events and changing it themselves by extra-economic action, had done nothing else except multiply and save. If it looks as it does, this is just as obviously due to the unremitting efforts of people to improve according to their lights upon their productive and commercial methods, i.e., to the changes in technique of production, the conquest of new markets, the insertion of new commodities, and so on. This historic and irreversible change in the way of doing things we call "innovation" and we define: innovations are changes in production functions which cannot be decomposed into infinitesimal steps. Add as many mail-coaches as you please, you will never get a railroad by so doing.

It is a question of some interest why the old type of economist, Marshall included, should, while recognizing this element and taking account of it in special cases, yet have persistently refused to face it squarely and to build an analytic apparatus fully descriptive of its mechanism and consequences. For our purpose it is both necessary and sufficient to list innovation, however much it may be linked to the other two, as a third and logically distinct factor in economic change, and to submit the propositions: The kind of wave-like movement, which we call the business cycle, is incident to industrial change and would be impossible in an economic world displaying nothing except unchanging repetition of the productive and consumptive process. Industrial change is due to the effect of outside factors, to the non-cyclical element of growth, and to innovation. If there be a purely economic cycle at all, it can only come from the way in which new things are, in the institutional conditions of capitalist society, inserted into the economic process and absorbed by it. In fact, the cycle seems to be the statistical and historical form in which what is usually referred to as "economic progress" comes about. This is why any serious attempt at analytic and even at practical control of the business cycle must be an historical one in the sense that the key to the solution of its fundamental problems can only be found in the facts of industrial and commercial history.

Prosperity and Depression

To simplify argument we will in this section make the hypothesis, presently to be discarded, that there is sense in speaking of only *one* "cyclical movement" in our material.

We can of course never expect to discover a definite date when the first cycle arose out of a state of perfect equilibrium, but it is essential, in order to avoid circular reasoning, to make our model describe such an event and, as far as historical and statistical description goes, to make it start from what has first to be identified as a neighborhood of equilibrium. We then get the picture of the system of economic quantities drawing away from this equilibrium or neighborhood under the impact of innovations which would supply, barring outside factors, the only possible "force." Let us visualize this by thinking of any of those booms in this country or in England which everyone would label as railroad booms. The new thing in this case takes years to get into working order and still longer to exert its full effects on the location of industry and agriculture, agglomerations of population, the evolution of accessories and subsidiaries, and so on. During this time there would, in strict logic and if the preceding equilibrium had been a perfect one, be little or no increase in the stream of commodities and services (there may in fact be a *decrease* in the output of consumers' goods), while producers' and consumers' expenditures would increase in consequence of credit creation and in other ways. The realistic complement of this is that, during this period, expenditure regularly expands more than output and that the non-innovating sectors of the economic system adapt themselves to this state of things. It is not possible to show here by the historical interpretation of the behavior of time series (neither should it be necessary to show, for it must be obvious to everyone who has ever, e.g., studied the charts published in this REVIEW) how perfectly this accounts for everything we mean when identifying a given interval as a time of business prosperity. After a period of gestation, which of course must be distinguished from what we may also designate by this term in the case of an individual firm, the products or services of the new business structures reach their markets, displacing either other such products and services, or methods of production and enterprises linked to them which have now become obsolete, and enforcing a process of liquidation, readjustment, and absorption. This would be so even if nobody ever made any errors and nobody ever misbehaved, although there is no difficulty whatever in understanding that the consequences of error and misbehavior will show up during this period in which the system struggles back to a new neighborhood of equilibrium. On the side of money and credit, the fundamental element which induces all others is the fact that as soon as the receipts stream in from the sale of the new products and as far as they are used to pay back bank loans, deposits will have to contract, in strict logic, down to the point of the previous neighborhood and, in reality, some way towards it. Again, there is no difficulty in inserting into this picture, as understandable consequences of this fundamental chain of events, all the accidental phenomena which experience tells us are usually associated with it. This not only gives a truer picture of the nature and the organic functions of cyclical down-swings, but also accords satisfactorily with statistical evidence.

Whatever starts a deviation of the system from equilibrium always, although not with logical necessity, gives rise to secondary phenomena which are mainly due to the fact that business men will act on the rates of change they observe. The sum total of these induced phenomena which are the center of the mass psychology of cycles and greatly intensify their amplitudes, we call "secondary waves." The expression, first used in 1911, is misleading and is kept only because Mr. Keynes has taken it up. But the thing is very important, so much so that the majority of students of the business cycle see nothing else. Whilst this accounts for many errors in diagnosis and remedial policy, it also helps to explain and partly to justify a large group of "theories" which, though missing the essential phenomenon, are yet perfectly satisfactory when viewed as descriptions of part of the mechanism of the secondary waves superimposed on the primary ones.

The units of the cyclical movements, then, lie necessarily between neighborhoods of equilibrium. In the simplest form of the model of economic change they have only two phases. But because of the fact that depressive forces gather momentum on the way back from the prosperity-excursion of the system, notably owing to the phenomena incident to the breakdown of the secondary wave, the system outruns usually the first neighborhood of equilibrium it strikes on its way back, and embarks upon a depression-excursion, from which it is forced up by the action of the equilibrium *ligamina* which bring it up again to another neighborhood from which the prosperity of the next cycle starts. Hence we have as a rule four phases: prosperity, recession, depression, and revival. This is almost generally recognized, but it is important to note that for purposes of fundamental analysis we are not free to count cycles from any point or phase we please, for instance, from peak to peak or trough to trough, but must always begin after the revival and at the beginning of a prosperity. It is, moreover, essential to distinguish these two, although it may be difficult to do so owing to the fact that they are both positive. The failure to do so, and especially to recognize that the "forces" at work in revival are entirely different from the "forces" at work in prosperity, is one of the main sources of faulty analysis.

The fundamental question still remains unanswered. Why should the carrying into effect of innovations (as distinguished from "invention" or experimentation which are quite another matter and do not in themselves exert any influence on business life at all—which is the reason why so little has come out of the Marshallian recognition of the element of invention) *cluster* at certain times, and not be distributed in so continuous a way as to be capable of being just as continuously absorbed as the current increase in the supply of labor is? One answer suggests itself immediately: as soon as the various kinds of social resistance to something that is fundamentally new and untried have been overcome, it is much easier not only to do the same thing again but also to do *similar* things in different directions, so that a first success will always produce a cluster. (See, e.g., the emergence of the motor-car industry.) This is indeed the method of *competitive* capitalism which has not as yet died out in *trustified* capitalism, to spread an improvement and to reap the social harvest—in the succeeding depression. But to carry full persuasion it would be necessary to go much deeper into this phenomenon, the roots of which stretch far beyond the economic field, than is here possible. However, as it has been the unfortunate experience of the present writer that even a very elaborate exposition has failed at times to convey to critics the picture he desired to convey, he prefers to ask the reader to consider the clustering of innovations as a postulate or hypothesis made to fit the facts in the same way as hypotheses are made in physics, irrespective of what might be adduced for or against their objective truth. Yet he feels entitled to say to anyone who doubts this proposition: Look around you in industrial life and see for yourself whether it is not so. Other writers have quite independently stressed the fact that it is possible to associate historically every business cycle with a distinct industry, or a few industries, which led in it and, as it were, applied the torch to what after becomes a flare-up covering a much wider surface.[1] The well established fact that fluctuations in investment goods are so much more marked than fluctuations elsewhere points, by virtue of its being explainable on the postulate mentioned, in the same direction.

It should be added that the above analytic model supplies an interpretation of economic trends which also bears on the technique of their determination. It follows, e.g., that barring the element of growth the trends of our time series are not due to influences distinct from those that create the cyclical fluctuations but simply embody the results of the latter. To these "result-trends," as the writer calls them in his workshop, it is entirely unwarranted to apply formal methods of the type of least squares. For extrapola-

---

[1] The first author to do this consciously was, as far as the present writer knows, Mr. D. H. Robertson (*A Study of Industrial Fluctuations*, published in 1915, and an earlier paper in the *Journal of the Royal Statistical Society*), who, equally independently, also developed a schema of the working of the credit mechanism, similar in many respects to the one implied above and developed in 1911, in his *Banking Policy and the Price Level* (1926).

tion there is, of course, no warrant in any case. But there are certain general characteristics which may be used in developing formal methods as more or less rough approximations. No general proposition is possible as to the relative or absolute lengths of the four phases, even apart from the fact that they will be influenced by outside factors. Partly but not wholly for the latter reason no great significance attaches to the mere height or depth of a peak or a trough, although we shall presently find a reason for expecting that certain depressions will be much more severe than others.

The Three-cycle Schema

The above analysis not only accounts for the fact that waves of prosperity always do arise whenever a neighborhood of equilibrium is reached "from below," and that they always do taper off into a new neighborhood of equilibrium, but, as far as the present writer is able to make out, also accounts for every single fact or characteristic ever proved to be associated with either up-swings or down-swings not provably due to the action of outside factors. The reader is invited to make the experiment of testing this assertion by drawing up a list of what he considers these characteristics to be and observing whether they fit into the model offered. But there is no ground to believe that there should be just *one* wave-like movement pervading economic life. On the contrary, it stands to reason that some processes covered by our concept of innovation must take much longer time than others to have full effect. The railroadization or electrification of a country, for instance, may take between one-half and the whole of a century and involve fundamental transformations of its economic and cultural patterns, changing everything in the lives of its people up to their spiritual ambitions, while other innovations or groups of innovations may arise and disappear within a very few years. Moreover, the former will generally be carried out in distinct steps and thus give rise both to shorter fluctuations and longer underlying swells. Under these circumstances it is not the most natural thing to assume the existence of a single cycle and to postulate that it will display any very marked regularities. This is in fact a very bold hypothesis which could be justified only if clearly imposed upon us by our material. But as this is not the case, even apart from what we may reasonably attribute to the outside disturbances to which our material is subject, it seems much more realistic (and also likely to do away with some spurious irregularities, that is to say, irregularities which are only due to the single-cycle hypothesis) to admit that there are *many* cycles rolling on simultaneously, and to face squarely the problem of analyzing their interference with each other. As, however, it is necessary for the purpose of handling our time series to settle on a moderate number of distinct movements which may be thought of as superimposed on each other and as passing their normals or neighborhoods of equilibrium *near* the points where they cross the path of the next higher cycle underlying them, the three-cycle schema is here suggested as a fairly useful working hypothesis. Nothing more than descriptive merits are claimed for it, but manifestly it fulfills the one condition which a device of this kind may reasonably be required to fulfill, the condition of carrying historical meaning, which—with material as exposed as ours is to disturbances by outside factors which are not small, independent, or "numerous" in the probability sense—is much more important than fulfillment of any formal criterion.

Historical knowledge of what actually happened at any time in the industrial organism, and of the way in which it happened, reveals first the existence of what is often referred to as the "Long Wave" of a period of between fifty-four and sixty years. Occasionally recognized and even measured before, especially by Spiethoff, it has been worked out in more detail by Kondratieff, and may therefore be called the Kondratieff Cycle. Economic historians of the nineteenth century have unconsciously and independently testified to the reality of the first of these waves our material allows us to observe, viz., the cycle from about 1783 to 1842, and they have also borne out in advance our interpretation of the phenomenon by coining the phrase of the "industrial revolution," which really implies everything we mean. The phrase is infelicitous and justly considered obsolete by now, but it pictures well how the happenings of the period struck entirely unprejudiced observers. The years 1842–1897 are readily interpreted as the age of steam and steel, particularly as the age of the railroadization of the world. This may sound superficial, but it can be shown in detail that railroad construction and work incident to it, connected with it, or consequential upon it, is the dominant feature both of economic change and of economic fluctuations during that time, and of every one of the four phases into which it is possible to divide it. Future historians finally will find no difficulty in recognizing the initiating importance of electricity, chemistry and motor cars for both the up-swing and the down-swing of the third Long Wave, which rose about 1897. Of course, if we prefer a more usual way of expressing the same thing, we may put these processes also into terms of "investment" and the expansion and contraction of credit: this is certainly a very important part of the mechanism. Unfortunately, this description is not only more usual but also more superficial, and opens the door to all the crudities and errors of the various monetary theories of the cycle. Any satisfactory analysis of causes must start with what induces that credit expansion, as every satisfactory analysis of effects must start by investigating what is done with the increased monetary resources—after which we immediately cease to wonder why the mere increase of credit facilities in or before a depression proves as ineffectual as we know it does. If, however, we stop at the process of investment and postulate that it has a mechanism of its own, we not only fail to get at the core of the matter but we also find it difficult to avoid such desperate logic as is implied in the conclusion that because increase of investment and expansion of credit are associated with a prosperity phase, we therefore can produce prosperity by expanding credit.

The majority of students of the business cycle does not consider the evidence alluded to sufficient to establish this particular cycle. But what does that mean? The term Kondratieff Cycle is for us but a name for a certain set of facts (a certain long-time behavior of the price level, the interest rate, employment, and so on), none of which is open to doubt. It is true that the term also implies an interpretation to the effect that this behavior of our series is amenable to interpretation on the same lines as their behavior in shorter cycles. But this again is merely an inference from historical facts, which have not so far been called in question either. Of course, experience of about two and three-fourths units of a phenomenon does not warrant much generalization, and still less prediction.

It is therefore *only as a statement of fact* that we venture to say that the two complete Kondratieff units within our range of statistical vision contain each of them six cycles of from nine to ten years' duration, equally well established by industrial history, though less clearly marked in our time series, which correspond as a matter of fact roughly to that cyclical movement which was the first to be discovered. Following the same procedure as in the earlier case, we may call them Juglar Cycles. As pointed out by D. H. Robertson,[1] it is possible in every instance to indicate the particular industry and the particular innovations which are responsible for the up-swing and the process of readjustment.

Finally, every Juglar so far observed (those of the present Kondratieff included) is readily, in most cases and in this country already by inspection, divisible into three cycles of a period of roughly forty months. The existence of this shorter cycle has been pointed out repeatedly these hundred years or more, and still oftener has it been felt and recognized implicitly, but one may remark that it was the two studies by Mr. Kitchin and Professor Crum in this REVIEW that were chiefly instrumental in establishing it.[2] Evidence about the commercial paper rate, this series being the most purely cyclical of all, is of course particularly important. That this cycle, as well as the others, is more clearly marked in this country than in any other and notably more marked than in England, is easily accounted for by the fact that cycles in most series will tend to be toned down or even ironed out the more a country's economic life is interwoven with international influences and the more its policy approaches Free Trade. The question of the statistical methods which arise out of this analysis (for statistical methods must arise out of our understanding of the phenomenon

---

[1] Cp. previous note, p. 11.
[2] This REVIEW, vol. v (1923), pp. 10–16 and 17–29.

they are to be applied to) will be taken up at another time. It is, of course, admitted not only that non-cyclical changes also create wave-like movements but that besides the three just mentioned there are other cyclical waves.[1] It is held, however, that the three-cycle schema works sufficiently well for the purposes of the stage of rough approximations in which we are, and are likely to remain for a considerable time.

A Research Program

If we coördinate available information, statistical and historical, in the light of the principles sketched out, we get not so much a picture as indications which give us an idea of what the real picture would be like. These principles do enable us to link up in a general way the behavior of those of our series which are most symptomatic of the pulse of economic life as a whole. These "systematic" series may be either "synthetic," as, for instance, series of price levels or of physical volume of production, or "natural," as, for instance, series of interest rates, clearing-debits, unemployment, pig-iron consumption, at least for the pre-war time, or the sum total of deposits. They all, also in a general way, behave as they would have to if the view outlined above were true to life. In the case of what, by way of distinction from "systematic," we may call "individual" series, such as the prices and quantities of individual commodities, our analysis becomes more complicated and perfect knowledge is necessary of the particular conditions in every branch of industry and commerce, of its lags, frictions and inertias, of the mentality of its men, of the particular random influences to which it is exposed, and especially of its active or passive rôle in any given cycle. As the outside factors impinge upon some phase of a process consisting of a number of superimposed wave-like movements, and as every one of these movements itself impinges upon a particular phase of some other movement underlying it, so all of this impinges on a particular resonator in the case of every individual industry or firm, *which responds according to its own structure.* This is perhaps

---

[1] As pointed out by Wardwell, Kuznets and others.

the best way of stating the problem in its full complexity. It also helps us to understand the many "special cycles" which some students have found or think they have found in various individual industries.

Now first, as regards a research program, it may be suggested that not a single one of the "systematic" series above spoken of represents adequately what it is meant to represent. And in no case is our historical or contemporaneous information adequate to account quantitatively for the fluctuations of the systematic series. It is only one side of the problem that this makes convincing verification of the result of any analysis impossible, and that all we can do at present is to say that the testimony of such facts as we have is compatible or incompatible with it. The other side is that many questions are not questions of principle and analysis at all, but simply of relative quantitative importance. The statement, e.g., that in the down-grade of any cycle inertia of wages counts for something in determining the amount of unemployment, is too obvious to require proof; but not only for practical but also for scientific purposes this is entirely irrelevant as long as we are unable to say whether this element accounts for one per cent or for ninety per cent of the unemployment figure observed in a given place at a given time. No wonder, therefore, that, if we are unable to be more precise than this, economics is considered as entirely useless by the practical man. Yet our analytic apparatus would turn out a definite answer all right, provided the necessary factual information were inserted into it, the assembling of which is, of course, much beyond the means of any individual worker or private group of workers.

Secondly, there is no reliable information at all on a number of subjects which are obviously of primary significance. Two examples must suffice. Waiving our objection to the present tendency to overstress the importance of price levels and monetary magnitudes in general, we may say that the stream of expenditure by households on consumers' goods is one of the most indispensable elements in the analysis of the business cycle. We have acceptable though far from satisfactory indicators for the post-war time but, owing to the exceptional circumstances present in this period, these are almost valueless for a fundamental understanding. And for the pre-war time we have to be content with pay-roll figures and the like, which might easily mislead even if they went further back than they do. Yet there is plenty of stray information stretching over centuries, which, if it could be brought together, would definitely clear up many pressing practical problems such as this one.

Again the process of investment and the corresponding process of credit contraction in down-grades can never, whatever the theorist may say, be fully grasped in its importance and consequences until we know more about the relative importance of its sources and the actual behavior of borrowers and lenders. The decisive figure here is the sum actually spent on the production of durable producers' goods *for new purposes*. It is in these last three words that our chief difficulty lies, which has so far been overcome only in a very few cases: we can follow up, for instance, how much was spent on railroad construction in England in the 'forties. It is difficult enough to find out how great the sum total is that newly enters industry and trade every year. It is still more difficult to find how much of this is spent on equipment. And even this would not be enough. However, an investigation lighting up this very important side of the past and present of capitalist society would be perfectly feasible.

Although, thirdly, the phenomenon of the cycle cannot be defined and understood as a sort of average between independent changes in individual industries, yet the behavior of individual industries, on the one hand causing and on the other hand responding to the sweep of changing business situations, requires a special study for each of them. Plenty of work has been done in this direction, but, as the decisive questions have hardly ever been in the minds of the writers to whom we owe that literature of industrial monographs, the evidence is incomplete and inconclusive. There is hardly any event, or peculiarity of structural pattern, in any industry which would be irrelevant to the question why the business cycle is what it is. Besides, if it be true that industrial change is at the bottom of the cyclical phenomenon, its mechanism can be established only by covering in detail all recorded cases of such change. To the thoughtful observer, for instance, a striking similarity reveals itself immediately between such different processes as the development of the English iron industry from the sixteenth to the end of the eighteenth century, and the rise of the motor-car industry in our time. In these, as in many other cases, we have even now advanced much beyond general impressions. There is, however, a long way between this and the goal of establishing the validity of the schema of innovation and showing how innovation produces, together with its monetary complement, the particular kind of waves inherent to the economic life of capitalist society and paralleled by similar phenomena in other fields of human activity.

2

THE LONG WAVES IN ECONOMIC LIFE*

By Nikolai D. Kondratieff‖

Foreword

The editors of the REVIEW OF ECONOMIC STATISTICS are happy to be able to present in translation the peculiarly important article by Professor Kondratieff, which, under the title "Die langen Wellen der Konjunktur," appeared in the *Archiv für Sozialwissenschaft und Sozialpolitik* in 1926 (vol. 56, no. 3, pp. 573–609). The combining circumstances of an increasing interest in "long waves" and the difficulty of securing access to the original article would alone justify translation and publication of Kondratieff's contribution to the theory of the trade cycle. In addition, the editors would take this means of indicating their intention from time to time of rendering available to the English-using world outstanding articles in foreign periodicals.

This translation of Professor Kondratieff's article was made by Mr. W. F. Stolper of Harvard University. Due to the limitations of space, the editors have taken the liberty to summarize certain sections of this translation. With the exception of a ten-page appendix of tabular material, however, all tables and charts have been included.

I. Introduction

The idea that the dynamics of economic life in the capitalistic social order is not of a simple and linear but rather of a complex and cyclical character is nowadays generally recognized. Science, however, has fallen far short of clarifying the nature and the types of these cyclical, wave-like movements.

When in economics we speak of cycles, we generally mean seven to eleven year business cycles. But these seven to eleven year movements are obviously not the only type of economic cycles.

---

* *The Review of Economic Statistics*, Volume XVII, Number 6, November 1935, pages 105–115. Reprinted by the courtesy of The Review of Economic Statistics.
‖ Formerly Business Research Institute, Moscow.

The dynamics of economic life is in reality more complicated. In addition to the above-mentioned cycles, which we shall agree to call "intermediate," the existence of still shorter waves of about three and one-half years' length has recently been shown to be probable.[1]

But that is not all. There is, indeed, reason to assume the existence of long waves of an average length of about 50 years in the capitalistic economy, a fact which still further complicates the problem of economic dynamics.

II–III. Method

[Sections II and III of Kondratieff's exposition may be summarized as follows:

The succeeding study is to be confined solely to an inquiry into various problems connected with these long waves. Investigation here is made difficult by the fact that a very long period of observation is presupposed. We have, however, no data before the end of the eighteenth century and even the data that we do have are too scanty and not entirely reliable. Since the material relating to England and France is the most complete, it has formed the chief basis of this inquiry. The statistical methods used were simple when no secular trend was present in the series. If the series displayed a secular trend, as was the case among physical series, the first step was to divide the annual figures by the population, whenever this was logically possible, in order to allow for changes in territory. Then the secular trend was eliminated by the usual statistical methods applied to each series as a whole; and Kondratieff refers specifically to the methods presented by Dr. Warren M. Persons in this REVIEW in 1919 and 1920. The deviations from the secular trend were then smoothed by a nine-year moving average, in order to eliminate the seven to eleven year business cycles, the short cycles, and random fluctuations possibly present.]

---

[1] Cf. J. Kitchin, "Cycles and Trends in Economic Factors," REVIEW OF ECONOMIC STATISTICS [hereafter referred to as "this REVIEW"], v (1923), pp. 10–16.

IV. The Wholesale Price Level

While the index of French prices goes back only to the end of the 1850's, the English and American indices date back to the close of the eighteenth century. In order not to overburden this study with figures, the statistical data are presented exclusively in the form of charts.[1]

The index numbers of prices plotted on Chart 1 have been neither smoothed nor treated in any other way. Nevertheless, a mere glance at the chart shows that the price level, despite all deviations and irregularities, exhibits a succession of long waves.

The upswing of the first long wave embraces the period from 1789 to 1814, i.e., 25 years; its decline begins in 1814 and ends in 1849, a period of 35 years. The cycle is, therefore, completed in 60 years.[2]

The rise of the second wave begins in 1849 and ends in 1873, lasting 24 years. The turning point, however, is not the same in the United States as in England and France; in the United States the peak occurs in the year 1866, but this is to be explained by the Civil War and casts no doubt on the unity of the picture which the course of the wave exhibits in the two continents. The decline of the second wave begins in 1873 and ends in 1896, a period of 23 years. The length of the second wave is 47 years.

The upward movement of the third wave begins in 1896 and ends in 1920, its duration being 24 years. The decline of the wave, according to all data, begins in 1920.

It is easily seen that the French prices after the close of the 1850's move generally parallel to the English and American prices.

---

[1] [Ten pages of tabular material were given by Kondratieff at the end of his article. The charts presented in this translation are not merely reproductions of those in the original article but have been drawn anew from the data given in his tabular appendix. A few slight discrepancies between the new charts and those of Kondratieff were discovered, but in no case were the discrepancies significant.—Editors.]

[2] In the upswing, the English index exhibits several peaks, which fall in the years 1799, 1805, 1810, and 1814; but since after the year 1814 a distinctly downward tendency can be observed, we regard this year as the turning point.

CHART 1.—INDEX NUMBERS OF COMMODITY PRICES*
(1901–10 = 100)

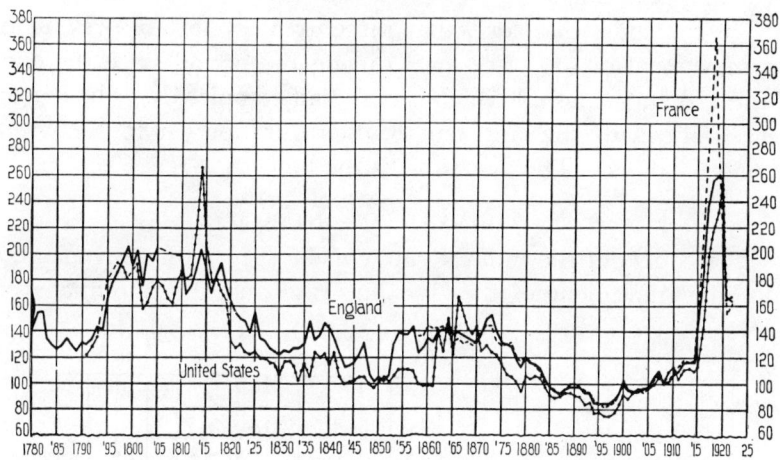

* The *French* data are taken from the *Annuaire Statistique* [Statistique Générale de la France], 1922, p. 341; the index number has been recalculated on a gold basis through use of dollar-franc exchange rates.

For *England*, there is for 1782–1865 the index of Jevons; for 1779–1850, a new index number, computed by Silberling and published in this REVIEW, v (1923); for the period after 1846, we have Sauerbeck's index, which at present is carried on by the *Statist*. Since Silberling's index is based upon more complete data of the prices of individual commodities than that of Jevons, we have used the former for the period 1780–1846. From 1846 on we use Sauerbeck's index number. Both indices have been tied together on the basis of their relation during 1846–50, for which period they are both available; after this procedure, we have shifted the series to a new base, 1901–10. For the period 1801–20 and since 1914, in which periods England was on a paper standard, the index numbers have been recalculated on a gold basis.

For the *United States*, we use the following series, which have been tied together: for 1791–1801, H. V. Roelse (*Quarterly Publications of the American Statistical Association*, December, 1917); 1801–25, A. H. Hansen (*ibid.*, December, 1915); 1825–39, C. H. Juergens (*ibid.*, June, 1911); 1840–90, Falkner (Report from the Committee on Finance of the United States Senate on *Wholesale Prices, Wages, and Transportation*, 52d Congress, 2d session, Report No. 1394, Part 1 [Washington: Government Printing Office, March 3, 1893]); since 1890, the B. L. S. index. All index numbers are on the base 1901–10. For the Greenback period (1862–78), they have been recalculated on a gold basis. All data [except Silberling's index] are taken from the *Annuaire Statistique*, 1922 [which utilizes the sources above cited].

It is, therefore, very probable that this parallelism existed in the preceding period as well.

We conclude, therefore, that three great cycles are present in the movement of the price level during the period since the end of the 1780's, the last of which is only half completed. The waves are not of exactly the same length, their duration varying between 47 and 60 years. The first wave is the longest.

V. The Rate of Interest

The course of the interest rate can be seen most conveniently from the movement of the discount rate and the quotations of

Chart 2.—Quotations of Interest-bearing Securities

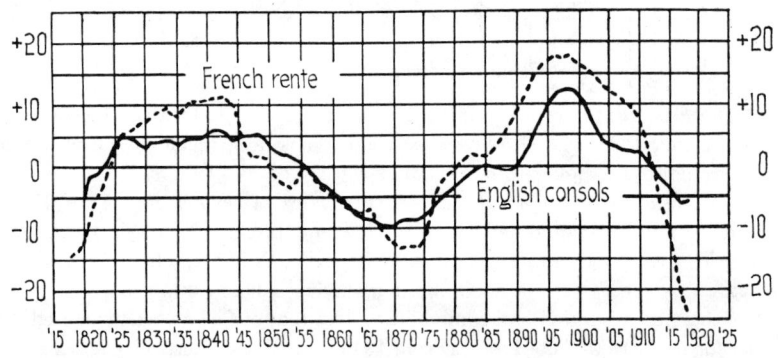

interest-bearing securities. Because the latter depend less on random fluctuations and reflect more accurately the influence of long-run factors, we use here only the quotations of state bonds.

Chart 2 shows the quotations of the French Rente[1] and of English consols.[2] Both have a secular trend during the period of

---

[1] Until 1825 the quotations of the five-per-cent Rente, after this the quotations of the three-per-cent Rente. In order to connect both series, we have first computed relatives with the base 1825–30 for both series. Then we shifted the base of the combined series to 1901–10, in order to make them comparable with the price curve. The original data are taken from the *Annuaire Statistique* [Statistique Générale de la France], 1922.

[2] According to the data in William Page, ed., *Commerce and Industry*, Vol. 2 (London, 1919), statistical tables, pp. 224–25. Relatives have been calculated from the figures, with the base 1901–10.

observation. The chart shows the deviations from the secular trend smoothed by means of a nine-year moving average.

The quotations of interest-bearing securities manifest, as is well known, a movement opposite to that of general business activity and of the interest rate. Therefore, if long waves are operative in the fluctuations of the interest rate, the movement of bond quotations must run in a direction counter to that of commodity prices. Just this is shown in our chart, which exhibits clearly the long waves in the movement of the quotations and consequently of the interest rate.

The chart starts only after the Napoleonic Wars, i.e., about the time that the first long wave of commodity prices had reached its peak; it does not cover the period of the upswing of the latter. Considering the data at hand, however, we may suppose that the quotations of state bonds took part in this movement also.

English consols actually manifest a decidedly downward tendency between 1792 and 1813. Their quotation in 1792 is 90.04; in 1813, on the other hand, it is 58.81. Although they drop most rapidly in the years 1797 and 1798, yet this steep decline is only an episode, and the general downward tendency from 1792 to 1813 stands out quite clearly.[1]

Accordingly, the period from the beginning of the 1790's up to 1813 appears to be the phase of rising interest rates. This period agrees perfectly with that of the rising wave of commodity prices.

The wave of bond quotations rises after 1813[2]—or the wave of the interest rate declines—even till the middle of the forties. (See the chart.) According to the unsmoothed data, consols reached their peak in 1844; the Rente, in 1845. With this, the first great cycle in the movement of the interest rate is completed.

The downward movement of bond quotations (or the rise of the interest rate) during the second cycle lasts from 1844–45 to

---

[1] Cf. N. J. Silberling, "British Financial Experience, 1790–1830," this REVIEW, 1 (1919), p. 289.

[2] The first years have disappeared from our chart because of the use of the nine-year moving average.

1870–74.[1] From this time onward until 1897, the market price of interest-bearing securities rises again, and consequently the interest rate goes down. With this, the second great cycle is completed.

The new decline of the quotations (rise in the rate of interest) lasts from 1897 to 1921. Thus the existence of great cycles in the movement of the interest rate appears very clearly.[2] The periods of these cycles agree rather closely with the corresponding periods in the movement of wholesale commodity prices.

VI–VII. Wages and Foreign Trade

[In Section VI, Kondratieff examines the course of weekly wages of workers in the English cotton-textile industry since 1806 and of English agricultural laborers since 1789.[3] The original wage data are reduced to a gold basis and then expressed in the form of index numbers with 1892 as the base year. Chart 3 presents these wage figures as deviations from trend, smoothed by use

---

[1] According to the original data, consols actually reach their lowest point in 1866, but the general tendency continues to be one of decline until 1874. The slump of quotations in 1866 is connected with the increase in the interest rate just preceding the money-market crisis of that year, and with the Austro-Prussian War.

[2] The existence of these cycles is also confirmed by several other studies: P. Wallich, "Beiträge zur Geschichte des Zinsfusses von 1800 bis zur Gegenwart," *Jahrbücher für Nationalökonomie und Statistik*, III. Folge, Vol. 42, pp. 289–312; J. Lescure, "Hausses et Baisses Générales des Prix," *Revue d'Economie Politique*, Nr. 4 (1912); R. A. Macdonald, "The Rate of Interest Since 1844," *Journal of the Royal Statistical Society*, LXXV (1912), pp. 361–79; T. T. Williams, "The Rate of Discount and the Price of Consols," *ibid.*, pp. 380–400. Also, *ibid.*, pp. 401–11, the discussion of the last-mentioned studies, especially the speech of E. L. Hartley, pp. 404–06.

[3] [Earnings of cotton-textile workers for 1806–1906 are taken from G. H. Wood, *The History of Wages in the Cotton Trade* (London, 1910), p. 127; beginning with 1906, they are from the *Abstract of Labour Statistics*.

For agricultural laborers, wage data for 1789–1896 are from A. L. Bowley, "The Statistics of Wages in the United Kingdom During the Last Hundred Years: Part IV, Agricultural Wages," *Journal of the Royal Statistical Society*, LXII (1899), pp. 555 ff. Thereafter, the figures are from Page, *op. cit.* The data refer to England and Wales.]

of a nine-year moving average. Kondratieff devotes the remainder of this section to a description of the series presented in Chart 3, from which analysis he concludes that, despite the scantiness of the available data, "long waves are undoubtedly present in the movement of wages, the periods of which correspond fairly well with those in commodity prices and the interest rate."

CHART 3.—WAGES IN ENGLAND

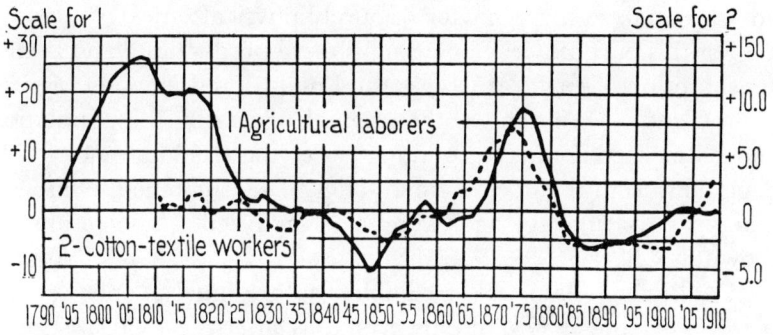

CHART 4.—FRENCH FOREIGN TRADE

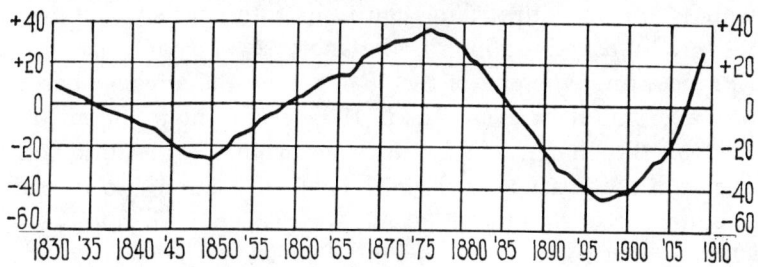

For his foreign-trade series presented in Section VII, Kondratieff takes the sum of French exports and imports. The figures were first corrected for population changes, and thereafter the secular trend (in the form of a second-degree parabola) was eliminated. The resulting deviations, smoothed by use of a nine-year moving average, are presented in Chart 4. After an examination of the chart, the author concludes that the data on foreign trade also show the existence of two great cycles, the periods of which coincide with those observed in the other data.]

VIII. The Production and Consumption of Coal and Pig Iron, and the Production of Lead

So far we have examined the movements only of such magnitudes, sensitive to changes in business conditions, as possess either a purely value character, e.g., commodity prices, interest rates, and wages, or at least a mixed character such as the data on foreign trade. Our study, however, would lose much of its force if we did not also analyze the behavior of purely physical series.

For this purpose we choose English coal production,[1] and French consumption of coal,[2] as well as the English production of pig iron and of lead.[3] We divided the original figures by the population, and eliminated from the resulting series the secular trends. The deviations from the lines of trend, after being smoothed by use of a nine-year moving average, were then analyzed. The results are shown in Chart 5.

Continuous data are available, unfortunately, only for the period after the 1830's, in part even only after the 1850's. Consequently, only one and one-half to two great cycles can be shown, but these appear with striking clarity in both charts.

There is a retardation in the increase of coal consumption [in France] until the end of the 1840's, then the advance becomes more rapid and reaches its peak in 1865, according to the smoothed curve (on the chart), and in 1873, according to the unsmoothed curve. In the latter year, English coal production also reaches a maximum, according to the unsmoothed curve. Then follows the decline, which comes to an end in 1890–94, giving way to a new long upswing. So we observe in the data relative to the rapidity in the increase of coal production and coal consumption nearly the whole of two large cycles, the periods of which correspond closely to the periods we have already found when considering other series.

Similarly, English production of pig iron and lead indicates sufficiently clearly the existence of one and one-half large cycles.

---

[1] According to the data of W. Page, *op. cit.*
[2] *Annuaire Statistique*, 1908 and 1922.
[3] According to *British and Foreign Trade and Industry*, and the *Statistical Abstract* [*for the United Kingdom*].

CHART 5.—CONSUMPTION OF COAL IN FRANCE AND PRODUCTION OF COAL, PIG IRON AND LEAD IN ENGLAND

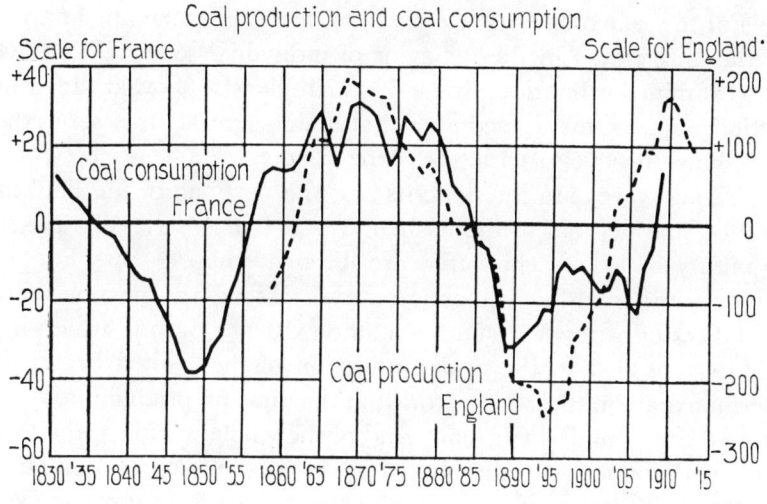

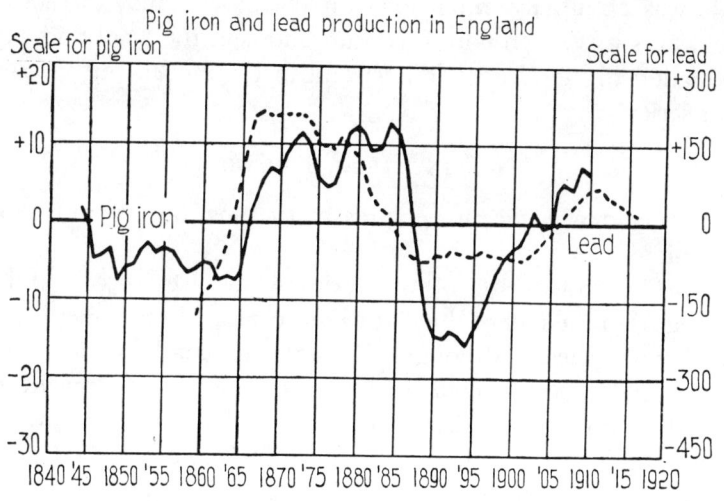

IX. Other Series

For the sake of brevity, we break off here the systematic analysis of the long waves in the behavior of individual series. We have also examined other data, some of which likewise showed the same periods as those mentioned above, although several other series did not show the cycles with the same clarity. Value series which show long waves are the deposits and the portfolio of the Bank of France, and deposits at the French savings banks; series of a mixed (quantity x price) character are French imports and English imports, and total English foreign trade. As regards the movement of indices of a physical character, the existence of long waves has been established in the coal production of the United States, of Germany, and of the whole world; in the pig-iron production of the United States and of Germany and of the whole world; in the lead and coal production of the United States; in the number of spindles of the cotton industry in the United States; in the cotton acreage in the United States and the oat acreage in France, etc.

It was absolutely impossible, on the other hand, to establish long waves in French cotton consumption; in the wool and sugar production of the United States; and in the movement of several other series.

X. Statistical Findings

The evidence we have presented thus far permits some conclusions.

(1) The movements of the series which we have examined running from the end of the eighteenth century to the present time show long cycles. Although the statistical-mathematical treatment of the series selected is rather complicated, the cycles discovered cannot be regarded as the accidental result of the methods employed. Against such an interpretation is to be set the fact that these waves have been shown with about the same timing in all the more important of the series examined.

(2) In those series which do not exhibit any marked secular trend—e.g., prices—the long cycles appear as a wave-like move-

THE LONG WAVES IN ECONOMIC LIFE

TABLE 1

Country and series	First cycle		Second cycle		Third cycle	
	Beginning of rise	Beginning of decline	Beginning of rise	Beginning of decline	Beginning of rise	Probable beginning of decline
France						
1. Prices.....................	....	....	....	1873	1896	1920
2. Interest rate................	....	1816*	1844	1872	1894	1921
3. Portfolio of the Bank of France	....	1810*	1851	1873	1902	1914
4. Deposits at the savings banks	....	....	1844	1874	1892	....
5. Wages of coal miners........	....	....	1849	1874	1895	....
6. Imports....................	....	....	1848	1880	1896	1914
7. Exports....................	....	....	1848	1872	1894	1914
8. Total foreign trade..........	....	....	1848	1872	1896	1914
9. Coal consumption...........	....	....	1849	1873	1896	1914
10. Oat acreage[1]................	....	....	1850*	1875	1892	1915
England						
1. Prices.....................	1789	1814	1849	1873	1896	1920
2. Interest rate................	1790	1816	1844	1874	1897	1921
3. Wages of agricultural laborers	1790	1812–17	1844	1875	1889	....
4. Wages of textile workers.....	....	1810*	1850†	1874	1890	....
5. Foreign trade...............	....	1810*	1842‡	1873	1894	1914
6. Coal production.............	....	....	1850*	1873	1893	1914
7. Pig iron production..........	....	....	....	1871§	1891	1914
8. Lead production.............	....	....	....	1870	1892	1914
United States						
1. Prices.....................	1790	1814	1849	1866	1896	1920
2. Pig iron production..........	....	....	....	1875–80	1900	1920
3. Coal production.............	....	....	....	1893	1896	1918
4. Cotton acreage..............	....	....	....	1874–81	1892–95	1915
Germany						
Coal production...............	....	....	....	1873‖	1895	1915
Whole world[2]						
1. Pig iron production..........	....	....	....	1872¶	1894	1914
2. Coal production.............	....	....	....	1873	1896	1914

[1] Reversed cycles.
[2] The data which refer to the whole world have not been corrected for population changes.
* Approximate dates.
† Another minimum falls in the year 1835.
‡ Other minima lie in the years 1837 and 1855.
§ Another maximum falls in the year 1881.
‖ Another maximum falls in the year 1883.
¶ Another maximum falls in the year 1882

32 BUSINESS CYCLE THEORY

ment about the average level. In the series, on the other hand, the movement of which shows such a trend, the cycles accelerate or retard the rate of growth.

(3) In the several series examined, the turning points of the long waves correspond more or less accurately. This is shown clearly by Table 1, which combines the results of the investigation not only of the data considered above but also of several other series.[1]

It is easy to see from this table that there is a very close correspondence in the timing of the wave movements of the series in the individual countries, in spite of the difficulties present in the treatment of these data. Deviations from the general rule that prevails in the sequence of the cycles are very rare. It seems to us that the absence of such exceptions is more remarkable than would be their presence.

(4) Although for the time being we consider it to be impossible to fix exactly upon the years that marked the turning points of the long cycles, and although the method according to which the statistical data have been analyzed permits an error of 5–7 years in the determination of the years of such turnings, the following limits of these cycles can nevertheless be presented as being those most probable:

First long wave
{ 1. The rise lasted from the end of the 1780's or beginning of the 1790's until 1810–17.
2. The decline lasted from 1810–17 until 1844–51.

Second long wave
{ 1. The rise lasted from 1844–51 until 1870–75.
2. The decline lasted from 1870–75 until 1890–96.

Third long wave
{ 1. The rise lasted from 1890–96 until 1914–20.
2. The decline probably begins in the years 1914–20.

(5) Naturally, the fact that the movement of the series examined runs in long cycles does not yet prove that such cycles also

---

[1] Table 1 enumerates the maxima and minima according to the original data. The problem of the most accurate method for the determination of the maxima and minima would deserve a special analysis; at present we leave this question open. We believe only that the indicated turning points are the most probable ones.

dominate the movement of all other series. A later examination with this point especially in mind will have to be made to show which ones of these share the described wave-like movement. As already pointed out, our investigation has also extended to series in which no such waves were evident. On the other hand, it is by no means essential that the long waves embrace all series.

(6) The long waves that we have established above relative to the series most important in economic life are international; and the timing of these cycles corresponds fairly well for European capitalistic countries. On the basis of the data that we have adduced, we can venture the statement that the same timing holds also for the United States. The dynamics in the development of capitalism, however, and especially the timing of the fluctuations in the latter country may have peculiarities.

XI. Empirical Characteristics

We were led to these conclusions by the study of statistical series characterizing the movement of the capitalist economy. From another point of view, the historical material relating to the development of economic and social life as a whole confirms the hypothesis of long waves. We neither can nor shall undertake here an analysis of this material. Nevertheless, several general propositions which we have arrived at concerning the existence and importance of long waves may be presented.

(1) The long waves belong really to the same complex dynamic process in which the intermediate cycles of the capitalistic economy with their principal phases of upswing and depression run their course. These intermediate cycles, however, secure a certain stamp from the very existence of the long waves. Our investigation demonstrates that during the rise of the long waves, years of prosperity are more numerous, whereas years of depression predominate during the downswing.[1]

(2) During the recession of the long waves, agriculture, as a rule, suffers an especially pronounced and long depression. This

---
[1] Cf. A. Spiethoff, "Krisen," (*Handwörterbuch der Staatswissenschaften*, 4th edition).

was what happened after the Napoleonic Wars; it happened again from the beginning of the 1870's onward; and the same can be observed in the years after the World War.[1]

(3) During the recession of the long waves, an especially large number of important discoveries and inventions in the technique of production and communication are made, which, however, are usually applied on a large scale only at the beginning of the next long upswing.

(4) At the beginning of a long upswing, gold production increases as a rule, and the world market [for goods] is generally enlarged by the assimilation of new and especially of colonial countries.

(5) It is during the period of the rise of the long waves, i.e., during the period of high tension in the expansion of economic forces, that, as a rule, the most disastrous and extensive wars and revolutions occur.

It is to be emphasized that we attribute to these recurring relationships an empirical character only, and that we do not by any means hold that they contain the explanation of the long waves.'

XII. THE NATURE OF LONG WAVES

Is it possible to maintain that the existence of long cycles in the dynamics of the capitalist economy is proved on the basis of the preceding statements? The relevant data which we were able to quote cover about 140 years. This period comprises two and one-half cycles only. Although the period embraced by the data is sufficient to decide the question of the existence of long waves, it is not enough to enable us to assert beyond doubt the cyclical character of those waves. Nevertheless we believe that the available data are sufficient to declare this cyclical character to be very probable.

We are led to this conclusion not only by the consideration of the factual material, but also because the objections to the assumption of long cyclical waves are very weak.

---

[1] Cf. Ernle, *English Farming Past and Present* (London, 1922), and G. F. Warren and F. A. Pearson, *The Agricultural Situation* (New York, 1924).

It has been objected that long waves lack the regularity which business cycles display. But this is wrong. If one defines "regularity" as repetition in regular time-intervals, then long waves possess this characteristic as much as the intermediate ones. A strict periodicity in social and economic phenomena does not exist at all—neither in the long nor in the intermediate waves. The length of the latter fluctuates at least between 7 and 11 years, i.e., 57 per cent. The length of the long cycles fluctuates between 48 and 60 years, i.e., 25 per cent only.

If regularity is understood to be the similarity and simultaneity of the fluctuations of different series, then it is present to the same degree in the long as in the intermediate waves.

If, finally, regularity is understood to consist in the fact that the intermediate waves are an international phenomenon, then the long waves do not differ from the latter in this respect either.

Consequently, there is no less regularity in the long waves than in the intermediate ones, and if we want to designate the latter as cyclical, we are bound not to deny this characterization to the former.

It has been pointed out [by other critics] that the long waves—as distinct from the intermediate ones which come from causes within the capitalistic system—are conditioned by casual, extra-economic circumstances and events, such as (1) changes in technique, (2) wars and revolutions, (3) the assimilation of new countries into the world economy, and (4) fluctuations in gold production.

These considerations are important. But they, too, are not valid. Their weakness lies in the fact that they reverse the causal connections and take the consequence to be the cause, or see an accident where we have really to deal with a law governing the events. In the preceding paragraphs, we have deliberately, though briefly, considered the establishment of some empirical rules for the movement of long waves. These regularities help us now to evaluate correctly the objections just mentioned.

1. *Changes in technique* have without doubt a very potent influence on the course of capitalistic development. But nobody has proved them to have an accidental and external origin.

Changes in the technique of production presume (1) that the relevant scientific-technical discoveries and inventions have been made, and (2) that it is *economically* possible to use them. It would be an obvious mistake to deny the creative element in scientific-technical discoveries and inventions. But from an objective viewpoint, a still greater error would occur if one believed that the direction and intensity of those discoveries and inventions were entirely accidental; it is much more probable that such direction and intensity are a function of the necessities of real life and of the preceding development of science and technique.[1]

Scientific-technical inventions in themselves, however, are insufficient to bring about a real change in the technique of production. They can remain ineffective so long as economic conditions favorable to their application are absent. This is shown by the example of the scientific-technical inventions of the seventeenth and eighteenth centuries which were used on a large scale only during the industrial revolution at the close of the eighteenth century. If this be true, then the assumption that changes in technique are of a random character and do not in fact spring from economic necessities loses much of its weight. We have seen before that the development of technique itself is part of the rhythm of the long waves.

2. *Wars and revolutions* also influence the course of economic development very strongly. But wars and revolutions do not come out of a clear sky, and they are not caused by arbitrary acts of individual personalities. They originate from real, especially economic, circumstances. The assumption that wars and revolutions acting from the outside cause long waves evokes the question as to

---

[1] One of the best and most compelling arguments for the assumption that scientific and technical inventions and discoveries are not made accidentally but are intimately connected with the needs of practical life is given by the numerous cases in which the same inventions and discoveries are made at the same time at different places and entirely independently of one another. Cf. the long list of such cases in W. F. Ogburn, *Social Change* (New York, 1924), p. 90. Cf. also Dannemann, *Die Naturwissenschaften in ihrer Entwickelung und in ihrem Zusammenhange* (Leipzig, 1923).

why they themselves follow each other with regularity and solely during the upswing of long waves. Much more probable is the assumption that wars originate in the acceleration of the pace and the increased tension of economic life, in the heightened economic struggle for markets and raw materials, and that social shocks happen most easily under the pressure of new economic forces.

Wars and revolutions, therefore, can also be fitted into the rhythm of the long waves and do not prove to be the forces from which these movements originate, but rather to be one of their symptoms. But once they have occurred, they naturally exercise a potent influence on the pace and direction of economic dynamics.

3. As regards the *opening-up of new countries for the world economy*, it seems to be quite obvious that this cannot be considered an outside factor which will satisfactorily explain the origin of long waves. The United States have been known for a relatively very long time; for some reason or other they begin to be entangled in the world economy on a major scale only from the middle of the nineteenth century. Likewise, the Argentine and Canada, Australia and New Zealand, were discovered long before the end of the nineteenth century, although they begin to be entwined in the world economy to a significant extent only with the coming of the 1890's. It is perfectly clear historically that, in the capitalistic economic system, new regions are opened for commerce during those periods in which the desire of old countries for new markets and new sources of raw materials becomes more urgent than theretofore. It is equally apparent that the limits of this expansion of the world economy are determined by the degree of this urgency. If this be true, then the opening of new countries does not provoke the upswing of a long wave. On the contrary, a new upswing makes the exploitation of new countries, new markets, and new sources of raw materials necessary and possible, in that it accelerates the pace of capitalistic economic development.

4. There remains the question whether the *discovery of new gold mines*, the *increase in gold production*, and a consequent *increase in the gold stock* can be regarded as a casual, outside factor causing the long waves.

An increase in gold production leads ultimately to a rise in prices and to a quickening in the tempo of economic life. But this does not mean that the changes in gold production are of a casual, outside character and that the waves in prices and in economic life are likewise caused by chance. We consider this to be not only unproved but positively wrong. This contention originates from the belief, first, that the discovery of gold mines and the perfection of the technique of gold production are accidental and, secondly, that every discovery of new gold mines and of technical inventions in the sphere of gold production brings about an increase in the latter. However great may be the creative element in these technical inventions and the significance of chance in these discoveries, yet they are not entirely accidental. Still less accidental—and this is the main point—are the fluctuations in gold production itself. These fluctuations are by no means simply a function of the activity of inventors and of the discoveries of new gold mines. On the contrary, the intensity of inventors' and explorers' activity and the application of technical improvement in the sphere of gold production, as well as the resulting increase of the latter, depend upon other, more general causes. The dependence of gold production upon technical inventions and discoveries of new gold mines is only secondary and derived.

Although gold is a generally recognized embodiment of value and, therefore, is generally desired, it is only a commodity. And like every commodity it has a cost of production. But if this be true, then gold production—even in newly discovered mines—can increase significantly only if it becomes more profitable, i.e., if the relation of the value of the gold itself to its cost of production (and this is ultimately the prices of other commodities) becomes more favorable. If this relation is unfavorable, even gold mines the richness of which is by no means yet exhausted may be shut down; if it is favorable, on the other hand, even relatively poor mines will be exploited.

When is the relation of the value of gold to that of other commodities most favorable for gold production? We know that commodity prices reach their lowest level toward the end of a long wave. This means that at this time gold has its highest purchasing power, and gold production becomes most favorable. This can be illustrated by the figures in Table 2.

Gold production, as can be seen from these figures, becomes more profitable as we approach a low point in the price level and a high point in the purchasing power of gold (1895 and the following years).

TABLE 2.—SELECTED STATISTICS OF GOLD MINING IN THE TRANSVAAL, 1890–1913*

Year	Cost of production	Profit
	Per ton of gold ore	
1890	42 sh. 2 d.	7 sh. 2 d.
1895	33 sh. 5 d.	11 sh. 11 d.
1899	28 sh. 0 d.	14 sh. 3 d.
1903	24 sh. 9 d.	14 sh. 11 d.
1906	22 sh. 2 d.	11 sh. 6 d.
1913	17 sh. 11 d.	9 sh. 10 d.

* Cf. W. A. Berridge, "The World's Gold Supply," this REVIEW, 11 (1920), p. 184.

It is clear, furthermore, that the stimulus to increased gold production necessarily becomes stronger the further a long wave declines. We, therefore, can suppose theoretically that gold production must in general increase most markedly when the wave falls most sharply, and vice versa.

In reality, however, the connection is not as simple as this but becomes more complicated, mainly just because of the effect of the changes in the technique of gold production and the discovery of new mines. It seems to us, indeed, that even improvements in technique and new gold discoveries obey the same fundamental law as does gold production itself, with more or less regularity in timing. Improvements in the technique of gold production and the discovery of new gold mines actually do bring about a lowering in the cost of production of gold; they influence the relation of these costs to the value of gold, and consequently the extent of gold production. But then it is obvious that exactly at the time when the relation of the value of gold to its cost becomes more unfavorable than theretofore, the need for technical improvements in gold mining and for the discovery of new mines necessarily becomes more urgent and thus stimulates research in this field. There is, of course, a time-lag, until this urgent necessity, though already recognized, leads to positive success. In reality, therefore, gold discoveries and technical improvements in gold mining will reach their peak only when the long wave has already passed its peak, i.e., perhaps in the middle of the downswing. The available facts confirm this supposition.[1] In the period after the 1870's, the following gold discoveries were made: 1881 in Alaska, 1884 in the Transvaal, 1887 in West Australia, 1890 in Colorado, 1894 in Mexico, 1896 in the Klondike. The inventions in the field of gold-mining technique, and especially the most important ones of this period (the inventions for the treatment of ore), were also made during the 1880's, as is well known.

Gold discoveries and technical improvements, if they occur, will naturally influence gold production. They can have the effect that the increase in gold production takes place somewhat earlier than at the end of the downswing of the long wave. They also can assist the expansion of gold production, once that limit is reached. This is precisely what happens in reality. Especially after the decline in the 1870's, a persistent, though admittedly slender, increase in gold production begins about the year 1883;[2] whereas, in spite of the disturbing influences of discoveries and inventions, the upswing really begins only after gold has reached its greatest purchasing power; and the increased production is due not only to the newly discovered gold fields but in a considerable degree also to the old ones. This is illustrated by the figures in Table 3.

---

[1] Berridge, *loc. cit.*, p. 181.
[2] Cf. *Statistical Abstract of the United States*, 1922, pp. 708-09.

TABLE 3.—GOLD PRODUCTION, 1890-1900
(Unit: thousand ounces)

	World total	Transvaal	United States	Australia	Russia	Canada	Mexico	India
1890	5,749	440	1,589	1,588	1,135	65	737	9
1895	9,615	2,017	2,255	2,356	1,388	101	290	230
1900	14,838	3,638	3,437	4,461	1,072	1,029	411	412

Source: Berridge, *loc. cit.*, p. 182.

From the foregoing one may conclude, it seems to us, that gold production, even though its increase can be a condition for an advance in commodity prices and for a general upswing in economic activity, is yet subordinate to the rhythm of the long waves and consequently cannot be regarded as a causal and random factor that brings about these movements from the outside.

XIII. CONCLUSIONS

The objections to the regular cyclical character of the long waves, therefore, seem to us to be unconvincing.

In view of this circumstance and considering also the positive reasons developed above, we think that, *on the basis of the available data, the existence of long waves of cyclical character is very probable.*

At the same time, we believe ourselves justified in saying that the long waves, if existent at all, are a very important and essential factor in economic development, a factor the effects of which can be found in all the principal fields of social and economic life.

Even granting the existence of long waves, one is, of course, not justified in believing that economic dynamics consists only in fluctuations around a certain level. The course of economic activity represents beyond doubt a process of development, but this development obviously proceeds not only through intermediate waves but also through long ones. The problem of economic development *in toto* cannot be discussed here.

In asserting the existence of long waves and in denying that they arise out of random causes, we are also of the opinion that the long waves arise out of causes which are inherent in the essence of the capitalistic economy. This naturally leads to the question as to the nature of these causes. We are fully aware of the difficulty and great importance of this question; but in the preceding sketch we had no intention of laying the foundations for an appropriate theory of long waves.[1]

---

[1] I arrived at the hypothesis concerning the existence of long waves in the years 1919-21. Without going into a special analysis, I formulated my general thesis for the first time shortly thereafter in my study, *The World Economy and Economic Fluctuations in the War and Post-War Period* (*Mirovoje chozjajstvo i jego koniunktury vo vremja i posle vojny* [Moscow, 1922]). During the winter and spring of 1925, I wrote a special study on "Long Waves in Economic Life" ("Bol'schije cykly konjunktury"), which was published in the volume of the Institute for Business Cycle Research, *Problems of Economic Fluctuations* (*Voprosy konjunktury*, Vol. 1). Only at the beginning of 1926 did I become acquainted with S. de Wolff's article "Prosperitäts- und Depressionsperioden," *Der lebendige Marxismus, Festgabe zum 70. Geburtstage von Karl Kautsky*. De Wolff in many points reaches the same result as I do. The works of J. van Gelderns, which de Wolff cites and which have evidently been published only in Dutch, are unknown to me.

3

BUSINESS CYCLES*

By Wesley C. Mitchell‖

The great mass of the unemployed in periods like that which led President Harding to call the Conference on Unemployment are workers who have been "laid off" because of business depression. The reason why millions of men lose their jobs at such times is that employers are losing money. Hence it is best to begin a study of methods of stabilizing employment by looking into the processes which every few years throw business into confusion.

I. The Nature of Business Cycles

Fifteen times within the past one hundred and ten years, American business has passed through a "crisis." The list of crisis years (1812, 1818, 1825, 1837, 1847, 1857, 1873, 1884, 1890, 1893, 1903, 1907, 1910, 1913, 1920) shows that the periods between successive crises have varied considerably in length. Further, no two crises have been precisely alike and the differences between some crises have been more conspicuous than the similarities. It is not surprising, therefore, that business men long thought of crises as "abnormal" events brought on by some foolish blunder made by the public or the government. On this view each crisis has a special cause which is often summed up by the newspapers in a picturesque phrase "the Jay Cooke panic" of 1873, "the railroad panic" of 1884, "the Cleveland panic" of 1893, "the rich man's panic" of 1903, "the Roosevelt panic" of 1907.

---

* *Business Cycles and Unemployment*, National Bureau of Economic Research, 1923, pages 5–18. Reprinted by the courtesy of the McGraw-Hill Book Company, Inc., and the author.

‖ Columbia University and National Bureau of Economic Research.

Longer experience, wider knowledge of business in other countries, and better statistical data have gradually discredited the view that crises are "abnormal" events, each due to a special cause. The modern view is that crises are but one feature of recurrent "business cycles." Instead of a "normal" state of business interrupted by occasional crises, men look for a continually changing state of business—continually changing in a fairly regular way. A crisis is expected to be followed by a depression, the depression by a revival, the revival by prosperity, and prosperity by a new crisis. Cycles of this sort can be traced for at least one century in America, perhaps for two centuries in the Netherlands, England, and France, and for shorter periods in Austria, Germany, Italy, Spain, and the Scandinavian countries. Within a generation or two similar cycles have begun to run their courses in Canada and Australia, South America, Russia, British India, and Japan.

At present it is less likely that the existence of business cycles will be denied than that their regularity will be exaggerated. In fact, successive cycles differ not only in length, but also in violence, and in the relative prominence of their various manifestations. Sometimes the crisis is a mild recession of business activity as in 1910 and 1913; sometimes it degenerates into a panic as in 1873, 1893, and 1907. Sometimes the depression is interrupted by an abortive revival as in 1895, sometimes it is intensified by financial pressure as in 1896 and 1914. Sometimes the depression is brief and severe as in 1908, sometimes it is brief and mild as in 1911, sometimes it is both long and severe as in 1874–1878. Revivals usually develop into full-fledged prosperity, but there are exceptions like that of 1895. Prosperity may reach a high pitch as in 1906–1907 and 1916–1917, or may remain moderate until overtaken by a mild crisis as in 1913, or by a severe panic as in 1893.

These differences among business cycles arise from the fact that the business situation at any given moment is the net resultant of a complex of forces among which the rhythm of business activity is only one. Harvest conditions, domestic politics, changes in monetary and banking systems, international relations, the making of war or of peace, the discovery of new industrial methods or resources, and a thousand other matters all affect the prospects of profits favorably or adversely and therefore tend to quicken or to slacken the pace of business. The fact that the rhythm of business activity can be traced in the net resultants produced by these many factors argues that it is one of the most constantly acting, and probably one of the most powerful, factors among them.

To give a sketch of the business cycle which will be applicable to future cases, it is necessary of course to put aside the complicating effects of the various special conditions which at any given time are influencing profits, and to concentrate attention upon the tendency of the modern business system to develop alternate periods of activity and sluggishness.

Even when the problem is simplified in this way, it remains exceedlingly complex. To keep from getting lost in a maze of complications, it is necessary to follow constantly the chief clue to business transactions. Every business establishment is supposed to aim primarily at making money. When the prospects of profits improve, business becomes more active. When these prospects grow darker, business becomes dull. Everything from rainfall to politics which affects business exerts its influence by affecting this crucial factor—the prospects of profits. The profits clue will not only prevent one from going astray, but will also enable one to thread the business maze slowly, if he chooses, taking time to examine all details, or to traverse the maze rapidly with an eye only for the conspicuous features. Needless to say, in this chapter we shall have to move rapidly.[1]

---

[1] The literature of business cycles is large and rather controversial. The differences among recent writers, however, are mainly differences in the distribution of emphasis. Among the best of the recent books upon the subject are the following: AFTALION, A., "Les Crises Périodiques de Surproduction," 2 vols., Paris, 1913; HANSEN, A. H., "Cycles of Prosperity and Depression," Madison, Wisconsin, 1921; HAWTREY, R. G., "Good and Bad Trade," London, 1913; HULL, G. H., "Industrial Depressions," New York, 1911; MITCHELL, W. C., "Business Cycles," Berkeley, California, 1913; MOORE, H. L., "Economic Cycles," New York, 1914; ROBERTSON, D. H., "A Study of Industrial Fluctuation," London, 1915.

II. Plan of Discussion

Since business cycles run an unceasing round, each cycle growing out of its predecessor and merging into its successor, our analysis can start with any phase of the cycle we choose. With whatever phase of the cycle we start, we shall have to plunge into the middle of things, taking the business situation as it then stands for granted. But once this start has been made, the course of the subsequent discussion is fixed by the succession of phases through which the cycle passes. By following these phases around the full cycle we shall come back to the starting point and end the discussion by accounting for the situation of business which we took for granted at the beginning.

With full liberty of choice, it is well to start with the phase of the cycle through which American business is passing at present—the phase of revival after a depression. The first task will be to see how such a revival gathers momentum and produces prosperity. Then in order will come a discussion of how prosperity produces conditions which lead to crises, how crises run out into depressions, and finally how depressions after a time produce conditions which lead to new revivals.

This whole analysis will be a brief account of the cycle in general business. But it is important to note that different industries are affected by business cycles in different ways. Some industries, for example, are hit early and hit hard by a decline in business activity, while other industries are affected but slightly. This aspect of the subject has received scant attention from investigators so far, and it cannot be adequately treated until the various industries have collected far more systematic records of their changing fortunes than are now available outside a narrow field. But with the cooperation of trade associations and certain business men we have collected some data that show how important and how promising is further work along similar lines. This material concerning the effect of business cycles upon particular industries will be presented in the next chapter after the cycle in general business has been traced.

III. Revivals and the Cumulation of Prosperity[1]

A period of depression produces after a time certain conditions which favor an increase of business activity. Among these conditions are a level of prices low in comparison with the prices of prosperous times, drastic reductions in the cost of doing business, narrow margins of profit, ample bank reserves, and a conservative policy in capitalizing business enterprises and in granting credits.

These conditions are accompanied sooner or later by an increase in the physical volume of purchases. When a depression begins, business enterprises of most sorts have in stock or on order liberal supplies of merchandise. During the earlier months of dullness they fill such orders as they can get mainly from these supplies already on hand, and in turn they buy or manufacture new supplies but sparingly. Similarly, families and business concerns at the end of a period of prosperity usually have a liberal stock of clothing, household furnishings, and equipment. For a while they buy little except the perishable goods which must be continuously consumed, like food and transportation. But after depression has lasted for months, the semi-durable goods wear out and must be replaced or repaired. As that time comes there is a gradual increase of buying, and as the seller's stocks are gradually reduced, there is also a slow increase of manufacturing.

Experience indicates that, once begun, a recovery of this sort tends to grow cumulatively. An increase in the amount of business that a merchant gets will make him a little readier to renew his shabby equipment and order merchandise in advance of immediate needs. An increase in the number of men employed by factories will lead to larger family purchases and so to more manufacturing. The improving state of trade will produce a more cheerful state of mind among business men, and the more cheerful state of mind will give fresh impetus to the improvement in trade. It is only a question of time when such an increase in the volume of business will turn dullness into activity. Sometimes the change is acceler-

---

[1] In this and the three following sections free use has been made of material from the writer's book, "Business Cycles," published in 1913.

ated by some propitious event arising from other than business sources, for example, good harvests, or is retarded by some influence, such as political uncertainties. Left to itself, the transformation proceeds slowly but surely.

While the price level is often sagging slowly when a revival begins, the cumulative expansion in the physical volume of trade presently stops the fall and starts a rise. For, when enterprises have in sight as much business as they can handle with their existing facilities of standard efficiency, they stand out for higher prices on additional orders. This policy prevails even in the most keenly competitive trades, because additional orders can be executed only by breaking in new hands, starting old machinery, buying new equipment, or making some other change which involves increased expense. The expectation of its coming hastens the advance. Buyers are anxious to secure or to contract for large supplies while the low level of quotations continues, and the first definite signs of an upward trend of quotations brings out a sudden rush of orders.

Like the increase in the physical volume of business, the rise of prices spreads rapidly; for every advance of quotations puts pressure upon someone to recoup himself by making a compensatory advance in the prices of what he has to sell. The resulting changes in prices are far from even, not only as between different commodities, but also as between different parts of the system of prices. In most but not all cases, retail prices lag behind wholesale, the prices of staple consumers' behind the prices of staple producers' goods, and the prices of finished products behind the prices of raw materials. Among raw materials, the prices of mineral products reflect the changed business conditions more regularly than do the prices of raw animal, farm, or forest products. Wages rise sometimes more promptly, but nearly always in less degree than wholesale prices; discount rates rise sometimes more slowly than commodities and sometimes more rapidly; interest rates on long loans move sluggishly in the early stages of revival, while the prices of stocks—particularly of common stocks—generally precede and exceed commodity prices on the rise. The causes of these differences in the promptness and the energy with which various classes of prices respond to the stimulus of business activity are found partly in differences of organization among the markets for commodities, labor, loans, and securities; partly in the technical circumstances affecting the relative demand for and supply of these several classes of goods; and partly in the adjusting of selling prices to changes in the aggregate of buying prices which a business enterprise pays, rather than to changes in the prices of the particular goods bought for resale.

In the great majority of enterprises, larger profits result from these divergent price fluctuations coupled with the greater physical volume of sales. For, while the prices of raw materials and of wares bought for resale usually, and the prices of bank loans often, rise faster than selling prices, the prices of labor lag far behind, and the prices which make up overhead costs are mainly stereotyped for a time by old agreements regarding salaries, leases, and bonds.

This increase of profits, combined with the prevalence of business optimism, leads to a marked expansion of investments. Of course the heavy orders for machinery, the large contracts for new construction, etc., which result, swell still further the physical volume of business and render yet stronger the forces which are driving prices upward.

Indeed, the salient characteristic of this phase of the business cycle is the cumulative working of the various processes which are converting a revival of trade into intense prosperity. Not only does every increase in the physical volume of trade cause other increases, every convert to optimism make new converts, and every advance of prices furnish an incentive for fresh advances, but the growth of trade helps to spread optimism and to raise prices, while optimism and rising prices both support each other and stimulate the growth of trade. Finally, as has just been said, the changes going forward in these three factors swell profits and encourage investments, while high profits and heavy investments react by augmenting trade justifying optimism, and raising prices.

IV. How Prosperity Breeds a Crisis

While the processes just sketched work cumulatively for a time to enhance prosperity, they also cause a slow accumulation of stresses within the balanced system of business—stresses which ultimately undermine the conditions upon which prosperity rests.

Among these stresses is the gradual increase in the costs of doing business. The decline in overhead costs per unit of output ceases when enterprises have once secured all the business they can handle with their standard equipment, and a slow increase of these costs begins when the expiration of old contracts makes necessary renewals at the high rates of interest, rent, and salaries which prevail in prosperity. Meanwhile the operating costs rise at a relatively rapid rate. Equipment which is antiquated and plants which are ill located or otherwise work at some disadvantage are brought again into operation. The price of labor rises, not only because the standard rates of wages go up, but also because of the prevalence of higher pay for overtime. More serious still is the fact that the efficiency of labor declines, because overtime brings weariness, because of the employment of "undesirables," and because crews cannot be driven at top speed when jobs are more numerous than men to fill them.[1] The prices of raw materials continue to rise

---

[1] Compare the discussion of fluctuations of production and of numbers employed in Section V of Chap. IV, below. Mr. Berridge there shows that physical output rises more in booms and declines more in depressions than do numbers of employees. But he agrees with the view here expressed regarding changes in efficiency of labor, thinking that these changes are more than offset by other factors—notably the prevalence of overtime in booms and of part time in depressions. Nevertheless, as George Soule of The Labor Bureau, Inc. who has kindly read this manuscript points out, the changes in efficiency of labor here referred to have never been statistically proved on a large scale. There are factors which tend to decrease efficiency in dull times, such as the desire to spread out slack work as long as possible, and inability to keep men on the processes for which they are best fitted. Mr. Soule knows personally some cases in which these causes have caused a decline of production in depression. He adds that if production does show a decline during booms per hours worked, "management or some other factor may be partly or even wholly responsible."

For evidence supporting the text, see the writer's "Business Cycles," pp. 476–80.

faster on the average than the selling prices of products. Finally, the numerous small wastes, incident to the conduct of business enterprises, creep up when managers are hurried by a press of orders demanding prompt delivery.

A second stress is the accumulating tension of the investment and money markets. The supply of funds available at the old rates of interest for the purchase of bonds, for lending on mortgages, and the like, fails to keep pace with the rapidly swelling demand. It becomes difficult to negotiate new issues of securities except on onerous terms, and men of affairs complain of the "scarcity of capital." Nor does the supply of bank loans grow fast enough to keep up with the demand. For the supply is limited by the reserves which bankers hold against their expanding liabilities. Full employment and active retail trade cause such a large amount of money to remain suspended in active circulation that the cash left in the banks increases rather slowly, even when the gold supply is rising most rapidly. On the other hand, the demand for bank loans grows not only with the physical volume of trade, but also with the rise of prices, and with the desire of men of affairs to use their own funds for controlling as many business ventures as possible. Moreover, this demand is relatively inelastic, since many borrowers think they can pay high rates of discount for a few months and still make profits on their turnover, and since the corporations which are unwilling to sell long-time bonds at the hard terms which have come to prevail try to raise part of the funds they require by discounting notes running only a few years.

Tension in the bond and money markets is unfavorable to the continuance of prosperity, not only because high rates of interest reduce the prospective margins of profit, but also because they check the expansion in the volume of trade out of which prosperity developed. Many projected ventures are relinquished or postponed, either because borrowers conclude that the interest would absorb too much of their profits, or because lenders refuse to extend their commitments farther.

The credit expansion, which is one of the most regular concomitants of an intense boom, gives an appearance of enhanced prosperity to business. But this appearance is delusive. For when the industrial army is already working its equipment at full capacity, further borrowings by men who wish to increase their own businesses cannot increase appreciably the total output of goods. The borrowers bid up still higher the prices of commodities and services, and so cause a further expansion in the pecuniary volume of trade. But they produce no corresponding increase in the physical volume of things men can consume. On the contrary, their borrowings augment that mass of debts, many protected by insufficient margins, which at the first breath of suspicion leads to the demands for liquidation presently to be discussed.

The difficulty of financing new projects intensifies the check which one important group of industries has already begun to suffer from an earlier-acting cause. The industries in question are those which produce industrial equipment—tools, machines, plant—and the materials of which this equipment is made, from lumber and cement to copper and steel.

The demand for industrial equipment is partly a replacement demand and partly a demand for betterments and extensions. The replacement demand for equipment doubtless varies with the physical quantity of demand for products; since, as a rule, the more rapidly machines and rolling stock are run, the more rapidly they wear out. The demand for betterments and extensions, on the other hand, varies not with the physical quantity of the products demanded, but with the fluctuations in this quantity.

To illustrate the peculiar changes in demand for industrial equipment which follow from this situation, suppose that the physical quantity of a certain product varied in five successive years as follows:

First year	100,000 tons
Second year	95,000 tons
Third year	100,000 tons
Fourth year	110,000 tons
Fifth year	115,000 tons

This product is turned out by machines each of which will produce one hundred tons per year. Thus the number of machines in operation each year was:

First year	1,000 machines
Second year	950 machines
Third year	1,000 machines
Fourth year	1,100 machines
Fifth year	1,150 machines

Each year one-tenth of the machines in operation wears out. The replacement demand for machines was therefore:

First year	100 machines
Second year	95 machines
Third year	100 machines
Fourth year	110 machines
Fifth year	115 machines

The demand for additional machines was far more variable. Neglecting the first year, for which our illustration does not supply data, it is plain that no additions to equipment were required the second year when fifty of the machines in existence stood idle, and also none the third year. But after all the existing machines had been utilized new machines had to be bought at the rate of one machine for each one hundred tons added to the product. Hence the demand for additions to equipment shown by the number of machines in operation was:

First year	No data
Second year	None
Third year	None
Fourth year	100 machines
Fifth year	50 machines

Adding the replacement demand and the demand for additions to equipment, we find the total demand for industrial equipment of this type to be:

First year	No data
Second year	95 machines
Third year	100 machines
Fourth year	210 machines
Fifth year	165 machines

Of course the figures in this example are fanciful. But they illustrate genuine characteristics of the demand for industrial equipment. During depression and early revival the equipment-building trades get little business except what is provided by the replacement demand. When the demand for products has reached the stage where it promises soon to exceed the capacity of existing facilities, however, the equipment trades experience a sudden and intense boom. But their business falls off again before prosperity has reached its maximum, provided the *increase* in the physical quantity of products slackens before it stops. Hence the seeming anomalies pointed out by J. Maurice Clark:

> The demand for equipment may decrease . . . even though the demand for the finished product is still growing. The total demand for [equipment] tends to vary more sharply than the demand for finished products. . . . The maximum and minimum points in the demand for [equipment] tend to precede the maximum and minimum points in the demand for the finished products, the effect being that the change may appear to precede its own cause.[1]

When we add to the check in the orders for new equipment arising from any slackening in the increase of demand for products, the further check which arises from stringency in the bond market and the high cost of construction, we have no difficulty in understanding why contracts for this kind of work become less numerous as the climax of prosperity approaches. Then the steel mills, foundries, machine factories, copper smelters, quarries, lumber mills, cement plants, construction companies, general contractors, and the like find their orders for future delivery falling off. While for the present they may be working at high pressure to complete old contracts within the stipulated time, they face a serious restriction of trade in the near future.

The imposing fabric of prosperity is built with a liberal factor of safety; but the larger grows the structure, the more severe become these internal stresses. The only effective means of preventing disaster while continuing to build is to raise selling prices time after time high enough to offset the encroachments of costs upon profits,

---

[1] Business Acceleration and the Law of Demand, *Journal of Political Economy*, March, 1917. Also see GEORGE H. HULL, "Industrial Depressions," 1911. Some materials concerning the sharp fluctuations in the activity of the equipment trades are given in Chap. II.

to cancel the advancing rates of interest, and to keep producers willing to contract for fresh industrial equipment.

But it is impossible to keep selling prices rising for an indefinite time. In default of other checks, the inadequacy of cash reserves would ultimately compel the banks to refuse a further expansion of loans upon any terms. But before this stage has been reached, the rise of prices may be stopped by the consequences of its own inevitable inequalities. These inequalities become more glaring the higher the general level is forced; after a time they threaten serious reduction of profits to certain business enterprises, and the troubles of these victims dissolve that confidence in the security of credits with which the whole towering structure of prosperity has been cemented.

What, then, are the lines of business in which selling prices cannot be raised sufficiently to prevent a reduction of profits? There are certain lines in which selling prices are stereotyped by law, by public commissions, by contracts of long term, by custom, or by business policy, and in which no advance, or but meager advances can be made. There are other lines in which prices are always subject to the incalculable chances of the harvests, and in which the market value of all accumulated stocks of materials and finished goods wavers with the crop reports. There are always some lines in which the recent construction of new equipment has increased the capacity for production faster than the demand for their wares has expanded under the repressing influence of the high prices which must be charged to prevent a reduction of profits. The unwillingness of producers to let fresh contracts threatens loss not only to contracting firms of all sorts, but also to all the enterprises from whom they buy materials and supplies. The high rates of interest not only check the current demand for wares of various kinds, but also clog the effort to maintain prices by keeping large stocks of goods off the market until they can be sold to better advantage. Finally, the very success of other enterprises in raising selling prices fast enough to defend their profits aggravates the difficulties of the men who are in trouble; for to the latter every further rise of prices for products which they buy means a further strain upon their already stretched resources.

As prosperity approaches its height, then, a sharp contrast develops between the business prospects of different enterprises. Many, probably the majority, are making more money than at any previous stage of the business cycle. But an important minority, at least, face the prospect of declining profits. The more intense prosperity becomes, the larger grows this threatened group. It is only a question of time when these conditions, bred by prosperity, will force some radical readjustment.

Now such a decline of profits threatens worse consequences than the failure to realize expected dividends, for it arouses doubt concerning the security of outstanding credits. Business credit is based primarily upon the capitalized value of present and prospective profits, and the volume of credits outstanding at the zenith of prosperity is adjusted to the great expectations which prevail when the volume of trade is enormous, when prices are high, and when men of affairs are optimistic. The rise of interest rates has already narrowed the margins of security behind credits by reducing the capitalized value of given profits. When profits themselves begin to waver, the case becomes worse. Cautious creditors fear lest the shrinkage in the market rating of the business enterprises which owe them money will leave no adequate security for repayment; hence they begin to refuse renewals of old loans to the enterprises which cannot stave off a decline of profits, and to press for a settlement of outstanding accounts.

Thus prosperity ultimately brings on conditions which start a liquidation of the huge credits which it has piled up. And in the course of this liquidation, prosperity merges into crisis.

V. Crises

Once begun, the process of liquidation extends very rapidly, partly because most enterprises which are called upon to settle their maturing obligations in turn put similar pressure upon their own debtors, and partly because, despite all efforts to keep secret what is going forward, news presently leaks out and other creditors take alarm.

While this financial readjustment is under way, the problem of making profits on current transactions is subordinated to the more vital problem of maintaining solvency. Business managers concentrate their energies upon providing for their outstanding liabilities and upon nursing their financial resources, instead of upon pushing their sales. In consequence, the volume of new orders falls off rapidly; that is, the factors which were already dimming the prospects of profits in certain lines of business are reinforced and extended. Even when the overwhelming majority of enterprises meet the demand for payment with success, the tenor of business developments undergoes a change. Expansion gives place to contraction, though without a violent wrench. Discount rates rise higher than usual, securities and commodities fall in price, and as old orders are completed, working forces are reduced; but there is no epidemic of bankruptcies, no run upon banks, and no spasmodic interruption of the ordinary business processes.

At the opposite extreme from crises of this mild order stand the crises which degenerate into panics. When the process of liquidation reaches a weak link in the chain of interlocking credits and the bankruptcy of some conspicuous enterprise spreads unreasoning alarm among the business public, then the banks are suddenly forced to meet a double strain—a sharp increase in the demand for loans, and a sharp increase in the demand for repayment of deposits. If the banks prove able to honor both demands without flinching, the alarm quickly subsides. But if, as in 1873, 1893, and 1907, many solvent business men are refused accommodation at any price, and if depositors are refused payment in full, the alarm turns into panic. A restriction of payments by the banks gives rise to a premium upon currency, to the hoarding of cash, and to the use of various unlawful substitutes for money. A refusal by the banks to expand their loans, still more a policy of contraction, sends interest rates up to three or four times their usual figures, and causes forced suspensions and bankruptcies. Collections fall into arrears, domestic exchange rates are dislocated, workmen are discharged because employers cannot get money for pay-rolls or fear lest they cannot collect pay for goods when delivered, stocks fall to extremely low levels, even the best bonds decline somewhat in price, commodity markets are disorganized by sacrifice sales, and the volume of business is violently contracted.

VI. Depressions

The period of severe financial pressure is often followed by the reopening of numerous enterprises which had been shut for a time. But this prompt revival of activity is partial and short-lived. It is based chiefly upon the finishing of orders received but not completely executed in the preceding period of prosperity, or upon the effort to work up and market large stocks of materials already on hand or contracted for. It comes to an end as this work is gradually finished, because new orders are not forthcoming in sufficient volume to keep the mills and factories busy.

There follows a period during which depression spreads over the whole field of business and grows more severe. Consumers' demand declines in consequence of wholesale discharges of wage-earners, the gradual exhaustion of past savings, and the reduction of other classes of family incomes. With consumers' demand falls the business demand for raw materials, current supplies, and equipment used in making consumers' goods. Still more severe is the shrinkage of producers' demand for construction work of all kinds, since few individuals or enterprises care to sink money in new business ventures so long as trade remains depressed and the price level is declining. The contraction in the physical volume of business which results from these several shrinkages in demand is cumulative, since every reduction of employment causes a reduction of consumers' demand, and every decline in consumers' demand depresses current business demand and discourages investment, thereby causing further discharges of employees and reducing consumers' demand once more.

With the contraction in the physical volume of trade goes a fall of prices; for, when current orders are insufficient to employ the existing industrial equipment, competition for what business is to be had becomes keener. This decline spreads through the regular commercial channels which connect one enterprise with another, and is cumulative, since every reduction in price facilitates, if it does not force, reductions in other prices, and the latter reductions react in their turn to cause fresh reductions at the starting point.

As the rise of prices which accompanies revival, so the fall which accompanies depression is characterized by marked differences in degree. Wholesale prices usually fall faster than retail, the prices of producers' goods faster than those of consumer's goods, and the prices of raw materials faster than those of manufactured products. The prices of raw mineral products follow a more regular course than those of raw forest, farm, or animal products. As compared with the general index numbers of commodity prices at wholesale, index numbers of wages and interest on long-time loans decline in less degree, while index numbers of discount rates and of stocks decline in greater degree. The only important group of prices to rise in the face of depression is that of high-grade bonds.

Of course, the contraction in the physical volume of trade and the fall of prices reduce the margin of present and prospective profits, spread discouragement among business men, and check enterprise. But they also set in motion certain processes of readjustment by which depression is gradually overcome.

The operating costs of doing business are reduced by the rapid fall in the prices of raw materials and of bank loans, by the increase in the efficiency of labor which comes when employment is scarce and men are anxious to hold their jobs, by closer economy on the part of managers, and by the adoption of improved methods. Overhead costs, also, are reduced by reorganizing enterprises which have actually become or which threaten to become insolvent, by the sale of other enterprises at low figures, by reduction of rentals and refunding of loans, by charging off bad debts and writing down depreciated properties, and by admitting that a recapitalization of business enterprises—corresponding to the lower prices of stocks —has been effected on the basis of lower profits.[1]

---

[1] George Soule comments: "I should like to see a specific warning against the theory—so often resorted to by banks and employers in efforts to 'deflate' wages— that business cannot revive unless all levels of wages and prices bear exactly the same relation to each other as before the depression—a sort of 'normal' or mathematically balanced relation. I do not believe the existence of such a normal relationship has ever been proved. Certainly, it has not been proved that there can be no permanent changes in price and wage relationships."

While these reductions in costs are still being made, the demand for goods ceases to shrink and begins slowly to expand—a change which usually comes after one or two years of depression. Accumulated stocks left over from prosperity are gradually exhausted, and current consumption requires current production. Clothing, furniture, machinery, and other moderately durable articles which have been used as long as possible are finally discarded and replaced. Population continues to increase at a fairly uniform rate; the new mouths must be fed and new backs clothed. New tastes appear among consumers and new methods among producers, giving rise to demand for novel products. Most important of all, the investment demand for industrial equipment revives; for, though saving slackens it does not cease, with the cessation of foreclosure sales and corporate reorganizations the opportunities to buy into old enterprises at bargain prices become fewer, capitalists become less timid as the crisis recedes into the past, the low rates of interest on long-term bonds encourage borrowing, the accumulated technical improvements of several years may be utilized, and contracts can be let on most favorable conditions as to cost and prompt execution.

Once these various forces have set the physical volume of trade to expanding again, the increase proves cumulative, though for a time the pace of growth is kept slow by the continued sagging of prices. But while the latter maintains the pressure upon business men and prevents the increased volume of orders from producing a rapid rise of profits, still business prospects become gradually brighter. Old debts have been paid, accumulated stocks of commodities have been absorbed, weak enterprises have been reorganized, the banks are strong—all the clouds upon the financial horizon have disappeared. Everything is ready for a revival of activity, which will begin whenever some fortunate circumstance gives a sudden fillip to demand, or, in the absence of such an event, when the slow growth of the volume of business has filled order books and paved the way for a new rise of prices.

Such is the stage of the business cycle with which the analysis began, and, having accounted for its own beginning, the analysis ends.

4

ECONOMETRIC BUSINESS CYCLE RESEARCH*
By Jan Tinbergen‖

1. Introductory

In recent years various attempts have been made to construct econometric models of the business cycle mechanism.[1] Some of them are very simple, others more complicated; some pay more attention to the mathematico-economic set-up, others give special care to a statistical determination of the coefficients involved. The latter group is notable for, in particular, the model by Radice of the post-war United Kingdom,[2] that by De Wolff of post-war Sweden,[3] and my own attempts for the Netherlands and the United States.[4] As far as I am myself concerned, a "model under con-

---

* *The Review of Economic Studies*, Volume VII, 1940, pages 73–90.
‖ Graduate School of Economics, Rotterdam.

[1] Apart from the examples to be quoted in notes 2 to 5 we may mention the following:

R. Frisch: "Propagation Problems and Impulse Problems in Dynamic Economics," *Economic Essays in Honour of Gustav Cassel*, London, 1933.

M. Kalecki: "A Macrodynamic Theory of the Business Cycle," *Econometrica*, 3 (1935), p. 327.

E. Lundberg: *Studies in the Theory of Economic Expansion*, London, 1937.

B. A. Chait: *Les fluctuations économiques et l'interdépendance des marchés*, Brussels, 1938.

[2] E. A. Radice: "A Dynamic Scheme for the British Trade Cycle, 1929–1937," *Econometrica* 7 (1939), p. 1.

[3] To be published in the near future.

[4] J. Tinbergen: *An Econometric Approach to Business Cycle Problems*, Paris, 1937, and *Business Cycles in the United States of America, 1919–1932* (Statistical Testing of Business Cycle Theories, II), League of Nations, Geneva, 1939.

struction" is that for the United Kingdom between 1870 and 1914.[1]

An essential feature of an econometric model is, I think, that it combines mathematico-economic treatment with statistical measurement of some type. The ultimate objectives of these models are the same as of any system of business cycle research, viz. (i) to explain historical events; (ii) to forecast future developments under certain conditions; and (iii) to indicate the probable consequences of measures of business cycle policy. Within the framework of these ultimate objectives, one may distinguish more proximate objectives. These may be separately stated for the economic and the statistical parts of the task. The objectives of the economic part are, to my mind:

(*a*) to clarify notions and assumptions of various theories and to localise differences of opinion;

(*b*) to find the complete implications of any set of assumptions as to type of movement resulting, influence of given types of policy, etc.

The objectives of the statistical part are:

(*a*) either, more modestly, to find such values for coefficients, etc., as are not contrary to observation;

(*b*) or, more ambitiously, to prove, under certain conditions, something to be true or not true.

It goes without saying that the use of mathematics is only a question of language; it does not imply any *a priori* choice of economic theory.

The statistical instruments used may be different. A frequent misunderstanding is that only multiple correlation analysis is used, or even admitted. Any method yielding results may be used, of course.

Recently there has been some discussion on the nature and the limitations of the econometric method.[2] I gladly accept, there-

---

[1] G. Lutfalla is working on a similar model for France.

[2] Cf. especially Mr. Keynes's review of Vol. 1 of my League of Nations study: "Statistical Testing of Business Cycle Theories, I: A Method and its Application on Investment Activity," in the *Economic Journal* of September, 1939, p. 558.

fore, the invitation of the editors of this REVIEW, to go into some more detail concerning the method. Since the subject is almost ripe for a text-book—at any rate as far as its extent is concerned—I must necessarily restrict myself. I shall try to do this in an efficient way, and to fill some gaps by references to other papers.

2. MATHEMATICAL BUSINESS CYCLE THEORY: THE FOUNDATIONS

2.1. *The "Arrow Scheme" and Elementary Equations*

Turning, first, to the mathematico-economic part of the work, I think this may be characterised as the construction of a scheme for

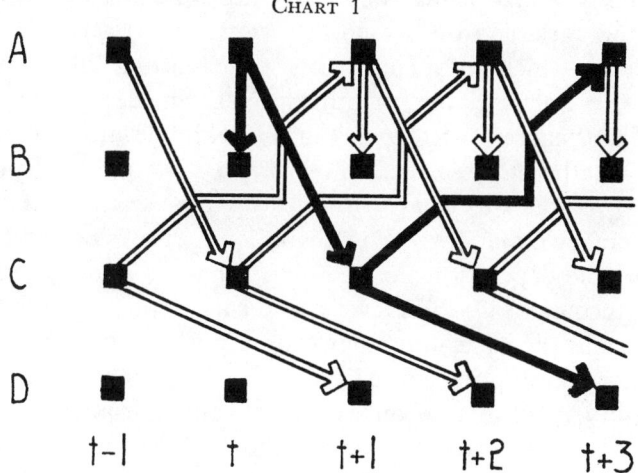

CHART 1

the utilisation of business cycle theories. It consists in indicating the logical structure of the business cycle mechanism. A graphic representation, given in Chart 1, may serve as a starting point. This scheme shows, in each (vertical) column the list of phenomena (variables) included: A, B, C . . . In each (horizontal) row the course of time is represented; i.e. the consecutive dots represent one phenomenon at consecutive unit time intervals. Denoting these by a suffix, the dots represent, e.g. A_1, A_2, A_3, A_4, etc. The extent of each of them, if A is a measurable phenomenon, could be plotted in a third dimension, e.g. perpendicular to the plane. We shall not, however, go into that now. Any definite theory tells us how a given change at moment t in A acts on other phenomena at other moments. Suppose the theory is that it acts on B without lag and on C with a lag of one time unit, i.e. $A(t)$ acts on $C(t+1)$. This is indicated by the arrows from $A(t)$ to $B(t)$ and from $A(t)$ to $C(t+1)$. If, e.g. changes in C are assumed to work on D and A, both with a lag of two time units, this will again be indicated by arrows. A change in $A(t)$ may be said to be a "first" or "direct" "cause" to a change in $C(t+1)$, and a "second" or "indirect" cause to a change in $D(t+3)$. All the arrows repeat themselves as long as the model's structure is supposed to remain the same. The more details are considered, the greater the number of arrows. The totality of arrows may be "listed" in two ways, viz. (i) according to the variable from which they start, or (ii) according to the variable at which they end. In the first listing all "effects" of changes in one variable on others are grouped together; in the second all "causes" of changes in one variable are put into one group. Both lists describe, however, the same mechanism. The latter corresponds to what will, in this paper, be called the system of elementary equations. Each equation indicates how changes in one variable depend on the "causing" changes in other variables.

Let income be Y, price level p, and consumption outlay U'; and let a certain theory assume that consumption outlay depends only on income and price level one time unit before. The arrows ending in U'_t will then be only two, one coming from Y_{t-1}, and one from p_{t-1}. The corresponding equation will be[1]

$$U'_t = f(Y_{t-1}, p_{t-1}) \qquad (1)$$

The function may be given a definite mathematical shape, it may, e.g., be linear:

$$U'_t = v_1 Y_{t-1} + v_2 p_{t-1} \qquad (2)$$

In that particular case, and in some other cases, it is possible to indicate the "influence" of a change ΔY_{t-1} on U'_t; it will be $v_1 \Delta Y_{t-1}$; similarly the "influence" of a change Δp_{t-1} will be $v_2 \Delta p_{t-1}$.

---

[1] By unbarred symbols I indicate deviations from the average over the period studied. For the present equation this is indifferent, but for some of the further equations it is essential.

A complete theory will contain as many such equations as unknown variables. The economic character of these equations may be one of the following:

(i) a definition, e.g. value equals price times quantity;
(ii) a balance equation, e.g. production = consumption + increase in stocks;
(iii) a technical, natural or institutional connection;
(iv) a reaction equation. The above example on consumption outlay belongs to this class. In general, the more "interesting" equations belong to this class, such as supply and demand equations. They always represent the reaction of groups of individuals or firms on certain economic conditions (incomes, prices, costs, etc.).

2.2. *Variables, Coefficients, Unsystematic Terms*

The example given was a very simple one. In its most complete form elementary equations may contain the following elements:

1. the variable "explained" by that equation (in the example U');
2. "explanatory" variables (in the example: Y and p);
3. constant coefficients and lags, representing the "structure" of the model (v_1 and v_2);
4. additional unsystematic terms. These are to be understood in the following way. All the possible causes of changes in the variable to be explained may be subdivided into systematic and non-systematic ones. The subdivision is to some extent arbitrary in that it may depend on the objectives of the study as well as on the behaviour of these causes. Purely accidental causes "obeying the probability laws" will always be classified as non-systematic. The influence of certain types of policy (e.g. tax changes) may, however, be classified in either group, depending on the problems to be solved. Indicating by $R_t^{U'}$ the total influence of non-systematic forces, equation (2) may be given the more complete form.

$$U'_t = v_1 Y_{t-1} + v_2 p_{t-1} + R_t^{U'} \tag{3}$$

Since these unsystematic terms as a rule change suddenly, they are sometimes called "shocks."

5. It may happen that a fifth category of terms appears in an elementary equation, viz. a given function of time $F(t)$. Various possibilities may be distinguished:

   (i) $F(t)$ may be a trend of any form being a catch-all of all causes moving only slowly and therefore not interesting for the analysis of rapid fluctuations;

   (ii) or it may take the form of a rapidly changing function of time standing for some given "external variable"; as a special case, this function may be or be assumed to be periodic. External variables are variables relating to non-economic phenomena or to economic variables outside the area considered. If a national economy as a whole is studied, foreign phenomena are external: if one market is studied, phenomena concerning other markets.

2.3. *The Determination of the System's Movements: the Elimination Process*

If all elementary equations describing the logical structure of a model are known, it is, in principle, possible to find the movements of the system as long as we are given:

(a) the "structure" of the model, represented by the coefficients, the lags, and the trends in the equations;
(b) the values of the "external variables" for all time units;
(c) the "disturbances" represented by the residuals for all time units; and
(d) the "initial values" of one or more of the variables of the problem. Exactly what initial values must be given can only be indicated in each particular case.

The technique by which these movements may be ascertained may be different. The simplest technique is that of "numerical extra-polation." An example is given in section 3.2. Here the propagation of the movements is followed step by step; in turn each elementary equation is used to compute one new value for one of the variables.[1] A more advanced technique consists in the "elimination process." Any two equations containing one variable in common may be combined into a new equation without that variable. In particular this elimination has a meaning if, in any equation, one of the explanatory variables is replaced by the equation explaining that variable. This means that instead of considering a "first cause" we are considering "second causes."

If the price level p_{t-1} in equation (3) is itself determined by the equation

$$p_t = \pi_1 r_{t-1} + \pi_2 l_{t-1} + R_t^p \qquad (4)$$

involving that

$$p_{t-1} = \pi_1 r_{t-2} + \pi_2 l_{t-2} + R_{t-1}^p \qquad (4')$$

where r is the level of raw material prices, and l that of wage rates, and, hence, $\pi_1 r_{t-2} + \pi_2 l_{t-2}$ represent cost of production, we may insert this equation into (3), yielding

$$U_t' = v_1 Y_{t-1} + v_2(\pi_1 r_{t-2} + \pi_2 l_{t-2}) + R_t^{U'} + v_2 R_{t-1}^p \qquad (5)$$

As far as a change in U_t' is to be attributed to changes in the price level, this change in U_t' has now been brought back to "deeper causes," viz. "second causes."

The elementary equations may be said to represent "elementary economic laws," the elimination results in representing "deduced economic laws." The laws of demand and supply, or Mr. Keynes's "psychological law of consumption" are examples of "elementary laws." The law of demand relates quantity demanded to price and other variables (such as e.g. income), that may be called "demand factors." Combining the law of demand and that of supply we get an equation by which either the price or the quantity handled is expressed as a function of "demand factors" and "supply factors." This may be called a deduced law. Similarly a deduced law might be obtained by substituting in the consumption equation (2) the equation telling how incomes depend on other economic phenomena.

---

[1] Good examples are to be found in Lundberg, loc. cit.

In this train of thought there is a whole hierarchy of deduced economic laws of different order. Most of these laws would not be known under separate names. This is one of the reasons why it is so difficult to give a verbal account of the process of elimination and why this process has been called "night train analysis." The final stage is reached if we are left with one single equation containing only one variable. This equation will be called the final equation. It is not always possible to obtain, without using approximates, only one final equation. At a certain stage, a system of equations may be obtained that cannot further be reduced and may be called an irreducible system.

The final equation contains, apart from the values at various time points of the one variable left, a number of terms with unsystematic influences. In equation (5) we already find two such terms; in the final equation there will, in general, be a greater number. Each step in the elimination process brings new ones. Each separate unsystematic influence R is multiplied by one or more coefficients; only the R-term originating from the elementary equation taken at the start has a coefficient equal to 1. Thus we see clearly how "shocks" applied to various elementary relations are cumulative and that their influence may be found back in the movements of any variable in the system, damped or magnified in dependence of the coefficients appearing before them. This is the bridge to calculations of "multipliers" in the Kahn sense.[1]

The performance of the elimination process exhibits very clearly one fundamental difficulty in business cycle theory. In order to be realistic it has to assume a great number of elementary equations and variables; in order to be workable it should assume a small number of them. It is the task of business cycle theory to pass between this Scilla and Charybdis. If possible at all the solution must be found in such simplifications of the detailed picture as do not invalidate its essential features. This should not be forgotten by those urging the introduction of many details into the elementary equations. Of course it may first be attempted to establish a system of very detailed elementary equations and then to simplify

---

[1] Cf. *Business Cycles in the U.S.A.*, pp. 162–5.

them in various alternative ways, in order to find out the differences in results. Such complicated systems as I tried to establish for the United States particularly lend themselves to this sort of experiment.

2.4. *The Flexibility of the Method*

I want to emphasise the great flexibility of the method under discussion. Often this is not sufficiently recognised by non-mathematical critics. I believe the following features in particular make it possible to fit the scheme to almost any theory:

(i) the number of variables and of equations is free;
(ii) the number of terms in each equation is free;
(iii) the shape of the functions is free;
(iv) the introduction of non-systematic terms is free. This circumstance opens up the possibility of introducing the influence of "imponderabilia."[1]

In particular, point (iii) deserves some further attention. It is often thought that the method, particularly if completed by statistical determination of the coefficients and lags, but also in view of the performance of the elimination process, is bound to the assumptions of constant coefficients and lags. The first of these two assumptions is equivalent to linear functions. I should like to recall briefly some remarks I have made, on various occasions, on this point.

1. It is not necessary to restrict ourselves to these hypotheses. There are various ways of avoiding them. We may introduce quadratic functions, or more complicated functions. Instead of (2) we may have an equation: $U' = v_1 Y_{t-1} + v_2 p_{t-1} + v_{22} p_{t-1}^2$. Or we may sub-divide the relevant interval of any variable into intervals in each of which separately the relations are linear.[2] A supply function showing the feature of saturation may be approximated

---

[1] I have gone into more detail concerning this equation in my reply to Mr. Keynes in the *Economic Journal*.

[2] As an example, cf. the treatment of stock exchange speculation in *Business Cycles in the U.S.A.*

by two straight lines. Lags may be assumed to be different in various conditions.

2. Using linear functions does not mean such a serious restriction as is often thought.

Linearity is not synonymous with proportionality.[1] Over small intervals almost any function may be approximated by a linear one. This is also true in the case where a coefficient is believed to depend on other variables. Suppose the influence of income on consumption outlay is assumed to be dependent on prices. This would mean that in our equation (2) v_1 would be a function of p_{t-1}, say; therefore $v_1 \equiv v_1(p_{t-1})$.

In order to make clear exactly what this means, it will be better to start with equation (2) in another form, viz. using absolute values of variables $\overline{\overline{U}}'_t$, $\overline{\overline{Y}}_t$, etc. instead of deviations from the average. It then runs:

$$\overline{\overline{U}}'_t = v_1(\overline{\overline{p}}_{t-1})\overline{\overline{Y}}_{t-1} + v_2\overline{\overline{p}}_{t-1} + C \qquad (2')$$

where C is a constant. As a first approximation for small intervals $v_1(\overline{\overline{p}}_{t-1})$ may be assumed to be a linear function:

$$v_1 = v_{10} + v_{11}\overline{\overline{p}}_{t-1}$$

Hence we get:

$$\overline{\overline{U}}'_t + v_{10}\overline{\overline{Y}}_{t-1} + v_{11}\overline{\overline{p}}_{t-1}\overline{\overline{Y}}_{t-1} + v_2\overline{\overline{p}}_{t-1} + C$$

This may again be brought into the form

$$\overline{U}' + \overline{U}_t = v_{10}\overline{Y} + v_{10}Y_{t-1} + v_{11}(\overline{p} + p_{t-1})(\overline{Y} + Y_{t-1}) \\ + v_2(\overline{p} + p_{t-1}) + C$$

or:

$$\overline{U}' + U'_t = (v_{10}\overline{Y} + v_{11}\overline{p}\overline{Y} + v_2\overline{p} + C) + v_{10}Y_{t-1} + v_{11}\overline{p}Y_{t-1} \\ + v_{11}\overline{Y}p_{t-1} + v_{11}p_{t-1}Y_{t-1} + v_2p_{t-1}$$

This may be contracted to:

$$\overline{U}' + U'_t = C' + v'_{10}Y_{t-1} + v'_2p_{t-1} + v_{11}p_{t-1}Y_{t-1}$$

---

[1] Cf. *A Method and its Application to Investment Activity*, p. 16.

where C', v'_{10} and v'_2 are new constants; if we use deviations from the average again, the terms $v_{11}p_{t-1}Y_{t-1}$ will consist, as a rule, of small terms of the second order, being a product of deviations which are, as a rule, not large in comparison to the average values. The last term may then be left aside; and the constant term C' will cancel out against $\overline{U}'$:

$$U'_t = v'_{10}Y_{t-1} + v'_2 p_{t-1}$$

The influence of p on the coefficient of Y_{t-1} is not, by these approximations, neglected, but hidden in the new coefficient v'_2 which is different from v_2.

3. Even if we assume curvilinearity in our relations and "coefficients depending on other variables," etc., we come back, in the end, to coefficients that are constant (v_{22} and v_{11} in the above examples). But that is essential for any theory that really deserves the name. Theory always means reducing variable things to constancy. In the simplest example of theoretical economics, viz. the use of the concept of demand curve, it takes the form of reducing fluctuations in quantity to given fluctuations in prices by some *constant* scheme. Complicated theories will establish the constancy in a complicated way, but will, in the end, also look for something constant. Describing phenomena without any sort of regularity or constancy behind them is no longer theory. An author who does not bind himself to some "laws" is able to "prove" anything at any moment he likes. But then he is telling stories, not making theory.

3. Mathematical Business Cycle Theory: Some Results

3.1. *Results for the Setting of the Problem*

What, now, is the sort of knowledge we can obtain by mathematical business cycle theory?

First, we can already achieve considerable improvement *in the setting of the problems*.

(i) We are able to find whether a given theory is complete in the sense of using a number of equations equal to the number of unknowns. In itself it is not very important to reach this stage, and the Lausanne school has sometimes—and rightly, I think—been ridiculed for stopping after having found that there are as many equations as unknowns. Nevertheless, there is one thing that is worse, viz. finding that there are not the same number! In how many well-known essays on the cycle has it been stated carefully what their number is?

(ii) We are forced to state clearly what relations we assume to exist. For example, I find it difficult to understand whether some theories that assume an influence of the interest rate on commodity stocks have in mind:

(*a*) an influence of interest rates on stocks, or
(*b*) an influence of interest rates on the increase in stocks during the unit time period considered.

Another example: many authors do not state whether or not they assume lags to exist in the relations they use. Mathematical treatment would force them to choose.

(iii) Mathematical treatment in the way indicated above provides a good means of "locating" differences of opinion between different theories. One can tell in what relation or, as the case may be, in what term the theories diverge. Logical classification of theories becomes possible.[1] One example of classification of outstanding importance is the distinction to be made between theories that consider the systematic terms as more essential, and theories that consider the non-systematic ones as more essential—explicitly or implicitly. As a rule, current information on the economic situation gives much more attention to "new events," corresponding to our non-systematic terms; it seems to be based upon the implicit assumption that these new events are very important.

---

[1] I tried to work out this idea in *Business Cycles in the U.S.A.*, pp. 181–3.

(iv) Apart from the general remarks just made, one or two special examples of the advantages of our method may be given.

What does the term "a flexible economy" mean? I think two elements are hidden in this concept, which are often not disentangled sufficiently, although they differ pretty much in their relation to the expected advantages (or disadvantages) attached to them. The reaction on one variable or another may be
(a) strong or weak, and, independently of this,
(b) rapid or slow.

Strength as well as rapidity seem to be elements of "flexibility"; their influence on the damping of business cycles may differ, however, considerably.

For instance, what should we do about the famous catch-all that two phenomena are "mutually related"?—a statement sometimes arrived at as the philosophical endpoint of a discussion—dark as so much philosophy. I believe it can be given a clear interpretation with our "arrow diagram." It may then be stated far better in the following way—taking one relation as a possible example: $A(t)$ influences $B(t + 1)$, and at the same time $B(t)$ influences $A(t + 2)$.

3.2. *The Types of Movements; Theories of the Cycle v. Theories of the Cumulative Process*

The second type of insight we can get, I think, from mathematical treatment, is a systematic insight into the types of movements that economic systems may perform. There is a piece of science of considerable extent—and use, I think—to be built on the basis of our system of equations even before any special economic meaning is given to the variables involved. I shall try to give some examples.

(i) The nature of the central problem in dynamic economics is different from that in static economics. In the latter it is:

what is the (constant) value of any variable if the system is in equilibrium? In the former it is: what is the course in time of each variable?

(ii) What movements does a given economic system (i.e. an economy of which the elementary equations are given) show?

(*A*) It is useful to distinguish between undisturbed and disturbed movements. *Undisturbed* movements occur during any period where no new unsystematic external causes occur. New unsystematic external causes are synonymous with disturbances. We start by considering undisturbed movements.

(*B*) Further, we provisionally restrict ourselves to systems of linear equations. It may then be shown in a general way that the movements that any variable in the system shows are superpositions of one or more of the following types of components:

(*a*) a constant level (this in a sense is not a movement, but, if one likes, a basis level from which the other movements may be measured);

(*b*) an external trend movement, given by the evolutionary external factors (e.g. growth of population —if we assume it to be independent of the economic situation—or of technical knowledge; but not, strictly speaking, growth of capital);

(*c*) an external periodic movement (e.g. seasonal fluctuations) or other non-trend movement (e.g. due to systematic external causes such as international prices);

(*d*) damped exponential movements, i.e. deviations forming a geometric series of falling absolute values;

(*e*) anti-damped exponential movements, i.e. deviations the values of which form an increasing geometric series;

(f) damped periodic movements; i.e. movements whose time shape is a damped sine curve;
(g) anti-damped periodic movements.[1]

The constant level (a) would alone be present if the system of equations were static in the strict sense, i.e. that only (1) variables that relate to one and the same time unit and (2) constant coefficients and additional terms are present.

The external trend movement (b) will appear as soon as e.g. a term growing linearly with time, representing e.g. the movement of population or of knowledge, comes into one or more of the equations. Similarly, the external non-trend movements will come in with the introduction of *given* functions of time.

The internal or endogenous movements (d) to (g) are only possible if not all the variables relate to the same time unit (or if differential coefficients or integrals occur, which, in a sense, means the same). Even then they may, for some special values of the initial values of the variables, be absent. In simple cases, these special values are comparable to equilibrium values in the static sense, i.e. values that would remain if no data were to change. In more complicated cases, things are less easy.[2] One can only get an idea of this type of problem by "playing" with some of the models. I have given a very simple example in *Business Cycles in the United States* (pp. 15–18). This example may be given a somewhat different form in order to demonstrate one or two principles of outstanding importance.

Let the total of all expenditure on final consumption and net investment in unit time period t be X_t, and income Z_t. Then, as a first elementary equation we have:

$$Z_t = X_t$$

---

[1] Strictly speaking, a linear movement in time, due to internal causes, should be added for the case where two roots of the characteristic equation coincide, etc. This will be disregarded.

[2] I treated some questions relating to this matter in *An Econometric Approach* and particularly in *Fondements mathématiques de la stabilisation des affaires*, Paris, 1938, and in "Sur la détermination statistique de la position d'équilibre cyclique," *Revue de l'Institut International de Statistique*, 1936, p. 173 (with English summary).

indicating that income will simply be equal to these expenditures. The second equation has to answer the question, How are these expenditures themselves determined? Here, in order to state our present problem in the simplest way possible and to couple it as little as possible to specific economic theories, we start from some very general principles. Expenditure will be based—directly or indirectly—on income some time ago; there will be a lag. This lag may be a distributed one, so that in the simplest case there are two lags included, say, of one and of two time units. The coefficients corresponding to these two lags may be of opposite sign. In this general principle the special case is included where expenditure is based on expected income, so far as these expectations are themselves based on

(*a*) income at prior moments, and even on

(*b*) the rate of increase in income formerly observed.

Non-systematic causes are disregarded for the moment. As our second equation we therefore get:

$$X_t = \xi_1 Z_{t-1} + \xi_2 Z_{t-2} + C \qquad (\xi_1, \xi_2, C, \text{constants})$$

Using the first equation, we have at once the final equation:

$$Z_t = \xi_1 Z_{t-1} + \xi_2 Z_{t-2} + C$$

The elimination process is very simple now, since we purposely combined direct and indirect influences without further discussion and so came back at once to Z_{t-1} and Z_{t-2}. For the moment our problems lie elsewhere.

In order to fix the ideas, we choose some particular values, viz. $\xi_1 = +1.6$, $\xi_2 = -1$, $C = 4$.

We now have a case without external movements, since trends or non-trend external movements are assumed not to occur. Components (*b*) and (*c*) are absent, therefore. It would not however, complicate matters to introduce (*b*) into C, by assuming C to depend linearly in time.

Component (*a*) is present. It can be shown to be $Z = 10$. It may be tested by the non-mathematical reader by giving all Z's this value; then the equation is satisfied:

$$10 = 1.6 \times 10 - 1 \times 10 + 4$$

The other components are found in the simplest manner by measuring Z in a new way, viz. as deviations from 10. Writing Z' for $Z - 10$, we get the following equation for Z':

$$Z'_t = 1.6 Z'_{t-1} - Z'_{t-2},$$

i.e. an equation without constant terms. This equation enables us to determine the development of Z', if two values are given. It is worth while to give an example. Let $Z'_0 = 0$, $Z'_1 = 1$. We easily find the figures of the following table (to be called "*example I*"):

Z'_2	Z'_3	Z'_4	Z'_5	Z'_6	Z'_7	Z'_8	Z'_9	Z'_{10}	Z'_{11}
+1.6	+1.56	+0.9	−0.1	−1.1	−1.6	−1.5	−0.8	+0.2	+1.1

It can be shown that this periodic movement will occur irrespective of the initial values chosen.

Suppose now that the structure of the model were different and that the coefficient 1.6 were 2.2. If again $Z'_0 = 0$ and $Z'_1 = 1$, we should now find the following development (to be called "*example II*"):

Z'_2	Z'_3	Z'_4	Z'_5	Z'_6	Z'_7
+2.2	+3.84	+6.2	+9.8	+15.3	+23.8

The movement is now one-sided (anti-damped exponential) and can equally be shown to be so, independently of the initial values. (The movement may, however, be directed towards $-\infty$ instead of towards $+\infty$.)

I want to draw two conclusions from the comparison of these two examples.

In economic terms, *example I contains a theory of the cycle, i.e. of the cumulative process as well as of the turning point; whereas example II only contains a theory of the cumulative process.* If example II had been the outcome of some set of economic hypotheses, a separate theory of the turning point would have been necessary. Generally speaking, it is sometimes necessary to give a separate theory of the turning point; sometimes, however, it is superfluous. There are scrupulous authors who give a theory of the turning point where it would perhaps not be necessary; there are other authors who think that they are giving a theory of the cycle, where they only give one of a cumulative process. *How can we know whether a theory is of type I or type II?* Often not by verbal treatment; our example II need not differ verbally from example I; the same phenomena may be included in both; only the intensity with which some of them act need be different.

Considering example I we may, then, ask with Mr. Keynes:[1] how does reversal come in? We see, before our eyes, that $z'_3 < z'_2$. What is the reason? It is not that some new phenomenon enters. Qualitatively the same forces are at work as before. It is "simply" the change in relative strength of the positive and the negative forces that alters the balance.

In order to see this in more detail, let us repeat the first two figures in example I and their genesis. For $t = 2$ and $t = 3$ we have:

$$z'_2 = 1.6z'_1 - z'_0 = 1.6 \times 1 - 0 = 1.6$$
$$z'_3 = 1.6z'_2 - z'_1 = 1.6 \times 1.6 - 1 = 1.56$$

In z'_2, the positive influence of z'_1 is large, the negative influence of z'_0 zero, since z'_0 is zero. In z'_3, the positive influence of z'_2 is even larger, but the negative force, $-z'_1$, has grown a little bit more.

That change in relative strength is itself a consequence of the laws governing—in our example—expenditure. It seems to be difficult, if not idle, to attribute it to some special cause. One may construct other examples where reversal does come in owing to some specific reason, some "ceiling" in credits or employment or still other things. *But it does not follow that turning points can only be explained that way.* I think this is a rather widespread misunderstanding among non-mathematical theorists.

Example II must not be misunderstood. Its ever-increasing figures may, perhaps, soon reach some impossible level. Does this prove that the theory behind it is erroneous and that, therefore, the

---

[1] Loc. cit.

example has no significance at all? I should prefer to put it in another way. The theory is only valid within a certain interval of values for z'. If that theory itself leads to values outside that range we must stop applying it. And the conclusion remains: that theory cannot explain a turning point.

3.3. *Stability of Equilibrium*

Much more could be said about movements of systems. I have done so on other occasions; and hope to unite all this within a larger framework. But it would take us too far now. We may proceed with another subdivision of the subject that equally illustrates what mathematical treatment teaches us.

(iii) What is to be understood by "business cycle stabilisation"? We shall try to give this notion a clear-cut meaning in the following way—which, of course, need not be the only possible way. Business cycle stabilisation is a set of measures changing the economic structure in such a way that the economy is able to perform *stable movements*. By a stable movement we mean a movement of which the cyclical components all show a high damping ratio, whereas the trend movements do not show too high a rate of growth. This means that the cyclic components soon come back to zero. New disturbances would not do much harm in such a system; its movements would be quiet; moderate trend movements would prevail.

Two important further questions arise; the first being how we can discern whether a system does or does not show only stable movements. From the foregoing it follows that the solution of the final equation or the final set of equations has to tell the story. If the complex roots of the characteristic equations all have a modulus well below one, the cyclic components will show a high damping ratio. This statement implies that, in order to know whether a given system shows stable movements, we must have information about some dynamic features of that system, e.g. the lags in the relations. Changing a lag means changing the characteristic equation and therefore its roots. Purely static information, e.g. knowledge on the slopes of demand and supply curves without knowledge on the lags, is insufficient. This conclusion brings us into conflict with a well-known statement that in any market the equilibrium is stable if the slope of the demand curve is less (in the algebraic sense) than that of the supply curve, unstable if the reverse is true.[1] The point is that the proof of this well-known statement assumes the lags of demand and supply reactions to be equal. The well-known cob-web theorem shows that if this hypothesis is abandoned, unstable equilibria may arise even if the slope of the demand curve is negative and that of the supply curve is positive. Suppose there is no lag in demand but a lag in supply; and that the supply curve has an absolute slope greater than that of the demand curve. Then the equilibrium will not be stable; ever wider fluctuations will occur after the smallest disturbance of equilibrium.

A second point on which we may pause for a moment is that of the level of the stable equilibrium. In the terminology used here, it is conceivable that a stable equilibrium could only be obtained at the expense of a lower value of the constant component in the solution; i.e. that general activity, e.g., would be, on the average, lower than before. If this is so, there arises a problem of choice which is a problem of policy rather than of business cycle theory. It is, however, far from certain that this situation presents itself. In view of the large number of structural constants it is more probable that these constants—even those that can be changed at will—can be chosen so as to make movements both more stable and on a higher average level. The latter objective is an end in itself; and an important one. But there is no guarantee, as some investigators seem to think, that measures leading to a higher level will, automatically, make the equilibrium more stable. Measures tending to make the average level of activity higher can be found and discussed with the help of static economics. Stability can only be obtained by measures to be found and discussed by dynamic theory.

4. Statistical Methods

4.1. *The Two Objectives of the Method of Multiple Correlation*

I shall now turn to some of the statistical problems involved in econometric business cycle analysis. The basic question is, What

---

[1] Cf. e.g. J. R. Hicks: *Value and Capital*, Oxford, 1939, ch. V.

do we want to obtain by statistical measurement? As I have mentioned already in the introduction to this paper, there are two possible ends, a more modest and a more ambitious one.

The modest one is to obtain such values for the constants in our relations as are not contrary to observation. This is already a useful result, since the number of possible theories is very large and would already be considerably restricted by taking only such relations. The whole subject is so complicated that further theoretical treatment without choosing numerical values for a number of the coefficients would be waste of time. Various examples could be given of theories using unrealistic relations. The frequent use of the acceleration principle for the explanation of investment fluctuations is one. Not only is this principle a bad explanation of most forms of investment activity, but even in the cases where it fits the facts (railways) the coefficient usually assumed is not in agreement with the facts.[1]

The first time I used multiple correlation analysis in business cycle theory[2] it was with this modest purpose in view. Afterwards the more ambitious objective, to measure with some degree of exactness the values of the coefficients, came in. Various pitfalls in this field have recently been discussed and I need not repeat them here. I think the matter has been discussed fairly completely and that it is now more useful to apply the method to concrete cases. That there are cases where it has yielded results is, I think, beyond question[3] and I hope to give some examples in § 4.3. There are one or two remarks I want to make that have, perhaps, not yet sufficiently been emphasised.

One is of a very elementary character. We should not forget, while talking so much about the statistical significance and the standard deviations of our regression coefficients, that even if these standard deviations are large, the most probable value for the

---

[1] Cf. J. Tinbergen: "Statistical Evidence on the Acceleration Principle," *Economica* V (1938), p. 164.

[2] The first very elementary attempts are to be found in my "Survey on Quantitative Business Cycle Theory," *Econometrica* 3 (1935), pp. 284–6.

[3] Even Mr. Keynes expresses this opinion (loc. cit.) notwithstanding the severity of his criticisms.

regression coefficient is the value we calculate. If no other information is available we can hardly avoid taking the regression coefficient we find, however uncertain it may be.

4.2. *Other Methods*

Another topic that may be considered somewhat more in detail is: are other methods available and what is their value? First, we have what may be called the common-sense method of business cycle research, to be found in most periodic surveys of economic conditions.[1] It consists in a careful cataloguing of facts and of the month-to-month fluctuations in a number of relevant economic time series. In a number of cases it attributes, with a fairly high degree of plausibility, certain given changes to certain events and by so doing succeeds in explaining, to some degree, the mechanism of cyclical movements. I think the successful cases of explanation are those where in the series to be explained a sudden rather marked change occurs at the same time, or shortly after, some sudden change in another series, or some new event happens. Just because the changes are rather sudden ones, we have approximately the situation that all other factors remain almost constant. Hence, in that short interval there is a simple correlation between the variable to be explained and the one explanatory variable that suddenly changes. It is evident that this method can be successful especially for the analysing of the influence of new events, i.e. of the—often small—disturbances of the movements. To my mind it is, therefore, especially favoured by those who attribute to these new events a great role. It is far more difficult, if not impossible, to apply it to the ever-present factors that do not change suddenly. These have not the courtesy to wait with their changes until other things remain unchanged; and prevent us from playing that most beloved game of *ceteris paribus*. Looked at in this way, the common-sense method reduces to simple correlation analysis, applied to special cases.

---

[1] A very good piece of work in this category, written with great skill, is S. H. Slichter: "The Downturn of 1937," *The Review of Economic Statistics*, XX (1938), p. 97.

There is another element in this common-sense method which has a methodological meaning in itself. This element is what I should like to call the *experimental method of determining relations*. Our relations often indicate how people *would* react *if* a certain change in prices, incomes, etc., were to occur. Instead of using multiple correlation analysis one might try an experiment, i.e. by some artificial means change only one factor at a time and see what people do. Large-scale and systematic experiments as in the natural sciences are, of course, excluded; but there are several forms of investigation that approximate to this method.

(i) One is the method of interview, described, e.g. by Mrs. Waterman-Gilboy and Frisch. Here we ask certain people what they would do in certain hypothetical circumstances. We could speak of a "virtual experiment." A counterpart of this method of interviewing is to ask people what was the reason for something they actually did.[1] This too, may, in principle, tell us something about the causes of a given change. It is this method that is frequently applied by common-sense business cycle research. The more informed the investigator is about the actual motives that have led people to react as they did, the better his approach will be.

(ii) There are other "experimental" investigations possible. In a sense, family budget statistics are an example. They tell us what the influence of income on expenditure is. Similar information may be obtained by comparing people living under different price situations, e.g. comparing the consumption of electricity in different localities; or comparing the ratio between labour and capital used in production in different countries. Data on cost curves for separate enterprises and on the distribution of enterprises over cost classes are a further important category in this class, which we may describe as "structural investigations."

---

[1] A splendid example is the Oxford inquiry on the factors influencing investment activity. *Oxford Economic Papers*, I (1938). For me, it is encouraging that this inquiry led to the same scepticism on the influence of the interest rate on investment activity as my investigation *A Method and its Application to Investment Activity*.

We have now to compare the accuracy of these methods with that of multiple correlation analysis. This can hardly be done in one general statement. There are certainly cases where "experimental investigations" are much more reliable than correlation investigations. In particular, good "structural investigations" deserve much attention. But there are also many pitfalls here. Even a good family budget inquiry may be a bad guide if the distribution of income in the group considered does not fit with that in the country as a whole; or it may give a wrong expression of the relation in time between income and expenditure, since changes in time need not have the same consequences as changes from one income group to another. In particular, it is very difficult to know whether any structural investigation based on a sample is representative.

The difficulties are considerably larger for the other types of "experimental investigations." The interview method, even if based on past events, must be somewhat superficial unless the utmost care is given to the formulation of questions—in order to make people conscious of what their own motives really have been. The way in which common-sense business cycle research uses this method is, in most cases, much more superficial still, since it is primarily based on newspaper information and personal opinions where even the best informed investigators only know a small part of the firms and individuals concerned. The way, moreover, in which accidental disturbances may influence the results of this type of explanation of fluctuations shows another danger of that method.

In conclusion, it would seem to me that the method of multiple correlation does not compare badly with the other methods. But we need not consider them as competitors. They can collaborate perfectly well. In most statistical determinations of demand curves I compared the results obtained—as far as the influence of income is concerned—with those of family budget investigations. Dr. Polak has given a very interesting example of collaboration of the two methods in the explanation of the fluctuations in farm prices.[1]

---

[1] In *Business Cycles in the U.S.A.*, section (3.4), which was entirely his work.

4.3 Results of Multiple Correlation Analysis

Most critics of multiple correlation analysis admit that it may serve some purposes, as e.g. the determination of a demand function for some specific commodity. Hence the difference of opinion is about where the limits lie. As a first step in the fixation of the demarcation line let me sum up some cases where I think the method has given useful results. I do not claim any degree of completeness, however.

Apart from one or two scattered applications, published in the *Journal of the Royal Statistical Society*, soon after Mr. Yule's inauguration of the method, the pioneer work on economic applications has been done in the United States. *Moore, Schultz, Ezekiel, Roos, Waugh* and several others have made important contributions; the first three authors particularly in the field of agricultural economics. The random movements of crops favour the application of the method, since there is little correlation between prices of particular agricultural commodities and incomes. They succeeded in determining elasticities of demand and supply in a number of cases. Important work on non-farm markets was done by Roos and his assistants; especially in housing and in the automobile market.

In Europe, *Prof. Frisch* and his followers (e.g. *Haavelmo*) have done much work in completing the method and applying it to demand studies for various consumers' goods. Part of Frisch's estimates of the marginal utility of income are based on multiple correlation analysis.

The German investigators *Donner* and *Hanau* have obtained several interesting results (cotton prices, German share prices; pig markets). *Dr. H. Staehle* has some very interesting (unpublished) investigations on the demand for labour in certain industries; further, in a discussion on the "propensity to consume" he gave an interesting example of multiple correlation calculus.

Of the Dutch group I may mention *T. Koopmans*, who has considerably contributed to the development of the theory of the significance of regression coefficients, *J. J. Polak, Derksen, De Wolff, Dalmulder, Rombouts, Mey, Smit, Van den Briel, Van der Schalk*, and

Van der Meer.[1] They and others have made numerous demand studies, not only for agricultural products, but also for industrial goods and services (e.g. motor cars, motor fuel, bicycles, postal services, tramway and railway traffic, electric current, cinema visits, shipping transport). In the League of Nations study (loc. cit.) the technique was, it seems to me, successfully applied to some new subjects as e.g. the monetary and banking sphere, the demand for investment goods and supply or price equations.

---

[1] I apologise for mentioning so many compatriots and forgetting many more foreign investigators; the reason being that I want to draw the attention to work that is, for linguistic causes, not so well accessible to other than Dutch readers.

5

SOME NOTES ON THE STOCKHOLM THEORY OF SAVINGS AND INVESTMENT*

By Bertil Ohlin‖

Owing to a coincidence of circumstances, already at an early stage of the depression Swedish economists came to deal with the problem of variations in employment, output and prices by means of a theoretical apparatus rather different from the price theory in economic textbooks. There are surprising similarities as well as striking differences between that apparatus and the conclusions reached in Sweden on the one hand and Mr. Keynes' "General Theory" on the other hand. Hoping that a discussion of two independent attacks on the same set of problems may throw some light on the latter, I intend in this and the succeeding paper to make some observations on these two theories. In view of the fact that the Stockholm approach and theories are only partly available in other languages than Swedish, I shall begin with some observations on this work—pointing out differences from and similarities with Keynes' position—and come in a second article to some critical notes on his theory. A more complete comparison between the two bodies of doctrines will have to wait until the Stockholm theory has been made available in English.

A. The Development and Characteristics of the Stockholm Theory

Among the circumstances which explain the present trend of theoretical analysis in Swedish economics one should, I think, first

---

* *Economic Journal*, Volume XLVII, 1937, Part I, March, 1937, pages 53–69; Part II, June, 1937, pages 221–240. Reprinted by the courtesy of the publisher and the author.

‖ Graduate School of Business, Stockholm; Former Visiting Professor, University of California, Berkeley.

mention the writings of Wicksell, which naturally attracted more attention in Sweden than elsewhere. His *Geldzins und Güterpreïse* of 1898 and his later books and papers on money contained the embryo of "a theory of output as a whole," although this fact was not clearly perceived until the late 'twenties, when Professor Lindahl presented his elaboration of Wicksell. Wicksell started from the fact that the price of an individual commodity is determined by supply and demand. If its price rises, one says that it is due to a rise in demand relative to supply. Naturally, if the prices paid for all commodities taken together rise—and thus the general price level is raised—a similar explanation should be possible. Wicksell attempted to give such an explanation through his analysis of saving and investment. Thus, he broke both with the Say doctrine that supply creates its own demand and with the accepted view that the theory of relative prices and the theory of money are two entirely different things, although he never arrived at a real unification of these theories.

Wicksell's analysis was concentrated on the process of price movements, in which credit plays a large rôle. Credit and savings have a time dimension. For this and other reasons he came to study time-using processes. The most famous is his so-called "cumulative" process, which proved to be an important "type model" of economic development, i.e., a "model sequence."

Professor Lindahl—as will be shown below—followed up the Wicksellian analysis. He showed that it was useful in a study of changes in employment and output as well as in prices. Furthermore, he showed that Wicksell's cumulative process depended on special assumptions concerning the entrepreneurs' expectations, thereby utilizing the analysis of "anticipations" which had been presented in Professor Myrdal's work, *Pricing and the Change Factor*, 1927. This work was the second of the circumstances which have vitally affected Swedish research in the field under discussion during the last decade. Myrdal discusses the influence of the uncertain future on price formation. To what extent are economic actions influenced by anticipations of future events, i.e. by expectations? In the static equilibrium price theory of the textbooks, this question had been neglected. Of the pre-depression treatises only Marshall seems to have had it in mind. If he did not make much progress himself in this field, at least he used a terminology which protects him from much of the criticism which can be directed towards other writers. In fact, Keynes' analysis of expectations in Ch. 5—which in many ways is similar to the general view in Stockholm—can be regarded as the following up of numerous suggestions in Marshall's "Principles."

Myrdal tries to build these expectations into the static price equilibrium, and thus to give a picture of the forces existing at a certain moment of time. He does not attempt to construct a dynamic price theory which considers the *rate* of change and thus gives an account of a process in time. His theory can be regarded as the last step which a static theory can take in the direction of dynamics. In constructing his equilibrium Myrdal eliminates time from change, but not anticipations of time. In other words, he assumes a timeless adjustment, but with all friction and cost and expectations.[1] While this may appear to be a peculiar construction, it is no doubt more realistic than the earlier static equilibrium. In any case, it enabled Myrdal to concentrate on the influence of expectations. This analysis was continued by him in Ch. V. of "Der Gleichgewichtsbegriff als Hilfsmittel in der Geldtheoretischen Analyse," in *Beiträge zur Geldtheorie*, published by Prof. Hayek in 1933. He there works out in some detail the vitally important distinction between "looking forward" and "looking backward," and shows its significance more clearly than he had done before in Swedish writings and discussions. This analysis of income and capital values with the aid of "*ex-post*" and "*ex-ante*" concepts is independent of the timeless equilibrium construction which is expounded in the paper and which is similar to that used in the book of 1927. In fact, it seems most useful in a *period analysis* of the type which Lindahl and myself are using, while Myrdal views it with some scepticism.

---

[1] Brinley Thomas, *Monetary Policy and Crises*, uses a different terminology from mine when he calls Myrdal's theory *the* dynamic theory and seems to have overlooked the need for a different theory of the sort I call "dynamic."

The third decisive factor in the development of the Stockholm theory was Lindahl's book on *The Means of Monetary Policy* (published in 1930 but circulated in proof a year earlier), which I have already mentioned. He used Myrdal's expectation analysis to follow the Wicksellian line of approach by means of periods of time, perhaps somewhat under the influence of Mr. D. H. Robertson in this latter respect. Some essential parts of Lindahl's theory can be briefly indicated.

Already Wicksell had stressed that consumption purchases are governed by that part of individual incomes which people want to consume, whereas investment purchases are not directly governed by the part of income people want to save. The decisions to save and the decisions to invest are taken largely by different individuals, and there is no mechanism which guarantees that the volume of savings and of investment will always be equal. This is the very essence of the Wicksellian approach. Wicksell goes on to investigate what rôle the rate of interest can play in making them equal, and what happens when they are not made equal. Lindahl does not concentrate his attention to the same extent on the investment activity. He starts from the formula:

$$E(1 - s) = PQ;$$

E is income, s savings ratio, P the price level of consumption goods, and Q the quantity of consumption goods. Regarded as a picture of a brief period, during which equilibrium exists, this equation is implicit in the equilibrium theory of prices. It can be used, however, for an analysis of a process in time, which is divided into different periods. Lindahl studies the conditions under which the components of the equation change, the volume of consumption goods as well as their prices. In so doing he naturally has to pay a great deal of attention, although not in my opinion sufficient, to the volume of real investment. He does not confine his discussion of policy to monetary policy in a narrow sense, but analyses also the effects of changes in the financial policy of the State, e.g. the financing of deficits by borrowing. Thus, he departs a long way from the quantity theory of money approach, by which it was natural in any discussion of price problems, etc., to ask how the quantity of money could be affected. In fact, he follows Wicksell in assuming a perfect credit economy, where the quantity of money has no significance. It would carry me too far to describe his argument concerning Wicksell's cumulative process. Among other things he introduces the hypothesis of unused resources and discusses alternative "models," based on different assumptions as to the disposition to save, etc., demonstrating that they behave rather differently under the impact of the same original change. He also investigates the importance of long- and short-term interest rates, and finds Wicksell's concept of a "normal" rate of interest to be of little or no use.

These Wicksell-Myrdal-Lindahl writings were the theoretical background for the work done by four economists, who were asked by the Unemployment Committee late in 1931 to write monographs on different aspects of economic policy in relation to unemployment. What the Committee asked for amounted to an extensive treatment of the "economics of unused resources." What will be the effect of this or that policy in conditions in which considerable quantities of the industrial agents are unemployed? The fact that the Committee put the question in this way is the fourth and last of the circumstances which influenced the direction of Swedish research in the field under discussion. I should, however, mention also the fact that Professor Bagge, a leading member of the Committee, had himself in 1930 published an excellent survey of the causes of unemployment, based on an assumption which one might call relatively constant demand in terms of money or "stable monetary conditions." Hence, it was possible for the writers of the four monographs to concentrate on the processes of general expansion and contraction of economic activity, connected with variations in total demand in terms of money. These questions were, of course, the ones which attracted the greatest general interest at this time of severe depression.

The titles of the four investigations, all published late in 1933 and early in 1934, were the following: Hammarskjöld, *On the Spread of Conjunctures;* Johansson, *Wage Development and Unem-*

ployment; Myrdal, *The Economic Effects of Public Financial Policy;* and my own book, *Monetary Policy, Public Works, Subsidies, and Tariff Policy as Remedies for Unemployment.* In spite of considerable differences in the methods and the terminology used, there is a certain unity between the theories developed and the conclusions reached in all the reports, including also the Final Report of the Committee on *Remedies for Unemployment,* published in 1935 and written by Dr. Hammarskjöld on the basis of discussion in the Committee. This report covers on the whole the same field of theoretical problems as those in Keynes' "General Theory." While there is only a scanty discussion of the determination of the rates of interest, there is an extensive analysis of "frictional" unemployment and possible remedies, matters which arc almost entirely ignored by Keynes.

The high degree of unanimity between the writers mentioned, and the fact that they were all influenced by the Wicksell-Myrdal-Lindahl writings and by Cassel with regard to the anticlassical approach to price and distribution theory, make it justifiable to talk about a Stockholm school of thought. (The only non-resident in Stockholm is Lindahl, who worked in Stockholm for many years.) It must not be supposed, however, that the different members of this school agree on everything. As in my attempt below to illuminate certain aspects of the Stockholm[1] theory I shall follow the version used by myself, I have to add that my terminology has been viewed with great scepticism by some of the younger Stockholm economists, chiefly because of my way of defining income so as to make savings and investment always equal *ex definitione.* Personally, however, I am to-day more than ever convinced that this set of definitions permits a simpler, more realistic and more easily understandable description of economic processes than the rather different definitions used by other members of the Stockholm school.

---

[1] There is considerable similarity between my terminology and analysis and that presented by Myrdal in Ch. V. of "Gleichgewichtsbegriff" (1933). I learned a great deal trom the Swedish, less complete, version of this paper. To some extent we arrived at similar conclusions independently of one another.

Let me begin by enumerating the characteristics of what I propose to call the "Stockholm Theory of Processes of Contraction and Expansion," meaning thereby the analysis of changes in employment, output and prices. Firstly, in the discussion of special partial processes attention is concentrated on the reaction of the economic system as a whole, i.e. possible influence on the *total* volume of output and monetary demand.[1] Monetary theory is therefore made a part of the general price theory. The analysis has not as yet been pushed far enough to make it include a theory of business cycles. A book by Dr. Lundberg on cycle problems (*Studies in the Theory of Economic Expansion*) will, however, appear before this paper is published. Secondly, care is taken to state clearly when concepts like income and savings refer to plans or expectations for the future and when they are concerned with a period that is already finished. Thirdly, with the exception of Myrdal (whose position is not quite clear) all use a period method of analysis. In this respect the procedure is similar to D. H. Robertson's. Fourthly, as in Hawtrey's and Keynes' theories, attention is concentrated on the action of the individual entrepreneurs or consumers, and not much is said about what this involves with regard to the movements of the currency units. The exception is Dr. Hammarskjöld, who in his book of 1933 uses a velocity of money approach. Fifthly, it has been found that the reasoning to be precise enough must be casuistic. Wide use is, therefore, made of "type models" like Wicksell's cumulative process. For the construction of such models, simplifying assumptions are necessary. Hence each of them throws light on only one aspect of the processes of expansion or contraction.

B. Some Aspects of Process Analysis[2]

1. To analyse and explain what happens or what will happen in certain circumstances it is necessary to register the relevant

---

[1] Compare my remarks on Keynes' position in this respect: Section C. 1 below.

[2] Section B, §§1–8, is almost exactly the contents of a lecture given at University College, Dublin in May 1934. It also formed part of the Marshall lectures at the University of Cambridge in November 1936. It is a summary—with insignificant changes—of certain parts of my book of 1934.

events. One needs a system of book-keeping which is relative to time. Not only is the time sequence of events as a rule important, the same is often true of the time-lags. It is therefore practical to use periods of time as a basis for the book-keeping. At the end of each period one can survey the registrations which refer to that period. This answers the question what has happened during a passed period. It is an account *ex-post*.

This, however, explains nothing, for it does not describe the causal or functional relations. As economic events depend on man's actions, one has to investigate what determines these actions. They always refer to a more or less distant future. Hence, one must study those expectations about the future which govern the actions, keeping in mind that expectations are based on the experience of the past, although only partly the *immediate* past. This analysis of the forward-looking type can be called *ex-ante*, using Myrdal's convenient expressions. It goes without saying that actions depend not only on ideas about the future, but also on actual conditions at the moment of action; e.g. the supply of capital instruments and commodity stocks, the character of existing contracts, etc. The *ex-post* description supplies knowledge about these things directly, and at the same time it throws light on those past events, which influence expectations to a greater or smaller extent. Obviously a combination of *ex-post* and *ex-ante* analysis amounts simply to this: after a description of actual events during a certain, finished period, and of the differences between these events and the expectations which existed at the beginning of the period, follows an account of those expectations for the future which more or less govern actions during the next period. The registration of events during this second period reveals again that expectations do not all come true, a fact which influences expectations and actions during the third period, etc.

2. Let me indicate briefly the concepts required for the *ex-post registration* in the general process analysis. For each individual or firm one has the following equation:

$$R - O - D = E = S + C;$$

R is *revenue*, i.e. the value of sales; O is *current costs*, i.e. payments to factors of production and to other firms for goods used up during this period; D is *depreciation items*, i.e. the computed costs for the period in question which are due to the use of things which are reckoned as products of earlier periods, minus corresponding appreciation items, which I leave out for the sake of simplicity; E is *net income*, of which one part C has been *used for consumption* while the rest is *savings* S. $R - O$ may be called *gross income* G, which is equal to $D + E$. I shall, however, not make use of this concept below.

These definitions are based on the picture of the transactions looked at from the "income side." If we now regard it from the "expenditure side" we get

$$X = I + C;$$

X is *total expenditure*, I is *investment expenditure*, and C is *consumption expenditure*. I includes both O (which is, of course, a kind of investment, but for a space of time shorter than one period) and the investment of a more durable kind. I consists of *reinvestment* I^r and *new investment* I^n.

Returning to the income side, we see that the revenue which is not net income is the return of money which has earlier been invested, either during the same period—this sum is equal to O—or during earlier periods—which sum is equal to D. $O + D$ can be called "old savings made available" or "*free capital*." These sums indicate a flow which is "available" for new investment expenditure. "Free capital" plus the new savings can be called "*waiting*," W, which is thus equal to: $O + D + S$.

If we sum up all these things for all firms and individuals—that is, for society as a whole—we get the following identities. The distinction between reinvestment and new investment is made in such a way that the sum of investment, which is equal to free capital, is called reinvestment, while the rest is new investment.

Revenue R = Total expenditure X.
Free capital $O + D$ = Reinvestment I^r.

Savings S = New investment I^n.
Waiting W = Investment I.
Net income E = New investment I^n + Consumption C.

The net income is, of course, equal to the sum total of all individual positive net incomes after deduction of all negative net incomes. Similarly, savings for society as a whole are equal to the sum of all positive savings minus all negative ones. An individual has a negative saving when he uses for consumption more than his income. This occurs always when his income is negative. But in other cases also—if his consumption exceeds his net income—he has to use a part of his fortune or take credit. Thus the savings for society are the sum of all positive savings minus negative incomes, consumption of one's own fortune and consumption credit.

This set of definitions, which refers to industrial, not financial transactions, is somewhat similar to Keynes' new terminology, which is based on the same type of identities. My investment I includes, however, more than Keynes' investment. I shall put off the discussion of the depreciation term D until a later part of this paper, where I comment on Keynes, who has made the important distinction between automatic depreciation—which can be called "time depreciation"—and depreciation caused by use of the different assets—"use depreciation." It should be mentioned already here that the computation of the depreciation terms depends upon the expectations, and that therefore book-keeping, including the closing of the accounts—the registration, grouping together, and interpretation of events—is not a pure *ex-post* manœuvre, but a combination of *ex-post* and *ex-ante*.

3. I come now to the *ex-ante phenomena*—that is, the psychological causation. Purchases of goods and services are either intended for investment or for consumption purposes. Consider first investment purchases. The entrepreneur has certain *expectations* concerning future events beyond his control and a certain knowledge about his productive apparatus, contracts, etc. On this basis he makes certain *plans* concerning his own investments during the coming periods, and these plans are actually carried

out as far as *his own* actions during this period are concerned. For the period is chosen so that he does not change his plans until the beginning of the next period. Much ought to be said about the implications of this assumption, and about the necessity for periods of different lengths, but I must pass over it here. Plans are regarded as a special sort of expectations. The difference is that plans concern his own actions, while other expectations do not. Plans are often in terms of alternatives, to be realised under different sets of expected conditions.

The investment plans are of course based on expected revenue from the investment in question and on the expected costs entailed, including the expected rates of interest. In brief, the plans are based on *the profit expectations*. But it would be wrong to assume that entrepreneurs plan to carry out all the investments which they think will yield a return, exceeding the rate of interest which they expect to pay. (Keynes' statement that the investment demand for capital depends on the relations of the marginal efficiency of capital to the interest rates, amounts practically to this.) Of all the possible investments which seem profitable, only some are planned for the next period and actually begun. This may be due to the fact that the present cash and credit resources of the firm are not large enough to permit more, or that the expected cash and credit resources put a check on the investments. Sometimes, however, strong business firms which could easily borrow huge sums for profitable-looking investment prefer not to do so. They are averse to an increase of their indebtedness. It is an open question whether this can be regarded as evidence that they reckon on unfavourable developments, which would make the investment unprofitable, as probable enough to make it not worth while, or whether the explanation must run in other terms. (I am looking forward to a paper by Dr. Kalecki on this subject.) In any case it is clear that the cash and credit resources, which the firm has at its disposal at the beginning of a period and acquires during the period, provide an upper limit for its *ability to buy*, and that the expectations concerning them set a limit to its investment plans; while the profit expectations and the expectations with regard to future cash and credit resources influence the *desire to buy*. As long as the latter does not touch the former limit, it determines the investment plans. (The above refers to investment in producers' goods. A similar, but somewhat different, reasoning explains the investment in durable consumers' goods.)

Like investment purchases, *the demand for non-durable consumption goods and services* is influenced by expectations and by knowledge concerning the actual situation of the consumer. On the basis of these circumstances consumption plans are made for the future, and as far as purchases during the first coming period are concerned, these plans are realised. Of course, the plans are not definite, for the consumer has not one precise expectation, e.g. about what prices will be during the next period or how much cash he will receive. But he usually plans to spend a certain sum for consumption purposes, and has alternative purchase plans concerning the distribution of this sum between different lines of consumption. The important thing for an analysis of changes in employment, output and prices is the sum total he plans to spend and does actually give out. On what does this sum total of planned consumption depend? First of all on the consumer's income expectations. Not his expected income during the first coming period only, but on what he expects to earn over a long period in the future. If a man gets a temporary, well-paid job which gives him a much higher salary than he is used to and more than he can expect to earn later on, his standard of consumption will obviously be much affected by consideration of this latter fact.

As a parenthesis let me observe that Keynes' analysis on this point seems a little superficial. On p. 28 he indicates that consumption depends on the relationship between the community's income and the propensity to consume. And on p. 57 he writes about the *causal* significance of net income: "Net income is what we suppose the ordinary man to reckon his available income to be when he is deciding how much to spend on current consumption"; Keynes adds that the consumer also considers, e.g., windfall gains. There are two objections to this standpoint. The income which has causal significance is *not* Keynes' *ex-post* concept, the realised income during the last period, but the *expected* income. Secondly, the expectations for many coming periods influence considerably the consumption plans and actual consumption during the next period. To make the relation between consumption and *last* period's income the central thing in a *causal* analysis, which should explain why people act as they act, is to overlook that these actions are determined by expectations, which often have only a loose connection with last period's realised income. This fact every American would willingly testify to-day; most of them expect growing incomes and base their consumption plans thereon. The term "propensity to consume" could well be used to indicate the relation between expected income and planned consumption. But even so it has the disadvantage of leading people to think that consumers plan a certain relation between the expected income during the *next* period and that period's consumption, whereas they actually correlate consumption plans and income expectations for many future periods. Therefore, it is better to indicate their attitude, when they are relating consumption plans to these expectations, with the term "propensity" or "disposition to save." The relation between expected income and planned consumption (or planned saving) during the *next* period can be called the "planned consumption ratio" (or the "planned savings ratio"). The consideration of income expectations for many future periods is, of course, the principal reason why people during depressions often consume much more than the income they expect or actually earn during the periods at the bottom of the depression. Note that the reasoning above takes into account the influence of windfall gains or losses. Having changed the individual's fortune, they directly influence his long-term expectations concerning income from interest, and they may set up expectations about future similar gains or losses.

Returning to the other circumstances which affect consumption plans, one must list chiefly two types: the expectations concerning future prices, and the expectations concerning future needs in comparison with the consumer's present needs. It is not necessary to dwell on these factors, the importance of which is obvious.

The latter has been much discussed in the standard works on the theory of interest. The present and expected future position with regard to cash or credit plays the same rôle for consumption demand as for investment demand.

The above reasoning, in my opinion, provides a solution to the problem which bothered Wicksell a great deal, as seen from his last paper on "The Scandinavian Crowns," published as an appendix in the English edition of *Geldzins und Güterpreise*. He there expresses doubts about the limitation of purchasing power, which, in the absence of an inflationary credit policy that gave new credit exceeding the simultaneous saving, was supposed to prevent prices from rising more than in proportion to the reduction in the supply of commodities due to war-time scarcity. If one man buys butter at high prices, his ability to buy other goods is reduced, but at the same time the farmer who sells the butter becomes in a position where he is able to increase his purchases. Hence it is not clear that a doubling of the price of butter, when its supply is reduced by one-fourth, should have any depressing influence at all on other prices.

Obviously Wicksell is right in this: there is no upper limit for purchases, which is fixed by the available purchasing power. The more people buy, the greater the total purchasing power in use. The holdings of cash and the amount of unused, available credit can be said at any given moment to indicate "unused purchasing power"; it is not reduced by purchases, only transferred. What, then, determines purchases and thus price movements as far as the demand side is concerned? The answer is given above. An individual's present cash or credit, plus what he receives during a period, sets the upper limit for what he can spend during that period, i.e., governs his ability to buy. His expectations, etc., determine his willingness to buy within that limit.

It goes without saying that a similar analysis of expectations, etc., is required to explain supply as to explain demand. But this is chiefly only another side of the entrepreneurs' investment plans, and need not detain us. I also pass over the analysis of the so-called period of investment. To be of any use this must be an *ex-ante* concept. One deficiency of the Vienna theories about the period of production is that it was not made clear when the concept was used *ex-post* and when *ex-ante*.[1]

4. Let us turn now to *a comparison of the ex-post and the ex-ante concepts*. Every one of the former has got a corresponding one among the latter. Thus we may simply fix an *a* at the bottom of each letter to indicate that it is *anticipated*, i.e., *expected or planned* income, savings, investment, etc., instead of *realised*. E.g. $E_a = S_a + C_a$.

Consider the relation of planned savings S_a to planned new investment I_a^n. There is no reason for assuming that they should be equal. But when the period is finished, new investment I^n is equal to savings S. How does this equality "come about"? The answer is that the inequality of S_a and I_a sets in motion a process which makes realised income differ from expected income, realised savings from planned savings and realised new investment differ from the corresponding plan. These differences we can call: *unexpected income E_u, unexpected new investment I_u and unintentional savings S_u* ("unintentional" is preferable to unexpected in this connection). The business man who, after the closing of his accounts, finds that he has had a larger net income than he expected and that therefore the surplus over and above his consumption is greater than his planned savings, has provided "unintentional savings" which is equal to this extra surplus. Unexpected new investment which, like unintentional saving, may, of course, be negative, can mean simply that stocks at the end of the period are different from what the entrepreneur expected.

All this is very simple. Many readers may wonder if it is worth bothering about in such detail. The answer is that unless the difference between *ex-ante* and *ex-post* concepts is kept quite clear, confusion is bound to ensue. The profit concept in Keynes' *Treatise on Money*—which in most places was an *ex-post* concept

---

[1] See the illuminating paper on "The Period of Production and Industrial Fluctuation," by Martin Hill, in the ECONOMIC JOURNAL, 1933.

where certain items had been deducted and reckoned as belonging to the next period, but which was used in the causal analysis as if it had been an *ex-ante* concept—is a case in point. Subsequently I shall demonstrate that even in Keynes' "General Theory" a similar though perhaps less important lack of precision is to be found.

To avoid misunderstanding of the above terminology, I wish to stress the fact that income has nothing to do with the actual receipt of cash. The term is used very much in the sense of the ordinary business account. It is not surprising, therefore, that—according to my experience—people with practical experience of business but with no training in economic theory find the system of terms I have sketched and their use in analysis of real problems relatively easy.

Finally, it is obvious that one has to make a distinction between income and "*Capital gains or losses.*" This latter is a little wider than Keynes' "*Windfall gains or losses.*" I return to this question later.

5. Let me now indicate very briefly how an account of various processes can be given with the above terms. Considerations of space force me to make it somewhat "short-hand." Assume that people decide to reduce their savings and increase their consumption during the next period by 10 million, as compared with the realised savings and consumption during the period which has just finished. They expect their income to be unchanged. Assume further that the planned investment is equal to the realised investment during the last period. What will be the result? Retail sales of consumption goods will rise 10 million and the stocks of retailers will at the end of the period be down, e.g. 7 million, the remaining 3 million being the extra income of the retailers. This latter sum is "unintentional" savings. Thus realised saving is down only 7 million, or the same amount as realised investment. For the next period planned investment by retailers will be higher. Furthermore, their income expectations will be more favourable, and therefore their planned consumption greater also. Both investment purchases and consumption purchases will be greater

during this second period than during the former, if consumers' disposition to save is the same. Output will rise, or prices go up, or both. While planned savings will be a little greater than during the former period—owing to the retailers' expectations of greater income—planned investment will go up more. For stocks of consumption goods will need refilling. Thus, during this period also, planned new investment will exceed the planned savings, and the process of expansion of the sum of transactions—and thereby quantities, or prices, or both—will go on.

The discrepancy between planned savings and planned investment can be regarded as the cause of the process. A similar development will follow if the original change is an increase of planned investment unaccompanied by any growth in planned savings.

This, however, is only one side of the story. Even if planned savings and planned investment should happen to be equal, a process of expansion is possible. The only thing then required is that expected incomes grow, and that consequently consumers increase their purchases. This fact has often been overlooked by writers who, under the influence of Wicksell or Keynes, start from the saving-investment analysis.

6. *The Speed of Reactions*

Obviously, in each case one has to study the actual transactions in their relation to the plans and expectations. The different reactions depend on that. As these reactions often go in opposite directions, it is necessary to consider the relative strength and speed of these tendencies. What happens first?

Take a simple case. Assume that the wheat crop in important producing countries promises to be unusually large, as in 1928. The price of wheat then falls so heavily that the expected total value of the crop is lower than its average value, and lower than in previous years. Consequently farmers expect lower incomes during the next year. (This is one illustration of the impossibility of making any general assumption that everybody expects his income during the next period to be what it was during the last one.) So far nobody else expects higher incomes. On the contrary, wheat merchants are apt to have more pessimistic income expectations owing to the fall in the value of their stock of wheat. Farmers and perhaps merchants decide to reduce their consumption purchases, and carry this out. But does not a compensatory increase in demand for consumption goods come from consumers who get their bread cheaper, and therefore have more money left for other things? Perhaps, but not at once. Mills do not reduce their prices immediately nor bakers their bread prices. Hence, to begin with, a decline in the total demand for consumption goods ensues. This may set up pessimistic profit expectations in some lines of industry—those selling to the farmers—and lead to a decline in investment, employment, and workers' income expectations, etc. Some such thing may have happened during the period immediately before the great depression, contributing towards its outbreak and severity. (A more complete analysis should, of course, as pointed out to me by Prof. Rogin, deal also with the speed of the reaction of supply. The above is only an illustration.)

Turn for a moment to the case above of a reduction in planned savings. I tacitly assumed that the banking system did not change its credit conditions. If, however, banks should immediately curtail credit—perhaps because they find that the flow of money into savings accounts is reduced—then investment purchases may be curtailed to the same extent as consumption purchases are increased. Hence, total purchases do not grow during the first period, compared with the last one, and what happens during the second one is uncertain. There is no greater probability that an expansion is caused than a contraction.

Obviously, the effects of a certain primary change varies with the time sequence and the speed of the secondary reactions. The consequences of changes in wage rates, tariffs, etc., will be different under different conditions.

The alternative processes which are caused do, of course, assume different developments with regard to the quantity or the velocity of the means of payments. But it is the time sequences and the time-lags between the various reactions—both the psychological reactions and the actual transactions—which govern the process much more than the construction of the monetary and banking system. Except when the latter reacts by causing a change in credit conditions, it has very little influence. It does not, therefore, seem very practical—although it is quite possible—to study the processes in terms of what happens to the velocity of money, i.e. by following the monetary units round their way in the economic system, in order to find out whether they are hoarded or not, etc. It is better to direct attention to the circumstances which make people change supply and purchases, and to analyse the speed of these reactions, studying the monetary mechanism only as one factor among several. The reactions of purchases depends, e.g., on (1) the speed with which profit and other income expectations are affected (see the crop-variation case above); (2) the speed with which (*a*) the amounts of cash in the hands of different firms or individuals are changed, and (*b*) the willingness of credit institutions and others to give credit is affected; (3) the actual cash and credit position when the primary change occurs. The latter circumstances concern the ability to buy, the first one the willingness to buy within the limits of ability. If the actual resources of many people are ample, then factor No. (2) is of little consequence.

It seems probable that in many cases the changes in the willingness to buy exercise the decisive influence. Hence, it is not then the speed with which the means of payments move, but rather the speed of the psychological reactions which is the governing factor. E.g. during a severe depression many firms have more cash and credit facilities than they need for any purchases under consideration.[1]

7. *The Sources of Increased Savings during an Expansion*

If the interest level is reduced, or the profit expectations raised or public works started, and thereby the total volume of investment expanded, while the planned saving is, to begin with, unchanged,

---

[1] The reader may expect some discussion of the speed of supply reactions and their relation to stocks, unused capacity, etc. But as the reasoning above is only an illustration, I have felt free to leave these things out.

how then is a larger volume of saving—corresponding to the increased investment—called forth? The answer is simple. At the end of each period some individuals and firms find that they have had larger incomes than they expected. In other words, realised savings exceed planned savings. Secondly, the negative incomes which reduce the net savings for society as a whole are reduced. Thirdly, as incomes and expected incomes rise, planned savings grow also.

There is in this explanation no room for such expressions as the common one, that "the expansion of investment has been financed by credit expansion," e.g. the printing of new notes, "injection of new money," and the like. Whether the note circulation is increased or not is immaterial, and has nothing to do with the question how the savings which correspond to the increased investment are called forth. Even when the State finances public works with the printing of new notes, the increased investment is matched by increased "real" savings. At the end of the period some people hold more cash than at its beginning. This is evidence that they have had an income which they have not consumed, i.e. that they have saved. *Ex-post* there is *ex definitione* equality between savings and investment. The usefulness of this construction is that one has to show through what process it is "brought about," even though, as in this case, planned savings differed from planned investment. This process has little or nothing to do with the question whether new notes are printed or not. It is just as possible during a period of constant quantity of money. Naturally, in that case the velocity increases. But to say that either the quantity of money or its velocity, or both, must increase in a truism and no explanation. It amounts to saying that in order that the total money value of transactions shall be able to rise, MV must rise; but MV *is* the total money value of transactions. Hence, it would seem that the quantity theory of money approach and the "injection of new money" idea have led to some confusion.

Are the new savings called forth by the larger investment "forced"? This is, of course, a matter of terminology. To talk about forced savings seems, however, unfortunate, as the people with fixed incomes who reduce their consumption when prices go up, nevertheless probably save less than before. A "forced levy" is therefore a better term. But it is not certain that prices go up. Output may expand at constant prices. In any case, the extra savings come from people who get larger incomes than they expected. Hence, the thing to be stressed is this "unintentional" saving. As already explained the decline in negative incomes and the later rise in planned positive savings and reduction in planned negative savings are also part of the process.

The character of the further process depends on which kind of new savings are created. To the extent that increased investment leads to larger planned savings, without any increase in expected income, it is void of expansionary force. Consumption demand is then reduced as much as investment purchases expanded. If this condition is not fulfilled, total purchases grow, incomes rise, unintentional savings rise, and later planned savings also. But this latter increase in planned savings comes later than it should have done to prevent the process of expansion from continuing.

SOME NOTES ON THE STOCKHOLM THEORY OF SAVINGS AND INVESTMENTS II[1]

8. *The Rate of Interest*[2]

Obviously the rate of interest cannot—with the terminology used above[3]—be determined by the condition that it equalises the supply of and the demand for savings, or, in other words, equalises savings and investment. For savings and investment are equal *ex definitione*, whatever interest level exists on the market. Nor can one say that the rate of interest equalises planned savings and

---

[1] The first part appears in the ECONOMIC JOURNAL for March, 1937. This second part is with particular reference to Mr. Keynes' *General Theory of Employment, Interest and Money*.

[2] The Swedish books contain only a scanty analysis of interest theory, so I do not know to what extent the *second* half of this section—which goes beyond my book of 1934 and may be influenced to some extent by Keynes' *General Theory*—is accepted by my Stockholm colleagues.

[3] *Cf.* Part I of this article.

planned investment, for it obviously does not do this. How, then, is the height of the interest level determined?

The answer is that the rate of interest is simply the price of credit, and that it is therefore governed by the supply of and demand for credit. The banking system—through its ability to give credit—*can* influence, and to some extent does affect, the interest level. As a matter of fact, it is often useful as a first approximation to analyse practical problems on the assumption that the banking system fixes the rates of interest which make the interest "level." Does this mean that its height has no connection with the disposition of individuals and firms to save and with other elements in the price system? Of course not. But it has such a connection only indirectly. One object of interest theory is to explain the nature of this connection.

Given a certain disposition to save and certain income expectations, i.e. certain consumption and savings plans, the level of the rate of interest relatively to profit expectations, etc., determines the volume of investment and the way in which production, trade and prices develop. Thus, incomes are made to differ from expected incomes, savings from planned savings, and investment from planned investment in such a way that savings and investment agree. *Ceteris paribus*, increased investment without a corresponding increase in planned savings raises the sum total of purchases and, thus, production or prices or both. But it should be noted that the "*ceteris paribus*" assumption includes "constant income expectations." If they rise, and consumption with them, an expansion will result even if planned saving should happen to be equal to planned investment. The essence of the matter is simple: how do consumption purchases plus investment purchases vary from one period to another? But to explain this, plans and expectations and their relation to the "realisations" of earlier periods have to be considered.

Other things being equal, a change in the interest level will cause a different kind of economic development. An important conclusion follows. Which rate of interest one wants to call "normal" depends on what kind of economic development one considers "normal." Some people regard a constant price level of some sort as natural, and they are then entitled to call the rate of interest "normal"—if there is one—which leads to this constancy. But there is, of course, no special reason for looking at the price situation alone instead of at the economic situation in general. In brief, the rate of interest, or rather the combination of rates of interest, which is compatible with the economic development one chooses to call "normal," is also normal, and so is the volume of savings and of investment which goes with it. If the interest level should be lower and the volume of investment greater than what corresponds to this development, then a process of relative expansion—of output or prices or both—is the outcome. Thereby the total quantity of savings is increased. As this economic development is *ex definitione* not "normal," the extra savings can also be called "not normal." Part of them is of the "unintentional" kind, the rest is planned on the basis of income expectations which are enlarged by the process in question.

According to Wicksell, who used different, somewhat ambiguous terms, a cumulative process of expansion was bound to ensue as long as the actual rate of interest was lower than the normal rate. What is the situation in this respect with the above terminology? Obviously, to say that the process of relative expansion continues so long as the actual rate falls short of the normal rate is a mere tautology, at least if we assume, as Wicksell did, that a lower rate always leads to greater investment than a higher rate. Wicksell's idea was that the normal rate—which he thought of as closely related to a natural rate corresponding to the marginal productivity of capital or of round-about methods of production in some Böhm-Bawerkian sense—changed very slowly if at all through the increase in savings caused by the process of expansion. Hence, he expected prices to continue to rise until the actual rate of interest on the market was raised. This latter opinion is not tenable, except perhaps if certain special assumptions are made as to expectations concerning the future. In a general analysis one has to stress the point that expectations and, thereby, the "normal" rate can change any day. There is, in my opinion, nothing more "physical" about it, as the Austrian theory wanted us to believe. The cumulative process—meaning a continuing rise in total purchases relative to the "normal" development—goes on as long as *expectations are such* that the investment purchases and the consumption purchases involve a relative rise in total purchases. This rather meaningless conclusion is not without importance, as it shows clearly that the "cumulative" character of the process depends on the fact that certain kinds of expectations are set up. A rise in the prices of consumption goods will, under certain conditions—e.g. if entrepreneurs at every moment expect existing prices to continue—raise the subjective value of capital goods and increase the demand for them, leading indirectly to greater income expectations and incomes and to a higher demand for consumption goods, etc., independently —in my opinion—of any shift of productive agents from one line of industry to another.

The important thing to stress is that the distinction between "normal" and "not normal" interest rates and savings depends on arbitrary assumptions that one kind of economic development, e.g. a constant wholesale price level, is "normal." Besides, it is far from certain that there is always one interest level which guarantees the existence of this normal development. On the one hand, it is possible that *no* interest level can do this. On the other hand, a great many and rather different interest levels may satisfy the condition of being compatible with this development. Obviously, in a dynamic analysis one has to give up the idea of an equilibrium rate of interest in the sense of the static equilibrium theory.

The fact that no sharp distinction is possible between "normal" and "not normal" savings throws some light on the above-mentioned attempts to distinguish between "true savings" ("*echte Sparmitteln*") and other savings, usually called "forced." On static assumptions it is possible to define a certain interest level and the corresponding volume of savings which is compatible with the maintenance of static equilibrium. Savings and interest rates which are not compatible with this equilibrium get a flavour of being "abnormal" or "artificial." But on dynamic assumptions such ideas have to be given up. It is, of course, conceivable that someone may in the future define a dynamic equilibrium in such a way as to make it useful for the analysis of practical problems, and that thus the distinction between equilibrium and non-equilibrium interest rates and savings may become important. But until this has been done—I doubt if it will ever happen—it seems necessary to emphasise the looseness of all ideas about "normalcy" in connection with interest rates, etc., and to attempt the study of time-using processes with the aid of more relativistic terms.

The reasoning so far is only an indication of the effects produced when the banking system fixes certain interest rates. But does the banking system actually alone determine the height of these rates? Of course not. Only the discount rate is usually fixed by the central bank. As to the other rates, e.g. the bond yield, the banking system is only one of many factors which affect demand, supply, and price. This requires further explanation.

Here again it is important to distinguish between an *ex-post* and *ex-ante* analysis. *Ex-post* one finds equality between the total quantity of new credit during the period, and the sum total of positive individual savings. (Of course, a person who uses his own savings is then said to give credit to himself; this supply and this demand offset one another and exert no influence on the price of credit.) Thus, there is a connection between the rate of interest, which is the price of credit, and the process of economic activity, of which the flow of saving is a part.

To explain how the rates of interest are actually determined, we need, however, a causal analysis which runs chiefly in *ex-ante* terms. What governs the demand and supply of credit? Two ways of reasoning are possible. One is *net* and deals only with *new* credit, and the other is *gross* and includes the outstanding *old* credits. The willingness of certain individuals during a given period to *increase* their holdings of various claims and other kinds of assets *minus* the willingness of others to *reduce* their corresponding holdings gives the supply curves for the different kinds of new credit during the period. Naturally, the quantities each individual is willing to supply depend on the interest rates. In other words, the plans are in the nature of alternative purchase and sales plans.

Similarly, the total supply of *new* claims *minus* the reduction in the outstanding volume of *old* ones gives the demand—also a function of the rates of interest—for the different kinds of credit during the period. The prices fixed on the market for these different claims—and thereby the rates of interest—are governed by this supply and demand in the usual way.

The demand for claims of different sorts can be explained partly in terms of the same expectation-analysis as demand for investment goods. In discussing this latter question above nothing was said about the former, i.e. the way people planned to handle their own savings and "free capital." Except when they want to use them for direct investment—purchases of goods for investment purposes—they must decide in favour of acquiring claims, including cash. The psychology behind the choice between the different possibilities in this respect has been much illuminated by Keynes' discussion of "liquidity-preference."

A similar kind of reasoning can, of course, be applied *gross*, i.e. including the old claims which were outstanding when the period began. People's willingness to hold the different claims and other kinds of assets every day governs the supply of credit. The total supply of claims, etc., governs the demand for credit. In each market for the different claims, etc., supply and demand are made equal by price. These prices for interest-bearing claims on certain fixed sums determine the rates of interest. It is quite obvious that this reasoning in gross terms leads to the same result as the net analysis above.

I must pass over the question about the differences between the different kinds of credits, e.g.—(1) the length of the contract and the right to get the sum back on short or long notice and (2) the security given and the credit-worthiness of the borrower. The changing valuation of these things, and the ideas concerning the profit possibilities of other assets than claims, affect demand, supply, and price in the different markets.

Let me add a few words about the market which is given a special position by Keynes, the demand and supply for cash and claims "quickly" convertible into cash. It goes without saying, that the interest rates existing at any given moment fulfil the condition that they make people willing to hold as cash—which term in the following includes the last-mentioned claims—the total amount outstanding. But the same is true of all other claims and assets. The total quantity of cash is not fixed by the banking system at a certain figure, but depends on the economic development and on the actions of a number of individuals just as does the quantity of bonds outstanding. The "market" for cash has no key position in relation to the other markets. It is not even certain that the rate of interest obtained on cash holdings is zero. Up to a few years ago the Swedish banks used to pay interest on cheque deposits. In many countries sums on savings accounts could be withdrawn readily and, therefore, could serve as money. Of course, one can ask: how intensively does each individual prefer holding a certain part of his fortune in form A (cash) rather than in form B? It is simpler and clearer to ask directly what sums people want to hold in form A, what in form B, etc., in a certain price situation and with certain expectations, e.g. with a certain constellation of interest rates, share prices, etc.[1] There is no need of a theory of interest in terms of differentials, similar to the Ricardian theory of rent.

In my opinion, the theory of interest can be regarded as falling into three parts: (1) An analysis of the markets for claims and other assets, where their prices and, thus, the rates of interest are determined. This includes the phenomena of credit policy by banks, e.g. open-market operations. (2) An explanation of what kinds of processes with regard to the quantities of planned and unintentional savings and investment result from the existence of certain interest rates or, rather, from certain movements in interest rates. (3) An account of the connection between these processes and the transactions on the markets first mentioned. One process is apt to increase the willingness to hold long-term bonds, while another process reduces it, and this changed willingness is much dependent on the changes in incomes and in planned savings. Consumers buy

---

[1] Dr. Johan Åkerman some years ago in conversation outlined some such approach to interest theory. I am not aware whether he has followed it up.

consumption goods, business men buy capital goods, i.e. invest in a real sense, but there is a third kind of purchases to be explained—namely, "financial investment," i.e. the purchases of bonds, shares and bank deposits and the failure to use savings either for real or financial investment, which is identical with an increase in cash. It is noteworthy that Keynes, who has presented so interesting an analysis of the desire to vary cash holdings and of the psychology of financial investment, i.e. the willingness to buy bonds, shares, etc., on the one hand, pays so little attention to the connection between changes in production, income and savings on the one hand and the *ability* to make financial investments on the other. Without a consideration of this latter circumstance, the analysis of the markets for claims of different maturity, where the rates of interest are determined, is incomplete. Such a theory as I have here only briefly indicated is of course different from any equilibrium theory of the text-book kind. But it agrees with that theory and differs from Keynes' construction in one essential respect: it brings out the relation of the rates of interest to the other elements of the price system and to their movements, whereas Keynes' construction—unless it is interpreted in a way which he probably does not accept—seems to regard the rates of interest as determined largely "outside" the price system, or at least as having almost no connection with the system of mutually interdependent prices and quantities.

9. *Some Aspects of a Theory of Employment*

As Mr. Keynes has—rightly, I think—put much emphasis on the consequences of his theoretical approach for the theory of employment and unemployment, I shall add a few words about the attitude towards this problem in the Stockholm theory. What I say is naturally much influenced particularly by Dr. Alf Johansson's monograph on *Wage Development and Unemployment*. Points (*a*) and (*b*) below are a summary of some of his argument. To be as brief as possible I shall only enumerate some of the salient conclusions.

(*a*) Permanent unemployment need not be "due to" a failure to reduce wages. In other words, it is far from certain that a reduction in wage rates would reduce unemployment to what one calls a "frictional" minimum. In the post-war discussion economists have sometimes *assumed* that there is an equilibrium wage which would make demand equal the available quantity of labour and, thus, lead to a state of no unemployment, except of the frictional type. Thereafter, they have proceeded to state that the existence of permanent unemployment is a *proof* that "wages are too high." It is evident that nothing is proved and that the latter statement is simply a repetition of the original assumption. Once the static equilibrium reasoning is given up, it becomes obvious that the relation between wages and unemployment is much more complicated. The level of wage rates is only one element of many, which have to get into certain relationships in order that the available labour force shall be employed. Discussing the unemployment during a period of prosperity, Dr. Johansson writes: "*A priori* one cannot expect that under all conditions—independently of the character, strength and speed of the structural changes and their relation to one another—a flexible wage should be completely effective as a regulator of equilibrium on the labour market for each period, which is longer than the business cycle. Why should the time-using . . . adaptations of the elements which govern supply and demand on the labour market and which are called forth by an adaptation of wages . . . have exactly the strength and time to develop exactly so far as is needed, in order that unemployment shall be reduced to an 'irreducible minimum' at the culminating stage of a business cycle, which may develop during a period of secular decline in prices and an intense technical rationalisation of a labour-saving sort?" (*op. cit.*, p. 9). If this is true of a period of prosperity, how much more uncertain must it not be that wage flexibility can prevent continued unemployment during a long depression?

(*b*) When labour is set free through labour-saving technical changes there is no automatic compensation in increased employment elsewhere. What is set free is not "purchasing power," which will buy more of other goods than those cheapened by the invention, so that the expansion of output of such goods will provide employment for the discarded labourers. On the contrary, it is "productive power" which is made available, and it will not be re-employed unless some new impulse to expansion comes forward.

(c) Wage increases can lead to larger output and employment. The effect depends chiefly on how the investment demand of entrepreneurs reacts. Under certain conditions it will grow when wages go up, e.g. because people expect prices to rise later on. Under other conditions the opposite is true. The reaction of consumption demand is easier to determine. The outcome with regard to output and employment depends much on the speed of the various reactions of different kinds of investment demand as well as consumption demand. The possible rise in employment has nothing, as such, to do with a rise in prices or costs of living. The Stockholm theory thus denies the validity of the "orthodox" thesis which Keynes defends—namely, that an increase in employment must be accompanied by a reduction in the real wage. Elsewhere I hope to point out wherein, in my opinion, Keynes' mistake lies.

Obviously, wage changes affect the course of events differently during different cyclical processes. As a first approximation one can say that wage changes are in the short run "neutral" towards employment, as they increase the "cost side" of output as much as the "demand side." It depends on the price policy pursued by the sellers and on the effects of wage changes on investment and consumption demand, whether the quantity of labour employed goes up or down in the short run. (To analyse a great many such processes is the essential part of a "dynamic" theory of wages and employment.) In the "longer run" the tendencies towards a change in the combination of productive factors must of course also be considered. A similar reasoning shows that an increase in import duties may well increase employment considerably, without any reduction in the "real wage."[1] As a matter of fact, wage reductions during depressions have usually been very small. There is no evidence of any *general* reductions in wage rates from the end

---

[1] My book of 1934 contains an extensive discussion of this problem and a criticism of the opposite view taken by Harrod in his *International Economics*.

of the eighteen-eighties up to the World War. This speaks against the Austrian argument that wage reduction, with the consequent decline in consumption, is the decisive factor which starts recovery.

It would carry me too far to describe—in terms of the above period-analysis—different courses of events which may follow upon changes in wage rates. The interested reader can, no doubt, do that for himself. Neither can I attempt to summarise the analysis in the Final Report of the Unemployment Committee, where the "frictional" types of unemployment are considered together with those connected with variations in the sum total of "monetary demand," i.e. with processes of general expansion and contraction. The Committee emphasises the fact that the total demand in terms of money will·be increased (1) if foreign countries buy more of our products, (2) if investment is increased, and (3) if consumption purchases are increased. For obvious reasons the possibilities of increasing investment during a depression are particularly studied. But the Committee is careful not to assume that measures to maintain investment are all that is needed to guarantee practically complete employment. Even the largest volume of investment which is during a certain period compatible with a desirable stability in price conditions and in the external value of the currency may leave considerable unemployment if the mobility of labour is small, or if wage rates are "too high." It is not much less dangerous to concentrate attention exclusively on the volume of investment in its relation to the propensity to consume than to think only about some of the other relationships involved, e.g. wage flexibility.

After this brief survey of some salient aspects of the Stockholm theory, I shall turn to a discussion of Keynes' analysis of the same set of problems with a somewhat different set of tools.

C. Some Observations on Mr. Keynes' Theory

1. *The Characteristics of the New Approach*

As I see it, the two outstanding characteristics of Keynes' theoretical system are the following. First, his reasoning runs in monetary terms instead of in "real" terms, as do the theories of

Marshall, Pigou and their followers, who regard money as a "veil" which one has to take away to see things clearly. A reasoning in monetary terms does not prevent any amount of considerations of the "real" implications, whenever such considerations may be desirable, e.g. in a discussion of policy. But it has the advantage of permitting a much simpler and less sophisticated explanation of the market phenomena, which are *price* phenomena. For this reason, it has long ago been accepted by almost all schools of economic thought outside England. One sometimes gets the impression that Keynes is unaware of this. Professor P. Douglas—in well-known works—and Professor Bagge[1] have both given us extensive treatments of wage and unemployment problems by means of reasoning in monetary terms.

The second and more important aspect of Keynes' work is that it is free from some basic assumptions tacitly made, I believe, in all systematic treatments of the pricing of commodities and productive factors, i.e. in the so-called theory of price and distribution (but not in money and cycles theory). In price theory it is assumed that the changes which are studied—e.g. changes in the supply and demand for a particular commodity—*do not react on the price system as a whole sufficiently for these repercussions outside the field of analysis to need to be considered*.[2] A special type of repercussion, which is thereby eliminated, is that which would occur if general processes of expansion and contraction—in terms of quantity or value of output—were to be started or affected by the *partial* processes under examination. E.g. in a study of the influence of a new invention the possibility that it will cause an expansion in the total volume of investment leading to inflation is not considered. This, no doubt, is a useful and fruitful method. However, this simplification would be quite absurd in the discussion of the prices and employment of the factors of production, e.g. in the determination of the wage and interest level, total employment, etc. The analysis there touches upon

---

[1] Professor Bagge's *Causes of Unemployment* (published in Swedish), 1930, gives an excellent survey of all those aspects of unemployment, which are independent of instability in the field of money, and touches upon some other aspects.

[2] This is the well-known method of the analysis of "particular equilibrium."

considerable changes in the whole price system, and is no longer chiefly concerned with a small part of it, as in the case of a particular commodity market. Hence, to avoid the consideration of such phenomena as general contraction and expansion processes, which is deferred to sections dealing with monetary and business cycle analysis, price and distribution theory proper is made to rest on the tacit assumption of what might be called "*monetary stability.*" It is not possible to say what meaning is given to this in the various textbooks, for the authors do not seem to be aware of the assumption they have made. The loose idea behind their discussion has some similarity with the Say doctrine, that supply creates its own demand, but involves something more than that, for there is nothing in this assumption—that total proceeds from sales equal total costs—which prevents changes in the volume of employment and output and in price-levels. (Say's assumption rules out "profit inflation," but not "income inflation." See Keynes' *Treatise on Money*.) Perhaps the tacit assumption means "a constant sum total—in terms of money—of all industrial transactions," or "a constant national income in terms of money" or "a national income which only changes in proportion to the variation in the quantities of productive factors."[1] Through some such assumption all other causes of incomplete employment than those connected with monopoly—including monopolistic trade union policy—and "friction" are ruled out, as well as movements in the general price-levels. Thus, the basic assumption in conventional price and distribution theory is—in my opinion—*not* one of relatively full employment. The simplification includes more than that, inasmuch as it also eliminates changes in general price-levels, i.e. that kind of process which is commonly called inflationary and deflationary.[2]

---

[1] See my *Interregional and International Trade*, p. 376.

[2] It follows from the above that, in my opinion, Keynes' attempt to explain why the textbook theories of price and distribution deal only with frictional and monopolistic unemployment is unsuccessful. Few twentieth-century writers have assumed that "the utility of the wage is equal to the marginal utility" of the existing amount of employment. But all writers on price and distribution, so far as I know, rule out the general processes of expansion and contraction in the value

An economic analysis on this basis ("monetary stability") can throw light upon a number of phenomena both in the labour market and in other markets. But the larger the size of the phenomena and processes considered, the greater is the probability that in the real world reactions will follow which change the total volume of output and national income, both in monetary and real terms. Hence the greater is the need for studying what this change will be. When this is done, we get a theory both of "variations in employment and output as a whole" and of movements in price-levels. Not that the conclusions concerning the pricing and employment of the factors of production, based on the assumption of "monetary stability," are entirely wrong. But only under special conditions are they sufficiently correct to be interesting, except as an introduction.

What we need is an analysis which makes no such assumption of monetary stability and which concentrates attention on the effects which all kinds of *partial processes* have on the *total* volume of employment and national income, the latter in terms of money as well as in terms of quantities of goods and services. An analysis of this type involves a consideration in price and distribution theory of those problems which have hitherto been discussed in the sections on money and business cycles in textbooks on economic principles. Thereby, the whole theory of the pricing process—which must be an account of the *time-using* process—can be given a unity which it has so far lacked. And the theory of wages, employment and interest becomes rather different from the theory built up on the basis of the "monetary stability" assumption. (See §§ 8–9 above.) The works by Lindahl, Hammarskjöld, Johansson, Myrdal and myself, that were published during the depression, represent an attempt to provide pieces of such a theory.

---

of output, and, *thereby*, both changes in employment and output—with the above-mentioned exceptions—and changes in general price-levels. In Chapter 19 Keynes mentions that the changes "in the amount of aggregate effective demand" have been ignored in conventional distribution theory. But this fact is not considered in the earlier part of the book, where the criticism of the "classical" theory is based on its utility assumptions.

In a world of booms and depressions such a discussion of wages, unemployment and the rates of interest, as well as the study of all kinds of economic policy, is—as already observed—apt to be more useful than an analysis based on an assumption of some sort of "monetary stability." But it would be foolish to dispense with the latter altogether, especially as an introduction. I believe that it represents one of the most fruitful simplifications that are used in economic science. Take, e.g., the analysis of certain phenomena within the individual firm or the study of so-called "frictional" unemployment, with all its considerations of different labour qualities, the various kinds of labour mobility, etc. Certainly, a number of conclusions concerning these phenomena hold good also under less stable monetary conditions, but are more easily reached when the difficulties concerning processes of general expansion and contraction are not introduced. Such knowledge concerning the labour markets as has been reached on the basis of monetary stability has to be incorporated in any *general* theory of employment worthy of its name.

It is understandable that Keynes, in writing his treatise, has concentrated on those aspects which had to do with the changes in output as a whole, and, therefore, pays very little attention to the other aspects. But it is all the more important that the relation of his reasoning to the "old" one shall be made quite clear. In comparing his theories with what he calls the "classical" theory, Keynes seems to me to mix together and confuse the differences arising from two distinct sources, mentioned above: (1) Those which depend on the fact that what he calls the "classical" theory is a Cambridge type of analysis in "real" terms and based on certain specific assumptions as to the supply of labour, whereas he thinks in monetary terms and has given up some—though not all—of these assumptions. In this respect his attitude resembles that of Cassel and several other contemporary economists. (2) Those differences which arise because both this "classical" theory and textbooks in price and distribution theory from U. S. A., Vienna, Stockholm, etc., rest on some such assumption as I have called "monetary stability," which rules out most of the large changes in the volume of output, while Keynes' own analysis—like the books by Stockholm economists mentioned above—is concentrated on a world where there are frequent and large changes in the total volume of employment and national income. From the point of view of economists who are used to discussing in monetary terms without the special "classical" assumptions about labour supply— I believe this is true of the overwhelming majority of economists in the world since the war—the former aspect of Keynes' book is simply the long-awaited conversion of a Cambridge economist to the almost generally accepted standpoint elsewhere. It is the second characteristic which gives the book a somewhat "revolutionary" flavour, from the point of view of economic theory. In my opinion, Keynes' greatest achievement in this work lies in the fact that he attempts—and in spite of his special assumptions concerning wage inflexibility etc. to a great extent succeeds—to provide a theory for changes in total employment and price-levels, which can also be called the theory of processes of general contraction and expansion.

Of course, not all the knowledge thereby reached is new. The theories of money and business cycles, even before the present depression, and still more in recent years, have given us much knowledge concerning changes in employment and rates of interest. What Keynes calls the "classical" theory does not seem to include any theory of money and cycles, otherwise it is difficult to see how he can say that this theory has "never given a single thought" to the question: "Will fluctuations in investment have any effect on the demand for output as a whole and, consequently, on the scale of output and employment?" Business cycle theory has also taught us much about the influence of wage changes, which Keynes has failed to notice. Few economists, at least outside the Vienna school, maintained that during the severe depression of 1932–33 a reduction in wages and an increased willingness to save would have been certain to increase employment. Theoretical discussion was concentrated on the effect on the entrepreneurs' expectations about the future course of prices, wages and profits, and upon the possibility that, thereby, wage reductions would give fresh impetus to a process of deflation and contraction of economic activity. Keynes makes the statement: "The idea that we can safely neglect the aggregate demand function is fundamental to the Ricardian economics, which underlie what we have been taught for more than a century" (p. 32). While some such idea underlies the price and distribution theories—as I have already argued—it is certainly not so with monetary and cycles theory, which is based on the very opposite idea. Recent discussion in this field has resulted in conclusions—e.g. on the effects on wage changes—which can be regarded as pieces of a theory of output as a whole. Economists who have followed this discussion will find Keynes' analysis of wage reductions (on pp. 262–64) and the stress on their influence on profit expectations and the volume of investment very familiar. I am sure, therefore, that most readers of the *General Theory* have been much surprised in finding (on p. 21) that the classical theorists —this expression seems to cover all others than Keynes himself and the "underworld" of economists—"are fallaciously supposing that there is a nexus which unites decisions to abstain from present consumption with decisions to provide for future consumption." Practically all monetary theorists take account of the fact that saving accompanied by "hoarding" by some people need not lead to investment by other people. Furthermore, it is the very essence of Wicksell's theory of money and "cumulative processes" that there is no such nexus between plans to save and decisions to invest. It has become the basis for most of the recent analyses of processes of expansion and contraction. Besides, D. H. Robertson, next door to King's College—and probably not much under the influence of Wicksell—has since 1926 presented several substantial pieces of "process analysis," obviously not based on the above-mentioned fallacy. The same is true of Hawtrey. Yet Keynes (p. 32) expresses the opinion that the correct idea "could only live on furtively, below the surface in the underworlds of Karl Marx, Silvio Gesell or Major Douglas."

Let us return for a moment to the two sources of differences between Keynes and the so-called "classical" theory. It is not a mere chance that he fails to distinguish between them. In fact, he maintains explicitly that there is only one such source (pp. 21-22). The classical theory is said to depend on the assumption that "the real wage is equal to the marginal disutility of existing employment," and that "supply creates its own demand in the sense that the aggregate demand price is equal to the aggregate supply price for all levels of output and employment." But these assumptions and a third one "all amount to the same thing, in the sense that they all stand and fall together, any one of them logically involving the other two." Surely, however, the Say doctrine that supply creates its own demand has nothing to do with the psychology of the labourer. Even if a universal thirty-hours week were fixed by law, and the workers had no disutility whatsoever from work—the first assumption would then be absurd—Say's doctrine would not be affected thereby. It runs in terms of total supply and total demand, *in terms of money*, at prices which cover money costs. Conversely, even if the special assumptions concerning the supply of labour are accepted, this does not preclude an analysis of processes which are incompatible with Say's assumption.

In my opinion the vitally important distinction between the "old" type of analysis, as represented by conventional price and distribution theory, and the "new" one, represented by Keynes, the Stockholm school, and—to some extent—more or less the whole theory of money and business cycles, lies in the former's fundamental assumption (not identical with the Say doctrine) which rules out the *general* processes of expansion and contraction of employment, output and prices, thereunder all other changes in the volume of employment than those connected with monopoly and friction. The central task for economic theory to-day, towards the solution of which Keynes has made such important contributions, is the construction of a body of analysis, free from such assumptions. This amounts to a co-ordination of the theories of price, money and cycles.

2. *Keynes' Equilibrium Theory versus a Process Theory of the Stockholm Type*

If Keynes' theoretical system is modern in the respect I have touched upon above, it is equally "old-fashioned" in the second respect which characterises recent economic theory—namely, the attempt to break away from an explanation of economic events by means of orthodox equilibrium constructions. No other analysis of trade fluctuations in recent years—with the possible exception of the Mises-Hayek school—follows such conservative lines in this respect. In fact, Keynes is much more an "equilibrium theorist" than such economists as Cassel and, I think, Marshall.

The central thesis in Keynes' theory is that the volume of employment depends upon the volume of investment. As most theories of business fluctuations, in their explanation of changes in employment, concentrate attention on changes in the volume of investment, Keynes' emphasis on this latter point is not new. The novelty lies in his construction of an *equilibrium*, governed by the quantity of money, the propensity to consume, the marginal efficiency of capital, and the liquidity preference. These "independent" variables determine the rate of interest, the volume of investment and, thus, the volume of employment.

The most fundamental objection to this theory is the following. The propensity to consume expresses "the functional relationship between a given level of income in terms of wage units and the expenditure on consumption out of that income." Given a certain propensity to consume, which we can call k, we obtain $E(1 - k) = I$. The income E will vary in the same proportion as the volume of investment I. However, this holds good only in reference to a period which is finished, i.e. *ex-post*. It would have been better, therefore, to talk about the "realised consumption ratio," instead of the "propensity" to consume, expressing the relation between the volume of consumption and the realised income. $(1 - k)$ is the "realised savings ratio," which can be defined as the relation between realised income and realised saving, i.e. $\frac{E}{S}$. But the latter is the same as realised investment. Hence, $(1 - k) = \frac{I}{E}$. The equation above only expresses a truism, showing that the definitions are consistent with one another, and explains nothing. The relationship in question does not throw any light on the question "what *determines* the position of employment at any time," as Keynes claims his theory to do. Neither does it indicate an equilibrium position, towards which the economic system tends and which, if reached, will remain stable, in the absence of new changes in the independent variables. As a matter of fact, this equation holds true for *every* period, even in the most *unstable* situations.[1]

To explain the development or the actual tendencies one must use terms which refer to the expectations, plans and actions based thereupon, an *ex-ante* terminology, as indicated in the first part of my paper in the last issue of this JOURNAL. Keynes probably has had a feeling of this, as he has used such a word as "propensity." But he has defined his terms income, investment and propensity to consume as *ex-post* concepts. Perhaps he has meant them *ex-ante?* But there is no such relation between expected income, planned consumption and planned investment as he indicates. Thus, either Keynes' reasoning is *ex-post*, and then it explains nothing, or it is *ex-ante*, and then it is entirely wrong. There is no reason why the planned investment plus the planned consumption should be equal to the expected total income for society as a whole. In other words, the planned investment will differ from the planned saving, unless they should happen to be equal by mere chance. Owing to this difference, expectations will not be fulfilled. At the end of the period people will find that their incomes, investment and savings during that period have not been what they expected them to be. Consequently, the expectations, plans and actions with reference to the next period will differ from what they were in the last period. The economic situation will change in a way which can only be explained through a study of how these differences between expectations and the actual course of events during one period influence expectations and actions in the future.[2]

---

[1] See p. 23 on "the income resulting from a certain employment." See also pp. 28, 57, 62, and 115.

[2] Note the difference between the equation above and Lindahl's, which is in *ex-ante* terms: $E_a(1 - s_a) = C$, where s_a is the planned savings ratio and C is consumption. Only for consumption can one assume that plans are always realised.

Should, however, by mere chance, planned saving and investment be equal, then expectations will come true, not for each individual or firm, but as far as total income, saving and investment are concerned. This is consistent with, but does not necessarily mean a stable situation. For people may have been expecting growing employment and income, and when these expectations are fulfilled, they may expect still further growth in income and employment. This is an exemplification of the fact that the series of events during the preceding periods may well lead to a change in planned savings or planned investment for the next period, even if expectations during the last period came true. Take another example. The volume of investment during the last period may have been influenced by old contracts which have now expired. In a thousand and one ways the situation at the beginning of the new period may be different from what it was at the beginning of the preceding period. Hence, the plans concerning savings and investment may be different also. A change in the economic situation will follow.

Let us start from a position where expectations have on the whole been fulfilled for some time and conditions have been subject only to relatively small changes. If we want to know the effects of a certain reduction in the planned volume of investment[1]—caused, e.g., by some political changes leading to pessimism in general—then one evidently has to follow the process through a study of the successive changes in expectations and plans in actual events, in the differences between them, and in the consequent reactions of the new expectations, plans, and actions, etc. In such a sequence leading to a considerable reduction in total employment and output it is *a priori* probable that many elements in the price system will be affected. The rate of interest will probably fall as a result of the smaller willingness to invest, given a certain willingness to save. (This is in accordance with the interest theory which has been briefly indicated above, and which is different from

---

[1] Investment plans, like consumption plans, are realised, as far as *purchases* go. But investment is influenced also by sales from stock of goods, and these sales may differ from expectations.

Keynes' theory.) Furthermore, the willingness to save will decline, although this may only start at a later stage than the fall in the interest level. When people come to regard their expected income as *temporarily* unusually low, the consumption will be a greater percentage of their expected income than under other conditions. (Keynes does not accept this; see p. 95.) Much here depends on the speed with which their realised incomes and income expectations fall. Investment will be affected by the rapidity of the reactions in prices, quantities and interest rates, and in the willingness of banks to give credit to firms and individuals with declining solvency. Thus, I cannot find that the economic system tends towards a stable equilibrium described by simple reference to the change in the volume of investments. It is highly improbable that the system ever gets to a state where expectations are fulfilled, in the above-mentioned sense. Nor is there a tendency to move in the direction of some such position. And if the system should happen to get into such a position, this does not mean that it tends to remain there.

Keynes' opposite view, that his so-called equilibrium will indicate a stable position towards which the system tends—a position determined by the four independent variables—is due to the facts that he (1) *assumes* that the other three elements will not vary when the fourth one changes, even though the situation may shift from boom to depression; (2) overlooks the fundamental difference between the *ex-post* and *ex-ante* concepts, using a relation between the realised consumption and income as if it meant the planned consumption ratio. It is a consequence of this latter defect that he ignores the influence of *the speed* of the various reactions. A comparison of two equilibria—consistent with different volumes of investment—supplemented with some indications concerning certain repercussions is, of course, unable to take into account this speed of reactions, the importance of which I have illustrated in the first part of this paper and shall return to in the discussion of wage changes.

The fact that the realised savings ratio, which is identical with the relation between the volume of investment and the volume of income, varies a great deal when general business conditions change, needs no other proof than reference to the well-known fact that the production of capital goods fluctuates much more than the production of consumers' goods. Changes in the quantity of commodity stocks are small in comparison therewith, and cannot make the volume of investment reach anything like the same proportion of total income during depressions as during booms. Hence, even if the psychological willingness to save were somewhat constant, it becomes absurd to assume a relatively constant multiplier. As a matter of fact, the willingness to save fluctuates, for reasons already mentioned, and the unintentional positive or negative savings, partly connected with losses, make the realised savings fluctuate more than the planned savings, but in the same direction.

This seems to me to be a rather damaging criticism of the theory of the multiplier, and this criticism holds also if the theory is stated in terms of the *marginal* propensity to consume. Even if the marginal willingness to save—the marginal planned savings ratio—were somewhat constant during varying conditions of good and bad trade, the marginal realised savings ratio, which is identical with the relation between the increase in investment and in total production, would not be constant; for the unintentional savings come in. As a matter of fact, however, people do not decide to save the same percentage of an expected increase in income during the beginning of a recovery as they do during a boom. The necessity to pay off debts, or doubts whether the increase in income is going to be lasting, may make them decide to save 50 per cent. of the expected increase in income during the first year of recovery, whereas they would want to save only 10 per cent. at a later stage of the recovery. Thus, if we want to form some idea as to the size of the effects of an increase in investment, e.g. in public works, we can only be misled by figures concerning some normal multiplier from which the actual effect is supposed to differ only slightly. Keynes mentions some circumstances which make for changes in the marginal consumption ratio and multiplier, but the whole tendency of his argument (see p. 121) is that it varies only little. The chief reason why the multiplier theory can tell us but little about the effects of a certain increase in investment is not its fluctuation, but the fact that it leaves out of account the reaction of a certain change in the volume of output and in the general business situation on profit expectations and the willingness to invest (the marginal efficiency of capital). At the bottom of a depression public works for a moderate sum may start a recovery, which would not otherwise have come, at least for a year or two. Hence the total increase in production due to these public works may during a certain period be ten times the sums spent. In another situation an increase in public works may scare the business world to such an extent that private investment activity declines, and total output is therefore increased by less than the sum allocated to public works. Thus, the multiplicatory effect may easily—if the reactions of private investment are included—at one time be ten or more, and at another time considerably less than one.[1]

---

[1] "Since the business cycles are mainly characterised *by variations* in this relation—between the value of new investments and consumption expenditures . . . *the theory must explain the changes in the multiplier* instead of assuming that the latter is given." Erik Lundberg, *Studies in the Theory of Economic Expansion*, p. 37. Mr. Lundberg's criticism of Keynes' *General Theory* is partly the same as mine, which was worked out before I had occasion to read his book. I shall, however, refer to it in some footnotes.

6

THE OUTCOME OF THE SAVING-INVESTMENT DISCUSSION*

By Friedrich A. Lutz‖

At first glance it is difficult to understand why the participants in the discussion of the relation between saving and investment should be unable to reach agreement as to how to define these two concepts. One reason, no doubt, is that the central figure in the discussion has been Mr. Keynes, who has as many champions prepared to defend every word he has written as he has opponents ready to challenge every phrase. But this psychological tendency towards contrariness is certainly not the only explanation. The more important element is the fact that not all of the writers concerned seem to realize that the problem at issue is not so much a question of which definitions are "right" or "wrong," as a question of which definitions are the most useful. There is, for example, little point in arguing that Keynes' terminology, according to which saving and investment must necessarily be equal, is wrong because it can be "proved" that there are circumstances in which they can be unequal. Those who attempt to give such a "proof" simply have other concepts of saving and investment in mind. It is equally purposeless, on the other hand, for Keynes' followers to reason that only their concepts express the "true" relationship between the two magnitudes. If all the participants in the discussion could be persuaded to drop this kind of argument, the

---

* *Quarterly Journal of Economics*, Volume LII, August 1938, pages 588–614. Reprinted by the courtesy of the Quarterly Journal of Economics and the author.
‖ Princeton University.

discussion would undoubtedly lose its uncompromising character and gain in fruitfulness.

If we are to analyze the various concepts so far developed from the point of view of their usefulness, we need a standard according to which we can decide which of them is to be preferred. This may be obtained by going back to the origin of the discussion, which, in the heat of the controversy about definitions, has apparently been completely forgotten by many authors. Wicksell held that a cumulative process of the economic system upwards or downwards is set into motion when saving is smaller or greater respectively than investment. It thus appeared that the relation between saving and investment had an important rôle to play in any attempt at a theoretical analysis of such processes. Moreover, it was inferred that the equality of saving and investment could be taken as a criterion of credit policy which, if followed, would eliminate these processes, and hence the trade cycle.[1] We shall therefore examine the different concepts of saving and investment in the light of their usefulness for the theoretical analysis of the cumulative process and for dealing with the problem of credit policy.

Keynes I

There is not much purpose in going back to Wicksell's treatment, as he did not give any clear definition of the concepts. We may begin therefore with the work which gave the impetus to the whole discussion—Keynes' Treatise on Money. Altho there is probably nobody who still favors the terminology used in that book, it cannot be omitted from a survey of the development of the doctrine. Moreover, the importance which Wicksell originally ascribed to the two concepts is given more emphasis in Keynes' Treatise than it has received in the discussion which followed.

According to this earlier formulation (hereafter referred to as Keynes I), a divergence between saving (S) and the value of investment (I) is supposed to give rise to total profits (when $I > S$) or

---

[1] Wicksell, although he argued in favor of such a policy, did not think that it would entirely eliminate the trade cycle, as he did not identify the latter with the cumulative process.

total losses (when $S > I$) in the system, and therewith produces a tendency to a cumulative expansion or contraction in the Wicksellian sense. Monetary equilibrium, if we may use the expression in opposition to the ordinary static equilibrium concept,[1] prevails then, just as in Wicksell's treatment, when $I = S$, which is identical with the condition that the total profits of the system must be equal to zero. Accordingly, it is the task of the banking system to control the supply of credit in such a way as to keep the value of new investment equal to new saving. Thus in Keynes I the relation between the two quantities is, as pointed out above, not only significant as an analytical tool for purposes of monetary theory, for the reason that it indicates whether the system is in an expansionist or contractionist phase, but is also important for practical monetary policy, which, it is inferred, should aim at keeping I equal to S and so preventing cumulative processes.

In what sense are the concepts "saving" and "investment" used here? As is by now familiar, the discrepancy between the two quantities in Keynes I is made possible by the fact that Keynes counts only "normal" profits as part of income: neither abnormal profits nor losses have any effect on income. Let us take an example. Suppose we start from an equilibrium in which

$$\text{Income } (E) = 50$$
$$\text{Consumption } (C) = 30$$
$$\text{Saving } (E - C) = 20$$
$$\text{Investment } (I) = 20$$

Assume that in the next period consumption increases by 10 at the expense of saving, with the consequence that prices of consumers' goods rise correspondingly, so that the dealers in these goods make profits of 10. Then according to Keynes I

$$E = 50$$
$$C = 40$$
$$S = 10$$
$$I = 20$$

---

[1] In static equilibrium the relative prices remain constant, whereas this is not necessary for the existence of monetary equilibrium. Whether the *price level* has to remain constant is a controversial question, which does not concern us here.

Investment,[1] half of which must in this case have been financed either by additional credit or by "dishoarding," exceeds saving by 10, which is equal to the total profits.[2] If we had counted the "abnormal" profits as income, we should of course have had $S = I$, which is the result reached later by Keynes in the General Theory.

What is the significance of these concepts for purposes of monetary theory? According to Keynes the difference between S and I is supposed to be the cause of the profits or losses of the system as a whole, and consequently of the inception of a cumulative process. It is obvious, however, that the difference between S and I arises only because abnormal profits are not counted as income, and losses are not deducted from income. This has a corresponding influence on the savings item, which is calculated as the difference between income and consumption. In other words, it is only by this treatment of profits and losses that Keynes can arrive at a difference between savings and investment. As Hawtrey has remarked, "a difference between savings and investment cannot be regarded as the *cause* of a windfall loss or gain, but *is* the windfall loss or gain."[3] Consequently the concepts as defined by Keynes I cannot be used for purposes of causal analysis.

Nonetheless the interpretation of the figures used in our example seems to work out quite satisfactorily; the diminution of saving, while investment remains constant, appears as the cause of profits. But if we look closer we see that this interpretation of the example is

---

[1] Keynes I understands by I only new investment, and does not include the value of capital goods produced for replacement purposes. Correspondingly S does not include the amortization quotas. The difficulties underlying this treatment will be discussed later.

[2] If we had assumed that the dealers in consumers' goods had sold 6 out of stocks and made profits of only 4, then the net investment would have been 14, that is 4 in excess of saving, a difference which would again correspond to the profits. If 6 out of the new receipts of dealers in consumers' goods had been passed on to producers, and had thence gone into higher wages in the same period, we should have had $E = 56$, $C = 40$, $S = 16$, $I = 20$, the excess of I over S again being equal to the profits of 4.

[3] Hawtrey, The Art of Central Banking, p. 349. See also Hansen and Tout, "Annual Survey of Business Cycle Theory," Econometrica, 1933, pp. 126, 127.

not really based on Keynes' own definitions. The assumption is that the income of the *last* period—the equilibrium period—is disposed of in the *next* period, so that in this next period the stream of money flowing on to the consumers' goods market is enlarged by 10, while the stream of consumers' goods remains the same as before; and since nothing has changed on the market for capital goods during this period, a total profit of 10 arises, which, it is assumed, is not disposed of during the same period. Thus, if we want to use the savings-investment relation for purposes of causal analysis, we have to interpret Keynes I in such a way as to understand by E the income of the *last* period, i.e., we have to introduce a time-lag. This marks a step in the direction of Robertson's treatment, with which we shall deal in the next section. In Keynes I, however, such an interpretation is possible only for the first period after the equilibrium, because it is only then that income from the last period is identical with the "normal" income from which Keynes I proceeds. In the analysis of later periods such an interpretation cannot be adopted, and Hawtrey's argument is unavoidable.

Let us ignore this difficulty and assume that a discrepancy in Keynes' sense can be regarded as the causal factor which, via profits, sets the cumulative process in motion. In what sense is this factor supposed to be "causal"? Keynes describes a discrepancy between S and I as the "mainspring" of change.[1] This is, to say the least, very imprecise. Such a discrepancy does not fall from heaven, as Keynes himself of course emphasizes, but goes back to some primary change, such as a rise in the marginal efficiency of capital due to inventions. Thus, strictly speaking, we can only say that a discrepancy between S and I is *symptomatic* of a cumulative movement or at most an intermediary cause; we cannot say that it is the primary cause.[2] If we wish to speak of monetary equilibrium in terms of saving and investment, all that the argument so far developed allows us to say is that the relation between them serves as an indicator which shows whether the system is in equilibrium or in a cumulative process upwards or downwards.

---

[1] Keynes, Treatise on Money, 1930, Vol. I, p. 160.
[2] See also footnote on p. 141.

Even this formulation, however, is not free from objections within the framework of Keynes' system. In the first place, even if investment exceeds saving, i.e., even if there are total profits in the system, this does not necessarily mean that a cumulative process upwards is in progress. Such a conclusion would be justified only if we could assume that entrepreneurs always act on the basis of the experience of the immediate past, i.e., that they always expand when they make profits.[1] But it is conceivable that the entrepreneurs may not expand, even tho they are making profits, because for some reason they are pessimistic about the future.[2] It is thus possible for a discrepancy between S and I to exist *without* any tendency towards a further cumulative development. Secondly, when $S = I$ profits are "normal," i.e., the economic system is in an equilibrium situation which is regarded as being in some sense "normal." Every other situation is then related to this normal and its degree of abnormality measured by comparison with it.[3] When $S > I$, we know that the economic system is in a situation below "normal," but we do not know whether the system has a tendency to move upwards or downwards. S can still be greater than I as related to the "normal" situation, even when the bottom of the depression has been passed and an upswing has already begun.[4]

---

[1] Keynes, it is true, *defines* windfall profits, as opposed to normal profits, as that part of entrepreneurs' net receipts which induces the entrepreneurs to expand. This definition is of course based on the assumption that entrepreneurs always act on the basis of the experience of the recent past. Otherwise we should have the result that however high the profits were, so long as they failed to lead to expansion (because of pessimism amongst entrepreneurs) they would be not profits but "normal" remuneration.

[2] Keynes himself was already conscious of this difficulty in his Treatise when he wrote, "Thus when I say that the disequilibrium between saving and investment is the mainspring of change I do not deny that the behaviour of entrepreneurs at any given moment is based on a mixture of experience and anticipation." Loc. cit., p. 160.

[3] Cf. Robertson, "Saving and Hoarding," Economic Journal, 1933, p. 411.

[4] This exposition may appear inconsistent with Keynes' definition of losses, since according to this definition a contraction follows from losses *ex definitione*. The real explanation is not that the exposition is inconsistent but that the definition of losses is self-contradictory. According to Keynes, **the remuneration of entre-**

Therefore the relationship between S and I does *not* say anything about the tendency for the system to expand or contract, as compared with the *preceding* situation, unless this preceding situation is one of "normal" equilibrium. Our conclusion, then, is that the concepts "saving" and "investment," as used by Keynes I, cannot be utilized for purposes of sequence analysis: their divergence is *not* the cause of profits and losses and therefore of total changes in the system, and a discrepancy between them is not even a symptom indicating whether the system is in process of expansion or of contraction.

The concepts are also valueless for dealing with problems of monetary policy. Keynes' definitions of saving and investment are derived from the concept of the "normal." The prescription that the aim of monetary policy should be to maintain equality between them therefore means nothing else than that monetary policy should be aimed at perpetuating "normal" conditions, a proposition which obviously tells us nothing. Keynes defines the "normal situation" with the help of the concept "normal profits." "The 'normal' remuneration of entrepreneurs at any time is that rate of remuneration which, if they were open to make new bargains with all the factors of production at the currently prevailing rate, would leave them under no motive either to increase or decrease their scale of production."[1] Entrepreneurs can only be in this situation if, under conditions of free competition, their production in the aggregate[2] is at that level for which average costs, including

---

preneurs is normal if the entrepreneurs, supposing that they had to hire all productive factors anew, would use the same amount of these factors as are actually used in their firms as at present constituted. Now it is probable that, even after recovery is under way, the entrepreneurs, if they could start their firms anew, would not invest the same amount in fixed capital as they invested in the existing firms. According to Keynes' definitions, there will be "losses" in this situation; but in spite of these "losses" there is a tendency to expand by hiring more of the non-fixed factors. Keynes himself remarks in his General Theory that profits and losses were not sufficiently defined in the Treatise, "if we allow for the possibility of changes in the scale of output." General Theory, p. 61.

[1] Keynes, Treatise on Money, Vol. I, p. 125.

[2] This does not need to be true for single entrepreneurs. Whether such an "aggregate" concept has any real sense is a question which cannot be discussed here.

normal remuneration for their own services, are just covered. Probably no objections will be raised against the proposition that this is the situation at which we should aim; but it is certain that the supposed criterion of the equality of S and I, since these concepts are *defined* by reference to the idea of "normal" profits, does not tell us anything which we did not know before, and consequently does not provide us with a rule on which monetary policy could be based.

ROBERTSON

Robertson's concepts of saving and investment need to be considered against the background of his general method of analyzing economic events through time. He first adopted this method of analysis in "Banking Policy and the Price Level," in which, however, the concepts saving and investment were not explicitly linked together. Whereas the usual procedure in general economic analysis, implicitly at least, is to treat the income of the economic subjects as being disposed of in the period in which it is received, Robertson divides the process into two periods, assuming that the income which is received in one period is not used until the next period. For the sake of brevity he calls the periods "days": the "day" is "a finite but indivisible atom of time."[1] The definition of saving which derives from this approach is that saving is equal to the disposable income of the period—i.e., the income which was received in the preceding period—minus the consumption of the period. In this treatment saving can differ from investment. If $I > S$ on any "day," either additional credit must have been granted or "dishoarding" must have taken place on that "day"; and vice versa if $S > I$. Reverting to our numerical example, we obtain the same figures for S and I after the disturbance of the equilibrium as in Keynes I, because we start out from the same income (50). The "normal" income in the Keynes I sense is here equivalent to Robertson's "disposable" income. If we carry the example further, differences of course arise. Let us assume that

---

[1] Robertson, Banking Policy and the Price Level, p. 59.

in the next period consumption is still 40, but investment rises to 30 as a result of the profits made in period 2. In this case we obtain different results according as we take the Keynes I version or Robertson's version, since Keynes' "normal" income remains constant at 50, whereas Robertson proceeds from a "disposable" income of 60. (In the following table, E in Robertson's sense always means disposable income.)[1]

PERIOD 1
Equilibrium
Keynes I and Robertson
$E = 50$
$C = 30$
$S = 20$
$I = 20$

PERIOD 2
Keynes I and Robertson (since here the "normal" income
is equal to the "disposable" income)
$E = 50$
$C = 40$
$S = 10$
$I = 20$

PERIOD 3

Keynes I
$E = 50$
$C = 40$
$S = 10$
$I = 30$

Robertson
$E = 60 \ (= I + C \text{ of period 2})$
$C = 40$
$S = 20$
$I = 30$

But not only do we get different figures; the discrepancy between I and S may also have a different meaning. Whereas the magnitude of the excess of I over S (or S over I) in the Keynes I sense is always exactly equal to the amount of the profits (or losses), this is not so in Robertson's version. For instance, if $I > S$, part of the new money created during the period may go into wage-payments in that same period, in which case the difference between

---

[1] In algebraic terms the Robertsonian version gives us the following series (E_e = earned income, E_d = disposable income); $E_{d_1} = C_0 + I_0$; $E_{e_1} = C_1 + I_1 = E_{d_2}$; $E_{e_2} = C_2 + I_2 = E_{d_3}$ and so on.

I and S will be greater than the profits. This is so because the higher income of the wage-earners does not appear as (disposable) income in this period as it does in the Keynes I version.[1]

The change which Robertson has made in the definitions of S and I, altho seemingly small, obviously leads to a completely different result. In his view, an equality between S and I can exist both at the top of the boom and at the bottom of the depression; and the same would be true of an equality between the money rate of interest and the natural rate, if this is supposed to be identical with an equality between S and I.[2] The situation on each "day" is not compared with any "normal" situation but is considered against the background of the preceding "day." This produces a characteristic difference as compared with Keynes I. If we apply the Keynes I formula, we do not know whether we are still on the downswing or already on the upswing; we only know whether we are at the "normal" level or above or below it. If we use Robertson's approach, however, we know that if S is greater than I, for example, this will produce a fall in the price level[3] compared with the day before and consequently a tendency to contraction. The concepts can therefore be used as instruments for analyzing economic events over time, showing how the events of one period influence the events of the next. The relation between S and I at each moment tells us whether the system contains a tendency to an upswing or a downswing.

Since S and I may be equal in the depression, it is evident that their equality cannot provide a norm of monetary policy, at least not by itself. We can use it solely as an instrument of theoretical

---

[1] As to the rôle of movements in stocks in this connection see p. 146.

[2] See Robertson, "Industrial Fluctuations and the Natural Interest Rate," Economic Journal, 1933.

[3] Robertson is mainly concerned with the movements of the price level. Here we are investigating his treatment of S and I from the point of view of whether they have anything to say about the stability of a situation. Since Robertson does not talk in terms of a cumulative process, what is said in the text applies not so much to the use which Robertson himself has made of the twin concepts as to the use which might be made of them, and has been made by others, in the theory of the cumulative process.

analysis, which is the only use to which Robertson himself puts it. For this purpose Robertson's definitions, as will appear later, are the most appropriate of any that have been put forward in the course of the discussion.[1] But, even so, we have to be wary in applying these concepts to the theory of the cumulative process. According as S is less than, greater than, or equal to I in the current period, expansion, contraction or stability, respectively, will follow in the next period only under certain conditions.[2]

(1) The first of these conditions has already been mentioned in the previous section: it has to be assumed that the entrepreneurs always expand, if they make profits, i.e., that they always act on the basis of the experience of the recent past. But it is not realistic to base the theory of the trade cycle on the assumption that entrepreneurs' expectations will always be of this kind.

(2) It is necessary to assume that the reactions to the situation in the current period ("day") take place quickly enough to show themselves in the next period. Otherwise the system can show an expansion or contraction in the next period, even tho $S = I$ in the current period, simply because of the operation of forces

---

[1] Robertson's terminology is also favored by Hansen ("Mr. Keynes on Underemployment Equilibrium," Journal of Political Economy, October 1936, p. 673ff.) and by Haberler ("Prosperity and Depression," p. 197ff.). Miss Curtis ("Is Monetary Saving Equal to Investment," Quarterly Journal of Economics, August 1937) uses the same concepts when she tries to show (in the table on p. 109) that S can diverge from I. Here she tacitly assumes that in any period people dispose of the income which they earned in the preceding period.

[2] In the section on Keynes I we pointed out that a discrepancy between I and S is never a "primary" (or original) cause of a movement in the system, but only an intermediate cause, which has itself been set to work by an original change in data, e.g., inventions. Here we are abstracting from new "primary" changes and considering only those movements of the system which are due to the *cumulative effect* of an initial discrepancy between I and S brought about by some such "primary" change in data. It is possible, of course, to describe the whole of the cumulative process in terms of shifts in the marginal efficiency of capital; but it has to be remembered that the shift at any stage of the process is *dependent* on the relation between I and S at the previous stage. It is thus inherent in the situation, and cannot be called "primary" in the sense in which we use this term to describe a rise in the marginal productivity of capital due to inventions, etc.

which were set in motion in earlier periods, but which only took effect after a time-lag which was longer than our "day." On the basis of the same reasoning, cases can be constructed in which an excess of I over S (or vice versa) need not lead to an expansion (or contraction) in the next period. The point is that the Robertsonian period does not take the reaction-times of the various elements in the situation as determinants of the length of the period. It seems to me that it is impossible to do this, given the fact that all the elements have different velocities of reaction.

(3) Because of the working of the acceleration principle, it is possible for a cumulative process upwards to come to an end altho no new changes in data (e.g., the raising of interest rates by the banks) occur.[1] In this case a point may automatically be reached in the expansionist process where I becomes equal to S, but where this relation leads to the commencement of a contractionist process in the next period. This is due to the fact that when investment is solely dependent on the working of the acceleration principle, the absolute amount of investment falls off as soon as the rate of increase in expenditure on consumers' goods slows down (assuming, of course, that the replacement demand does not increase sufficiently and in time to fill the gap). In this case we cannot conclude from the existence of an equality between S and I in any period that the equilibrium will be preserved in the next period. This also shows that a banking policy which was aimed at keeping I equal to S after an expansionist period could only succeed for a short time, after which a contraction would ensue (stabilization crisis).

The general conclusion, then, is that the relation between S and I on any single "day" does not always tell us what is going to happen on the next "day."

Many authors make use of the concepts "saving" and "investment" without taking the trouble to define them. I think, how-

---

[1] There are two different types of explanation of the turning-point. The one explains it as the automatic outcome of the mechanism of the cumulative process; the other ascribes it to some exogenous change. Within these broad types there are again various patterns, of which the explanation alluded to in the text is only one.

ever, that the definitions they have in mind are the same as those used by Robertson. When, for example, it is said that new savings, if put into hoards, lead to a deflationary process, because they mean an excess of S over I, the writer is undoubtedly thinking in terms of some kind of period analysis. Not only does the human mind instinctively think of things as happening with a certain order in time, but it is natural, in an economic system where incomes are paid out discontinuously, to suppose that the earning of income and the disposal of income are not completely concurrent processes. It would make no sense to say that new savings which take the form of hoarding make S greater than I, and therefore lead to a deflationary process, unless we assumed that the income which is disposed of during the current period was already in the hands of the economic subjects at the beginning of the period. If we were to adopt the procedure of assuming that the income is received concurrently with its disposal (part of it being hoarded in the case we are considering), we should have the result that, as under Keynes in the General Theory, the hoarding would not appear anywhere under the calculation of S and I, but would only show its effect in the form of a diminished E. A difference between S and I could not occur. If, in our standard example, we assume that in the second period 10 out of the 20 savings are hoarded, and also assume that the E which is being disposed of is the income of the same period, we obtain the following results for period 2:

$E = 40$ (showing a diminution of 10 in comparison with the initial period, as the result of the deflationary effect of hoarding)
$C = 30$
$S = 10$ (since losses of 10 occur which have to be deducted from saving)
$I = 10$ (the value of investments equals the "invested" saving out of which they are financed)

We then have $S = I$, which is a denial of the proposition that hoarding produces a discrepancy between them.[1] The only distinction

---
[1] If we were to introduce Robertson's time-lag, we should have $E = 50$, $C = 30$, $S = 20$, $I = 10$, so that $S > I$, giving rise to the deflationary effect in the next period.

between the everyday usage and Robertson's use of the terms is that the former makes no explicit reference to the time-lag.

It appears, also, that not all of those who use the concepts in this way are as conscious as Robertson of the fact that they have to abandon the idea that there is such a thing as monetary equilibrium, defined simply by the equality of savings and investment, which could be set up as a norm of banking policy. It is customary to treat an equality between the natural interest rate and the money rate as identical with the equality of S and I, and then to propose that the banks should keep the money rate equal to the natural rate. This is meaningless, however, unless we start out from a stable equilibrium (with full employment) and then advocate that this equilibrium should be maintained. If this equilibrium does not prevail, as it never does in reality, and if S may be equal to I in the above sense, and consequently the natural interest rate equal to the money rate, even at the bottom of the depression, then the equality between them cannot, by itself, be taken as the aim of monetary policy. The adoption, consciously or unconsciously, of an equilibrium position as a starting point seems to me to be an essential reason for believing that the importance of the concepts has been overrated.[1]

The Ex Ante and Ex Post Concepts

In the course of the foregoing exposition we have several times encountered the expectations element. Some authors have tried to embody expectations in their definitions of savings and investment. They do this by introducing the notion of *ex ante* values of

---

[1] There are, of course, still other concepts of investment which have not been dealt with here, e.g., according to Bresciani-Turoni ("Theory of Saving," Economica 1936) and Armstrong ("Saving and Investment," 1936) new investment begins when a new longer production process is started, even if the first stages are still being financed out of the amortization quotas of those production processes which are gradually being liquidated. In this case investment can, and usually will, precede saving, and there will be discrepancies over certain periods. But it is plain that this concept is not applicable to an analysis of the cumulative process.

S and I, which they compare with the *ex post* values. The distinction is due to Swedish economists and was first used by Myrdal.[1] Reference may be made in particular to the publications (in English) of Ohlin[2] and Lundberg.[3] Let us first examine Myrdal's position, which differs from that of the two other authors mentioned to the extent that he regards the concept of monetary equilibrium as a fruitful one, and places it in the center of his analysis.

A Wicksellian cumulative process is set up, according to Myrdal, when monetary equilibrium is disturbed, and he attempts to work out the conditions which have to be satisfied if monetary equilibrium is to exist, and to reduce these conditions to a formula which can be applied both theoretically and practically. It has to be borne in mind that he is always thinking of a certain *moment* of price formation, and that he is interested in determining whether the system is in equilibrium or not at that moment. The condition which must be fulfilled for equilibrium to be present is that the net yield of real capital should be equal to the money rate of interest or, what amounts to the same thing, that saving should be equal to investment. Here we are concerned only with the latter formulation.

"Saving" and "investment" here refer to saving and investment as *planned* in a moment of price formation for the succeeding unit-period, and are thus to be understood in the *ex ante* sense. Investment is conceived of as the discounted value at the present moment of the production costs of *gross* investment; and saving consists of the new saving plus the depreciation minus the appreciation of the value of the existing stock of real capital. It is necessary to take gross investment because of the impossibility of drawing a clear distinction between new investment and replacement. There is a corresponding difficulty, on the other side, of differentiating between new saving and the amortization quotas (for simplicity's sake we leave the appreciation item out of account). If the amortization

---

[1] Myrdal, "Der Gleichgewichtsbegriff als Instrument der Geldtheoretischen Analyse," in Beiträge zur Geldtheorie, edited by Hayek, pp. 427ff.

[2] Ohlin, "Some Notes on the Stockholm Theory and Economic Policy," in Economic Journal, March and June, 1937.

[3] Lundberg, Studies in the Theory of Economic Expansion, Chapter 6.

quotas are set at a low figure, the income of society appears to be higher than it would be if the amortization quotas were set at a high figure. As saving is, by definition, equal to income minus consumption, we also obtain a higher savings figure.. Saving becomes higher by the amount by which the amortization quotas are lower, the sum of the two items remaining the same.[1] It is therefore necessary to compare gross real investment with the total volume of investable funds (i.e., saving + amortization quotas), where both are calculated at a moment of time *ex ante*, of course. If planned saving and planned investment in this sense are equal, then monetary equilibrium prevails.

While saving and investment may, of course, be unequal *ex ante*, they will always, as Myrdal himself emphasizes, be equal *ex post*. According to Myrdal, this equalization is brought about via profits or losses. If, reverting to our old example, we assume that planned S equals 10 and planned I equals 20, we find that

ex ante	*ex post*
$E = 50$	$E = 60$
$C = 40$	$C = 40$
$S = 10$	$S = 20$
$I = 20$	$I = 20$

The way in which the *ex post* position derives from the *ex ante* position is as follows: the dealers in consumers' goods make profits of 10 which enter the accounts for the period *ex post* as savings, making $S = I$.[2]

How useful are these *ex ante* concepts of savings and investment as the analytical tools which Myrdal intends them to be?

---

[1] The figure for the savings item is therefore partly dependent on accounting methods.

[2] In Ohlin's version (and also Lundberg's) the *ex post* equality may also be due to unplanned increases or decreases in stocks. Myrdal seems to have abstracted from these items. If we assume (where $I > S$) that part of the difference goes into increased wage-payments which have not yet been spent by the workers, then when we make the *ex post* calculation, we have to count these unspent wages as savings in order to obtain equality between S and I. (See the section on Keynes II below.)

In Myrdal's treatment saving and investment are calculated *ex ante* for a unit-period the length of which is arbitrarily chosen. It is clear, however, that we are not at liberty to choose the unit-period arbitrarily. If we wish to talk about plans being fixed in advance for a certain period of time, our period must be so chosen that no changes in plans occur within it. This is the definition of the unit-period which Ohlin and Lundberg adopt. But this is significant only when applied to an individual enterprise; there is no such period for all entrepreneurs in the aggregate. Both the length and the "timing" of their individual planning periods vary, so that plans are stopping and starting at every moment.[1] Any attempt, therefore, to analyze the *ex ante* concepts leads logically to the identification of the period with an extremely short "finite but indivisible" unit of time. This seems to me to mean, in effect, the abandonment of the *ex ante* idea in favor of Robertson's approach.

Let us assume, however, that, even tho the period has ultimately to be reduced to a very small unit of time, it is still sensible to speak of plans being made *ex ante* for this period. What differences are there, then, between the *ex ante* treatment and Robertson's? In the first place, the *ex ante* concepts relate to saving and investment which are planned in a moment of time to be executed over the succeeding period of time, whereas Robertson is looking at the *process* of saving and investment as it takes place *during* the period. This does not, however, mean that Robertson's terms include unintentional saving or dissaving (profits or losses) and unintentional investment or disinvestment (accumulation or depletion of stocks) which may be made during the period. Unintentional saving (or dissaving) is not included, because Robertson does not add profits (or subtract losses) made during the period to the disposable income of that period but carries them forward to the disposable income of the next period. Unintentional investment (or disinvestment) is not included, because he abstracts from stocks, on which this item depends.[2] If he were to include stocks, he would have specifically to define his

---

[1] It is clear from his discussion (loc. cit., p. 47) that Lundberg, himself, felt uneasy about this treatment.

[2] Robertson, "Saving and Hoarding," Economic Journal, 1933, p. 401.

investment as *intended* investment carried out during the period, in order to arrive at consistent results.[1]

Secondly, it looks as if the magnitude of S, according to the *ex ante* calculation, might differ from the magnitude of S according to Robertson's calculation for the reason that, as pointed out before, the *ex ante* saving is conceived of as being determined on the basis of the income that people *expect* to receive in the forthcoming period, whereas Robertson's saving is made out of the income actually received in the preceding period. But the difference is illusory. It is immaterial, from Robertson's point of view, whether the saving which people decide to do in the forthcoming period is determined by them as some proportion of the income received in the last period or as some proportion of the income which they hope to receive in the forthcoming period. Robertson is not concerned with the factors which influence people's decisions as to the amount of saving they want to do, but only with the actual carrying out of their plans; and these plans can only be executed out of (and are limited by) the amount of income already received.

Thirdly, the *ex ante* concepts refer explicitly to expectations, whereas Robertson's concepts do not. The results of applying the concepts, however, are the same in both cases. If, for instance, investment *ex ante* is greater than saving *ex ante*, we have an expansion in the period to which the plans *ex ante* relate. In Robertson's treatment, also, an excess of I over S shows an expansion for this

---

[1] If the $I + C$ of the current period is to equal the earned income of this period (and therefore the disposable income of the next period), unintentional investment cannot be included under I in Robertson's formula, as is shown by the following example. Let us suppose that new saving in the form of hoarding takes place, with a corresponding accumulation of stocks of consumers' goods. If we were to include this increase in stocks under I, then in spite of the hoarding we should have $S = I$, and consequently no change in the earned income of this period as compared with the last period, and no fall in the disposable income for the next period. This would mean counting an unintentional increase in stocks as income-creating. Moreover, if we were to calculate in this way, we should of course find that S can be equal to I in the current period, but that there will be a contractionist process in the next period owing to a reduction in I designed to work off excess stocks (and vice versa in the case of credit inflation and depletion of stocks).

period. But in neither case do we know whether the expansion will continue in the following period in response to the profits to which the initial excess of I over S has given rise (unless we make a specific assumption to this effect, as Lundberg does).

For all practical purposes it does not matter, therefore, whether we use Robertson's concepts or the *ex ante* concepts. Accordingly, the criticism advanced in the last section is equally applicable here. The relation between S and I *ex ante* in any period does not necessarily tell us how the system will move in the next period. In particular, an equality between the two magnitudes in any period does not guarantee a stable situation, even in the absence of new primary changes.[1] Lundberg also feels obliged to drop the idea that an equality between S and I guarantees monetary equilibrium.[2] Similarly Ohlin remarks that the equality of S and I *ex ante* "is consistent with but does not necessarily mean a stable situation."[3] Moreover, the equality between S and I *ex ante*, since it may occur at the bottom as well as at the top of the trade cycle, cannot by itself be taken as a criterion of credit policy. It would be undesirable to stabilize the equality between S and I at the bottom of the depression; and to recommend stabilization at the top of the boom is an equally unhelpful suggestion, since, as has been shown, a banking policy which attempted to achieve this end would be likely to produce a contraction instead.

Active and Passive Investment and Saving

Some authors[4] distinguish between "active" (intended) and "passive" (unintended) investment, and also between "active"

---

[1] This point is also illustrated in Lundberg's model sequences; several of these show that at some point following a period of expansion an equality of I and S may arise, but that this situation is inherently unstable, itself leading to a reduction of I below S in the next period. This is explained in his examples by the working of the acceleration principle.

[2] Lundberg, op. cit., p. 249.

[3] Ohlin, loc. cit., p. 238.

[4] Hawtrey, Capital and Employment, pp. 176ff. Hawtrey uses the terms "active" and "passive" only in connection with investment. According to him, saving is always equal to active plus passive investment. Lundberg, op. cit., pp. 140ff., in discussing this terminology applies it both to investment and to

and "passive" saving. According to these authors, equilibrium exists if active I is equal to active S. When active S exceeds active I, the result will be "passive" investment due to unintentional accumulation of stocks or, assuming that there are no stocks, passive dissaving due to losses. Conversely, if active I exceeds active S, we get passive disinvestment due to depletion of stocks, or passive saving in the form of profits. Assume that, in our example on page 146, we conceive of S and I in the *ex ante* column as active saving and active investment. Then in the *ex post* column we have passive saving of 10, i.e., unintentional saving in the form of profits of 10. This shows at once that the concepts under consideration may be used interchangeably with the *ex ante* and *ex post* concepts of saving and investment, and that they give rise to the same difficulties, altho in another terminological dress. If one chooses a long period, the passive savings which are made within the period can become active savings within the same period, since those who happened to make the passive savings may *decide* within this period whether to spend them or to save them "actively." The same can be said of passive investment. If we want to avoid this consequence, we are forced to take a very short period. If we do this, we are back again at Robertson's concepts. The lack of any counterpart, in the latter's terminology, to "passive" saving and "passive" investment is due, as was shown above, to the fact that he carries the profits or losses (passive saving or dissaving) of any period forward to the next period, and that he disregards stocks, the movements of which alone make passive investment or disinvestment possible.

All that has been said in the two previous sections about the usefulness of the concepts for the purposes of monetary analysis and monetary policy therefore applies here also.

Keynes II

According to Keynes' new terminology, put forward in his "General Theory," saving is necessarily equal to investment by

---

saving. A similar distinction is made by Miss Curtis ("Are money savings equal to investment?" Quarterly Journal of Economics, August, 1937, p. 606) when she speaks of "the amount of money which saving individuals *decide* to save and the amount which investing individuals *decide* to invest."

definition. Since, on the one hand, investment equals value of output (income) minus the value of the output of consumption goods, while, on the other hand, saving equals income minus consumption, saving must always be equal to investment. It is the *ex post* equality discussed above. One might feel inclined to accept this terminology simply because it relegates the two concepts to the background, where they ought perhaps to remain. But the decision is not so easy as that. Keynes himself has confused his definitions in two ways: first, by associating the doctrine of the saving-investment relation with the multiplier; secondly, by asserting that his terminology marks a return to the classical doctrine of the relation between saving and investment.[1]

Altho S equals I by definition, Keynes holds, at the same time, that the multiplier makes them equal. "An increment of investment in terms of wage-units cannot occur unless the public are prepared to increase their savings in terms of wage-units. Ordinarily speaking, the public will not do this unless their aggregate income in terms of wage-units is increasing. Thus their effort to consume a part of their increased incomes will stimulate output until their new level (and distribution) of income provides a margin of saving sufficient to correspond to the increased investment. The multiplier tells us by how much their employment has to be increased to yield an increase in real income sufficient to induce them to do the necessary extra saving, and is a function of their psychological propensities."[2]

Keynes' multiplier is supposed to be the reciprocal of the "marginal propensity to save."[3] If the latter is $\frac{1}{4}$, i.e., if the public has the propensity to save $\frac{1}{4}$ of an increment of income, the multiplier

---

[1] See Keynes, "Alternative Theories of the Interest Rate," Economic Journal, June, 1937, p. 249.

[2] Keynes, General Theory, p. 112.

[3] For simplicity's sake we avoid the détour which Keynes makes round the "marginal propensity to consume": the latter is equal to 1 minus the "propensity to save," i.e., in the example in the text $1 - \frac{1}{4}$. The problems raised by the measurement of money values in terms of wage-units do not concern us in the present context.

is 4. An act of new investment financed with new credit would therefore lead to an additional income four times as great as the new investment (provided we assume that no disinvestment is taking place at the same time). If, for example, the state invests the sum of 1000 by way of public works, income of 4000 will be created. Since, given a propensity to save of ¼, the amount of this income that will be saved is 1000, which is equal to the value of the investment, the equality of S and I seems to be brought about by the working of the multiplier. If we look more closely into the matter, however, we find that the saving-investment relation is independent of the multiplier.

Keynes tells us that his theory of the multiplier holds good for any period of time we may choose.[1] He would presumably say that in the first moment, when the money has been invested but has not yet been spent by the workmen to whom it was paid, the marginal propensity to save is 100% and the multiplier 1. In the next moment, when the workmen have spent their money, the multiplier will have risen. If we assume that the expenditure of the money on consumers' goods increases the profits of the dealers in those goods by the amount spent, the multiplier for the whole of the period so far taken becomes 2 and the "propensity to save" ½, and so on. From this it is easily seen that the "propensity to save" is far from being an independent psychological datum which determines the multiplier[2] and, through the latter, the income that will be created by an increment of investment. On the contrary, both the "propensity to save" and the multiplier, instead of being determinants of this income, are resultants of an *ex post* calculation. We have first to find out how much income has been created within a certain period of time by an act of investment (and Keynes tells us nothing about the real determinants of the amount of income so

---

[1] Keynes, op. cit., p. 123t. See also Harrod, The Trade Cycle, p. 72.

[2] Haberler, "Mr. Keynes' Theory of the Multiplier" (Zeitschrift für Nationalökonomie 1936, pp. 301f.) says: "Keynes expresses the multiplier in terms of the 'marginal propensity to consume' and treats the latter as if it were a thing in the real world which is independent from the former, whilst in fact the two are closely connected by definition."

created) and if we then divide this income by the value of the investment, the result gives us the multiplier. Now since saving is equal to investment (by definition), the reciprocal of the multiplier, which tells us the ratio that the newly created income bears to the original increment of investment, also tells us the ratio of savings to the newly created income, i.e., the "marginal propensity to save." Both the multiplier and the "marginal propensity to save" are thus shown to be *ex post* concepts.[1] The conclusion is that it is the equality of saving and investment which makes the reciprocal of the multiplier equal to the "marginal propensity to save," rather than the other way round.

If we return to our concrete case, we find that the reason why saving is always equal to investment is that in every moment of

---

[1] It is not only to the transition period, before "things have settled down," that this criticism applies. In the long run various results are conceivable, lying between two extremes as follows:

(*a*) All of the money created by the original act of investment may become part of the regular *flow* of money which is being continually received and continually spent. The multiplier will then be identical with the income velocity of money, and will have to be related to a definite period of time as otherwise it will be infinite. If the income velocity is 2 per year, the multiplier will be 2 and the "marginal propensity to save" ½ per year. It seems obvious that this income velocity is not determined by the "marginal propensity to save," since in the case considered nobody "saves" in any useful sense of the term. Moreover, even if there were saving, this would not influence the income velocity, if the money saved were invested.

(*b*) The other extreme is the case (which is only conceivable in time of depression) where each successive set of entrepreneurs to whom the new money flows uses part of it to pay back bank debts or to hoard, so that the money gradually leaks out of circulation until finally all of the new money is taken up by hoards. At the end of this process the income in the system will have fallen back to the old level. This is the case which Keynes' treatment fits best, since it is here not as necessary as in the previous case to take a definite period in order to make sense of the multiplier; moreover, the multiplier seems to be determined by the propensity to save, because the income created in the system will vary inversely with the proportion of their new receipts that entrepreneurs on the average hoard. But even here it would be more correct to say that the multiplier is determined by the "marginal propensity to hoard," since savings, if they were invested, would exert the same effect as expenditure on consumption.

time an amount of new money corresponding to the new net investment is somewhere in the cashholdings of the system, and has to be counted as saving according to Keynes' definition of this term. In the first moment after the new investment of 1,000 has taken place, the workmen hold the 1,000 additional money in their cash balances, so that there is 1,000 "savings" corresponding to the value of the additional investment. If these balances are then spent on consumers' goods, and create profits to the same amount, they become cashholdings in the hands of the sellers and have to be counted there as "saving" of 1,000. If dealers satisfy part of the increased demand by selling from stocks, with the result that only part of the 1,000 new cashholdings can be counted as profits, saving still corresponds to the *net* new investment (i.e., the original increment of investment minus depletion of stocks). The same analysis applies each time the new money changes hands.

Keynes contends that his terminology is a return to the classical view, according to which S (supply of savings) is always equal to the demand for S (investment). What the classical writers meant, however,[1] was that the volume of funds demanded and the volume of savings offered are made equal by the working of the interest rate, whereas Keynes' equality between I and S is not dependent on any such process of adaptation. The classics treat the case as completely analogous to the demand-supply-price adjustments on a commodity market. What the price makes equal in the commodity market is the amount demanded and the amount offered for sale; but this amount is not necessarily equal to the amount produced, since some potential sellers may have a "reserve price" for their holdings of the commodity. Similarly, if the classics had conceived of the possibility of savers having a "reserve price" for their "commodity" (savings), they would have said, unlike Keynes, that the amount of savings made may exceed the amount of savings invested. Likewise neo-classical writers, who recognize that the volume of funds offered on the capital market can be swollen by inflationary bank credit, would of course agree that the volume of funds lent is

---

[1] See Robertson, "Alternative Theories of the Interest Rate," Economic Journal, September, 1937, pp. 429ff.

equal to the volume of funds borrowed, but not that all the funds borrowed and invested are necessarily derived from savings: they would certainly not count the new money, which comes into the hands of workers *after the transactions on the capital-market are over*, as savings and in this way arrive at a necessary equality between savings and investment.

To object to the use which Keynes himself makes of his concepts is not, however, to judge their appropriateness in general. One of the drawbacks, altho perhaps a minor one, of adopting his terminology is that it means departing from the ordinary usage. It is an uncommon use of terms to say that a newly employed workman who receives his wage at the beginning of the week, and spends it entirely in the course of the week, "saves" the money in the meantime, and that as soon as he spends the money it is "saved" by the next recipient (so long as the latter does not sell from stocks of course) and so on. Nevertheless, we might concede this unusual terminology, if it had compensatory advantages. The main advantage of Keynes' definitions is, no doubt, that they get rid of the problem of how to define the unit-period. On the other hand, they do not allow us to distinguish investment which is financed out of inflationary credit or dishoarding from investment that is financed out of the current supply of voluntary savings. There is no doubt, however, that it makes a lot of difference whether investment is financed from the one source or the other; and a terminology which conceals this difference hardly seems to be commendable. It is clear, moreover, that Keynes' definitions do not fit the standard of reference put forward at the beginning of this article, since they are neither useful for the analysis of the cumulative process nor of any help in dealing with the problem of credit policy.[1]

---

[1] A. P. Lerner's article "Saving Equals Investment," Quarterly Journal of Economics, February 1938, p. 292ff, came into my hands when this article was already in type. Mr. Lerner favors the Keynes II definitions. I entirely agree with his statement that the identity between I and S "follows from and is implicit in our definitions of income, consumption, savings and investment and the postulate that in any period moneys paid out are equal to moneys received." He concedes that if we assume inequality between money receipts and expenditure

The results of our discussion may be summarized under two main heads:

1. It has been shown that, disregarding the concepts of Keynes' "Treatise," which no longer find any favor, there are only *two* essentially different concepts of saving and investment. On the one side we have Robertson's definitions, which are interchangeable both with the *ex ante* and with the "active" saving and investment definitions; on the other side we have the definitions of Keynes' "General Theory," according to which saving is always necessarily equal to investment. The latter have the advantage that they avoid the difficulty of defining the "period," which is the crucial problem connected with the other group of definitions. Keynes' definitions, however, have the disadvantage (*a*) that they cannot be used for causal analysis, (*b*) that they force us to say that all investment is financed out of saving and that all saving goes into investment, so that inflationary credit, dishoarding, and hoarding fall completely out of the picture, whereas nobody doubts that these things have a decisive influence on the course of events. As regards these two points, Robertson's concepts are more satisfactory, and on balance, therefore, they seem to be the more useful.

2. In applying these concepts, however, we have to bear in mind (*a*) that an equality between I and S in any period does not guarantee "monetary equilibrium," even in the absence of new "primary" changes; (*b*) that this equality can exist in any stage of the trade cycle, so that it cannot by itself be made the aim of monetary policy; (*c*) that a difference between S and I does not necessarily mean that the cumulative process will continue in the next period in the direction indicated by the positive or negative sign of this difference.

The saving and investment relation furnishes us with little more than a handy formula. On the whole, the twin concepts

---

due to a time lag, we may have a difference between S and I. The question therefore is which assumptions are the more realistic and therefore the more fruitful. In contradiction to Lerner's view it is the contention of this article that the assumption of a time lag between receipts and expenditure in Robertson's sense is closer to reality than the assumption of simultaneity between them and is necessary for the analysis of economic events over time.

seem to deserve the fate of actors who, after having been supernumeraries for a long time, are suddenly "discovered" and given the principal rôles in the play, but unfortunately do not turn out to be as good as they were supposed to be. Like such "new stars," they should again be relegated to the position of supernumeraries who attract relatively little attention.

7

SAVING AND INVESTMENT: DEFINITIONS, ASSUMPTIONS, OBJECTIVES*

By Abba P. Lerner‖

In a recent article in this Journal[1] Dr. F. A. Lutz has done much toward the elimination of a fruitless disputation that has been going on about the "proper" definitions of saving and investment. His method is to examine a number of sets of current definitions of S (saving) and I (investment), to consider the meaning, if any, of $I - S$ on each of these sets of definitions, and then to discuss "their usefulness for the theoretical analysis of the cumulative process and for dealing with the problems of credit policy."[2]

Of these three tasks the first two are carried out very well. The final discussions and conclusions seem, however, to be open to serious criticism. It will be convenient, in preparation for this criticism, to set out the definitions and the corresponding meanings of $I - S$. Except for the differences indicated in footnote 2, page 160, this will agree with Dr. Lutz's presentation. For simplicity of exposition $I - S$ and its various constituents on the different definitions will be taken as positive, though they may just as well be negative. The reader might find it is a useful exercise to go through the analysis transposing all the signs.

Definitions

1) If, as in Mr. Keynes' General Theory of Employment Interest and Money, S is defined as the income earned in a period

---

* *Quarterly Journal of Economics*, Volume LIII (1938–39), pages 611–619. Reprinted by the courtesy of the Quarterly Journal of Economics and the author.

‖ Graduate Faculty, New School for Social Research; Formerly London School of Economics.

[1] August, 1938, pp. 588–613.
[2] Ibid., p. 589.

minus the consumption in the same period, and I is defined as the expenditure in this same period on investment (and therefore also the income in that period earned other than in the production of consumption goods), then I is always equal to S. Any talk of the difference between saving and investment must be based either upon other definitions or upon confusion.

(2) If, as in Mr. Keynes' Treatise on Money, S_t is defined as "normal" (instead of actual) income *minus* consumption, and is therefore less than the S of the General Theory by as much as "normal" income is less than actual income; while I_t is defined just like I in the General Theory, then $I_t - S_t$ (which is the same as $S - S_t$) will represent the excess of actual over "normal" income—"abnormal profits."

(3) If, as in Mr. Robertson's writings, S_r is defined as income earned yesterday (instead of today—and therefore "disposable" today) *minus* today's consumption, and is therefore less than S by as much as income earned yesterday is less than income earned today; while I_r is defined in the same way as I, then $I_r - S_r$ (which is the same as $S - S_r$) will represent the excess of income earned today over income earned yesterday.

(4) If, as in the work of the Swedish writers, Ohlin, Lundberg, and especially Myrdal, S_e is defined as *expected* or *ex ante* saving and I_e is defined as *expected* or *ex ante* investment, it is possible to give an almost unambiguous meaning to these concepts by so interpreting them that they fall into the Robertsonian scheme of discrete and extremely short "days." S_e is equal to income *minus* consumption as expected at the beginning of the "day" by the recipients of the income and the spenders on consumption. The "day" is so short that the plans for consumption are always carried out, expected consumption is always equal to actual consumption, and expected saving, S_e, is less than S by the extent to which expected income is less than actual income. The difference $(S - S_e)$ may be called "unexpected income."[1] I_e, investment as expected at the

---

[1] Dr. Lutz fails to distinguish between the excess of actual over expected income and the excess of actual over "normal" income, calling them both "profits."

beginning of the day by the investors, is greater than I to the extent that there is an unexpected depletion of stocks arising from a discrepancy between what sellers expect to sell and what buyers expect to, and actually do, buy. $I_e - S_e$ therefore represents unexpected depletion of stocks *plus* "unexpected income."

(5) If, as in Mr. Hawtrey's Capital and Employment, I_a is defined as "active" or intended investment and S_a is defined as "active" or intended saving,[1] so as to leave out "passive" or unintended investment, which arises when an unexpectedly large demand leads to a depletion of stocks, and "passive" or unintended saving, which is the result of an unexpectedly large income earned in the period, the procedure is identical with the above described interpretation of *ex ante*. $I_a - S_a$, like $I_e - S_e$ represents unexpected depletion of stocks *plus* "unexpected income."

These are the five different sets of definitions that Dr. Lutz examines for their usefulness. He finally dismisses (2) as not being defended by anybody now and decides against (1) (or what are now known as the Keynesian definitions) in favor of (3) (Mr. Robertson's procedure) which he regards as practically equivalent to (4) (*ex ante*) and therefore also to (5) ("active").[2]

---

[1] Mr. Hawtrey does not apply this distinction to saving.

[2] In the scheme as set out above (3) is clearly quite different from (4). $I_r - S_r$ in (3) represents the excess of income earned today over income earned yesterday, whereas $I_e - S_e$ in (4) represents unexpected depletion in stocks *plus* "unexpected income." Dr. Lutz tries to establish equivalence between these, in the first place, by declaring that if Mr. Robertson had not, for the sake of simplicity, ignored all variations in stocks, it would have been necessary for him, for the sake of consistency, to exclude from I_r any unintended variation in stocks (p. 148 and n. 1). The argument is that a positive $I_r - S_r$, representing a greater income earned today than yesterday, and therefore an equally greater income "disposable" tomorrow than today, is an indication of a tendency towards economic expansion in the next period when the income is spent. An unexpected depletion of stocks is also an indication of an expansionist tendency in the next period when the stocks will be replenished. Therefore $I_r - S_r$ should, like $I_e - S_e$, include unexpected depletion of stocks.

This syllogism would seem to fail on account of its middle term being undistributed, as in the argument: bread is a food, milk is also a food, therefore bread must be understood to include milk. The deficiency in the argument could be

Assumptions

In general Dr. Lutz steers clear of the confusion between differences of definition and differences in assumptions which is not uncommon in this field of discussion. Indeed, throughout the article he considers only the differences in definition of S and I and judges these appropriately by their usefulness for certain purposes. But a footnote,[1] added after the article was completed, which refers to an article by myself, contains a serious lapse from this admirable procedure in the form of a new reason for preferring the Robertson-*ex ante* definitions to the Keynesian terminology. Here it is declared that "In contradiction to Mr. Lerner's view it is the contention of this article that the assumption of a time lag between receipts and expenditure in Robertson's sense is closer to reality than the assumption of simultaneity between them and is necessary for the analysis of economic events over time."

Simultaneity between receipts and expenditures is implicit in the proposition that $I = S$ only in the sense that there is no interval between the moment that A receives a payment from B and the moment when B makes this same payment to A. Between this receipt and expenditure there can be no time lag, because they are

---

filled by the assumption that Mr. Robertson wished $I_r - S_r$ to include *all* tendencies to expansion in the next period, but whether this is his intention seems doubtful.

But even if I_r could be taken to be equivalent to I_e, Dr. Lutz's argument for the equivalence between S_e, which is measured with respect to income earned yesterday, and S_e, which is measured with respect to income expected to be earned today, remains unconvincing. For in this case the unsatisfactory argument that both procedures indicate a tendency toward expansion when I is greater than S is made even weaker by Dr. Lutz's observation a few pages earlier that "it is conceivable that entrepreneurs may not expand when they make profits, because for some reason they are pessimistic about the future" (p. 136). In the same way an excess of actual over expected income does not necessarily mean that there has already been an expansion in income earned (which is what $I_r - S_r$ does in fact indicate). Such an excess may arise from an unfulfilled, or incompletely fulfilled, expectation of a decline in demand.

The failure to substantiate the equivalence between (3) and (4) does not, however, appreciably affect the main thesis of Dr. Lutz's article.

[1] Page 155, note 1.

merely different names for the same event. This simultaneity is hardly open to dispute, least of all by people who, like Dr. Lutz, have made use of it in showing that I is always equal to S. Mr. Robertson's time lag is, however, something quite different. It is the time elapsing between the moment that A receives his income from B and the moment when he spends this income (appropriately defined) on (consumption) goods purchased from C. Simultaneity between such receipt and expenditure would be not merely unrealistic, as Dr. Lutz suggests, but impossible, as I have pointed out in the very article referred to.[1] However, this kind of simultaneity is nowhere assumed by Mr. Keynes or by myself, so that criticisms of the Keynesian definitions and approach on this score[2] must be based on a confusion between the two meanings of a time lag between receipts and expenditures. The difference between the two approaches is in definition and in method, not in any conflicting assumptions about the real world. (Even the special assumptions that the Robertson method has to make about the nature of the time lags, so as to be able to fit them into "days," are not contradicted by the absence of any such special assumptions on the other approach as to the nature of the time lag between an individual's receipts and his subsequent expenditures.) We may, therefore, in judging between the usefulness of different sets of *definitions* of I and S, dismiss as irrelevant any alleged differences in assumptions, since any set of assumptions may go with any set of definitions, and to consider the realism of assumptions at the same time as the usefulness of definitions can hardly have any other effect than to confuse the issues.

OBJECTIVES

Apart from the digression on assumptions discussed above, the main reasons given by Dr. Lutz for rejecting the Keynesian in

---

[1] "Saving Equals Investment," Quarterly Journal of Economics, February, 1938, pp. 306–307.

[2] As e.g. by Dr. Haberler in "Mr. Keynes' Theory of the Multiplier," Zeitschrift für Nationalökonomie, 1936, where he declares that the Multiplier doctrine implies an infinite velocity of circulation.

favor of the Robertson-*ex ante* definitions are based upon an examination of the suitability of the different definitions for three different purposes: (*a*) to provide some indication of either the level of economic activity or any tendency for it to expand or contract; (*b*) to provide a guide for credit policy; and (*c*) to develop a dynamic or causal or process analysis of economic activity through time. It is granted that the Keynesian definitions have the advantages of simplicity and of freedom from the difficulties associated with the concept of a period which is supposed to be simultaneously identical with time lags of different length. Against this is set the disadvantage of the absence of any difference $I - S$ which might act as a guide for the purposes enumerated above. What is surprising is that the disadvantage is rated higher than the advantagfes after a demonstration that the difference $I - S$ cannot be used for any of these purposes.

Whatever the manner in which Dr. Lutz would like to have the different procedures (1) to (5) compounded to form his interpretation of the Robertson-*ex ante* definition, $I - S$ will consist of some or all of the four elements: abnormal profits, excess of income earned today over income earned yesterday, unexpected income, and unexpected depletions in stocks. Dr. Lutz has shown that none of these can tell us unambiguously what is the level of economic activity or whether economic activity is going up or down in the near future, that they cannot provide anything that can seriously be considered as a guide for credit policy, and that their usefulness for dynamic analysis is vitiated by the impossibility of fitting all the relevant time lags into the Robertsonian "day." Furthermore, insofar as any of these concepts are of some use, it would appear to be more reasonable to call them by recognizable names—such as those used in this paragraph—rather than to speak of $I - S$, which might stand for any or all of them. In this way it would be possible to utilize such of these concepts as may be useful without confusing them with each other and without giving up any of the advantages of the Keynesian terminology.

Dr. Lutz gives two subsidiary reasons for his conclusions and one final argument that belongs to quite another universe of discourse. He declares that "Keynes himself has confused his definitions in two ways: first, by associating the doctrine of the saving-investment relation with the multiplier; secondly, by asserting that his terminology marks a return to the classical doctrine of the relation between saving and investment."[1]

The second point can be dismissed as a misunderstanding for which Mr. Keynes' mischievous style might perhaps be blamed. Mr. Keynes and his followers will completely agree about the differences that Dr. Lutz points out between the classical and the Keynesian theories of the rate of interest. The first of these two points is, however, based on a complete misunderstanding of the concept of the Multiplier which is so common that Mr. Keynes' presentation cannot escape the suspicion of lack of clarity.

Since S is equal to I by definition, it is as impossible for the Multiplier to "bring them into equality" as it is for the rate of interest (which is supposed to do this on the classical theory). The phrase is unfortunate but almost unavoidable in attempts to describe the mechanism by which a change in the level of investment brings about a change in the level of income or employment that is indicated by the multiplier. Neither Mr. Keynes nor any of his followers would deny that "the saving-investment relation (in the sense of their equality) is independent of the multiplier."[2] More significant is the suggestion[3] that the multiplier (and therefore also its inverse, the marginal propensity to save) are *ex post* concepts and so cannot be identified with any previously known *ex-ante* psychological propensities, which alone could provide any independent, non-tautological, information as to the effect of an increase in the rate of investment on the level of income or employment.

It is true that Mr. Keynes claims that the multiplier holds good for any period of time we may choose, and that if he is taken up on this and very short or otherwise non-typical periods are

---

[1] Ibid., p. 151.
[2] Ibid., p. 152.
[3] Also put forward by Dr. Haberler, op. cit.

considered, some very strange results appear. By appropriately choosing a very short period the marginal propensity to consume, and consequently the multiplier, too, can be "discovered" to have almost any desired value. At one extreme will be the period in which there is an increase in income (compared with some corresponding previous period) but no increment in (expenditure on) consumption (because the shops are shut or because such expenditures as are made in this period are rigid). This would give a marginal propensity to consume of zero and a multiplier of unity. If a period is chosen in which the increment in consumption is equal to the increment in income, the marginal propensity to consume will be unity and the multiplier equal to infinity. At the further extreme would be the case where the period taken was a Saturday evening, when there is no increment of income from investment but an increase in expenditure on consumption as compared with a previous Saturday evening following a week in which earnings were less. In this case the marginal propensity to consume is infinite and the multiplier might be anything.

I think Mr. Keynes can legitimately be criticized for making it appear plausible that he would consider such "propensities to save" to represent a useful form of psychological generalization about human behavior. But surely this is merely a matter of presentation. Consumption and saving can be considered to be stable functions of income only if periods are considered that are long enough for the elimination of the discontinuities that give such strange results. In other words, unless some special period is indicated, *the* marginal propensity to consume which gives *the* multiplier, and which is based upon "psychological law," must be understood to refer to *short period equilibrium*, where the abnormalities due to discontinuities and to failure of adjustment of the output of consumption goods to the new level of investment will have been overcome. Thus "except in conditions where the consumption industries are already working almost at capacity, so that an expansion of output requires an extension of plant, there is no reason to suppose that more than a brief interval of time need elapse before employment in the consumption industries is advanced *pari passu* with employment in the capital-goods industries, with the multiplier operating near its normal figure."[1] If we consider periods long enough for short period equilibrium to be reached, the propensity to save will correspond closely enough to the habits of the people to enable us to say how much the level of employment will have moved up as a result of a given increase in the level of investment and saving. Saving will be greater by the increase in investment, not because people have received income and are waiting for the shops to open so they can spend it, but because the greater rate of saving is in correspondence with the greater level of employment and income.[2]

This brings us to a legitimate criticism, or rather limitation, of Mr. Keynes' approach which would seem to underlie much of the criticism that it has received. It is not as dynamic as some would wish. It is concerned most of the time with short period equilibrium and with the movement of such an equilibrium through time. In assuming such equilibrium to be continuously maintained, it gives up, for the sake of simplicity, the process analysis that the Robertson approach attempts. If successfully carried out the latter would be more complete and more realistic than Mr. Keynes' equilibrium analysis, but it seems at the moment to be

---

[1] Keynes, "General Theory," pp. 124–5.

[2] In another unfortunate footnote (n. 1, p. 153) Dr. Lutz tries to show that the propensity to save "is far from being an independent psychological datum which determines the multiplier," even in the long run, by considering two extreme cases; (a) where the money created by the original act of investment remains permanently in circulation, when the multiplier would equal the income velocity of money, and (b) where the money all flows out of circulation and income falls to the original level and the multiplier is, presumably, zero. This treatment forgets that the multiplier is a relationship between a rate or *flow* of investment and a corresponding rate or *flow* of employment, both going on at the same time in short period equi-(brium. It mixes this up with the effects of increases in the amount of money lwhich might of course influence employment by lowering the rate of interest, which might increase the level of investment and in this way indirectly increase the volume of employment by an extent measured by the multiplier) and in other ways reverts to obsolete confusions as to the operations of hoarding, saving and velocities of circulation.

stalemated by the complexity of the problem and the multiplicity of the time lags which have to be considered. Mr. Keynes' greatest fault is perhaps his failure to point out with sufficient emphasis that he is in the main concerned with equilibrium analysis. This has led to much wasted argument. But there is no reason whatever for supposing an indissoluble bond to exist between the static or equilibrium approach that characterizes the greater part of Mr. Keynes' General Theory of Employment Interest and money and the Keynesian definitions of saving and investment.

Those who are optimistic as to the possibilities of dynamic or process analysis have not only the right but the duty to carry on with their work, and there can be no quarrel between workers on the different approaches who will continue to be of service to each other. It would be well, however, if the difference between equilibrium and process analysis approaches were not hampered by traditional loyalties to particular terminologies. The high respect that all economists have for Mr. Robertson's work has made his definitions, or some definitions that can be made to look something like his, almost imperative for workers on process analysis. I would like to submit, with all the diffidence of one who has been working almost entirely on the other line, that the greater clarity of the Keynesian definitions and the necessity, if these are used, for finding specific names for the various things that might be hidden under $I - S$ would prove advantageous even in process analysis. Dr. Kalecki's work[1] would seem to substantiate this view.

The final argument raised by Dr. Lutz against the Keynesian definitions is that "they do not allow us to distinguish investment which is financed out of inflationary credit or dishoarding from investment that is financed out of the current supply of voluntary savings. There is no doubt, however, that it makes a lot of difference whether investment is financed from the one source or the other; and a terminology that conceals this difference hardly

---

[1] "A Theory of the Trade Cycle," Review of Economic Studies, February, 1937.

seems commendable."[1] If this means that the use of the Keynesian terminology prevents us from discussing the effects of increases in the amount of money or of diminutions in liquidity preference or increases in the marginal efficiency schedule of investment, it clearly is incorrect. It would seem rather that these matters can be discussed so clearly in the Keynesian terminology that the bogey of "forced saving" loses the portentousness lent to it by a dimmer light. Dr. Lutz appears to lament the theoretical capital lost in the "forced saving" venture, but until a clear and significant meaning is discovered for "voluntary" saving it would be best to call it a bygone and to leave open the question whether the undefined distinction makes "a lot of difference" or not.

---

[1] Op. cit., p. 155.

8

THE RATE OF INTEREST AND THE OPTIMUM PROPENSITY TO CONSUME*

By Oscar Lange||

1. By introducing liquidity preference into the theory of interest Mr. Keynes has provided us with an analytical apparatus of great power to attack problems which hitherto have successfully resisted the intrusion of the economic theorist. In this paper I propose first to elucidate the way in which liquidity preference co-operates with the marginal efficiency of investment and with the propensity to consume in determining the rate of interest and to point out how both the traditional and Mr. Keynes's theory are but special cases of a more general theory. Further I propose to show how the analytical apparatus created by Mr. Keynes can be used to handle the problem which bothered the under-consumption theorists since the time of Malthus and Sismondi.

2. The economic relations by which the rate of interest is determined can be represented by a system of four equations.[1]

---

* *Economica*, Volume V (New Series), Number 17, February 1938, pages 12–32. Reprinted by the courtesy of The London School of Economics and Political Science and the author.

|| University of Chicago.

[1] A similar system of equations has been given for the first time by Reddaway, "The General Theory of Employment, Interest and Money," *The Economic Record*, June, 1936, p. 35. While writing this there has come to my notice a forthcoming paper of Dr. Hicks on "Mr. Keynes and the Classics," in the meanwhile published in *Econometrica*, April, 1937, which treats the subject in a similar and very elegant way. The form chosen in my paper seems, however, more adapted for the study of the problems it is concerned with. Cf. also Harrod, "Mr. Keynes and Traditional Theory," *Econometrica*, January, 1937.

The first of these equations is the function relating the amount of money held in cash balances to the rate of interest and to income. This is the liquidity preference function. If M is the amount of money held by the individuals, Y their total income and i the rate of interest we have[1]:

$$M = L(i, Y) \qquad (1)$$

It is convenient to take M and Y as *measured in terms of wage-units*, or of any other *numéraire*. Thus Y is the real income while M is the real value of the cash balances, both in terms of the *numéraire* chosen. This presupposes, of course, that the ratio of the price of each commodity or service to the price of the commodity or service which is chosen as the *numéraire* is given. These ratios may be thought of as determined by the Walrasian or Paretian system of equations of general economic equilibrium. Thus index numbers are *not* involved in this procedure. We assume that the real value, as defined, of cash balances decreases (or, in the limiting case, remains constant) in response to an increase of the rate of interest and that it increases (or, in the limiting case, remains constant) in response to an increase of real income, i.e., $L_i \leq 0$ and $L_Y \geq 0$.

The second equation expresses the propensity to consume. The total expenditure on consumption depends on the total income and, possibly, on the rate of interest. Denoting by C the total expenditure on consumption during a unit of time, we have the function:[2]

$$C = \phi(Y, i) \qquad (2)$$

where C and Y are measured in wage-units (or in some other *numéraire* chosen). The expenditure on consumption increases

---

[1] This function is obtained by summation of the liquidity preference functions of the individuals in the same way as a market demand function is obtained from the demand functions of the individuals. It holds only for a given distribution of incomes.

[2] This function is the sum of the functions expressing the propensity to consume for each individual. It holds only for a given distribution of incomes.

in response to an increase of income, though less than the income, i.e., $0 < \phi_Y < 1$, while no general rule can be stated as to the reaction of this expenditure to a change in the rate of interest, so that $\phi_i \gtreqless 0$.

The investment function which relates the amount invested per unit of time to the rate of interest and to the expenditure on consumption provides us with a third equation. If I is the investment per unit of time the function is:

$$I = F(i, C) \tag{3}$$

Both I and C are measured in wage-units. The investment function is based on the theorem that the amount of investment per unit of time is such as to equalise the rate of net return on that investment (the marginal efficiency in Mr. Keynes' terminology) to the rate of interest. This rate of net return is derived from the rate of net return (marginal efficiency) on capital but it is not identical with it.[1] The lower the rate of interest the larger the investment per unit of time, i.e., $F_i < 0$. Investment per unit of time depends, however, not only on the rate of interest but also on the expenditure on consumption. For the demand for investment goods is *derived* from the demand for consumers' goods. The smaller the expenditure on consumption the smaller is the demand for consumers' goods and, consequently, the lower is the rate of net return on investment. Thus, the rate of interest being constant, investment per unit of time is the larger the larger the total expenditure on consumption, i.e., $F_c > 0$.

---

[1] They are frequently confused. However, the marginal efficiency of capital relates the rate of net return to a *stock* of capital while the marginal efficiency of investment relates it to a *stream* of investment per unit of time. As to how the marginal efficiency of investment is related to the marginal efficiency of capital cf. a forthcoming paper by Mr. Lerner. It also ought to be observed that the investment function holds only for a given capital equipment and for a given distribution of the expenditure for consumption between the different industries.

Finally we have the identity:

$$Y \equiv C + I \qquad (4)$$

which provides us with the fourth equation.[1]

If the amount of money M (in wage-units) is given these four equations determine the four unknowns, i, C, I and Y. Alternatively, i may be regarded as given (for instance, fixed by the banking system) and M as determined by our system of equations. These equations determine also the income-velocity of circulation of money which is $\frac{Y}{M}$.[2] It must, however, be remembered that C, I and Y are measured in terms of a *numéraire* (wage-units). If we want them to be expressed in money we need an additional equation which expresses the money price of the commodity or service chosen as *numéraire* (a unit of labour in our case). If w is this money price and Q the quantity of money we have:

$$Q = wM \qquad (5)$$

which is equivalent to the traditional equation of the quantity theory of money.

3. The process of determination of the rate of interest according to the four equations above is illustrated by the three following diagrams.

---

[1] This identity is the sum of the budget equations of the individuals. It can also be written in the form $Y - C \equiv I$ which expresses the equality of investment and the excess of income over expenditure on consumption, i.e., saving. The identical equality of investment and saving holds for investment and saving actually performed. Investment or saving *decisions* can be different. The identity above states, however, that, whatever the decisions, income is bound to change so as to make equal saving and investment actually realised.

[2] It is interesting to notice that the income-velocity resulting from these equations is the "hybrid" corresponding to the definition of Professor Pigou (cf. *Industrial Fluctuations*, 1927, p. 152) and of Mr. Robertson (*Money*, new edition, 1932, p. 38) and not the ratio of income to income deposits only which Mr. Keynes calls income-velocity (cf. *A Treatise on Money*, Vol. II, pp. 24–25).

RATE OF INTEREST AND PROPENSITY TO CONSUME   173

Fig. 1 represents the relation between the demand for cash balances and the rate of interest. The quantity of money (in wage-units) being measured along the axis OM and the rate of interest along the axis Oi, we have a *family* of liquidity preference curves: one for each level of total income (measured in wage-units).

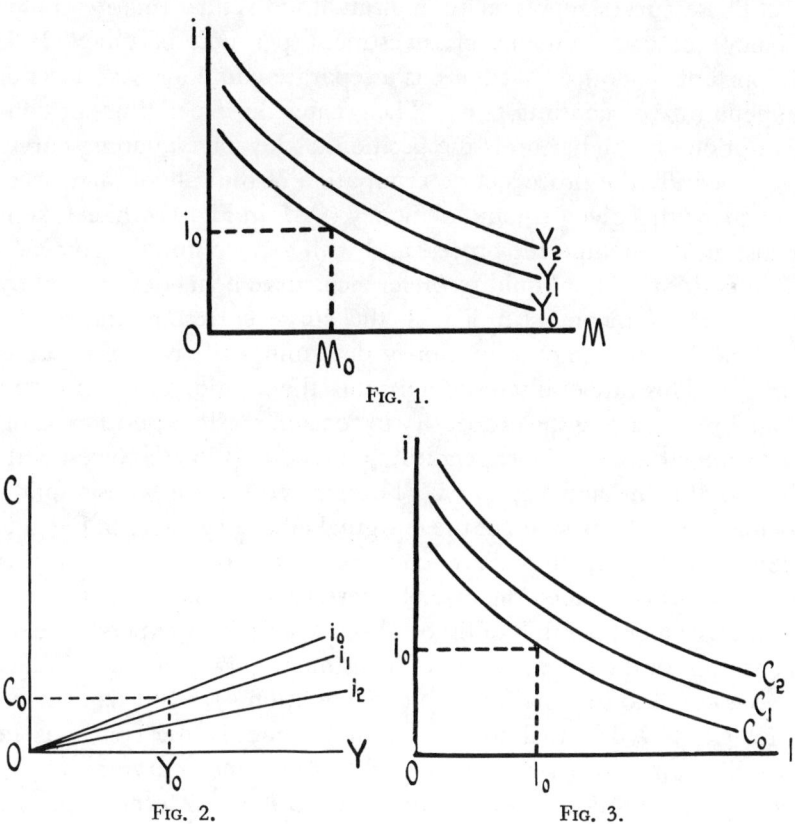

FIG. 1.

FIG. 2.   FIG. 3.

The greater the total income the higher up is the position of the corresponding curve.

Further we have a family of curves (one for each rate of interest) representing the relation between income and expenditure on consumption (Fig. 2). Income is measured along OY and expenditure on consumption along OC.

The relation between investment and the rate of interest is represented by Fig. 3. Measuring investment per unit of time along the axis OI and the rate of interest along Oi we have a family of curves indicating the investment corresponding to each value of the rate of interest.

These curves represent the marginal net return (marginal efficiency) of each amount of investment per unit of time. It is important to notice that there is a separate curve for each level of expenditure on consumption. The greater the expenditure on consumption the higher up is the position of the corresponding curve.

To study the process of determination of the rate of interest let us start with a given amount of money (OM_o in Fig. 1) which is kept constant throughout the process and with a given initial income Y_o. The position of the liquidity preference curve being determined by the level of income (in Fig. 1 the curve corresponding to the income Y_o), the amount of money determines the rate of interest, say i_o. This rate of interest determines the position of the curve in Fig. 2 representing the propensity to consume. This position being determined, we get the expenditure on consumption C_o corresponding to the initial income Y_o. The expenditure on consumption being given, the position of the marginal efficiency curve in Fig. 3 is determined (i.e., the curve corresponding to C_o). When this position is determined the rate of interest i_o determines the amount I_o of investment per unit of time. We have thus the expenditure on consumption and the amount of investment. But the sum of these two is equal to the total income (*vide* equation 4). If it happens so that $C_o + I_o$ is equal to the initial income Y_o the system is in equilibrium. Otherwise the liquidity preference curve in Fig. 1 changes its position so as to correspond to the new level of income $C_o + I_o$. This gives us a new rate of interest. As a result of this and of the changed income we get a new level of expenditure on consumption. This in turn changes the position of the marginal efficiency curve in Fig. 3 and the new rate of interest determines another amount of investment which, together with the expenditure on consumption, determines a third level of total income. As a result the liquidity preference curve shifts again, etc. This process of *mutual adjustment* goes on until the curves in our three diagrams have reached a position compatible with each other and with the quantity of money given, i.e., until equilibrium is attained.[1]

4. Let us now consider how changes in the curves of the marginal efficiency of investment and in the curves representing the propensity to consume affect the rate of interest.

If the marginal efficiency curves are all shifted upwards (which, ultimately, must be due to an increase of the marginal net productivity of capital), then a larger amount of investment corresponds to any given rate of interest and expenditure on consumption. Therefore total income increases and the curve of liquidity preference in Fig. 1 shifts upwards. This causes a rise of the rate of interest. Thus, just as in the traditional theory, an increase in the marginal productivity of capital is accompanied by a rise of the rate of interest. The reverse happens when the marginal productivity of capital declines.

On the other hand, a decrease in the propensity to consume (or, in other words, an increase in the propensity to save) is accompanied by a fall of the rate of interest. For with a given initial income and a given rate of interest the expenditure on consumption is now lower. This causes the marginal efficiency curve in Fig. 2 to shift downward and a lower quantity of investment corresponds to any given rate of interest. Total income decreases both as a direct result of the decreased expenditure on consumption and because of the diminished quantity of investment. Thus a downward shift of the liquidity preference curve in Fig. 1 takes place. The consequence is a fall of the rate of interest. In a similar way an increase in the propensity to consume raises the rate of interest.

Thus the two traditional statements that the rate of interest rises together with the marginal net productivity of capital, and vice versa, and that it moves in the opposite direction to the propensity to save, hold fully in our generalised theory. Two limiting cases, however, deserve special attention.

---

[1] If this process of adjustment involves a time lag of a certain kind a cyclical fluctuation, instead of equilibrium, is the result. Cf. Kalecki, "A Theory of the Business Cycle," *Review of Economic Studies*, February, 1937.

The theory put forward is quite general and formal. The actual reactions, however, depend on the concrete shape of the functions (1), (2) and (3). We are concerned at present with the consequences of different shapes of the liquidity preference function. For the general case it has been assumed that the demand for liquidity is a decreasing function of the rate of interest and an increasing function of total income. The demand for liquidity (i.e., for cash balances) has thus two elasticities: an interest-elasticity which is negative and an income-elasticity which is positive. These two elasticities determine the reaction of the rate of interest to changes in the marginal efficiency of investment (which is correlated to the marginal net productivity of capital) and in the propensity to consume; for the reaction of the rate of interest to these is due to the influence which the change of income caused by them exerts upon liquidity preference. The greater the income-elasticity of the demand for liquidity the more the curve of liquidity preference is shifted when income changes and, consequently, the greater is the reaction of the rate of interest. The shift of the liquidity preference curve changes the demand for liquidity corresponding to any given rate of interest. If, however, the amount of money (in wage-units) is fixed, the rate of interest must change so as to equalise the demand for liquidity to the quantity of money available. The change of the rate of interest which thus follows is the greater the smaller the interest-elasticity of the demand for liquidity. Therefore, the reaction of the rate of interest is the greater the smaller the interest-elasticity of the demand for liquidity.

In the special case in which the income-elasticity of the demand for liquidity is zero the rate of interest does not react at all to changes other than in the quantity of money (measured in wage-units). The demand for liquidity is in this case a function of the rate of interest alone:

$$M = L(r) \qquad (1a)$$

There is but one curve of liquidity preference and the amount of money determines the rate of interest independently of the level of total income. Changes in the marginal efficiency of investment and in the propensity to consume do not affect the rate of interest at all. The whole brunt of such changes has to be borne by the other variables of the system (i.e., expenditure on consumption, investment and income). The same result is also reached when the interest-elasticity of the demand for liquidity is infinite. In this case, too, the rate of interest does not react to changes in the marginal efficiency of investment or in the propensity to consume. For the change of the rate of interest which is necessary to balance a given change in the demand for liquidity caused by a change of total income is nil in this case. This is Mr. Keynes' theory. Since Mr. Keynes recognises *expressis verbis* the dependence of the demand for liquidity on total income[1] it is obviously the last case he must have in mind.

The other special case is when the interest-elasticity of the demand for liquidity is zero. The demand for cash balances is in this case a function of income alone:

$$M = L(Y) \qquad (1b)$$

Both Y and M being measured in wage-units (or in any other *numéraire*, for instance, wheat[2]) this equation states simply the proportion of their real income people hold in cash (in real balances). If this proportion is regarded as constant our function becomes:

$$M = kY$$

(where k is a constant) which is the well known Cambridge equation of the quantity theory of money. Taking into account equation (5) this can be written $Q = kYw$, or $Q = wL(Y)$ in the more general case, where Q is the quantity of money and w is the money price of the commodity or service which has been chosen as *numéraire*. The latter being given, the total income is determined by the quantity of money. Total income being given, the rate of interest is determined exclusively by the equations (2), (3) and (4),

---

[1] Cf. *The General Theory of Employment*, etc., pp. 171–172 and pp. 199 *et seq.*
[2] The reader will be reminded that Marshall and Professor Pigou have used wheat as a *numéraire* in this connection. *Vide* Marshall, *Money Credit and Commerce*, p. 44, and Pigou, *Essays in Applied Economics*, p. 177.

i.e., by the propensity to consume, by the marginal efficiency of investment (which in turn depends on the marginal net productivity of capital), and by the condition that investment is equal to the excess of income over expenditure on consumption (i.e., saving). This is the traditional theory of interest.

Thus both the Keynesian and the traditional theory of interest are but two limiting cases of what may be regarded to be the general theory of interest.

5. It is a feature of great historical interest that the essentials of this general theory are contained already in the work of Walras.

Indeed, the demand for liquidity appears in Walras as the *encaisse désirée*. Walras is quite explicit about the fact that the demand for liquidity is a function of the rate of interest. This dependence is expressed as early as in the second edition of his *Eléments d'économie politique pure* which was published in 1889. "In a society—he writes—where money is kept in cash from the moment when it is received until the day when it is given into payment or loaned out, money renders few services and those who keep it, producers or consumers, lose needlessly the interest on the capital which it represents." ("Dans une société où on garde la monnaie en caisse depuis le moment où on la reçoit jusqu'au jour où on la donne en paiement ou jusqu'au jour où on la prête, la monnaie rend peu de services, et ceux qui la détiennent, producteurs ou consommateurs, perdent inutilement l'intérêt du capital qu'elle représente.")[1] This is emphasised even more in his *Théorie de la Monnaie* where we read about the service yielded by a given *encaisse monétaire:* "its satisfaction is obtained at the price of interest and this is why the effective demand for money is a decreasing function of the rate of interest" ("sa satisfaction se paie au prix d'un intérêt et c'est pourquoi la demande effective de monnaie est une fonction décroissante du taux d'intérêt").[2] He goes on, to quote again from the second edition of the *Eléments*, saying: "Suppose that on a cer-

---

[1] P. 382.

[2] P. 95 of the reprint in *Etudes d'économie politique appliquée* (published in Lausanne in 1898). This passage does not occur in the original edition in form of a separate book which was published in 1886 (Lausanne).

tain day the existing quantity of money Q_u has diminished or that the demand for cash H which represents the utility of money has increased. . . . Equilibrium will be re-established on the next day on the market at a new and higher rate of interest at which the demand for cash will be reduced." ("Supposons qu'un jour la quantité existante de monnaie Q_u ait diminué ou que l'encaisse désirée H représentant l'utilité de la monnaie ait augmenté . . . L'équilibre ne s'établirait, le lendemain, sur le marché, qu'à un nouveau taux d'intérêt plus élevé auquel l'encaisse desirée se reduirait.")[1]. Walras also uses the device of expressing the demand for cash balances in real terms. It is a certain real purchasing power over which the individual wants to have command and he expresses it in terms of a *numéraire*.[2] If H is the demand for liquidity in terms of the *numéraire* chosen and Q_u is the amount of money in existence, then the price p_u of money in terms of the *numéraire* is determined by the equation $Q_u p_u = H$, which is analogous to the equation (5) above.[3] Walras fails, however, to indicate whether the *encaisse désirée* depends also on the level of real income. But whatever the shortcomings of his presentation, the liquidity preference function has been indicated clearly by Walras.

Our remaining three equations are also contained in the system of Walras. There is, first of all, the propensity to save (instead of our propensity to consume). Saving is defined, as by Mr. Keynes, as the excess of income over consumption (l'excédent du revenu sur la consommation).[4] Now this excess of income over consumption is

---

[1] P. 383. In the last editions of the *Eléments* the exposition, though put into mathematics, is somewhat obscure. Walras introduces also the question of liquidity (i.e., of stocks) in other commodities. Of each commodity a stock is kept which renders a "*service d'approvisionnement*" (service of storage). The rate of interest is the cost of this service. Cf. *Eléments*, 4th ed., 1900, pp. 179, 298, 303.

[2] Pp. 377–78 of 2nd ed. and *Théorie de la Monnaie* (as reprinted in *Etudes d'économie politique appliquée*), p. 95.

[3] P 378 and p. 383 of 2nd ed.

[4] P. 281 of first edition published in 1874 (p. 269 of second ed. and p. 249 of final ed.). Walras uses throughout the term *excédent* and the word *épargne* is reserved to denote net saving. Cf. p. 282 of first ed. (p. 270 of 2nd ed. and p. 250 of final ed.).

conceived by Walras to be a function of both the rate of interest and income. He expresses the propensity to save by an equation and states explicitly that this equation "gives the excess of income over consumption as a function of the prices of the productive services and of consumers' goods and of the rate of interest" ("donnant *l'excédent* du revenu sur la consommation en fonction des *prix* des services et des produits consommables et du *taux* du revenu net").[1] By introducing the prices of all commodities he brings income indirectly into the equation expressing the propensity to save. His equation thus corresponds to our equation (2). As a counterpart to our investment function Walras has an equation which determines the total value of *"capitaux neufs"* produced. This value is determined by the condition that the selling price of the *capitaux neufs* (which is equal to the capitalised value of their net returns) is equal to their cost of production.[2] This equation determines the total volume of investment corresponding to any given rate of interest. Unfortunately, Walras fails to indicate on what the net return of the *capitaux neufs* depends. He takes it just for granted and as a consequence there is no relation between their net return and the expenditure on consumption.

Finally Walras expresses in a separate equation the equality of the value of the *capitaux neufs* and the excess of income over consumption.[3] This, however, is *not* equivalent to our equation (4) which states the equality of investment and the excess of income over consumption. For there is an important difference. In our system, as in the theory of Mr. Keynes, equation (4) is an identity. Whatever the investment and saving *decisions* are, the volume of total income always adjusts itself so as to equalise saving and investment *actually performed*.[4] This is a simple budget relationship, for the

---

[1] P. 271 of 2nd ed. "Taux du revenu net" must be translated by "rate of interest" in this connotation.

[2] Cf. 284 of first ed. (pp. 246-7 and p. 253 of final ed.).

[3] P. 284 of first ed. (p. 252 of final ed.).

[4] It ought to be mentioned here that this has been recognised by many economists before Mr. Keynes. If investment decisions exceed saving decisions "forced saving" takes place according to a widely accepted doctrine. And Mr. Robertson has pointed out (cf. *Money*, London, 1928, pp. 93-97) that if saving

individuals' incomes are equal to the sum of expenditure on consumption and investment. Walras, however, treats the equality of investment and saving not as an identity but as a genuine equation which holds true only in a position of equilibrium. Hence his investment (value of the *capitaux neufs*) and saving (excess of income over consumption) are to be interpreted as *decisions* which finally are brought into equilibrium by a change in the rate of interest and in total income.[1] But this equation does not show how total income changes so as to bring saving actually performed always into equality with investment.

This is done by our identity (4) which corresponds to the sum of the budget equations in the Walrasian system and shows how expenditure on consumption and investment *determine* the total income. When this budget relationship is taken account of, there is no need any more for a separate equation indicating the equilibrium of saving and investment decisions based on some *given* income, however defined. All the relevant relations are expressed by our equations (2), (3) and (4). Thus Mr. Keynes' apparatus involves a considerable simplification of the theory.

6. Having investigated the consequences which the introduction of liquidity preference has for the formulation of the theory of interest, let us see how the general theory outlined above can be applied to solve the problem which is the concern of all theories of underconsumption. Mr. Keynes has scarcely done justice to what is the core of the argument of those theories. "Practically—he writes—I only differ from these schools of thought in thinking that they may lay a little too much emphasis on increased consumption at a time when there is still much social advantage to be obtained from increased investment. Theoretically, however, they are open to the criticism of neglecting the fact that there are *two* ways to expand output."[2] Mr. Keynes treats investment and expenditure

---

decisions exceed investment decisions the excess cannot be saved. It becomes "abortive."

[1] P. 286–7 of 2nd ed. (pp. 266–67 of final ed.). In the process of *tâtonnements* described by Walras all the prices change and thus total income changes, too.

[2] *The General Theory of Employment, etc.*, p. 325.

on consumption as two *independent* quantities and thinks that total income can be increased indiscriminately by expanding *either* of them. But it is a commonplace which can be read in any textbook of economics that the demand for investment goods is *derived* from the demand for consumption goods. The real argument of the underconsumption theories is that investment *depends* on the expenditure on consumption and, therefore, cannot be increased without an adequate increase of the latter, at least in a capitalist economy where investment is done for profit.

Few underconsumption theorists ever maintain that *any* saving discourages investment.[1] Generally they maintain that up to a certain point saving encourages investment while it discourages it if this point is exceeded.[2] This is the theory of oversaving. If people would spend their whole income on consumption, investment would obviously be zero, while the demand for investment would be zero too, if they consumed nothing. Thus mere common sense suggests that there must be somewhere in between an *optimum* propensity to save which maximises investment. But no underconsumption theorist ever has shown what this optimum is and how it is determined. The problem, however, was put forward with unsurpassed clarity already by Malthus: "No considerable and continued increase in wealth could possibly take place without that degree of frugality which occasions, annually, the conversion of some revenue into capital, and creates a balance of produce over consumption; but it is quite obvious . . . that the principle of saving, pushed to excess, would destroy the motive to production . . . If consumption exceeds production, the capital of the country must be diminished, and its wealth must be gradually destroyed from its want of power to produce; if production be in great excess above consumption, the motive to accumulate and consume must cease from the want of will to consume. The two extremes are obvious; and it follows that there must be some intermediate point, though the resources of political economy may not be able to

---

[1] The most prominent among those who did so was Rosa Luxemburg in her famous book *Die Akkumulation des Kapitals* (Berlin, 1912).

[2] *Vide*, for instance, Hobson, *The Industrial System*, London, 1910, pp. 53–54.

ascertain it, where taking into consideration both the power to produce and the will to consume, the encouragement to the increase of wealth is greatest."[1]

The general theory of interest outlined in this paper enables us to solve this problem and to determine the optimum propensity to save which maximises investment. Since investment per unit of time is a function of both the rate of interest and expenditure on consumption a decrease of the propensity to consume (increase in the propensity to save) has a twofold effect. On the one hand the decrease of expenditure on consumption discourages investment, but the decrease in the propensity to consume also causes, as we have seen, a fall of the rate of interest which encourages investment on the other hand. The optimum propensity to consume is that at which the encouraging and the discouraging effect of a change are in balance.

The condition of such a balance is easily found. A change of the propensity to consume is mathematically a change of the *form* of the function (2) in our equations. We want to discover the conditions this function has to satisfy in order to maximise investment. Let δC be the variation of expenditure on consumption and δi the variation of the rate of interest which are caused by the change of the propensity to consume. Recalling the investment function (3), which is $I = F(i, C)$, the condition that investment be a maximum is then:

$$\delta I = F_i \delta i + F_c \delta C = 0 \qquad (6)$$

where δI is the corresponding variation of investment.

From equation (4) we derive the variation of total income caused by the change of the propensity to consume:

$$\delta Y = \delta C + \delta I$$

and since $\delta I = O$ when investment is a maximum we have in the maximum position:

$$\delta Y = \delta C \qquad (7)$$

---

[1] *Principles of Political Economy*, London, 1820, pp. 8–9 (Introduction). Cf. also pp. 369–70.

Now the change of the rate of interest due to the change of the propensity to consume can be obtained from equation (1), i.e., from the liquidity preference function. We have:[1]

$$\delta M = L_i \delta i + L_Y \delta Y \qquad (8)$$

If the sum of real balances available, i.e., the quantity of money measured in wage-units or in any other *numéraire*, is assumed to be constant[2] this reduces to:

$$L_i \delta i + L_Y \delta Y = 0 \qquad (8a)$$

whence:

$$\delta i = -\frac{L_Y}{L_i} \delta Y \qquad (9)$$

By substitution of (9) and (7) in (6) we arrive at the equation:

$$-F_i \frac{L_Y}{L_i} \delta C + F_c \delta C = 0$$

---

[1] The liquidity preference function holds only for a given distribution of incomes (cf. footnote 1 on p. 170 above). Similarly the investment function holds only for a given distribution of the expenditure for consumption between the different industries, for even if the total expenditure on consumption remains unchanged a shift of expenditure from goods requiring less to goods requiring more capital to produce, or vice versa, necessarily affects investment. Equations (6) and (8) in the text presuppose, therefore, that changes in the distribution of incomes and in the direction of consumers' expenditure to different industries are either absent, or that their effect on total investment and on the total demand for liquidity is of second order magnitude and can thus be neglected. Since a change of the propensity to consume certainly produces changes in the distribution of incomes and of consumers' expenditure the second assumption is the only realistic one. A more precise theory would have to take into account the effect of these changes, too.

[2] If the money wage (or, more generally, the money price of the *numéraire* chosen) is constant, this means that the nominal quantity of money is constant, too. If not, the nominal quantity of money has to change proportionally to the money price of the *numéraire*. If, however, labour is not regarded as a homogeneous factor the use of labour-units as *numéraire* involves really the use of a particular index number, i.e., the labour standard, and our assumption amounts to assuming that the purchasing power of money in terms of the labour standard is constant.

which can be transformed into:

$$-\frac{L_Y}{L_i} = -\frac{F_c}{F_i} \quad (10)$$

This equation, together with the equations (1), (3) and (4) of our system, determines the optimum propensity to consume under the assumption that the amount of money (measured in wage-units) is constant.[1]

Only such forms of the function representing the propensity to consume which satisfy this equation provide a maximum investment. A very simple economic interpretation can be given to the equation obtained. The right hand side of the equation is the marginal rate of substitution between a change of the rate of interest

---

[1] If the amount of money (as defined in the text) is allowed to change a more general condition is obtained. For this purpose we must add to our system of equations a supply function of money. Let this function be:

$$M = \psi(i, Y)$$

where M and Y are measured in terms of wage-units. We have then:

$$\delta M = \psi_i \delta i + \psi_Y \delta Y$$

and taking into account equation (8) in the text we obtain:

$$\psi_i \delta i + \psi_Y \delta Y = L_i \delta i + L_Y \delta Y$$

which can be written in the more convenient form:

$$(\psi_Y - L_Y)\delta Y = (L_i - \psi_i)\delta i$$

whence we get:

$$\delta_i = \frac{\psi_Y - L_Y}{L_i - \psi_i} \delta Y$$

Substituting this and (7) in (6) we arrive at:

$$F_i \frac{\psi_Y - L_Y}{L_i - \psi_i} \delta C + F_c \delta C = 0$$

which is, finally, transformed into:

$$\frac{\psi_Y - L_Y}{L_i - \psi_i} = -\frac{F_c}{F_i} \quad (10a)$$

This is the most general form of the equation which determines the optimum propensity to consume. Equation (10) obtained in the text is a special case of it when $\psi_Y + 0$ and $\psi_i = 0$.

and a change of the expenditure on consumption as inducements to invest. The left hand side is the marginal rate of substitution between a change of the rate of interest and a change of real income as determining the demand for liquidity. The optimum propensity to consume is thus determined by the condition that *the marginal rate of substitution between the rate of interest and total income as affecting the demand for liquidity is equal to the marginal rate of substitution between the rate of interest and expenditure on consumption as inducements to invest.*[1]

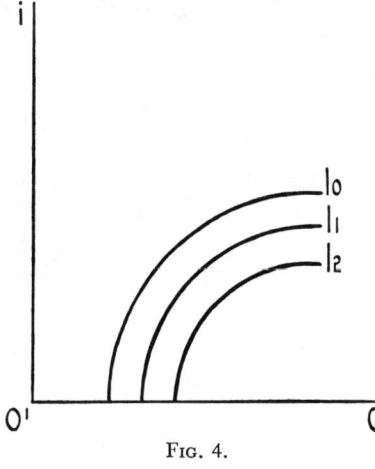

Fig. 4.

It is convenient to have a graphic illustration of this condition. On Fig. 4 we draw a family of indifference curves indicating the possible variations of the rate of interest and of the expenditure on consumption which do not change the level of investment per unit of time. We may call them *isoinvestment curves.* The expenditure on consumption being measured along the axis $O'C$ and the rate of interest along $O'i$ these curves slope upward[2] and the greater the

---

[1] The economic interpretation of equation (10a) is similar to that of equation (10), only the left hand side is here the marginal rate of substitution not along a curve of equal liquidity (isoliquidity curve; *vide* below) but along the curve corresponding to the equation:

$$\psi(i, Y) = L(i, Y)$$

Thus the left hand side of (10a) is the marginal rate of substitution between the changes of the rate of interest and of total income which are compatible with the maintenance of the equality of the supply of and the demand for money. The supply function of money depends on the behaviour of the monetary system.

[2] The slope of these curves is $-\dfrac{F_c}{F_i}$. Since $F_c > 0$ and $F_i < 0$ the slope is positive.

level of investment the more to the right is the position of the corresponding isoinvestment curve.[1] The curves can be expected to be concave downwards, for the stimulus to invest exercised by each successive increment of expenditure on consumption is weaker. This is explained by the increasing prices of the factors of production which diminish the net return derived by entrepreneurs from successive increments of expenditure on consumption (the curves of marginal efficiency of investment in Fig. 3 are shifted upwards less and less). Thus the greater the expenditure on consumption the greater is the increment of it which is necessary to compensate a given rise of the rate of interest. Finally, we reach a point where a further increase of the expenditure on consumption fails entirely to stimulate investment.

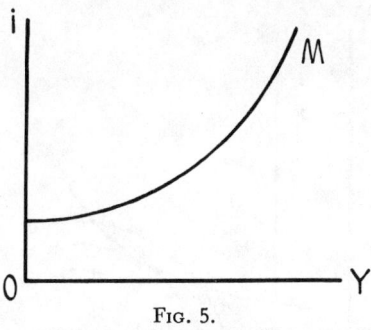

Fig. 5.

This happens when the elasticity of supply of the factors of production has become zero, so that an increase of the expenditure on consumption only raises their prices. Thus the isoinvestment curves become horizontal to the right of a certain critical value of the abscissa.[2]

On Fig. 5 we draw an indifference curve which represents all the variations of the rate of interest and of total income which do not affect the demand for liquidity (total income and the demand for liquidity being expressed in wage-units). We may call it the *isoliquidity curve*. Since the amount of money is assumed to be given we have only one such curve (the curve M in Fig. 5). It

---

[1] There are certain combinations of the expenditure on consumption and of the rate of interest at which the existing capital is just maintained by replacement. They determine the curve corresponding to zero investment (i.e., the curve I_o in Fig. 4). All curves to the right of it correspond to positive and all to the left correspond to negative investment.

[2] $-\dfrac{F_c}{F_i} = 0$ when $F_c = 0$.

slopes upward[1] and is straight, convex or concave downward, according as the demand for liquidity increases with an increase of real income at a constant, an increasing or a decreasing rate, respectively.[2] Downward convexity, however, seems to be the case which is practically most likely to occur.[3]

The optimum propensity to consume can now be determined in a simple way by combining the diagrams of Fig. 4 and Fig. 5.

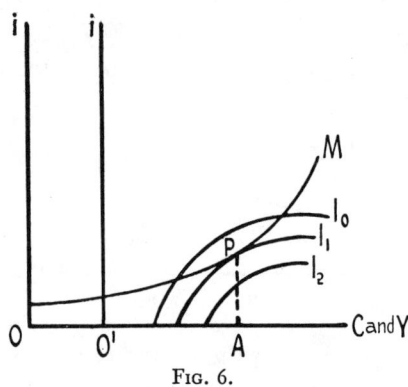

FIG. 6.

Equation (10) states that the slope of the isoliquidity curve has to be equal to the slope of the isoinvestment curve (*vide* the point P in Fig. 6). But the position of the origins O and O' in the combined diagram is not arbitrary. For OO' is the difference between total income and expenditure on consumption, i.e., represents the level of investment. Thus to each level of investment there belongs a special length of OO'. The optimum propensity to consume is, therefore, obtained by superimposing Fig. 5 upon Fig. 4 (as in Fig. 6) and moving it horizontally until the isoliquidity curve becomes tangent to the isoinvestment curve whose index (i.e., level of investment) is equal to the length of OO'. OO' is then the maximum investment, $O'A$ and OA are the expenditure on consumption and the total income which correspond

---

[1] The slope of the curve is $-\dfrac{L_Y}{L_i}$. It is positive because $L_Y > 0$ and $L_i < 0$. In the limiting cases, however, where either $L_Y = 0$ or $L_i = 0$ we have either $-\dfrac{L_Y}{L_i} = 0$ or $-\dfrac{L_Y}{L_i} = \infty$ and the isoliquidity curve degenerates into a horizontal or vertical straight line.

[2] We have $\dfrac{d^2i}{dY^2} = -\dfrac{L_{YY}L_i - L_{iY}L_Y}{L_i^2}$. Taking $L_{iY} = 0$ approximately and remembering that $L_i < 0$, we find that $\dfrac{d^2i}{dY^2}$ is of the same sign as L_{YY}. (Footnote added, 1943.)

[3] The last two sentences were revised by the author, 1943.

RATE OF INTEREST AND PROPENSITY TO CONSUME 189

to it. The isoinvestment curves[1] being concave downward, an optimum propensity to consume exists and is unique if the isoliquidity curve is convex downward or is a straight line, or even if it is concave downward, provided its concavity is less than that of the isoinvestment curves and its curvature does not change sign.[2]

From Fig. 6 we obtain the expenditure on consumption $O'A$ and the total income OA which correspond to maximum investment and which are, as we have seen, uniquely determined. Plotting them on a diagram (*vide* Fig. 7) we obtain a point R through which the curve representing the propensity to consume has to pass. Thus the function expressing the optimum propensity to consume is determined only by *one* point through which it has to pass. *Any* function which passes through the point R maximises investment. Any function, however, which does not pass through R makes total investment smaller.

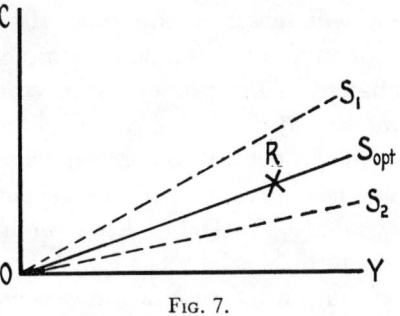

Fig. 7.

Generally we may expect that a decrease of the propensity to consume (i.e., an increase of the propensity to save) leads us from curves which pass above R to curves which pass below R (e.g., the curves S_1 and S_2 in Fig. 7). As long as they pass above R the propensity to consume is above optimum, when they

---

[1] Balance of this sentence was revised by the author, 1943.

[2] The graphic solution indicated in Fig. 6 is also applicable to the general case where the quantity of money (in terms of wage-units) is not constant. As shown in the footnotes 1 on pp. 185 and 186 the equation (10a) is substituted in this case for the equation (10). Instead of the isoliquidity curve we get a curve corresponding to the equation $\psi(i, Y) = L(i, Y)$. It is a projection on the Yi plane of the curve resulting from the intersection of the two surfaces representing the supply and the demand for money respectively (the isoliquidity curves are a special case of it obtained when the supply surface of money is a plane parallel to the Yi plane). The shape of the curve depends now also on the form of the supply function of money. The graphic solution is obtained as in the text by moving the diagram of this curve horizontally until the curve becomes tangent to the isoinvestment curve corresponding to the level of investment equal to OO'.

pass below R it is below optimum. Maximum investment is attained when we hit upon a curve which passes through R (e.g., the curve S_{opt} in Fig. 7). This is a curve of optimum propensity to consume. Any change of the shape of the curve which does not affect its passing through R is irrelevant.

7. Let us now apply the result obtained to two special cases.

When either the income-elasticity of the demand for liquidity is zero or the interest-elasticity of the demand for liquidity is infinite, which is the case corresponding to Mr. Keynes' theory, we have either $L_Y = 0$ (and $L_i \neq 0$) or $L_i = \infty$ (and $L_Y \neq 0$). It follows immediately from equation (10) that $F_c = 0$ in either case.[1] The economic interpretation is simple. As we have seen, in this case a change in the propensity to consume does not affect the rate of interest at all. The rate of interest remaining constant, the optimum propensity to consume is *when the expenditure on consumption is such that a further increase does not any more increase the marginal efficiency of investment.* It has been mentioned already that this happens when the elasticity of supply of factors of production becomes zero, so that an increase of the expenditure on consumption only raises their prices but cannot increase investment. This implies the absence of even voluntary unemployment of factors of production. If involuntary unemployment of a factor is defined by its supply being infinitely elastic, it is absent whenever the elasticity of supply is finite. A zero elasticity of supply, however, means that there are no more factors which would offer their services if the remuneration were greater, i.e., are voluntarily unemployed. Until this stage is reached any increase in the propensity to consume stimulates investment.[2] This fits well into the scheme of Mr. Keynes' theory.

---

[1] It seems, however, highly doubtful that $L_i = \infty$ over the whole range of the liquidity preference function.

[2] In the general case where the quantity of money is allowed to vary the same result is reached when $\psi_Y = L_Y$ (*vide* equation (10a)). In this case the income elasticity of supply of money is equal to the income-elasticity of the demand for liquidity; each change of total income is balanced by exactly such a change of the supply of money that the rate of interest remains constant.

The other special case is when the interest-elasticity of the demand for liquidity is zero which is, as we have seen, the case of the traditional theory. Then $L_i = 0$ (and $L_Y \neq 0$) and by rewriting equation (10) in the form:

$$-\frac{L_i}{L_Y} = -\frac{F_i}{F_c}$$

we obtain $F_i = 0$ for this case. *Any decrease in the propensity to consume stimulates investment* by causing an appropriate fall of the rate of interest. The propensity to save can never be excessive, for the rate of interest falls always sufficiently to make room for additional investment. The only limit is when a further decrease of the rate of interest stops increasing investment ($F_i = 0$), i.e., when the net return on investment becomes zero and the rate of interest is zero, too.

In the general case the optimum propensity to save is somewhere between these two limits and *it is the greater the greater the income-elasticity and the smaller the interest-elasticity of the demand for liquidity.* For the fall of the rate of interest due to an increase in the propensity to save is the greater the greater is the first and the smaller is the second of these two elasticities. The optimum propensity to save is also the greater the greater the elasticity of investment with respect to the rate of interest and the smaller the elasticity of investment with respect to expenditure on consumption.

Thus we arrive at the result that, with the exception of the special case covered by the traditional theory of interest, there exists an optimum propensity to save[1] which depends on the shape of the liquidity preference and of the investment functions. This imposes a maximum limit on investment per unit of time and any attempt to exceed it by raising the propensity to save above its optimum frustrates itself by leading to a diminution of investment.

---

[1] "Optimum" means here merely "maximising investment." This need not be the most desirable propensity to save from the point of view of social policy. From the latter point of view a propensity to save which maximises real income may be more desirable. My "optimum" propensity to save, however, maximises the speed of growth of wealth. (Footnote added in 1943.)

In a society where the propensity to save is determined by the individuals there are no forces at work which keep it automatically at its optimum and it is well possible, as the underconsumption theorists maintain, that there is a tendency to exceed it. Whether this is actually the case is a matter for empirical investigation and cannot be answered by the economic theorist.

The optimum propensity to save is, however, defined only with regard to a given quantity (or more generally: to a given supply function) of money. Therefore, if the propensity to save does exceed its optimum it need not be curbed to avoid its evil consequences. It can be made to benefit economic progress by an appropriate monetary policy which increases the quantity of money sufficiently to reduce the rate of interest so as to compensate the discouraging effect a high propensity to save has on investment.[1] How far such a policy is possible depends on the structure of the monetary and of the whole economic system.

---

[1] The requirement of an increase of the quantity of money to counteract an excessive propensity to save is *not* in contradiction with the teaching of Professor Davidson, Professor Hayek and Mr. Robertson that technical progress does not require an increase of the quantity of money to avoid deflation. If the increase in the propensity to save is accompanied by technical progress which increases the marginal efficiency of investment, investment is not discouraged and no increase of the quantity of money is necessary.

9

MR. KEYNES' THEORY OF THE "MULTIPLIER":
A METHODOLOGICAL CRITICISM*
By Gottfried von Haberler∥

I

According to Mr. Keynes, his analysis of the so-called "multiplier" is "an integral part" of his "General Theory of Employment" (p. 113). This multiplier, k, "establishes a precise relationship, given the propensity to consume, between aggregate employment and income and the rate of investment" (p. 113). "It tells us that, when there is an increment of aggregate investment, income will increase by an amount which is k times the increment of investment" (p. 115). "Before coming to the multiplier" Keynes introduces "the conception of marginal propensity to consume" (p. 114). He calls Y_w income in terms of wage units, C_w and I_w are consumption and investment respectively also in terms of wage units. For our purpose it is not necessary to go into the choice of the units—a matter which Keynes discusses carefully. He points out that changes in Y_w must not be identified with changes in income in terms of product and with changes in employment. "The fact that they always increase and decrease together," however, makes it, in certain contexts, possible "to regard income in terms of wage-units as an adequate working index of changes in real income" and in employment (p. 114). Since our argument is independent of the unit, we may accept Keynes' choice and in the following discussion use the symbols Y, C and I alone without the subscript w.

---

* *Zeitschrift für Nationalökonomie*, Volume VII, 1936, pages 299–305.
∥ Harvard University.

Keynes assumes that "when the real income of the community increases and decreases, its consumption will increase and decrease, but not so fast" (p. 114). That is to say, ΔC and ΔY have the same sign, but $\Delta Y > \Delta C$. The marginal propensity to consume is defined as $\frac{\Delta C}{\Delta Y}$. If e.g., the marginal propensity to consume is $9/10$, that means that $9/10$ of a small increment of income will be consumed. If it is 1 the whole increment will be consumed, if it is zero the whole will be saved.

"This quantity (the marginal propensity to consume) is of considerable importance, because it tells us how the next increment of output will have to be divided between consumption and investment" (p. 115). Now,

$$\Delta Y = \Delta C + \Delta I$$
$$= \frac{1}{1 - \frac{\Delta C}{\Delta Y}} \cdot \Delta I$$

$\frac{1}{1 - \frac{\Delta C}{\Delta Y}}$ is, by definition, the multiplier, k.

Or $1 - \frac{1}{k}$ is, by definition, the marginal propensity to consume (p. 115).

It follows that if e.g. the marginal propensity to consume is $9/10$ the multiplier is 10; "and the total employment caused (e.g.) by public works will be ten times the primary employment provided by the public works themselves, assuming no reduction of investment in other directions" (p. 116–117). This result is clearly implied by the assumption: if we assume that an increment in Y is divided in the proportion of 1:9 between I and C, then we assume that an increase in I by X units will mean an increase of $9X$ in C and an increase of $10X$ in Y. If we assume the marginal propensity to consume to be zero, in other words that an increment in Y is wholly confined to I, then we assume that an increment in I increases Y by no more than its own amount. If the marginal propensity to consume is assumed to be 1, that is if we assume that "the next increment of output will have to be divided between consumption and investment" in the proportion of 1 to 0, then, in order not to contradict this assumption, we must assume that any increase in I is accompanied by an infinite increase in C and Y— we assume the multiplier to be infinity.

II

We have now to ask, what is gained by this procedure? In reality nothing more than that a new name is given to the multiplier. The multiplier is defined in terms of marginal propensity to consume. Instead of the multiplier we can always say $\dfrac{1}{1 - \dfrac{\Delta C}{\Delta Y}}$ and for marginal propensity to consume we can always substitute $1 - \dfrac{1}{k}$. One and the same thing has got two names.

Now, I do not question that sometimes it may serve a useful purpose to have two names for the same thing, but it seems that Mr. Keynes has fallen into the trap of treating such a relationship by definition as a causal or empirical relationship between investment and income and that thereby a large part of what he says about the multiplier and its probable magnitude is vitiated. By assuming something about the marginal propensity to consume he assumes something about the multiplier, but this is no more an explanation of the multiplier that pauvreté is an explanation of poverty.

Mr. Keynes has adopted exactly the same procedure in his Treatise on Money in respect to differences between savings and investment. As Professor Hayek and Mr. Hawtrey have emphasised, Mr. Keynes there defines savings and investments in such a way that an excess of savings over investments is identical with an equal amount of losses and an excess of investment over savings is identical with an equal amount of profits, so that for excess saving we can always substitute losses and for excess investment profits. But although he has identified these magnitudes by his definitions, he treats them on numerous occasions as cause and effect by saying that a certain event or measure or factor can cause losses or profits only if and in so far as it leads to excess saving or excess investment. If we insert the definition for these expressions this amounts to saying that certain events will cause losses or profits only if and in so far as they lead to losses or profits.

This mistake of treating relationships by definition as causal relationships occurs rather frequently in economics,[1] not only in Cambridge, so that it might be useful to analyse the multiplier case, which constitutes an interesting specimen of this fallacy, a little further.

III

The problem was originally to get a quantitative idea about the secondary effects of a certain piece of investment on employment and income. If the Government spends a hundred millions on road construction and employs thereby directly and indirectly a certain number of workers, how large will be the secondary effect? This is certainly a very important question and since it is impossible to estimate the secondary effect offhand, the problem must be closely analysed and various cases distinguished.[2]

Now Keynes approaches the problem by means of a terminological roundabout way, that is to say, by giving the magnitude in which we are interested another name. He expresses the multiplier in terms of marginal propensity to consume and treats the latter as if it were a thing in the real world which is independent from the

---

[1] The general aspects of methodology are discussed by F. Kaufmann, Methodenlehre der Sozialwissenschaften, Vienna 1935, pp. 32, 43, 48, 257. See also his article "On the Subject-Matter and Method of Economic Science" in Economica, November 1933, p. 387 et seq.

[2] Mr. Kahn stated the problem clearly in his well known article in the Economic Journal. For a theoretically correct and at the same time realistic discussion of the factors on which the result depends, see J. M. Clark, Economics of Planning Public Works (1935), p. 80 and seq. and E. R. Walker's illuminating article "Public Works as a Recovery Measure" in The Economic Record, Vol. XI, Dec. 1935. See also M. Mitnitzky, "The Effects of a Public Works Policy on Business Activity and Employment" International Labour Review XXX (1934), and H. Neisser, "Secondary Employment: Some Comments on R. F. Kahn's Formula" in Review of Economic Statistics. Vol. 18, 1936.

former, whilst in fact the two are closely connected by definition—so closely indeed that the author himself on one occasion forgets that they are conceptually not the same and treats them by mistake as synonyms (p. 123 and erratum on p. 403).

I still believe in the superiority of longer over shorter roundabout ways of production of concrete goods, but I am highly suspicious of terminological roundabout ways in the construction of theories. They cannot always be avoided, but they are dangerous, and in the case under review the verbal roundabout method has led to a confusing terminological duplication.

This criticism will be contested. Probably it will be urged that the deprecated roundabout way proves to be fruitful, since it is possible to make, on the basis of psychological observations of a general nature, a number of statements about the approximate magnitude of the marginal propensity to consume—statements which cannot be made directly about the multiplier. To confirm this, chapters 8 and 9 may be pointed to, where Keynes discusses in detail the objective and subjective factors which influence the propensity to consume. I do not question either the validity or the usefulness of these observations, and I readily agree that these psychological considerations do not apply except very indirectly to the multiplier and that therefore, if they are to be used in determining the multiplier, a bridge must be constructed to link them to it. There is, however, this difficulty. If we really can, on the basis of psychological considerations, guess in what proportions an increment in Y, however brought about, will be divided between C and I, we do *ipso facto* estimate the proportion by which an increment in I will increase Y. If we say something about the marginal propensity to consume, we say thereby something about the multiplier. The premise that we can say something on the basis of such psychological considerations about the propensity to consume sounds very plausible: the inference that the multiplier too can be completely determined by such familiar psychological considerations is manifestly precarious. This strongly suggests that something is rotten in the State of Denmark! It is not very difficult to see what is wrong. Keynes has in fact two different concepts of propensity to consume. In his arithmetics he uses it in the formal sense which we have discussed; in this sense it is by definition directly related to, and is another aspect of, the multiplier. In the chapters 8 and 9 where he discusses on what circumstances depends the proportion of a man's income which he spends on consumption, he speaks of the marginal propensity to consume in the ordinary or "psychological"[1] sense without realising that this is an entirely different thing. About the latter, we can, of course, make generalizations on the basis of our everyday experience derived from our own attitude towards increases in income and our observations of the behaviour of other people in this respect under various attendant circumstances. But from this the multiplier cannot be directly deduced. Keynes achieves this deduction only by substituting the propensity to consume in the formal sense for the propensity to consume in the ordinary sense. In other words, he now uses the same word for two entirely different things having previously bestowed two words upon the same thing. His terminology exemplifies the paradox of poverty in the midst of plenty.

It is easy to see that marginal propensity to consume in the formal sense, that is $1 - \frac{1}{k}$, is not the same thing as marginal propensity to consume in the ordinary sense. Suppose the latter is unity, that is to say, people spend all their additional income on consumption. What, under this assumption, will be the secondary

---

[1] The words "formal" and "psychological" are not well chosen. It would be better to characterize the distinction as "aggregate," "*ex post*," relating to society as a whole *vs.* "individual," "*ex ante*," relating to individuals rather than to corporations and governments. Evidently behavior patterns derived from individual psychology cannot be confidently expected to hold of corporations, governments and government agencies. Individual propensities cannot even be applied to groups without paying attention to changes in income distribution. Moreover, in order to obtain *stable* individual propensities to consume, it would probably be better to define them in the Robertsonian sense, that is $\frac{C_t}{C_{t-1}}$ where t and $t-1$ stand for successive time periods. (This footnote was added by the author in 1943. For further elaborations see Haberler, *Prosperity and Depression*, 2nd or later editions, Chapter 8, §4, especially p. 228 *et seq*.)

effects of public works? What will be the multiplier, that is $\dfrac{1}{1 - \dfrac{\Delta C}{\Delta Y}}$? Will the multiplier necessarily be infinite and the marginal propensity to consume in the formal sense unity? Not at all! How it works out, in the end, depends on many other circumstances, a number of which have been treated by Keynes himself and by Kahn, and especially by J. M. Clark, and E. R. Walker. It depends on the leakages discussed by Mr. Kahn;[1] on the time which is allowed to elapse; on the effects of the primary investment on other investment, that is, in the terminology of Mr. Keynes, on the marginal efficiency of capital;[2] on the velocity, especially the income velocity of money. If we say that according to our psychological experience people spend a certain proportion or the whole of their income on consumption, we do not mean that they spend it instantaneously, we mean that they spend it during the income period as fixed by the habits of payment. A multiplier of infinity, that is a propensity to consume, in the formal sense, of unity would involve a velocity of circulation of infinity—an absurd consequence which is not involved by the assumption that the propensity to consume in the ordinary sense is unity. For various reasons which I cannot discuss here, I am inclined to believe that usually the secondary effects of public works will be larger, if the marginal propensity to consume, in the ordinary sense, is larger than if it is smaller. There is, however, no close and unique

---

[1] Some of these leakages, not all, involve the assumption that the propensity to consume in the ordinary sense is less than unity.

[2] I am aware that Keynes speaks of net changes in aggregate investments in which these secondary investments are to be included. But to assume these secondary investments as given detracts considerably from the value of the theory. This reveals a significant change in the meaning of the multiplier. Originally it was defined as the ratio of the secondary to the primary employment, when the primary employment is that which is required by the production of a concrete piece of investment. Now that the meaning has been changed, we can no longer speak of primary and secondary. This alteration is symptomatic for the transformation of the theory of the multiplier from an empirical statement into a barren identity.

relationship between the marginal propensity to consume in the ordinary sense (as determined by the objective and subjective factors discussed by Keynes in his chapters 8 and 9) on the one hand, and the multiplier (and the marginal propensity to consume in the formal sense) on the other hand.

It could conceivably be objected that even in chapters 8 and 9 Keynes does not mean marginal propensity to consume in the ordinary sense, but that in the formal sense, and this objection could be corroborated by pointing to the definition of marginal propensity to consume at the beginning of chapter 8 (p. 90). If, however, this were the case, then the analysis of the objective and subjective factors determining the marginal propensity to consume is simply besides the point because these factors have clearly no direct bearing on the marginal propensity to consume in the formal sense and, what comes to the same thing, on the multiplier. In that case it also follows that the guesses about the probable magnitude of the marginal propensity to consume (which are erroneously extended to the multiplier), which are based on the analysis of the objective and subjective factors just mentioned, are unsupported and unsubstantiated statements.

An interesting illustration of the state of confusion is afforded by the following statement on p. 117: "An increment of investment in terms of wage-units cannot occur unless the public are prepared to increase their savings in terms of wage units. Ordinarily speaking, the public will not do this unless their aggregate income in terms of wage-units is increasing. Thus their effort to consume a part of their increased incomes will stimulate output until the new level (and distribution) of incomes provides a margin of saving sufficient to correspond to the increased investment. The multiplier tells us by how much their employment has to be increased to yield an increase in real income sufficient to induce them to do the necessary extra saving, and is a function of their psychological propensities." It is not easy to interpret this statement, since we must remember that, according to Keynes' terminology, aggregate (net) saving is by definition equal to aggregate (net) investment. Suppose e.g. that roads are being built by the Government with the value of 100 (wage units) and assume further that there are no repercussions whatsoever on other investment which is Keynes' own assumption (first line p. 117). Then according to Keynes these 100 wage units constitute an addition to total income, investment and savings, all three are being increased by the same amount, whatever happens to consumption. For any net increase in investment constitutes by definition also saving. What is then the sense of saying that income must increase by so and so much in order to induce income-receivers to provide the necessary saving? If we adhere to all the definitions given, the meaning can be only this: On the basis of the objective and subjective factors mentioned above, certain assumptions are arrived at about the actual magnitude of the propensity to consume in the psychological sense. Then the propensity to consume in the formal sense is substituted for the propensity to consume in the psychological sense. The quantitative estimate about the latter is thereby extended to the multiplier. By now everything is assumed. An increase in investment cannot occur without an increase in aggregate income as determined by the multiplier, not, as Keynes says, because otherwise the public will not be prepared to provide the necessary savings,[1] but because we have assumed that it cannot occur otherwise. The quoted statement turns out to be not an empirical statement which tells us something interesting about the real world, but a purely analytical statement about the consistent use of an arbitrarily chosen terminology—a statement which does not explain anything about reality.

IV

I do not deny that there are interesting observations and helpful hints in these pages on the multiplier. But they are thrown out incidentally as by-products and are, so to speak, not put in the right perspective. The consequences are rather serious. On p. 118,

---

[1] If there is an additional investment this is in itself, by Keynes own definition, savings and nobody is called upon to provide savings.

e.g., in application of the theory, the following statement is made:[1] "In actual fact the marginal propensity to consume seems to lie somewhere between the these two extremes, though much nearer to unity than to zero; with the result that we have, in a sense, the worst of both worlds, fluctuations in employment being considerable and, at the same time, the increment in investment required to produce full employment being too great to be easily handled."

I do not wish to discuss the truth or falsehood of the proposition that, as a rule, under certain circumstances, the secondary effects of increments in investment are such as Mr. Keynes says. It is perhaps possible to demonstrate that our economic world is so organised that the multiplier sometimes works out according to the quoted statement. But Mr. Keynes offers no adequate proof, only a number of rather disconnected observations (which could be used for the construction of an adequate theory). His central theoretical idea about the relationships between the propensity to consume and the multiplier, which is destined to give shape and strength to those observations, turns out to be not an empirical statement which tells us something about the real world, but a barren algebraic relation which no appeal to facts can either confirm or disprove.

---

[1] It should be noted that after the theory has thus been applied to practical problems, Mr. Keynes finds it necessary to qualify his theory very severely. But these qualifications are not expressly extended to the applications. This procedure, which is adopted more than once, makes the book very dangerous for the unguarded reader.

10

PERIOD ANALYSIS AND MULTIPLIER THEORY*

By Fritz Machlup||

This article is not an exegesis of the theory of the Multiplier; nor is it a critique; it attempts merely to be an analysis of some essentials of that theory. I intend to place much emphasis on points which have received little emphasis, if any, by the founders of the Multiplier theory, Messrs. Kahn and Keynes; and I shall employ a terminology of which they disapprove. Not that I wish to criticize them for their distribution of emphasis or for their use of terms. I have found, however, in countless discussions that the choice of terminology is not always quite disassociated from the importance which one wishes to assign to various problems. For a discussion of time lags, transition phases, and other intertemporal relationships, Keynesian terminology is not well suited. The time element in the theory of the Multiplier is, I submit, of great importance. Hence the use of concepts more appropriate for "period analysis"—such as the concepts employed by D. H. Robertson—recommends itself.[1]

Significant "Periods"

The meaning of "period analysis" is ambiguous, and recent discussion has suffered from a confusion of various sorts of "periods."

---

* *Quarterly Journal of Economics*, Volume LIV, November 1939, pages 1–27. Reprinted by the courtesy of Quarterly Journal of Economics and the author.

   || University of Buffalo.

   [1] The main difference concerns the concepts of "income" and "saving." While Keynesian concepts compare rates of flow at simultaneous instants of time, we shall employ Robertsonian terminology, for which saving is the difference between "today's" consumption and "yesterday's" income. The meanings of "today" and "yesterday" will occupy us presently.

Especially these four groups of periods are often confused with one another: transaction periods, income periods, plan adjustment periods, and equilibrium adjustment periods. They all have their place in economic analysis. The following digression on economic periods has, of course, wider application than merely to the theory of the Multiplier, and it is for that reason more detailed than would be necessary for an understanding of Multiplier theory.[1]

The concept of a "transaction period" is useful in order to take account of the facts that dates of receipts and outlays are usually fixed, and that nobody can spend any part of his receipts (gross or net income) before he receives it. (That one can borrow in addition to ordinary receipts, or spend out of a balance carried over from the past, are obviously important matters which no period-analyst neglects.) For some persons the (individual) transaction periods may be more significantly determined by fixed dates of heavy expenditures, or, more correctly, by the intervals between these dates, than by dates of receipts. (Example: the weekly or bi-weekly pay rolls of firms whose wage payments constitute a considerable part of their total money transactions.) For other persons fixed intervals between the dates on which they receive the largest payments affect their individual transaction periods. There are at least three different transaction periods which ought to be distinguished.

Transaction period A is the length of the cycle of ebb and flow in the balances of the individual cash holder; or, in other words, the time interval between the peaks (or normally recurring troughs) in his cash balances.[2] This period does not reflect either large or small amounts held permanently idle (i.e., throughout the period under consideration), or long or short average intervals between receipt and outlay. (If a firm pays wages every Friday, its transaction period A may be a week, whether the bulk of receipts come in earlier or later in the week or at an even rate.)

---

[1] I am indebted to Mr. Abba P. Lerner for suggestions which helped me to improve an earlier formulation of these passages.

[2] "Money" or "cash balance" include both currency and check deposits.

Transaction period B is the time interval during which money, both the currently received funds and the funds carried as more permanent reserve, can be said to rest, on the average, in the cash balances of the individual cash holder; or, in other words, the ratio of average cash balance to total of outlays; or, again in other words, the period of time for which total outlays are equal to the average cash balance. This period can be calculated for individual persons (accounts) or for groups of persons. For the whole economy it is the reciprocal of the transaction velocity of circulation.[1] For individual accounts transaction period B will be shorter than transaction period A, if the individual holds only negligible minimum balances; it will be longer, if minimum balances are considerable. For the economy as a whole transaction period B is almost certain to be longer than average transaction period A.

Transaction period C is the time interval during which currently received money amounts can be said to rest, on the average, in the cash balances of the individual cash holder, neglecting those amounts which are carried as a minimum balance; it is, in other words, the ratio of average minus minimum balance to the total of outlays; or, again in other words, the period of time for which total outlays are equal to the active part of the average cash balance; i.e., to the excess of the average over the minimum cash balance. Transaction period C is shorter than transaction period B, because it neglects the inactive part of the cash balance; it is also shorter than transaction period A, because the average interval between receipt and outlay is shorter than the interval between consecutive

---

[1] Professor Robert A. Gordon, in an article on "Period and Velocity as Statistical Concepts," *Quarterly Journal of Economics*, Vol. 55, 1941, pp. 306-313, objected to my interpretation of "periods" as reciprocal of "velocities." His main point is that the average of the periods of all individual balances or accounts is not the same as the reciprocal of the velocity in the economy as a whole. But he shows himself that this reciprocal is equal to the *weighted* average of the individual periods, each period weighted by the total annual expenditures out of each account. Averaging the periods of individual balances without weighting them by expenditures would surely be of no help in describing the national money flow. The same point refers also to others of our transaction and income periods. (Footnote added by the author in 1943.)

dates of periodic receipts or periodic outlays. For a person whose receipts come periodically while his outlays take place at an even rate (or *vice versa*), transaction period C will be half of transaction period A; if the same person carries no minimum balances, i.e., if he exhausts his balances completely, so that the lows are zero balances, transaction periods B and C will be the same.[1]

For persons whose receipts constitute their net income, the transaction period is an "income period." There are at least five different "income periods" which ought to be distinguished. The first three are analogous to the three transaction periods.

Income period A is the length of the cycle of ebb and flow in the cash balance of the individual income recipient; or, in other words, the time interval between the consecutive peaks (or troughs) in his cash holdings. For the wage earner paid weekly, income period A is a week; for the recipient of a monthly salary, income period A is a month.

Income period B is the time interval during which money, both the currently received funds and the funds carried as more permanent reserve, can be said to rest, on the average, in the cash balances of the individual income recipient; or the ratio of his average cash balance to his total outlays; or the period of time for which his total outlays are equal to his average cash balance.[2] Income period B for the whole economy is not the reciprocal of the income velocity of circulation. Applied only to check payments, it is the reciprocal of the velocity of circulation of income deposits (see Keynes' Treatise on Money); applied to all sorts of money, it is the reciprocal of the velocity of circulation of the money balances carried by income recipients. Income period B is greater or smaller than income period A, according as minimum balances are large or small.

---

[1] On the necessity and practicability of distinguishing between active and inactive balances (working balances and idle balances) see the excellent article by Professor Howard S. Ellis, "Some Fundamentals in the Theory of Velocity," *Quarterly Journal of Economics*, Vol. 52, 1938, pp. 431–472. (Footnote added by the author in 1943.)

[2] Further modifications of this concept result, if "net income" or, on the other hand, "outlay for consumers' goods" is substituted for "outlay."

Income period C is the time interval during which currently received money incomes can be said to rest, on the average, in the cash balances of the individual income recipient, neglecting the amounts carried as minimum balance; or, in other words, the ratio of average minus minimum balances carried by the income recipient to his total outlays; or the period of time for which his total outlays are equal to the active part of his average cash balance.[1] The average income period C for the whole economy is a much less significant factor than the differences between the income periods C of different classes of people. These differences are relevant for discussions of problems connected with the income distribution between "fast spenders" and "slow spenders."

Income period D is the length of time which it takes for money, both active and inactive funds, to complete a circuit flow from income recipient to income recipient; or, more exactly, it is the ratio of the existing money volume (i.e., average total cash balances) to the sum total of money net incomes; or, again in other words, the period of time for which the sum total of net incomes is equal to the existing money stock.[2] Income period D is not meaningful with respect to individual accounts, it is a concept which relates only to the whole economy or to a group of individuals in a certain region. Income period D is the reciprocal of the income velocity of circulation, or the period of time for which the income velocity of circulation is equal to one. It is obvious that income period D is longer than any of the other income periods, because it relates not only to the balances of income recipients but to all balances in existence. It includes, therefore, the sum of all non-income transaction periods which lie between the receipts of consecutive incomes.[3]

---

[1] See preceding footnote.

[2] Further modifications of this concept result if "income recipients' total outlays" or, again, "total outlays for consumer's goods" is substituted for "total net income."

[3] Professor A. C. Pigou, in his book on *Industrial Fluctuations*, London, 1937, p. 136, discusses what is here the income period D under the term "circulating period." (Footnote added by the author in 1943.)

Income period E is the length of time which it takes for the money in active circulation to complete a circuit flow from income recipient to income recipient; or, more exactly, it is the ratio of the active part of all cash balances (average total cash balances minus total of minimum balances) to the total of money net incomes; or, again in other words, the period of time for which the sum total of net incomes is equal to the total of active money balances.[1] Income period E is, of course, shorter than income period D, but considerably longer than A, B or C. Since it refers to the flow of money as it creates the incomes of consecutive recipients, income period E might be called the "income propagation period."[2]

None of the transaction or income periods implies any assumptions regarding fixed plans or fixed propensities on the part of the persons involved. Transaction period A and income period A may be quite influential in shaping the normal planning periods, especially as to budgeting and expenditure planning. But normal planning periods are less significant than *plan adjustment periods*. The concept of a plan adjustment period rests on the fact that plans remain unchanged over a certain time interval, even if conditions change. In most cases plans may be easily changed within an income period (in all senses), whereas in some cases plans may be fixed over more than an income period. The length of the plan adjustment periods of various persons is a function of their speed of reaction, which is, in turn, the result of psychological, institutional and technical conditions.[3] The first change usually will not be the

---

[1] See footnote 2 on p. 207.

[2] Our income period E, or income propagation period, may be understood as the sum of two periods, the interval between income receipt and disbursement plus the interval between disbursement and the receipt of this full amount again as income. Paraphrasing Professor Angell's expression, one may speak of the income-expenditure period and the expenditure-income period, the sum of the two being the income propagation period. (Footnote added by the author in 1943.)

[3] Since writing this article I discover that Professor Hicks employs an almost identical concept in his Value and Capital, pp. 123 and 247. There he speaks of "the length of time necessary for entrepreneurs (and others) to wake up and change their plans."

final plan adjustment; the final adjustment may come about as the result of a succession of little adjustments; the time it takes to initiate the adjustment may affect seriously the path toward a new equilibrium and, indeed, the position of the new equilibrium.

The direction of the change of plans is determined by a "given" state of tastes and propensities. There is sense in talking about propensities in this connection only if we may assume these propensities and preferences to be stable in relation to the length of adjustment periods (or, at least, to change only in a predictable manner). The adjustment of plans to changes in data is supposed to take place according to given propensities. Little can be said about any adjustment or equilibrium of any sort, if we may not assume that the propensities and preferences will be constant over the adjustment period. The constancy of a state of propensity may be safely assumed for the initial plan adjustments; whether it may be assumed also for long-run equilibium adjustments has to be seriously considered.[1]

The *equilibrium adjustment period* is the time interval during which certain (predicted) adaptations to certain changes in data are expected to work themselves out, either completely or so far that further repercussions may be neglected. One may limit the analysis of certain problems to a certain degree of adjustment or to certain types of adjustment, ruling out a number of repercussions which are expected to take place in an adjustment period of different length. Marshallian period analysis is a case in point. The final adjustment (final in the sense that further repercussions are neglected) will mostly be reached by a succession of little steps, but it is a quite legitimate methodological procedure to skip intermediate phases of transition, and try to confine the hypothetical prediction to the ultimate outcome. It is imperative, however, for many practical problems to form an estimate as to the actual length of the equilibrium adjustment period, and to ascertain whether or not one may safely assume all "other circumstances"

---

[1] Some propensities, on the other hand, may be fairly stable only in the long run, while wide fluctuations are likely during short periods.

which have a bearing on the outcome to be invariant over that whole period.

All four groups of period concepts have their role in a period analysis of the theory of the Multiplier. Some of the periods may be needed as tools of reasoning, others may be needed only to aid in estimating the length of the periods which are themselves inherent parts of the theory. For an elementary understanding of the underlying monetary mechanism, that is, of the money flow which "multiplies" an initial outlay up to a higher level of income, an income period concept is fundamental.[1] Which of the various income periods is relevant, and how long is it in terms of clock-time?

The Relevant Income Period

Let us try to make up a little story of a money flow that is started by an outlay of "new money," say, for building a road.[2]

At the moment when that increase in investment takes place and the outlay of the new money is made, a money income of exactly the same amount is received by somebody, to wit, by the workers employed on the investment project. We assume, as is proper for such stories, that nothing else has changed. Thus there is at that moment (or short interval) an increase in income which equals the increase in investment; that is, the instantaneous Multiplier is one.

The recipients of the income thus created, our road workers, are likely to turn around and spend the greatest part of the income for their consumption. In our story they take advantage of a cheap sale and buy new boots. This expenditure implies, of course, the receipt of the money by the shoe dealer. It happens, however,

---

[1] All problems which are relevant for the "Investment-Multiplier," i.e. the ratio of total income increase to primary investment, are a fortiori relevant also for the "Employment-Multiplier," i.e. the ratio of total employment increase to primary employment.

[2] There are those who feel that primitive stories are unworthy of being embodied in a scientific article. I believe, however, that if more such stories were employed by writers when they develop their arguments, they might avoid a good many pitfalls, or their critics, at least, might discover them more quickly.

that the latter, who sold the boots out of his stock, regards no part of the proceeds as his net income. Strictly speaking, such a liquidation of inventory should be called a disinvestment, but we shall quickly repair this damage to the simplicity of our story by having the shoe dealer re-stock with little delay. The money goes to a wholesaler and from him, *via* a collecting agency, to a shoe factory which increases its production in order to fill the increased orders. New workers are employed by the shoe factory, and they receive the money as their net income. The money spent by our first income recipients, the road workers, has now reached second income recipients, the shoe factory workers. If our road workers have remained at their employment (i.e., if the rate of investment is continued at the increased level), they may receive another pay envelope at just the same time that their former expenditure reaches the shoe factory workers, our second income recipients. The total increase in the flow of income above its size before the increase in investment exceeds the investment of the moment (or short interval) by the income of the second income recipients; the Multiplier at the particular moment is, therefore, greater than one.

The time interval between the first and the second increase in income was determined by the number of persons through whose hands the money had to pass, and by their particular transaction periods C, in addition to the income period C of our road workers. We should also point out (and hope that we do not thereby confuse the issue) that the length of some plan adjustment periods was involved too; the store keeper and the wholesaler had to increase their orders, and the shoe manufacturer had to increase his output. We may, however, assume here for the sake of simplicity that the reactions of all the persons involved were so fast that we need not reckon with any longer intervals than those which result from the circuit flow of money. Simplicity commands that we also neglect at this point another problem which is often connected with the emergence of increased demand: the problem of windfall profits on the part of the sellers.

On the other hand, we seem now to be ready for other, unexpurgated, versions of our story to the effect that the time interval between first and second income recipient will be replaced by a series of intervals of different length. Our shoe dealer, in this version, regards a part of his gross receipts as net income; the wholesaler, the collecting agent, and the shoe manufacturer do likewise; the second income is, therefore, split among all these people together with the shoe factory workers, leather dealers, leather dressers, tanners, etc. The average interval between the income receipt by our road workers and the income receipts by all these people who receive income out of the road workers' purchases is not something easily measured. Moreover, if our road workers did not spend all their money on boots but on a number of different things, then the "second income recipient" is a composite of several hundred different persons who receive their income at very different moments of time.

Our composite "second income recipient" will again spend a part of "his" increased income on consumption. We know already that the second receipt took place at very different moments of time. The expenditure, in turn, will take place after very different intervals, depending on so many individual income periods C, and gradually a third income receipt will arise. The "recipient" this time is a composite of tens of thousands of different persons; they will receive the income increases after intervals which include a varied number of transaction periods of varied length. It is easily conceivable that a fraction of the primary outlay will arrive at a "sixth" income recipient when another fraction is just arriving at a "second" income recipient. It is clearly imperative to simplify the analysis by thinking in terms of an average income period.

This average income period cannot be any of our periods A, B or C, because it has become apparent from our story that intermediate non-income transactions are a part of the intervals between the income receipts. Should income period D, the reciprocal of the income velocity of circulation, be the relevant interval? The income velocity of circulation for the United States has frequently been estimated at approximately 2 per year; Professor Angell estimated it at approximately 1.6 per year as a long time normal,[1]

---

[1] James W. Angell, "Money, Prices and Production," Quarterly Journal of Economics, November, 1933, p. 75; also The Behavior of Money.

and Professor Clark arrived at a velocity figure of less than 1.1 for the depression year 1932.[1] These figures correspond to income periods D of 6 months, 7½ months, and 11 months duration respectively. These periods are clearly much longer than the income period germane to our story of the money flow.

Income period D is of so long a duration because it refers to both active and inactive money balances. The income period relevant for our purposes refers to active balances only. The income period relevant for the circuit flow of newly created or newly activated funds must neglect the existence of balances with zero velocity of circulation. The possibility that splinters of the new money flow may come to rest through hoarding on the part of successive income recipients is accounted for, in the theory of the Multiplier, by the assumption of a dwindling series of derivative incomes; it must not be counted a second time by applying the low income velocity figure. The long income period D is not relevant for our purpose.

Income period E refers only to the active, or circulating, part of money balances; the inactive minimum balances are deducted. Income period E, the period in which total incomes are equal to the total of active balances, is much shorter than income period D. Unfortunately we have no information concerning the actual sizes of the active and of the inactive portion of our monetary stock. Information might be obtained at not too great expense. For a representative sample of accounts, minimum balances, average balances, and debits could be obtained, and transaction periods B and C calculated. Since the difference between transaction periods B and C hinges on the same distribution between active and minimum balances which is responsible for the difference between income periods D and E; since, furthermore, transaction period B and income period D are known for the economy as a whole, income period E could be deduced from the rest.

So long as we have no information, we must have recourse to guesswork. If we assume that between 50 and 60 per cent of all

---

[1] John M. Clark, Economics of Planning Public Works, Washington, D. C., p. 88.

balances are minimum balances (with zero velocity of circulation), an income velocity of circulation of between 1.6 and 2 per year for all balances would correspond to an income velocity of 4 per year for active balances only. This would mean that income period E, or, as we called it, the income propagation period, had a duration of three months.

This does not settle the issue. The "marginal" income propagation period might be shorter than the average income propagation period. To use a metaphor, a new tributary to the existing money flow might cause some swifter currents within the flow.[1] Increased incomes (and increased gross receipts) may be passed on faster than the average of previous incomes (and gross receipts). However, the opposite is just as easily conceivable. Although the presumption seems to be more in favor of a shortened income propagation period, we shall assume for the further analysis that the marginal propagation period is the same as that of the (guessed) average period, i.e., of three months duration.[2,3]

[1] This does not mean (abandoning the metaphor again) that formerly inactive funds are activated. Induced dishoarding is a separate problem. Here we speak only of the accretion to the money flow that started directly from the primary investment.

[2] John M. Clark, op. cit., p. 87, estimated the relevant period at two months. He based his estimate more on income periods A and C, thus neglecting intermediate non-income transactions.

Another question was raised by Professor Alvin H. Hansen in private discussion: Is the income propagation period, which refers to new additions to the money flow, not altogether different from the regular income period E? Was the latter not defined as the period which elapses until a receipt of, say, $100 income of one person becomes again $100 income of other persons—while we are now satisfied with the arrival of $60 or $80 at other income recipients in case the first income recipient withholds $40 or $20 from consumption? There is, as far as I can see, no essential difference between the two income periods. In the "stationary" income propagation period $100 become again $100 income, while in the "dynamic" income propagation period $100 may become only $60 or $80 income; but, for that, the latter need not be different in length from the former. What is withheld from expenditure will not arrive at another recipient; but what is spent need not arrive there any faster.

[3] Mr. Colin Clark estimated that the relevant income period was negligible, probably less than a week. (C. Clark and J. G. Crawford, *The National Income of*

Two more points should be mentioned before we proceed. The pure theory of the Multiplier usually abstracts from induced changes in liquidity preference and investment propensities, hence from induced dishoarding and hoarding. Through the medium of induced dishoarding on the part of business firms the actual propagation of incomes may be much faster than that which is possible on the basis of the circuit flow of money. For the present, however, we shall rule out induced dishoarding, as it has been ruled out by most writers on the subject.

The second point is an anticipated qualification of several propositions in our further analysis. The length of the income period will be found to be an important factor in the determination of the length of the adjustment period. Yet there is nothing which assures that the income period shall not vary during transition phases. We do not refer here to the shortening of the income period D through activation of idle funds (dishoarding). Income period E is independent of this. What changes income period E is the emergence of new, or elimination of old, intermediate (non-income) transactions. An increase in transactions arising from the transfer of assets might lengthen the income period; an increase in the use of money substitutes and of clearing arrangements might shorten the income period. The effects on the propagation speed of the new income flow may be considerable.

Australia, London, 1939, p. 96.) He reasoned on the basis of what I called the income period C, and forgot all about intermediate non-income transactions.

Professor Pigou, on the other hand, in a discussion of a similar problem, considered his "circulating period," that is, my income period D, as the relevant period and, on the basis of the income velocity of circulation in England, estimated that it was 6 months. (*Industrial Fluctuations*, op. cit. p. 137.) Thus, he failed to make the correction for inactive balances.

Professor Henry H. Villard, employing the same reasoning as I, arrived independently at an estimate of the relevant period of $3\frac{1}{2}$ months. (*Deficit Spending and the National Income*, New York, 1941, p. 256.)

Professor James W. Angell, also reasoning in terms of an "average circulation period of active money alone," and using figures from 1899–1929, computed that the length was between 3.15 and 3.33 months. (*Investment and Business Cycles*, New York, 1941, p. 145.) (This footnote added by the author in 1943.)

The Length of the Adjustment Period

The statement that an increase in the rate of investment will raise the rate of income by an amount which is a certain multiple of the amount of the additional investment can be true only after the lapse of a certain period of adjustment. One factor which affects the length of the adjustment period is the length of the income period.[1] Another major factor is, as will be shown presently, the actual value of the Multiplier, the length of the adjustment period varying directly with the value of the Multiplier.

With the Multiplier equal to one, the final rate of income is, of course, reached simultaneously with the increased rate of investment, or without any time lag. The Multiplier is equal to one, if there is no secondary income, that is, if the primary income recipient uses no part of it for consumption expenditures. (If the reader finds it hard to assume such a thing, let him imagine that the income recipient has had pressing bank debts which he repays or reduces with the increment to his income.)

With the Multiplier equal to infinity the "final" rate of income would be reached only after a time lag of infinite length. Table 1 may illustrate this case, which is hardly a possible one, because the duration of fixed propensities (to consume, to save, to invest, to be liquid, etc.) will be shorter than the adjustment period: the propensities that would make for the infinite increase in income are likely to change after a finite time interval.

The assumptions which underlie the figures of Table 1—some of which are likely to be somewhat offensive to common sense—are these: (1) An additional investment at a rate of $100 per period is undertaken by the Public Works Authority and financed through the issue of securities which are bought by the Central Bank. (2) Every income recipient spends all of his income received on consumption goods.[2] (3) In spite of increased incomes, people do not

---

[1] By "income period" we mean here and in the rest of the article the period relevant for the propagation of income.

[2] We might say "domestic consumption goods." Foreign trade will be discussed in a later section.

wish to augment or reduce the absolute amount of their inactive money balances (i.e., their liquidity for speculative or precautionary purposes). (4) In spite of the increase in the public debt and in the monetary circulation, no change in "confidence" takes place, so that private investment incentives as well as speculative liquidity-preferences are unaffected by this influence. (5) In spite of the financing of the additional investment, interest rates and the availability of money capital remain unchanged, so that other investment activities are not affected by this influence. (6) In spite of increased incomes and increased demand, no increase in derived investment takes place, so that the extra-investment by the PWA

TABLE 1

Period	Income receipt												Total increase of income
	I	II	III	IV	V	VI	VII	VIII	IX	X	XI	XII	
1	100												100
2	100	100											200
3	100	100	100										300
4	100	100	100	100									400
5	100	100	100	100	100								500
6	100	100	100	100	100	100							⌄600
7	100	100	100	100	100	100	100						700
8	100	100	100	100	100	100	100	100					800
9	100	100	100	100	100	100	100	100	100				900
10	100	100	100	100	100	100	100	100	100	100			1,000
11	100	100	100	100	100	100	100	100	100	100	100		1,100
12	100	100	100	100	100	100	100	100	100	100	100	100	1,200

is not followed by any other investment increases. (This is really an impossible assumption, because there must be, at least for a time, increased investment in working capital.) (7) In spite of the increased demand for productive resources on the part of the PWA, cost of production remains unchanged, so that the extra investment by the PWA does not on this account change the rate of private investment.

These assumptions have merely the purpose of ruling out, for the time being, a number of problems which we prefer to deal with at a later stage of the exposition; problems which are usually hidden under two short-cut assumptions, viz., that the marginal propensity to consume is equal to one, and that there is a net increase in the rate of investment of $100.

It can easily be seen that, under these assumptions, the total increase in the rate of income rises in every income period. If marginal propensity to consume is to refer to the behavior of consumers, it makes no sense to state that with a marginal propensity to consume of unity the Multiplier is infinity: what is true only after a time lag of infinite length is not true in our world. If the length of the income period is three months, the Multiplier which corresponds to a propensity to consume of unity becomes 3 after half a year, 5 after a year, 9 after two years, 13 after three years, and so on.

We should point out, however, that we have here used the concept marginal propensity to consume in a sense in which it has been used by Keynes only in a few places in his General Theory, viz. as a psychological factor determining the behavior of consumers. Another definition is used when the relationship between the marginal propensity to consume and the Multiplier is said to be reducible to an algebraic expression between simultaneous rates of investment and rates of income. That an empirical phenomenon and an analytical (tautological) ratio cannot be one and the same thing is obvious. Professor Haberler has shown the difference in the logical nature of the two concepts of the marginal propensity to consume.[1] If one wished to apply the tautological concept of the marginal propensity to consume to the case of the gradual rise in the rates of income, one would have to state that the "marginal propensity to consume" is rising gradually from zero to unity—in spite of the fact that *every* successive income recipient spends *all* of his disposable income on consumption, that is to say, in

---

[1] Gottfried Haberler, "Mr. Keynes' Theory of the 'Multiplier': A Methodological Criticism," Zeitschrift für Nationalökonomie, Vol. VII, 1936, pp. 299–305.

spite of the fact that the "psychological propensity to consume" is unity throughout the transition period. It is, of course, the psychological propensity which will be referred to throughout the argument.

The thought that an infinite income corresponded to a propensity to consume of one prevented most writers from seeing that the marginal propensity to consume can be greater than one.[1] After all, the Multiplier cannot be greater than infinity! Yet the Multiplier can easily be greater than 3 after half a year, or 5 after a year, in spite of a three-month income-period—and it will be so if the marginal propensity to consume is greater than one. It is easily conceivable that income recipients increase their consumption by an amount which exceeds the rise of their received income. They can do this by borrowing or by dishoarding. Indeed, investigations in installment buying seem to indicate that increases of consumption in excess of increases in received incomes are actual occurrences.

If the marginal propensities to consume are between zero and unity, it is interesting to know the eventual Multiplier that would be approached after "full" adjustment.[2] But since the adjustment

---

[1] That the increase in consumption is absolutely greater than the increase in income, i.e. that $\frac{\Delta C}{\Delta Y} > 1$, refers to consumption compared with *received* income, hence to $\frac{\Delta C_t}{\Delta Y_{t-1}}$. If one applied Keynes' Multiplier formula of $K = \frac{1}{1 - \frac{\Delta C}{\Delta Y}}$ to the case of $\frac{\Delta C}{\Delta Y} > 1$, the Multiplier would be a *negative* value and the whole matter would refer to a diminished rate of investment (because if $\Delta C > \Delta Y$, then ΔI would be negative) instead of an increased rate of investment. The confusion arises from the fact that any increased consumption would, in turn, involve increased income, increased income again increased consumption—until the system would "explode." The crux is that it is not of much value to speak of simultaneous rates which are applicable to "any instant of time" and yet include all effects which take place only through time. In any finite period the Multiplier would, of course, be less than infinity, and the "tautological marginal propensity to consume," therefore, would be less than unity.

[2] We speak of "full" adjustment when further repercussions become so slight that they may be neglected.

period may exceed the calendar periods with which the Treasury and other authorities must deal, and, moreover, since we must not calculate with "given conditions" for too long a period, it is more important to know the Multiplier that may be expected to be reached after half a year, after a year, etc.

For small marginal propensities to consume, and hence small values of the Multiplier, the adjustment periods are short enough to be of practical significance. If the marginal propensity to consume were $\frac{1}{2}$ and the "full" Multiplier, therefore, equal to 2, the increased rate of income would come within 10 per cent of the full multiple after a lapse of only three income periods. (100 + 50 + 25 + 12.50 = 187.50.) This would mean that with an average income period of three months, the approximate adjustment period would be some nine months.

For a marginal propensity to consume of $\frac{2}{3}$, and a full Multiplier of 3, an increased income flow of 10 per cent below the full multiple of the extra investment would be reached after five income periods, or, according to our previous assumption, after fifteen months. (100 + 66.67 + 44.44 + 29.63 + 19.75 + 13.17 = 273.66.) The Multiplier after a quarter of a year would be only $1\frac{2}{3}$, the Multiplier after a year would be $2^{49}\!/_{81}$. Had the PWA, the Treasury, or the Banking authorities reckoned with the "long-run Multiplier," they would be considerably off the expected figures—even if all the other assumptions were less "incredible" than they unfortunately are.[1]

The Lag of Cumulative Income

For many problems the current rate of income is the significant factor. For other problems cumulative figures which include the

---

[1] Professor Paul A. Samuelson, in his article on "Fiscal Policy and Income Determination," *Quarterly Journal of Economics*, Vol. 56, 1942, p. 603, made the curious remark that I was among those attempting a "marriage" between the velocity and multiplier approaches and that my "velocity discussion of the first ten pages bears little or no relation to the . . . subsequent analysis." The relationship, I think, is clear: the velocity discussion serves merely to arrive at an estimate of the time dimensions of the multiplier effects. (This footnote added by the author in 1943.)

changing rates of income over a transition period are more significant. For an estimate of the income-tax proceeds for the next year or two, neither the full (long-run) Multiplier nor the value that the Multiplier may reach after certain dates is relevant. Since the rate of income rises gradually, a period of a year includes the low income figures which belong to the early phases of the adjustment period. The sum total of income increase of the first year after the beginning of the investment program bears to the sum total of additional investment a ratio which falls short of the ratio which the increase in the income *flow* bears to the *rate* of additional investment at the end of the year.

Let us assume, for example, a net increase in investment of $100 per income period and a marginal propensity to consume of $\frac{2}{3}$. The long-run Multiplier is 3; that is, the eventual increase in the rate of income would be $300. The Multiplier after one year would have reached, according to the above reasoning, $2^{49}/_{81}$, that is, the rate of income per period would have increased by about $260. The total income for the year would show a still more modest increase in relation to the total extra investment. With a total extra investment of $100 per income period, hence $400 for the whole year, the total increase of income would be $718.52 for the whole year $(100 + 166.67 + 211.11 + 240.74 + 718.52)$;[1] this is only a little more than $1\frac{3}{4}$ times the total investment increase.

The greater the long-run Multiplier, the more disappointing (relatively, of course) will be the short-run effects. A long-run Multiplier of 5, which would correspond to a marginal propensity to consume of four-fifths, would take an adjustment period of the length of 10 income periods in order to be approximated by a 10 per cent margin. (The income increase would reach $457 in the 11th period. See Table 2.) If the income period is three months, the adjustment period would be two and a half years. After a year and a quarter, i.e., in the sixth income period, the increase in the income flow would be about $3\frac{2}{3}$ times the rate of additional invest-

---

[1] The income level reached after the lapse of the fourth income period would not be included in the incomes realized during the first year.

ment; and the total increase in income since the beginning of the investment program would be about $2\frac{1}{2}$ times the total additional investment. These figures compare rather poorly with the full-fledged Multiplier of 5, yet they are, no doubt, the ones which have to enter into a realistic account.

If, therefore, the adjustment periods are longer as the Multiplier is higher, or, in other words, if high Multiplier values are not realized in short calendar periods, the short-run effects of public works will not differ so much as one might think for higher and lower marginal propensities to consume.

A Schematic Illustration

Some of the points discussed so far, and a few others to be dealt with presently, can be made much clearer with the help of a table showing the successive income payments. Table 2 assumes a marginal propensity to consume of four-fifths. We shall make again our whole series of assumptions, with the promise to drop most of them later. The second assumption (see above, p. 216) now reads thus: Every income recipient spends 80 per cent of his received income on consumption goods. Assumptions (3) to (7), which all had the purpose of ruling out any induced changes in private investment, may be retained here, except that assumption (3) should now read: In spite of the increased "savings" on the part of the individual income recipients, interest rates and the availability of money capital remain unchanged, so that other investment activities are not affected by this influence. If the marginal propensity to consume is defined in terms of wage units, we might add, for the sake of the simplicity of dealing in dollar figures, another assumption (8) to the effect that wage rates remain unchanged throughout the upswing of income which is created by the public investment program.

What Are the Leakages?

The marginal propensity to consume is, of course, not the same for all individuals; the value of the marginal propensity to consume for society as a whole will, therefore, depend on the distribution of the income flow among different individuals. We chose to conceal this problem—which is of importance because of the changes in income distribution resulting from the income change—by making the assumption that *all* individual marginal propensities to consume are four-fifths, so that each income recipient saved twenty cents out of each dollar received. These twenty cents represent the famous "leakage."[1]

Many of the critics of Multiplier theory were not able to interpret the leakage as anything but "hoarding." Accumulation of idle cash balances (and cancellation of bank deposits through debt repayment) was the only answer which these critics had for their query as to the nature of the leakages. This identification of the leakages with hoarding is liable to make full-blooded Keynesians furious. They usually react to it with an explanation of the meaninglessness of the concept of hoarding—in the Keynesian language—but they do not tell their misinterpreters "what happens to the leaked-out funds." They confine themselves to the contention that all that matters is the fact that these amounts are not spent on consumption. This answer, in turn, is apt to make their opponents furious.

As a matter of fact, it *is* irrelevant for the immediate effect what the nature of the leakage really is. It *is* true that it does not make any immediate difference "what happens to the leaked-out funds." But the critics have nevertheless a perfect right to know what happens if the funds are not "hoarded." Additional curiosity does more good than harm; and incidentally what happens to the leaked-out funds has its indirect bearing through its effects on liquidity, interest rates, debt structure, and other matters.

That the savings of individual income recipients may be used for debt cancellation, or for accumulating inactive savings deposits, or for piling up idle demand deposits are, of course, possibilities. If the banking system creates $100 in demand deposits by its acquisition of the securities which finance the PWA investment, and if (e.g.) the $36 which are "saved" in the third income period

---

[1] The problem of "leakages due to imports" will be discussed separately.

224   BUSINESS CYCLE THEORY

TABLE 2[1]

[1] See footnote on opposite page.

(Table 2) are used for bank debt repayments, the *net* increase in active balances in this period will be only $64. Exactly the same will be true if the $36 are employed to purchase securities from the banking system. And again the same will be true if the $36 are used to buy a part of the newly issued securities which finance the PWA investment. For if $36 of the new security issue is bought "out of current savings," only $64 will flow from new bank credit as a "contribution to income." The critics were not able to see that the $36 would constitute a leakage, even if they were "invested," because they overlooked the fact that it had been *assumed* that no additional investment over and above the $100 PWA investment was being made. Hence, if the $36 were not hoarded but "invested," they simply alleviated the demands on the banking system. As to the effects upon secondary income, it did not matter what happened to the saved funds, as long as the assumption was maintained that the total net increase of the rate of investment was no more and no less than $100.

The secondary saving, as the voluntary saving out of the secondary incomes may be called, increases with the secondary income from period to period. If the rate of total investment remains constant, as has been assumed, an increasing part of the public investment outlay will be financed out of voluntary saving, or, at least, offset by voluntary saving. The continuing PWA investment will, therefore, make smaller and smaller net contributions toward further increases in income. In the 12th income period, for example (to illustrate again with our Table 2), secondary saving is $91.40, so that only $8.60 of the public investment

---

[1] It should be kept in mind that in the table "income period" stands for "income propagation period," and not, as one might think, for the individual income periods "A" of the first income recipients. If the income propagation period were twelve weeks, but the primary investment were paid out in weekly periods, $100 per income period would mean $8.33 per week. (It would, of course, be possible to construct a table with weekly payments which reach the next income recipient after so many weeks as correspond to the income propagation period. The intermediate non-income payments might be entered in such a table. The gain for "realism" would be a loss for "simplicity.")

during that period is of expansionary character. Income in this period rises, accordingly, only by $8.60 above the income of the preceding period. In the 15th period more than 95 per cent of the public investment can be financed out of voluntary savings. The income flow approaches a new equilibrium level as the amount of voluntary additional saving approaches the amount of additional investment. When almost the entire outlay for the public investment can be financed directly or indirectly by voluntary saving, the continued investment outlay will not result in any further increase in income.

It will be noted that the rate of income reaches practically its new equilibrium level (the famous multiple of the rate of investment) at the time when the rate of investment no longer exceeds the rate of voluntary saving. This is a remarkable meeting of the timeless and the period analyses of Saving and Investment: the Multiplier principle will have worked itself out when saving out of received income becomes equal to investment. The emergence of a new equality of saving and investment (in the Robertsonian sense) marks the end of the adjustment period for the (Keynesian) Multiplier principle.

The Leakage Through Imports

The leakages in the income stream which were attributed to various forms of saving are different in nature from the leakages attributed to imports. In a superficial account, however, they look much alike. The part of income, for example, which is applied to the repayment of a bank loan will cause a reduction of bank assets ("loans and discounts") and an equal reduction of bank deposits. The part of income which buys imports will likewise cause a reduction of bank deposits and of bank assets (the reduced assets being "due from foreign banks" or "reserve with central bank," directly, and "gold," indirectly). Indeed, were the whole Multiplier theory not based on the condition of an elastic credit supply, one might enlarge upon the more stringent effects which the increased imports are likely to have owing to the loss of bank reserves.

The error in this type of reasoning lies in the neglect of the increase in foreign incomes derived from the increased domestic incomes. If it is assumed that a certain part of any domestic income increase will be used for purchasing not domestic but foreign consumers' goods, then we must go the whole length and assume that a certain part of any foreign income increase will be used for purchasing imports and will thus create, through "our" increased exports, a further domestic income increase. If the foreign country does not itself pursue expansionary policies, so that the increase in "our" imports is the only contribution to the foreign income increase, then we must, of course, not expect that our increased imports will bring forth an equal increase in exports; but they will bring forth some increase in exports. It is likely that the income propagation period becomes longer because of a time lag of exports behind imports, although the opposite result is also conceivable. If the foreign countries happen to engage in the same expansionary policies, the increase in exports might equal the increase in imports, and the "net-leakage" through foreign trade would then be absolutely zero.

One might hold that the increased imports which result from the increase in income constitute "leakages for the time being," and that an eventual increase in exports should be treated as a separate, new impulse. Such a procedure would be most arbitrary; it would involve coupling a timeless Multiplier theory with a time-conscious foreign trade theory. Consistent timeless analysis would have to include the increased exports no less than any other derived purchases in the aggregate income increase. If period analysis is applied, it becomes obvious that the increase in exports is likely to come about within the adjustment period and, therefore, that imports must not be treated as net leakages. Only when the country is very small in comparison with the rest of the world is the error involved in neglecting induced exports slight.[1] In this

---

[1] The problem of induced exports is fully treated in my book *International Trade and the National Income Multiplier*, Philadelphia, 1943. (Footnote added by the author in 1943.)

case the full "leakage through imports" may be accepted as a sufficient approximation.[1]

Dropping Some Assumptions

Any statement which "predicts" a certain income increase as the result of a certain amount of public works and of a given propensity of consumers to use a certain portion of their income increase for increased consumption is based on a fundamental assumption: viz. that the identical amounts which are spent by consumers are eventually received by income recipients. This implies that business firms expend no less and no more than they receive, which will be true only (1) if they do not increase or decrease their investments, and (2) if they do not change the minimum cash balances which they carry. These two conditions were the gist of those contained in the list of assumptions which we put as preamble to Tables 1 and 2. The probability that these conditions will be fulfilled is almost nil.

Equilibrium analysis is generally not vitiated by the discovery that things which in theory are assumed to be unchanged are likely to change in reality, if only these changes are either independent of the analyzed causal relationship or if their influence upon the outcome is negligible. That conditions *may* change is no argument against assuming them to remain unchanged. But conditions which *must* significantly change, or are most likely to change when a certain event occurs, should not be treated as unchanged in an applicable theory of the effects of that same event.

Several of the assumptions made in the theory of the multiplying effects of public works involve conditions which are liable to change, not only independently but as direct or indirect effects of the additional investment and the increased income. There is, first of all, the inducement to invest which is affected by the "primary investment," that is, in our case, by the outlays on public

---

[1] It ought to be mentioned at this point that other factors which are sometimes treated as leakages, such as "saving on the dole" or displacement of private investment, should be dealt with as factors influencing the rate of investment increase, not as leakages from the income flow.

works. Private investment will be affected on four counts: first, because of the change in effective demand; second, because of changes in the state of confidence; third, because of changed production costs; fourth, because of changes in interest rates and in the availability of capital. All of these may affect private investment in either direction, the net resultant being determined by the relative importance of the component forces.

Effective Demand

The income flow which is created by the public works may decrease private investment by facilitating disinvestment. In the early phases of a public works program, especially if it is started before the downswing has reached its bottom, private disinvestment may easily be the concomitant of public investment: firms sell out of inventories which they do not replace at the time; the new money flow then disappears immediately through the leak of liquidation (unless dividend payments are increased).

In a later phase of a public works program, when disinvestable inventories are exhausted, a tendency toward increasing the marginal efficiency of private investment seems to be obvious. To satisfy the increased consumers' demand through increased production of consumers' goods implies increased investment in *working* capital. Any appreciable increase in employment above the public works employment will clearly bring with it increased outlays for building up inventories: the principle of acceleration is set in operation with respect to working capital both more certainly and much earlier than with respect to durable equipment.

In a third phase increased investment in *durable* equipment will be induced by the continued rise in effective demand, unless such inducement is offset by opposite forces. The neglect of opposite forces and, therefore, the active interplay between Multiplier and Acceleration principle was perhaps the substance behind the pump-priming theories of recent years.

The assumption that private investment remains unchanged, and hence the theory that the income increase will tend toward its multiple of the public investment, would fit in our world only the conditions prevailing at the transition stage between the first and second phase, when disinvestment through inventory liquidation and induced investment in inventory accumulation just balance each other. A justification of the assumption of unchanged private investment might, however, also be found in the idea that the building up of inventories would merely be a temporary adjustment whose effects would not change that long-run equilibrium level of income which corresponds to a permanent rate of public investment.

For an analysis of aggregate income and aggregate spending it seems to be a rather arbitrary procedure to single out the marginal propensity to consume and to shove aside the marginal propensity to invest. A rise of a craftsman's income, for example, may induce him to buy a new hammer just as it may induce him to buy new boots. To include the boot purchase (through the assumption of increased consumption), but to exclude the hammer purchase (through the assumption of unchanged investment opportunities), has the sure advantage of making possible a theory with simpler formulæ but the disadvantage of making that theory less applicable.[1]

The State of Confidence

Prejudice more than experience and common sense often make for certain changes in the state of confidence, which may either reinforce or offset the effects of the public works outlays. "Confidence" is an aggregate of vague ideas about general prospects of profits or losses, influenced mostly by expectations as to general price movements, taxes, restrictions, and the like. Unbalanced budgets and a rising public debt, both involved in a public investment program, may easily affect the state of confidence and, thereby, the inducements for private investment. While the fear

---

[1] On the other hand, the marginal propensity to invest is much less likely to be stable than the marginal propensity to consume, the latter being based largely on consumers' habits, the former on entrepreneurs' conjectures. On this score, it is probably the wiser procedure to include induced consumption expenditures in the "model" while induced investment outlays are excluded. The latter would then have to be taken into account by special assumptions as circumstances may require. (Footnote added by the author in 1943.)

of an immediately imminent inflation might lead to a wave of heavy private investment, vague uneasiness and uncertainty might lead to a decline in investment offsetting the effects of the public outlays.

"Confidence" not only affects investment directly as a part of the investor's expectations (i.e. as a part of the marginal efficiency of capital); it enters in a second time through its influence upon lenders, the resulting effects upon interest rates and the availability of capital.

Cost of Production

Both primary public investment and secondary consumers' demand are likely to raise the prices of some factors of production. Higher cost tends to reduce the marginal efficiency of investment. While the expectation of quickly rising costs may temporarily increase private investment, the persistent effect of increased costs of production is certainly toward a diminution of private investment. The level of production cost may indeed be the critical factor in the whole question of private investment and employment. A mere sign-post must suffice here; a discussion of the point would go much beyond the scope of this article.

Interest Rates

It is conceivable that interest rates may remain unchanged in spite of the additional investment and its results; but this is not likely to be the case. The ways of financing the extra investment, on the one hand, and changes in liquidity-preference, on the other, would not be without influence. Higher interest rates would restrict, lower interest rates would enhance private investment activities. Of importance also, in a world of credit rationing, is the fact that the "internal rates of interest" of individual business firms may be higher than the rates at which they actually borrow. If, because of narrow lines of credit, firms cannot borrow as much as they would like to, the marginal efficiencies of the funds which are available to them constitute their internal interest rates. It has been mentioned above that changes in effective demand are likely to change the schedules of marginal efficiencies of investment. No matter whether and in what direction such changes occur, the internal interest rates of firms may be automatically diminished (along the revised schedules) when, through increased demand, increased proceeds (profits) make more funds available to the firms. The public investment may have been financed by a banking system with large excess reserves and, hence, perfectly elastic credit supply—in other words, under unchanged market rates of interest; yet internal interest rates to secondary money recipients may be reduced. Even a slight rise in the market rate of interest may be compatible with a reduction of many an internal interest rate, if the funds of the "primary" borrower—the PWA—reach secondary recipients who had been able to borrow only less than they demanded. It should be repeated that the "external" rates of interest charged to particular firms may also be changed simply as a result of changed risk estimates.

Ordinarily, however, the fact that the banking system may be able to finance the additional investment only under rising interest rates would imply—unless the marginal efficiency of capital had already risen—that private investment is encroached upon by the public investment. If the capacity of the banking system to create credit was small—as was the case in many Central European countries—public loan expenditures would be almost completely at the expense of private investment; and the Multiplier theory of public works would be of little use. To be more exact, one should state that, in a system incapable of creating money, the funds for public investment may be drawn, through increased interest rates, from three sources: (*a*) from the investment funds of private industry; (*b*) from dishoarded idle balances; (*c*) from increased voluntary saving. Only source (*b*) would have any multiplying effects upon income. The theory that the interest rate cannot rise unless "liquidity-preference" rises has no explanatory value. Those who hold this theory would readily admit that the funds drawn from inactive balances will be "held" in (consecutive) cash balances for transactions purposes, and will become available for inactive reserves only very slowly and to the extent that secondary savings are brought forth. If an increased income level is to be supported by a fixed quantity of money, with unchanged preference to be liquid for speculative purposes, the interest rate would have to remain at an increased level, and public investment would *for the larger part* be permanently at the expense of private investment.

If the banking system is capable of creating credit, and if a part of the public investment is directly or indirectly financed by the central bank, the liquidity of the member banks and, as secondary savings come forth, the liquidity of individuals and firms will be increased. A fall in interest rates will most likely ensue; and private investment may, therefore, become more attractive. There is another reason why interest rates may fall (or money capital become more easily available to potential investors). The increase in effective demand, which is the very essence of Multiplier theory, may lead to a fall in the liquidity-preference for speculative purposes. This would probably occur if price increases resulted from the increased demand and were expected to continue. Unfortunately, exactly the contrary development is not impossible either; "confidence" may change for the worse, and liquidity-preference may increase.

The complete unpredictability of changes with respect to idle balances deprives any statement about the multiplying effects of public works of most of its predictive value. And, incidentally, there are many cases for which the tools "liquidity-preference" and "marginal propensity to consume" fit only under strain. Take the case of business corporations which make increased profits from their sales of consumers' goods and retain a part of these profits in the form of idle cash and PWA-financing securities. Must we then speak of a decreased marginal propensity to consume (although corporations can never be said to consume at all, but merely to influence their stockholders' consuming power by greater or smaller profit distributions) and, at the same time, of an increased liquidity-preference (although the relative distribution of wealth between cash and other assets may not have changed)? Anyway, in whatever terms we put it, the fact would remain that the money spent on consumption by one income recipient would not reach the next income recipient to the full amount; and the Multiplier would be less than the "psychological marginal propensity to consume" would lead us to expect.[1]

Every proposition can be made "true under all circumstances," if it is reduced to an empty tautology. This can be easily done with the theory of the Multiplier. Instead of speaking of a certain amount of public works, one can speak of a certain net increase in the rate of aggregate investment. And instead of speaking of a certain psychological propensity to consume, one can speak (see above, p. 218) of a ratio between investment and total income. But it should be clear that the theory of the Multiplier is then of no use. It would not refer to the possible effects of public works, because public works are not likely to be identical with the "net increase in the rate of aggregate investment." And it would not refer to the typical behavior of consumers, but rather to an infinite number of possible events whose composite but wholly unpredictable effect is expressed by a term confusingly named "propensity to consume."

The theory of the Multiplier, if it is to be of use to those who wish to know the possible and the probable effects of public works, must renounce the attractive appearance of neatness and preciseness. The two variables which seem to play the main parts in the play of the Multiplier must be decomposed into the all too large number of variables which play the important rôles in the real world.

---

[1] That business firms retain part of their profits and hold them in cash or securities can, after all, not be said to be a function of an increase in real income and of the propensity to consume a certain part of it.

11

BUSINESS ACCELERATION AND THE LAW OF
DEMAND: A TECHNICAL FACTOR IN
ECONOMIC CYCLES*

By John Maurice Clark‖

I. Introduction

The publication of W. C. Mitchell's book, *Business Cycles*, has rendered obsolete all attempts to explain crises in terms of any one fact or any one narrow chain of causes and effects. The central problem, however, is as clearly defined throughout his remarkably comprehensive study of the details of the actual process as in more abstract treatments of single phases of it. It is the question why business adjustments do not stop at a point of equilibrium, but go on to a point from which a more or less violent reaction is inevitable, and so on without apparent end. And it seems probable that of all the many circumstances which at every stage of the cycle lead to the next stage, the greater part can hardly be held primarily responsible for this primary fact; certainly not all are responsible in equal measure.

Disturbances originating outside the business world, so to speak, such as wars and crop fluctuations, can scarcely be held primarily responsible. Some such disturbances there are bound to be, and our system seems capable of manufacturing its crises out of any raw material that comes to hand, when the crisis is due, and of rising superior to serious provocation at other times. Some forces act to spread the effect of prosperity or adversity from one industry to

---

* *The Journal of Political Economy*, Volume XXV, Number 3, March 1917, pages 217–235. Reprinted by the courtesy of the University of Chicago Press and the author.

‖ Columbia University.

another, thus insuring that a boom or sharp crisis will effect industry in general, but they cannot be held responsible for the condition which they merely transmit. Nor can the familiar "forces of equilibrium" be held responsible, though they are acting at all stages of the process.

There is one circumstance whose natural effect is different from all of these in that (1) it acts as an intensifier of the disturbances it transmits and (2) without any diminution of demand to start with it can produce a diminution. It can convert a slackening of the rate of growth in one industry into an absolute decline in another. This circumstance is not psychological, nor does it depend upon the nature of our credit system, nor upon the distribution of income, but rather upon the elementary technical necessities of the case. It is concerned with the way in which the demand for finished products is handed on in the form of a demand for machines, tools, construction materials, and unfinished goods in general. This circumstance is not to be erected into a "theory of crises," but it is put forward as indicating that the purely technical side of this phenomenon is of prime importance, though it has been somewhat overshadowed by the more spectacular features of credit inflation, speculation, capitalization, and mob psychology, while its details have been blurred in the more general theories of "overproduction" or "maladjusted production."

II. Chief Data to Be Interpreted

There are certain outstanding facts in the behavior of crises which point in one direction and can be linked together by one explanation. It appears, first, that raw materials and producers' goods in general vary more sharply both in price and in the physical volume of business done than do consumers' goods, while wholesale prices fluctuate more than retail.[1]

The work of constructing industrial equipment appears to fluctuate more intensely than other types of production.[2] Its

---

[1] Mitchell, *Business Cycles*, pp. 502–503, and charts and tables, pp. 97, 100–103.
[2] *Ibid.*, pp. 471–72, 483–84, 557.

revival coincides, naturally, with a sudden and very great increase of investments. The failures which precipitate a panic are likely to be among producers of industrial equipment, although as to this "there is no general rule."[1] Another fact closely connected with those already mentioned is the shrinkage of merchants' stocks of goods in hard times[2] and their expansion in times of prosperity. Raw materials for manufacture are also carried in larger quantities at times when production is more active.[3] In point of time, also, it appears that raw materials take the lead, beginning to fall in price before the finished products, while "technical journals usually report that the factories and wholesale houses are restricting their orders some weeks, if not months, before they report that retail sales are flagging."[4] Mr. Babson notes in one of his reports[5] that "the production of pig iron forecasts the condition of the whole building industry and construction of all kinds," and that "the turning point of the statistics on new building has been from two years to six months earlier than the general crisis."[6] In 1907 a comparison of prices indicates that certain goods bought by producers reached their highest point and began their decline earlier than the goods sold by the same producers.[7] These latter were in some cases goods for consumption and in some cases tools, etc., to be used in further production. Manufactured producers' goods are not shown to be especially quick in feeling the upward trend of prices, though they rise farther than other types of goods.[8] The demand for consumers' goods fluctuates quite decidedly, but the

[1] *Ibid.*, p. 512.
[2] *Ibid.*, p. 452.
[3] *Ibid.*, p. 482.
[4] *Ibid.*, pp. 502–503 and charts and tables, pp. 97, 100–103. (Quotation is from p. 502.)
[5] Babson, *Reports*, 1914, Charts Nos. 612 and 598, cited by Warren M. Persons, *Amer. Econ. Rev.*, IV, 741.
[6] *Ibid.*
[7] Mitchell, *Business Cycles*, p. 501 and table, p. 98. Professor Mitchell's classification into "producers' and consumers' goods" does not quite accurately describe the commodities included in the table.
[8] *Ibid.*, p. 461.

greater part of its fluctuations appears to be the result of the changes in the amount of unemployment which result from the business cycle itself. Some changes in consumption are independent of this cause, and these may well be among the independent causes of business cycles, but it would seem that only a comparatively minor part of the total fluctuations in consumption can be of this character.

III. Industrial Expansion and Derived Demands

These data suggest a unified explanation, and group themselves about one industrial fact: the production of capital goods. Its importance has long been recognized, and several theories of crises have turned upon it. The aim of the present study is to present the underlying technical facts in a definite quantitative formulation.

Every producer of things to be sold to producers has two demands to meet. He must maintain the industrial equipment already in use and the stocks of materials and goods on their way to the final consumer, and he must also furnish any new equipment that is wanted for new construction, enlargements, or betterments, and any increase in the stocks of materials and unsold goods. Both these demands come ultimately from the consumer, but they follow different laws. The demand for maintenance and replacement of existing capital varies with the amount of the demand for finished products, while the demand for new construction or enlargement of stocks depends upon whether or not the sales of the finished product are growing.[1] Normally, over a long period of years, there is a certain demand for new construction on which producers can rely, and hence the demand for new construction is a normal part of any demand schedule for this kind of goods. But it does not come regularly.

---

[1] If demand be treated as a rate of speed at which goods are taken off the market, maintenance varies roughly with the speed, but new construction depends upon the acceleration. (Comment added on occasion of reprinting, 1943: It does not, of course, depend on this alone, nor should one expect that the relationship would be quantitatively simple, except in the hypothetical "perfect machine" here used to isolate this particular relationship in pure form. Some of the actual complications appear at later points in this essay.)

The nature of the mechanical law at work can be emphasized by imagining the industry reduced to a mere machine. Price, for the time being, is to be disregarded. Finished goods are turned out as fast as wanted, and materials and means of production are instantly supplied as fast as the process of finishing requires them. On this simplified basis we can predict accurately how the speed of the different parts of the machine must needs vary, and the results will furnish an index of the varying strains that are put on the much less mechanic a system that does these things in real life.

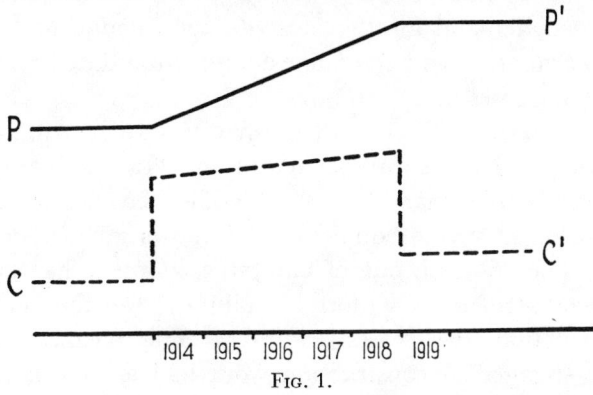

Fig. 1.

The figure represents the course of demand (measured vertically) over a period of years (measured horizontally). PP' represents the demand for the finished product and CC' the derived demand in an industry engaged in construction and maintenance.

The demand for a certain product, let us say, begins to increase steadily, each year seeing an increment equal to 10 per cent of the original demand. At the end of five years the increase stops and the demand remains stationary. If the productive equipment has kept pace with the need, it is now enlarged by 50 per cent and calls for 50 per cent more expenditure for maintenance and replacements. Meanwhile there has been an added demand for new construction equal in five years to half the entire original equipment. If renewals are at the rate of 5 per cent a year, the first effect of an increase in demand at the rate of 10 per cent in a year is to treble the demand for the means of production, since a demand for new construction has arisen twice as large as the previous demand for maintenance. At the end of a year the demand for maintenance has been increased because of the fact that there is now 10 per cent more capital to be maintained (see Fig. 1). Under practical conditions the increase in maintenance would probably be considerably less than 10 per cent, as it takes some time for the new machinery to be installed, and after that it is some time before it reaches its average condition of wear and tear. Until then the repair bills are comparatively light. However, this consideration does not affect the main feature of our problem, which is the suddenness of the increased demand for the means of production and the fact that it is far greater as a percentage change than the disturbance of demand that causes it.

What happens at the end of the five years when the demand stops growing? By this time the requirements for maintenance are 50 per cent greater than they were, while new construction has been going on at a rate equal to twice the original maintenance account. The total output of capital equipment has grown to three and one-half times its former volume. But the demand for new construction now ceases abruptly. This means that if the producers engaged in construction work had enough capacity to meet the demand of the fifth year, the sixth year would see them running with four-sevenths of their capacity idle.

This is a serious condition for any industry in the real world. It might well be serious enough to produce a panic if any considerable number of industries were in the same condition at the same time. And yet something like it is a normal effect, an inevitable effect, of changes in consumers' demands in a highly capitalistic industrial system.

Thus the law of demand for intermediate products states that the demand depends, not only on the demand for the final product, but on the manner in which that demand is fluctuating. A change from one year to the next in the rate of consumption has a temporary effect on the demand for the intermediate product which is greater than its permanent effect, in just about the proportion by which the total amount of investment in the intermediate product exceeds the amount annually spent for maintenance.[1] In order to bring about an absolute shrinkage in the demand for the intermediate product, all that may be needed is that the final demand should slacken its rate of growth. Making all due allowances for

---

[1] The assumption has been made that the new construction actually keeps pace with the demand for it, simply in order to have some figures that would not be too complicated. In fact, the supply is almost certain to fall behind the demand, thus lessening the amount of the overrun and of the ultimate revulsion without altering the principle at work. The law may be expressed algebraically, if the reader will remember that it represents only a purely mechanical view of the situation, and will supply for himself an allowance for the elements that are not included in the formula.

Let t = years elapsed between two dates, t_1 and t_2.

Let C = rate of consumption at time t_1.

Let $C + \Delta C$ = rate of consumption at time of t_2, the increase being distributed evenly through time t.

Let I = investment necessary to produce output at rate C.

Let L = average life of instruments included in I, in years. Then maintenance is required at the rate $\frac{I}{L}$. The demand for new construction during time $= I \frac{\Delta C}{C}$, an annual amount equal to $I \frac{\Delta C}{Ct}$. Demand for new construction is to previous demand for maintenance as $I \frac{\Delta C}{Ct} : \frac{I}{L}$, or as $\frac{\Delta C}{Ct} : \frac{1}{L}$, or as $L\Delta C : Ct$.

If L be large, as in the case of long-lived instruments, the disturbing effect is great. If it be small, as in the case of merchants' stocks of goods of sorts that are turned over rapidly, the disturbing effect is far less, though still appreciable.

The total demand for replacements and for new construction may be taken to have increased from $\frac{I}{L}$ annually, at time t_1 to an annual amount equal to $\frac{I}{L}\left(1 + \frac{L\Delta C}{Ct}\right) + \frac{I\frac{\Delta C}{C}}{L}$ or $\frac{I}{L}\left(1 + \frac{L\Delta C}{Ct} + \frac{\Delta C}{C}\right)$ at time t_2 after which it would drop to $\frac{I}{L}\left(1 + \frac{\Delta C}{C}\right)$.

The last term of this expression is exaggerated, as has been mentioned, by ignoring the fact that it takes some time for new equipment to reach its average condition of depreciation and renewal. Any attempt to avoid this would only complicate matters without any substantial increase in accuracy. If we are thinking of dealers' stocks of goods which change hands quite rapidly, the third term of the formula would hold substantially true.

mitigating factors in translating the illustration back into real life, it is still difficult to see how the building and machine-making industries can possibly avoid the disagreeable experience of outgrowing themselves in time of prosperity. For demand can never be expected to grow at an absolutely steady rate, and the slightest fluctuation seems destined to put the producer of capital goods in a situation comparable to that of a passenger forcibly carried by his station.

This principle may be illustrated by a town which grows rapidly up to the size at which its industrial advantages are fully utilized and beyond which its normal production can expand but slowly. When the point of transition is reached from rapid to slow expansion, the town may find that it has outgrown itself by the number of people engaged in the extra construction work involved in the process of growing. Houses to take them in, stores to feed and clothe them, trucks to haul the materials they work with, offices, etc., all will be demanded, and thus a boom may be created which is none the less temporary for being based on tangible economic needs. The experience of the boom town has been common enough in the growth of our western country, and the blame need not be laid entirely upon the vagaries of mob psychology. In a similar way the great work of rebuilding which must follow the present war will give rise to a huge temporary addition to the demand made upon the industries engaged in reconstruction, and as this special work is accomplished and a state of slower and more natural growth takes its place, these industries will have to count on a corresponding shrinkage, not merely relative, but absolute. This will almost inevitably lead to a depression, and, if unforeseen, it may lead to a crisis.

IV. Derived Demand Fluctuates First

This principle has another very interesting consequence. So far as the demand for new construction follows this law it not merely fluctuates more than the demand for the finished product;

it also fluctuates in a way which gives it all the appearance of leading instead of following in point of time. This can be clearly seen if the course of business activity is represented by a curve as in Fig. 2 instead of by the straight lines used in the previous diagram.

In this figure the curve which represents the rate at which the wholesalers take the finished product from the manufacturer is drawn on the assumption that the normal stock of goods in the hands of all the dealers is equivalent to four months' consump-

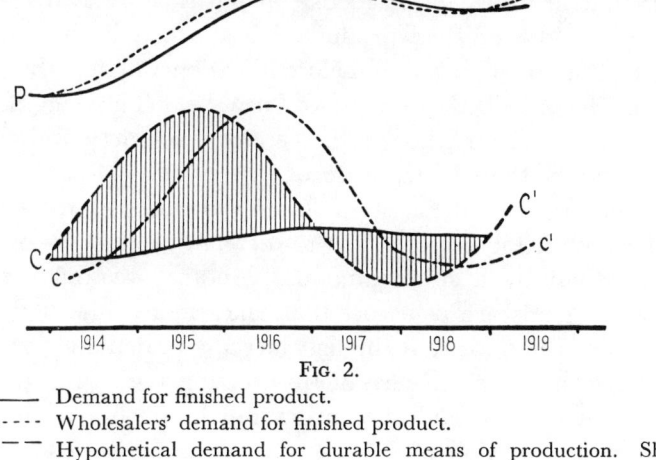

Fig. 2.

───────── Demand for finished product.
---------- Wholesalers' demand for finished product.
── ── ── Hypothetical demand for durable means of production. Shaded area shows excess or deficiency as compared to needs of maintenance.
─·─·─·─ Hypothetical demand for durable means of production with allowance for lagging.

tion. The curve which represents the course of demand for a durable instrument of production is drawn on the assumption that the life of the instrument is approximately eight years. Had a longer life been assumed, the disturbance shown would have been much more marked. No necessary relation is assumed between the absolute heights of the upper and lower pairs of curves, the significant thing in each pair being the percentage fluctuation.

The need for new construction, indicated by the shaded area, reaches its maximum when the demand for the final product is at its point of fastest growth. As soon as this rate of growth slackens and long before it has reached its highest point the need for new construction has started downward. The curve CC' represents the same impossibly fluid condition of industry that was previously assumed, in which the need for new construction is satisfied as soon as it arises. The curve cc' is closer to the facts, for it represents the work of supplying the derived demand as lagging somewhat. It shows that, even allowing for this natural lagging, one might well expect to find some, at least, of the businesses that furnish capital goods starting their revival before the demand for the finished products has reached its bottom point, and starting their reaction before the demand for the finished products has reached the crest of its wave. This lagging would naturally be more marked in the case of machinery and construction generally than in the case of raw materials, partly because the disturbance in the case of long-lived goods is more intense, and because it takes more time to increase production by a large amount than by a small amount. Another reason is that the long-lived goods are of a sort that takes more time to turn out, and a third reason is that the first increase in demand for finished products can be taken care of by utilizing the excess producing capacity which an industry using much machinery habitually carries over a period of depression. Thus they do not need to buy more equipment the instant the demand begins to increase.

The investment in long-lived instruments cannot be reduced as readily as it can be increased. It is reduced, if at all, by the slow process of starving the maintenance and replacement accounts in dull seasons, and this policy is conditioned by such complex technical relationships that it is impossible to reduce it accurately to any set formula. The deciding factor is economic rather than technical, it is the force with which the financial pinch is felt rather than the fact that the reduction in output has made some of the equipment technically superfluous. On the opposite side stand the optimism of the employer or his industrial pride, or other elements of the "personal equation." Thus the formula would be correct in representing replacements as diminished or postponed, but when it comes to estimating how much this postponement amounts to it is impossible to make any assumption that would not be quite arbitrary.

V. The Hypothesis Compared with Statistical Evidence

This hypothetical case agrees remarkably closely with the observed behavior of the demand for raw materials, manufactured producers' goods, and manufactured consumers' goods. It accounts for both the greater intensity and the greater promptness of the price movements of goods at the earlier stages of the productive process as compared to the final sale to the consumer, as well as for the fact that raw materials rise probably more promptly, if anything, though not more sharply, than finished instruments of production. The bigger the stock of goods as compared to the annual wastage and replacement, the greater this element of intensification becomes. Anything tending to reduce the size of stocks and to speed up the turnover would seem to be advantageous as tending to lessen this intensification, so long as the stocks do not become so slight as to create the danger of an absolute shortage in case of strikes, or poor harvests, or other unpredictable interference with the normal course of supply.

In attempting a more detailed test of this hypothesis, the railroads furnish the most favorable case, both because of the full statistics available and because the railroad is under obligation to carry whatever traffic offers at the time it offers, and so must needs adjust its facilities as best it can to the fluctuations of demand. It cannot "make to stock" in slack periods like the manufacturer. Thus the technical needs of the business are unusually free from disturbing financial influences. In the accompanying chart (Fig. 3) a comparison is made of railway traffic and purchases of cars over a period of fifteen years.[1] The results of this comparison may be briefly summarized.

---

[1] The data were taken from the Interstate Commerce Commission's *Statistics of Railroads in the United States*, with the exception of the line representing "cars ordered," which was taken from a chart made by the Brookmire service for Mr. E.

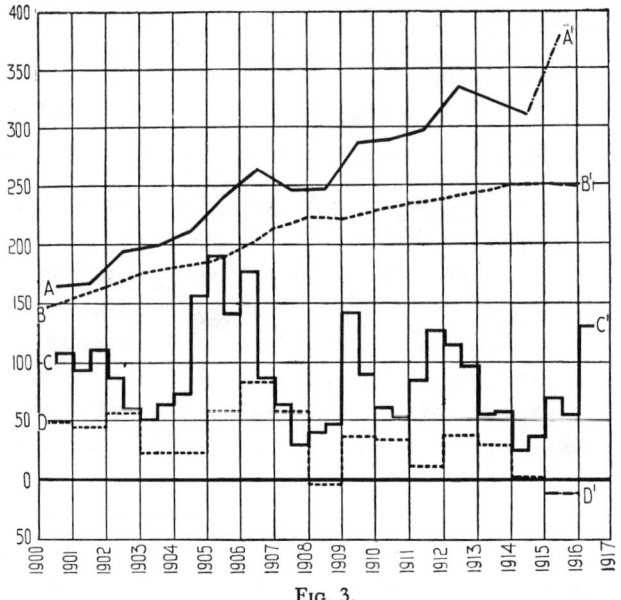

Fig. 3.

Line *AA'* represents traffic (ton-miles plus passenger-miles, 000,000,000 omitted) the total from July 1 to June 30 being plotted as one point at January 1.

Line *BB'* represents total cars in service June 30 (0,000 omitted).

Line *CC'* represents half-yearly orders for cars (000 omitted); taken from chart published by Mr. E. B. Leigh substituting horizontal lines covering an entire half-year for points located in the middle of each half-year.

Line *DD'* represents the yearly net increase in cars (000 omitted) divided by two in order to correspond with half-yearly figures for car orders.*

The vertical ordinates are drawn at June 30 of each year.

B. Leigh, of Chicago, and published by him in various pamphlets urging the importance of railroad purchases as a cause of general prosperity. The 1915–16 figures for traffic and the 1916 figures for total car equipment and net change in car equipment were taken from the preliminary report of the Bureau of Railway Economics, based upon the same figures published by the Interstate Commerce Commission. Since these reports cover fewer roads than the Commission's final figures, the totals would be misleading, and hence the net change between the 1915 and 1916 reports of the Bureau itself is used in placing the final points in lines *AA'*, *BB'*, and *DD'*. The resulting inaccuracy is so small as to be virtually imperceptible save in a chart drawn to a much larger scale than the one used here.

---

* By making the lower lines rectangular, a comparison is afforded of volume of demand for cars with rate of increase of traffic, and one that is fairer for judging

1. The percentage fluctuations in car manufacturing are vastly greater than in railroad traffic, though the line BB' indicates that they are still not nearly great enough to cause the equipment to keep pace with the needs of the traffic in its ups and downs, even if averaged over yearly periods.

2. The orders for cars have the appearance of fluctuating ahead of the movements of traffic. On the basis of this fact, Mr. E. B. Leigh, of Chicago, has urged in several addresses and pamphlets that railroad purchases are the cause of business prosperity. It seems undeniable that car orders reach their maxima and minima ahead of the index of general business activity, and even reach their maxima ahead of the maxima of railway traffic itself. As here analyzed, however, orders for cars do not move in

---

how the significant data compare in point of time than if two lines of the same sort, rectangular or otherwise, had been plotted against each other.

If both lines were made rectangular, the growth of traffic would appear as taking place at one instant. Car orders would have the appearance of growing a half-year ahead of traffic, merely because the first half of the period of growing traffic would not appear in the graph. If both lines were plotted as the upper one is, on the single-point system, a fairer result would be obtained with regard to the high and low points of car orders. In this case, however, another significant set of facts is wrongly dated; namely, the beginning of an upward or downward bend in the slope of the traffic curve as compared to the beginning of the rise or fall in the absolute volume of car orders, with which it is to be compared. The beginning of a bend in the traffic curve is postponed, while the beginning of an absolute rise or fall in car orders is dated ahead, if both are plotted in this way.

The method adopted makes the bends of the traffic curve and the rises and falls of car orders both appear as happening all at once, and shows them at their (probable) mid-point, ignoring the beginning of each movement. Thus a comparison between the two is not vitiated. With regard to the other sets of data, the attainment of a given rate of growth of traffic, and the attainment of a given volume of orders for cars, both phenomena appear too soon, in all probability, since the average for a period is shown as a uniform rate from beginning to end of the period. Thus the method adopted is one by which the data we are seeking to compare suffer similar distortions. By following other methods of presentation the writer has been able to give either set of data the appearance of lagging behind the other; a fact which serves to emphasize the conclusion that no proof of lag is contained in the figures.

any different manner from that which would naturally result if they were wholly guided by the need of moving the traffic—a result and not a cause.[1]

3. The direction in which the slope of the traffic curve deviates from the average slope agrees with the direction in which the yearly volume of car orders deviates from the average volume in twelve out of fifteen years. The disagreement is comparatively slight in one case (1904), and the failure of car orders to rise above the average in that year may be explained by the fact that car equipment had been catching up on traffic in the year preceding.

4. A change in the rate of growth of traffic is accompanied by a similar change in yearly volume of car orders ten times, by an opposite change once (1908), and in three cases one change or the other is so slight that the result may be regarded as neutral (1902, 1911, 1914). These four years of negative or neutral results are in each case years in which car orders are lower with reference to the previous year than the state of traffic growth calls for, and in each case the preceding year was one in which car supply caught up with traffic noticeably. These cases, then, involve a retarded adjustment for which the contemporary slope of the traffic curve makes no allowance.

5. The noticeable peaks of car orders fall within the years of maximum growth of traffic. The year 1916 is an exception, the growth of car orders being much delayed. Of the twelve half-years of fastest growth of traffic, eight correspond to the eight half-years of highest car orders, while two (1915–16) are periods of wholly abnormal conditions. Of the eighteen half-years of slowest growth of traffic (including those of absolute decline) thirteen correspond to the thirteen half-years of lowest car orders. Of the four half-years of lowest car orders, one comes at the end of a two-year decline in traffic, another follows this one, and the other

---

[1] No one would deny that activity in the production of railroad equipment has an effect upon other branches of business. The effects of any disturbance are widespread. The present contention is that the fluctuations are themselves natural results of the technical situation. Their effect is, of course, self-re-enforcing.

two follow immediately on the heels of the only other period when traffic absolutely declined.

6. In these minimum points the orders for cars appear to lag behind the shrinkage of traffic to which they correspond, thus supporting the contention that they behave as they would if they were governed by the needs of the traffic. The beginning of the recovery shows a similar lag. Apart from this there is no clear evidence of a tendency for either curve to lag behind the other when the level of car orders is compared with the *rate of growth* of the traffic, and the points of rise or fall in car orders are compared with the points of *increase or decrease in the rate of growth* of the traffic.

7. The general trend of car orders is slightly downward, in spite of a great increase in traffic.[1] The net yearly additions to the equipment of cars trend quite strongly downward.

In short, the figures, so far as they go, bear out the statement that the demand for cars varies with the rate at which traffic is increasing or diminishing rather than with the absolute volume of the traffic.

VI. What Governs the Size of Stocks

So far the assumption has been made that the need for productive instruments and materials varies with the output. It may be that this assumption will be challenged in some cases, however well it tallies with common experience in most situations. Where the rate of turnover can be easily increased, it may seem natural that producers should take their gains partly in this way rather than bear the burden of an increased investment. However, this could only happen if the producers had previously been either careless enough to let the turnover become unduly slow, or else had been unable to speed up the turnover in slack times by carrying a decreased stock. In production of a technical sort such as that of factories, machine-shops, railroads, etc., the length of the process cannot be reduced at will. It is the business of the staff, from

---

[1] This may be accounted for by an increase in the capacity of cars.

president to foremen, to keep the work moving at all times as fast as is reasonably possible, for waste time is waste time always. It is only in mercantile production that the rate of turnover can be increased more or less at will, and even here it is natural to increase the investment when the output increases.

The size of merchants' stocks is governed by many considerations, some psychological, some commercial, and some speculative. If a dealer knew beforehand just what goods would be demanded and just when, what kind and brand and quality and quantity, he would really have no need of keeping any stocks at all, save to serve as samples. If the static state means absolute steadiness in the demand for everything—if there were absolutely no change and hence no uncertainty in the matter of consumers' wants—dealers would be able to predict demand exactly. Even stock for sample purposes would hardly be needed, and the necessity for the investment of capital in large reserve stores of goods would virtually disappear. This need is the child of uncertainty, and uncertainty is a dynamic fact. Goods held against future demand are the playthings of chance and change.

The chief reasons for keeping a stock are, first, to give the customer a wide selection of goods which he can actually inspect and, secondly, to give assurance of being able to fill large orders without delay. What is the effect of expanding demand on the amount of stock needed to fulfil these functions? Obviously, the larger the orders, the greater the danger of being sold out, unless the stock is increased in a corresponding proportion, or something not too far short of it. The increase in demand would not seem to make it necessary to keep any wider range of goods in stock. But if we are thinking, not of what is necessary, but of what is profitable, we have a different situation. The range of goods a merchant carries is limited largely by a process of natural economic selection, by weeding out the "stickers," whose turnover is too slow to pay for keeping them in stock. With a quickened demand there are fewer "stickers." Some goods which were just below the line of toleration will become profitable to handle on the basis of the increased rate at which they can be sold, and the natural result is the carrying of a greater variety of goods as well as of more goods of each kind. If the dealer is in doubt whether or not to keep a certain line in stock at all, a brisk state of demand will be likely to decide him to keep it.

When we begin considering what is profitable, rather than merely what is physically necessary, we open up a wide range of considerations. The size of the stock is one element in the quality of service rendered by any dealer, which means that it is something in which he is likely to economize when business is poor, and to be liberal when he can afford it. When demand is expanding, merchants are in general prosperous enough to be able to afford to spend money for the purpose of improving the quality of their service. If the increase in demand is part of a general growth of business activity, the customers themselves will be in just such a prosperous state of mind as would put petty economics at a discount. They would be less influenced by a slight saving in price, which can only be made sure of after close study of the qualities of the goods, than by an obvious superiority in quality of service and range of selection. When the buyer's mind swings in this direction the merchant is invited to respond in kind if he wishes to attract his share of the increase in business, rather than to attempt to do it merely by keeping prices down and seeing that the quality of the goods themselves is maintained. A time of general activity in business is a time when large stocks are good tactics commercially.

One other fact which may make merchants more willing to invest in considerable stocks is that a time of growing demand for some one commodity, or a time of general increase in activity, are both times of rising prices for the intermediate products called for in the business affected. This makes these commodities a profitable investment[1] so long as credit can be had on easy terms with which to enlarge one's holdings. Merchants tend to assure their future supplies by buying either outright or for future delivery. Buying for future delivery is usually a cheaper way in which to combine

---

[1] Mitchell, *Business Cycles*, p. 459.

certainty of future supplies with a chance of a speculative gain if prices go up, but it is chiefly used by contractors, and by shops and factories, rather than by merchants dealing with finished products.

Each of these two ways of meeting the situation has its own effect on the demand as felt by the manufacturer. Buying outright intensifies it, while buying for future delivery has an effect which may at times prove even more disturbing. While not increasing the immediate effect of an upward swing, it puts the market in a condition in which, if the demand from consumers slackens or stops its growth, the demand for the same goods on the part of dealers cannot immediately shrink in full response. The boom is artificially prolonged for the manufacturer at the expense of the middleman, only to fall all the more suddenly when the future contracts have been filled. At such a time the same factory often sells the same goods at prices wide apart, the price on new contracts being cut to the barest minimum while good prices are still being received from middlemen unfortunate enough to have bought too far ahead.[1] Taking all these things into consideration, one is justified in concluding that an increase in demand naturally tends toward an increased investment in dealers' stocks, which is, if anything, more than in proportion to the increase in sales, unless limited by: (1) difficulty in getting added credit to carry the extra "working capital," (2) an extremely sharp rise in supply prices, (3) the fear that the prosperity is temporary, or (4) the inability of manufacturers to make deliveries.

VII. Conclusions. Some Dynamic Laws of Demand

So far we have considered only one big division of the process. If we imagine the effect of all this on those industries which produce the tools and machinery used in the construction industry itself, we have a further possibility of multiplying the effects of a change in demand. In fact, the possibilities multiply with every step backward, for every industry which produces the means of produc-

---

[1] *Ibid.*, p. 488.

tion for some other industry has its own demand for its own tools and machinery to be filled. These possibilities of intensification are soon mitigated, however, by the fact that as we get farther and farther back we reach industries which produce machinery and tools for a large number of other industries at once, so that they register the effect of the average of a great many changes in a great many particular lines of production. Thus we finally reach the steel industry, which produces the chief of all the raw materials used in making capital goods. This industry is so large that a change in the demand for any comparatively unimportant product, however much it may be intensified in the way we have just studied, has no appreciable effect on the great mass of steel production of the country. Only the largest industries buy enough steel to have a decided effect on the demand for this basic material. Railroading, which itself is to a very large extent engaged in the production of intermediate products, furnishes the steel industry with an outlet for its products which is so large as to be quite decisive and at the same time so fluctuating as to be a constant barometer of prosperity or of depression. And the steel industry itself is an equally important barometer, reporting in intensified form all general movements which originate with businesses closer to the final sale of the product.

In summary, the chief attempt of this study has been to give an exact formulation to the relationship, in quantity and in time, between demand for products and demand for the means of production; a relationship which plays a large part in several different theories of business cycles, and the results of which are so obvious that almost all descriptions of business cycles display them. The main principles contended for are as follows:

1. The demand for enlarging the means of production (including stocks of finished goods on the way to the consumer) varies, not with the volume of the demand for the finished product, but rather with the acceleration of that demand, allowance being made for the fact that the equipment cannot be adjusted as rapidly as demand changes, and so may be unusually scarce or redundant to start with in any given period. The demand for equipment may

decrease as a result of this law even though the demand for the finished product is still growing.

2. The total demand for producers' goods tends to vary more sharply than the demand for finished products, the intensification being in proportion to the average life of the goods in question.[1]

3. The maximum and minimum points in the demand for producers' goods tend to precede the maximum and minimum points in the demand for the finished products, the effect being that the change may appear to precede its own cause.

These are but a few of the dynamic laws of demand. Two others may be mentioned which have been brought incidentally into the current of the argument and which have been discussed by other writers. We have seen that the demand for durable goods depends, not merely on the price, but on the direction in which the price is expected to move in the near future, as judged chiefly by the direction in which it has been moving in the immediate past.[2] As this has been worked out by other writers, it need not be elaborated here, but may be listed as one of the dynamic laws of demand. Another fact clearly brought out by Mitchell's study is that the demand for materials is sometimes hindered from reacting promptly to a change in the demand for the finished product by the existence of standing contracts, which divide the market into open and closed sections. The result may be under certain conditions to accentuate the suddenness of changes.

ADDITIONAL NOTE ON "BUSINESS ACCELERATION AND THE LAW OF DEMAND"*

The foregoing essay is the writer's earliest treatment of this theme. Later treatments develop additional aspects. See *Studies in*

---

[1] The "life" of a finished product in this statement means the length of time it remains unsold.

[2] This fact is mentioned by Senior, *Political Economy*, 6th ed., pp. 17–20, esp. p. 18, as well as by Mitchell, *op. cit.*, p. 459. Cf. also G. B. Dibblee, *The Laws of Supply and Demand*, pp. 139–40.

* This additional note was inserted by the author when his article was reprinted in his book, "*A Preface to Social Economics*" New York, 1936, Farrar and Reinhart. Reprinted by the courtesy of Farrar and Reinhart and the author.

the *Economics of Overhead Costs*, University of Chicago Press, 1923, pp. 389–94; and *Strategic Factors in Business Cycles*, National Bureau of Economic Research, 1934, pp. 33–44, 170–182. In the latter volume the theory was extended to durable goods in general, and emphasis was laid on the way in which the effect of changes in activity in the durable-goods industries returns upon general consumer-demand, and so on, in a theoretically endless series of cycles. Thus the originating movement (which *may* occur at any point in the system) tends to be overlaid by these aftereffects, so that its original character cannot be traced statistically. This point is important for the discussion that follows. The principle at work is essentially the same as that treated in the essay: "Aggregate Spending by Public Works," *American Economic Review*, Vol. XXV, Mar., 1935, pp. 14–20. The original theory became the subject of a controversy with Professor Ragnar Frisch, *Journal of Political Economy*, Oct., Dec., 1931, Apr., 1932. More recently it has been discussed at length by Dr. Simon Kuznets, "Relation Between Capital Goods and Finished Products in the Business Cycle," in *Economic Essays in Honor of Wesley Clair Mitchell*, Columbia University Press, 1935, pp. 209–267.

Dr. Kuznets' challenging and penetrating discussion invites comment and commendation at many points; but I think I shall be doing as he would wish by going to the heart of his conclusions and bringing out the extent of our agreement and the nature and source of our differences, if any. At the end of an extended and laborious statistical verification, he finds that: "The statistical analysis shows a striking disparity between the expectations based on the hypothesis and the actual changes revealed by the quantitative evidence. In the data studied, the amplitude of cyclical changes in the demand for capital goods is far short of that indicated on the basis of net changes in the demand for services of these goods. Similarly, the lead of the cycles in the demand for capital goods is far short of that suggested by the turning points in the net changes in the demand for finished products." Now it happens that the first of these findings agrees with that of my own more rudimentary statistical test; and also with my expressed expectations (See footnote, pp. 333-4). And the second finding also agrees with my expressed expectations (See line cc' in chart, p. 336 and text commenting on it) although in my limited statistical sample, this line appeared to move more promptly than I should have expected.

The fact seems to be that the hypothesis which Dr. Kuznets is testing is, in those features which are essential for the present purpose, the one which I introduced by saying: "The nature of the mechanical law at work can be emphasized by imagining the industry reduced to a mere machine. . . . Finished goods are turned out as fast as wanted, and materials and means of production are instantly supplied as fast as the process of finishing requires them. On this simplified basis we can predict accurately how the speed of the different parts of the machine must needs vary,[1] and the results will furnish an index of the varying strains that are put on the much less mechanical system that does these things in real life" (p. 331). Again: "The assumption has been made that the new construction actually keeps pace with the demand for it, simply in order to have some figures that would not be too complicated. In fact, the supply is almost certain to fall behind the demand—" (p. 333, footnote). I should have added that actual demand in the shape of orders would also be morally certain in most cases to fall behind the hypothetically-indicated demand. Again: "Making all due allowances for mitigating factors in translating the illustration back into real life, it is still difficult to see how the building and machine-making industries can possibly avoid the disagreeable experience of outgrowing themselves in time of prosperity" (p. 334).

These citations may serve to show how the hypothesis in question was intended to be used. If taken as a picture of what must happen in real life, it would involve the absurd condition that producers of finished goods never have any excess or shortage of capacity (except when demand has shrunk faster than productive equipment can shrink by wearing out), while producers of productive equipment have always enough excess capacity to handle instantly any demand that may be put upon them. There is, of

---

[1] This refers to the *hypothetical* machine.

course, no reason for supposing that these two groups of producers behave in such diametrically opposite ways. Actually, each group has normally some excess capacity, part of which at least is likely to be of inferior quality and worth replacing or modernising if it comes into more constant demand. In respect to this and other matters Dr. Kuznets has contributed so substantially to elaborating the necessary qualifications and modifications of this provisional hypothesis that it causes some surprise to see him reverting to it to apply his statistical test and setting up as my theory what I had called "the impossibly fluid condition of industry that was previously assumed" (p. 337).

His use of this hypothesis affects his test in one way which might escape the casual reader. It controls the way in which the "theoretical demand" of his tables is constructed, and I shall not accept this as unqualifiedly valid (to say the least) for the purpose in hand. He works out a slowly moving normal ratio of equipment to traffic —one freight car to so many million net ton-miles—and applies this to the excess of traffic in any year over traffic the previous year (with allowance for the fact that new equipment has more-than-average capacity) to determine the number of new cars theoretically needed, above replacements. This amounts to assuming for each year that the ratio of equipment to traffic was normal the preceding year; in spite of the fact that the figures themselves show that production of new equipment did not fluctuate nearly enough, nor promptly enough, to keep this ratio normal; and each year would actually start with an excess or shortage left over from the preceding year. This initial excess or shortage should play a part in determining "theoretical demand" for new equipment, as well as the change in volume of traffic during the current year.

One method which would do this would be to apply the equipment-ratio to the total volume of traffic in the second of a pair of years, subtract the actual volume of equipment in existence the first year, and so get the volume of new construction needed to bring the ratio to normal (with allowance for increased unit capacity of new equipment as before). The result would be to shift the timing of movements in theoretical demand for new equipment, bringing it nearer to that of movements in total volume of traffic, and thus shifting the base-line of Dr. Kuznets' comparisons. It would incidentally introduce an allowance, of a sort, for the factor of overcapacity to which Dr. Kuznets has called attention. (Cf. also Sec. 4, pp. 341–2.)

However, I have no intention of contending that my original treatment is perfect. I find it especially faulty in its handling of maintenance and replacements, which should be distinguished from each other and more emphasis given to replacements which should not, for long-lived equipment, be assumed to vary with current rate of output of the finished product. On this point Dr. Kuznets has brought out what seem to be the chief factors to be taken into account, and has developed one of them mathematically. For one of them, credit should be given also to Thomas M. McNiece—cf. "Rhythmic Variations in Industry," *Mechanical Engineering*, Nov., 1933, pp. 659 ff.

The important thing is, of course, what behavior should be expected with the principle in question operating under actual conditions. For this purpose the behavior of replacements should be carefully reconsidered. But more important is the fact that the interaction between consumers' purchases and the production of capital goods runs in both directions; and that the greater part of the fluctuations in the total amount of consumers' spendings or purchases are the result of fluctuations in their incomes, in which fluctuations in the production of durable goods play an important or controlling part. (Cf. footnote 15, p. 341.) An original disturbing impulse may come from either side; in either case it can start a series of interactions, mutually reinforcing one another. In the case of the production of durable capital goods, some six to eight months might be expected to elapse after an original impulse before the activity of production showed anything like the full effects. It would presumably take a shorter time for the resulting income to be distributed and to take effect on movements of consumers' purchases—let us say, on the average, two or three months. This picture is still highly simplified, but may contain enough of the important elements to afford a basis for prediction of an approximate normal pattern of behavior. What would such a pattern be?

If we start with an upward inflection of consumers' purchases, then the first period of six to eight months would witness an upward curve in production of capital goods, reaching a substantial amount by the end of the period, while the first effects of the reaction on consumers' purchases would have begun to show themselves in a slight reinforcement of the original rise. In the second period, consumers' purchases would continue to rise, and production of capital goods also; but the latter might now be rising in something like a straight line. The natural result would be a straight-line rise in consumers' purchases, with a slight lag. As this continued, the production of capital goods might soon reach a point at which it would taper off and cease to increase, though remaining at a higher level than at first, the result would be to put an end to the derived increase in consumers' purchases; and bring about a downward (relative) inflection of this curve. The result of this, with a lag, would be to start a decline in production of capital goods, which would in turn result in a decline of consumers' purchases, relative to their secular trend, and probably a positive decline unless the secular trend is very strongly upward. This would in turn drive the production of capital goods below its initial level. This downward movement would then ultimately reverse itself as a result of a similar series of interactions in the reverse direction. The whole cycle might be expected to take an amount of time approximately equal to four times the sum of the two lags (from thirty-two to forty-four months), or possibly longer. The high points of production of capital goods would lag behind the midpoints of the rises in consumers' purchases by six to eight months (possibly more) and would lead the high points of consumers' purchases by two to three months, or more if the upward secular trend of the latter is substantial.

If the initial movement came from the production of capital goods, these would lead in the first period, but after that the pattern would be substantially the same. Or if at any time some fresh originating impulse entered from either side, it would temporarily alter the timing of the pattern. It would also be modified by the fluctuations in the need for replacements resulting from previous fluctuations in production of equipment, and by any unusual surplus or shortage of productive capacity left over from preceding periods. This last might cause additional lags or prolongations of movements. A particular type of durable goods might have a natural cycle-period different from that of general business, with the result that its individual pattern would be a complex one.

When considering a single class of capital goods confined to the making of a product or products the demand for which moves to some extent independently of the general cyclical curve of consumer-demand, the problem will be different, because the secondary effects of changes in the production of such capital goods on consumers' demand for the particular products which these goods make, will be relatively slight. The observable effects will be almost entirely those running from consumer demand to demand for means of production. But if consumer-demand for these products moves in harmony with general consumer-demand, the resultant pattern should show the same features as the more general one.

This note has grown too long, without doing justice to all of Dr. Kuznets' points which invite comment. As to the possibility of statistical verification of the theoretical expectations here formulated, they are known in advance to agree with the general type of observed behavior of the shorter business cycles (the "forty-month" variety) and leave possibilities of longer movements. It would be interesting to study discrepancies and variations and their causes. One subtle and interesting question is whether the sum of the two lags figuring in the pattern just suggested has any causal bearing on the length of the "forty-month cycle." Since both are of the nature of distributed lags and presumably with their tails lopped off, the question presents its difficulties. The direct and obvious method of statistical attack would amount to verifying a tautology.

12

INTERACTIONS BETWEEN THE MULTIPLIER ANALYSIS AND THE PRINCIPLE OF ACCELERATION*

By Paul A. Samuelson ||

Few economists would deny that the "multiplier" analysis of the effects of governmental deficit spending has thrown some light upon this important problem. Nevertheless, there would seem to be some ground for the fear that this extremely simplified mechanism is in danger of hardening into a dogma, hindering progress and obscuring important subsidiary relations and processes. It is highly desirable, therefore, that model sequences, which operate under more general assumptions, be investigated, possibly including the conventional analysis as a special case.[1]

In particular, the "multiplier," using this term in its usual sense, does *not* pretend to give the relation between total national income induced by governmental spending and the original amount of money spent. This is clearly seen by a simple example. In an economy (not necessarily our own) where any dollar of governmental deficit spending would result in a hundred dollars less of private investment than would otherwise have been undertaken, the ratio of total induced national income to the initial expenditure

---

* *The Review of Economic Statistics*, Volume XXI, Number 2, May 1939, pages 75–78. Reprinted by courtesy of The Review of Economic Statistics and the author.

|| Massachusetts Institute of Technology; Formerly Harvard University.

[1] The writer, who has made this study in connection with his research as a member of the Society of Fellows at Harvard University, wishes to express his indebtedness to Professor Alvin H. Hansen of Harvard University at whose suggestion the investigation was undertaken.

Table 1.—The Development of National Income as a Result of a Continuous Level of Governmental Expenditure When the Marginal Propensity to Consume Equals One-half and the Relation Equals Unity
(*Unit: one dollar*)

Period	Current governmental expenditure	Current consumption induced by previous expenditure	Current private investment proportional to time increase in consumption	Total national income
1	1.00	0.00	0.00	1.00
2	1.00	0.50	0.50	2.00
3	1.00	1.00	0.50	2.50
4	1.00	1.25	0.25	2.50
5	1.00	1.25	0.00	2.25
6	1.00	1.125	−0.125*	2.00
7	1.00	1.00	−0.125	1.875
8	1.00	0.9375	−0.0625	1.875
9	1.00	0.9375	0.00	1.9375
10	1.00	0.96875	0.03125	2.00
11	1.00	1.00	0.03125	2.03125
12	1.00	1.015625	0.015625	2.03125
13	1.00	1.015625	0.00	2.015625
14	1.00	1.0078125	−0.0078125	2.00

* Negative induced private investment is interpreted to mean that for the system as a whole there is *less* investment in this period than there otherwise would have been. Since this is a marginal analysis, superimposed implicitly upon a going state of affairs, this concept causes no difficulty.

is overwhelmingly negative, yet the "multiplier" in the strict sense must be positive. The answer to the puzzle is simple. What the multiplier does give is the ratio of the total increase in the national income to the total amount of investment, governmental and private. In other words, it does *not* tell us how much is to be multiplied. The effects upon private investment are often regarded as tertiary influences and receive little systematic attention.

In order to remedy the situation in some measure, Professor Hansen has developed a new model sequence which ingeniously combines the multiplier analysis with that of the *acceleration* principle or *relation*. This is done by making additions to the national income consist of three components: (1) governmental deficit spending, (2) private consumption expenditure induced by previous public expenditure, and (3) induced private investment, assumed according to the familiar acceleration principle to be proportional to the time increase of consumption. The introduction of the last component accounts for the novelty of the conclusions reached and also the increased complexity of the analysis.

A numerical example may be cited to illuminate the assumptions made. We assume governmental deficit spending of one dollar per unit period, beginning at some initial time and continuing thereafter. The marginal propensity to consume, α, is taken to be one-half. This is taken to mean that the consumption of any period is equal to one-half the national income of the previous period. Our last assumption is that induced private investment is proportional to the increase in consumption between the previous and the current period. This factor of proportionality or *relation*, β, is provisionally taken to be equal to unity; i.e., a time increase in consumption of one dollar will result in one dollar's worth of induced private investment.

In the initial period when the government spends a dollar for the first time, there will be no consumption induced from previous periods, and hence the addition to the national income will equal the one dollar spent. This will yield fifty cents of consumption expenditure in the second period, an increase of fifty cents over the consumption of the first period, and so according to the *relation* we will have fifty cents worth of induced private investment. Finally, we must add the new dollar of expenditure by the government. The national income of the second period must therefore total two dollars. Similarly, in the third period the national income would be the sum of one dollar of consumption, fifty cents induced private investment, and one dollar current governmental expenditure. It is clear that given the values of the marginal propensity to consume, α, and the *relation*, β, all succeeding national income levels can be easily computed in succession. This is done in detail in Table 1 and illustrated in Chart 1. It will be noted that the introduction of the acceleration principle causes our series to reach a peak at the 3rd year, a trough at the 7th, a peak at the 11th, etc. Such oscillatory behavior could not occur in the conventional model sequences, as will soon become evident.

CHART 1.—GRAPHIC REPRESENTATION OF DATA IN TABLE 1
(*Unit: one dollar*)

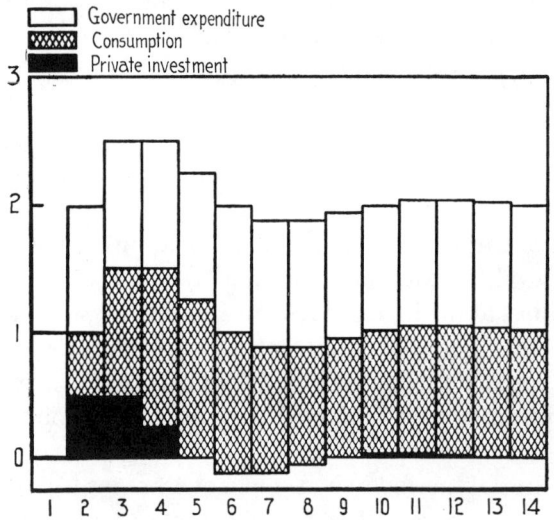

For other chosen values of α and β similar model sequences can be developed. In Table 2 national income totals are given for various selected values of these coefficients. In the first column, for example, the marginal propensity to consume is assumed to be one-half, and the *relation* to be equal to zero. This is of special interest because it shows the conventional multiplier sequences to be special cases of the more general Hansen analysis. For this case no oscillations are possible. In the second column the oscillations in the national income are undamped and regular. In column three things are still worse; the oscillations are explosive, becoming larger and larger but always fluctuating around an "average value." In the fourth column the behavior is no longer oscillatory but is explosive upward approaching a compound interest rate of growth.

By this time the investigator is inclined to feel somewhat disorganized. A variety of qualitatively different results emerge in a seemingly capricious manner from minor changes in hypotheses. Worse than this, how can we be sure that for still different selected values of our coefficients new and stronger types of behavior will not emerge? Is it not even possible that if Table 2 were extended to cover more periods, new types of behavior might result for these selected coefficients?

Fortunately, these questions can be given a definite negative answer. Arithmetical methods cannot do so since we cannot try all possible values of the coefficients nor compute the endless terms of each sequence. Nevertheless, comparatively simple algebraic analysis can be applied which will yield all possible qualitative types of behavior and enable us to unify our results.

The national income at time t, Y_t, can be written as the sum of three components: (1) governmental expenditure, g_t, (2) consumption expenditure, C_t, and (3) induced private investment, I_t.

$$Y_t = g_t + C_t + I_t.$$

But according to the Hansen assumptions

$$C_t = \alpha Y_{t-1}$$
$$I_t = \beta[C_t - C_{t-1}] = \alpha\beta Y_{t-1} - \alpha\beta Y_{t-2}$$

and

$$g_t = 1.$$

Therefore, our national income can be rewritten

$$Y_t = 1 + \alpha[1 + \beta]Y_{t-1} - \alpha\beta Y_{t-2}.$$

In words, if we know the national income for two periods, the national income for the following period can be simply derived by taking a weighted sum. The weights depend, of course, upon the values chosen for the marginal propensity to consume and for the *relation*.

This is one of the simplest types of difference equations, having constant coefficients and being of the second order. The mathematical details of its solution need not be entered upon here. Suffice it to say that its solution depends upon the roots—which in turn depend upon the coefficients α and β—of a certain equation.[1]

TABLE 2.—MODEL SEQUENCES OF NATIONAL INCOME FOR SELECTED VALUES OF MARGINAL PROPENSITY TO CONSUME AND RELATION
(*Unit: one dollar*)

Period	$\alpha = .5$ $\beta = 0$	$\alpha = .5$ $\beta = 2$	$\alpha = .6$ $\beta = 2$	$\alpha = .8$ $\beta = 4$
1	1.00	1.00	1.00	1.00
2	1.50	2.50	2.80	5.00
3	1.75	3.75	4.84	17.80
4	1.875	4.125	6.352	56.20
5	1.9375	3.4375	6.6256	169.84
6	1.9688*	2.0313	5.3037	500.52
7	1.9844	.9141	2.5959	1,459.592
8	1.9922	− .1172	− .6918	4,227.704
9	1.9961	.2148	−3.3603	12,241.1216

* Table is correct to four decimal places.

It can be easily shown that the whole field of possible values of α and β can be divided into four regions, each of which gives qualitatively different types of behavior. In Chart 2 these regions are plotted. Each point in this diagram represents a selection of values for the marginal propensity to consume and the *relation*. Corresponding to each point there will be a model sequence of national income through time. The qualitative properties of this

---

[1] Actually, the solution can be written in the form

$$Y_t = \frac{1}{1-\alpha} + a_1[x_1]^t + a_2[x_2]^t$$

where x_1 and x_2 are roots of the quadratic equation

$$x^2 - \alpha[1 + \beta]x + \alpha\beta = 0,$$

and a_1 and a_2 are constants dependent upon the α's and β's chosen.

MULTIPLIER ANALYSIS—PRINCIPLE OF ACCELERATION   267

sequence depend upon whether the point is in Region A, B, C, or D.[1] The properties of each region can be briefly summarized.

Region A (relatively small values of the relation)

If there is a constant level of governmental expenditure through time, the national income will approach asymptotically a value $\frac{1}{1-\alpha}$ times the constant level of governmental expenditure. A single impulse of expenditure, or any amount of expenditure followed by a complete cessation, will result in a gradual approach to the original zero level of national income. (It will be noted that the asymptote approached is identically that given by the Keynes-Kahn-Clark formula. Their analysis applies to points along the α axis and is subsumed under the more general Hansen analysis.) Perfectly periodic net governmental expenditure will result eventually in perfectly periodic fluctuations in national income.

Region B

A constant continuing level of governmental expenditure will result in damped oscillatory movements of national income, gradually approaching the asymptote $\frac{1}{1-\alpha}$ times the constant level of government expenditure. (Cf. Table 1.) Governmental expenditure in a single or finite number of periods will result eventually in damped oscillations around the level of income zero. Perfectly regular periodic fluctuations in government expenditure will result eventually in fluctuations of income of the same period.

Region C

A constant level of governmental expenditure will result in *explosive*, ever increasing oscillations around an asymptote computed as above. (Cf. column 3 of Table 2.) A single impulse of

---

[1] Mathematically, the regions are demarcated by the conditions that the roots of the equation referred to in the previous footnote be real or complex, greater or less than unity in absolute value.

expenditure or a finite number of expenditure impulses will result eventually in explosive oscillations around the level zero.

Region D (large values of the marginal propensity to consume and the relation)

A constant level of governmental expenditure will result in an ever increasing national income, eventually approaching a com-

CHART 2.—DIAGRAM SHOWING BOUNDARIES OF REGIONS YIELDING DIFFERENT QUALITATIVE BEHAVIOR OF NATIONAL INCOME

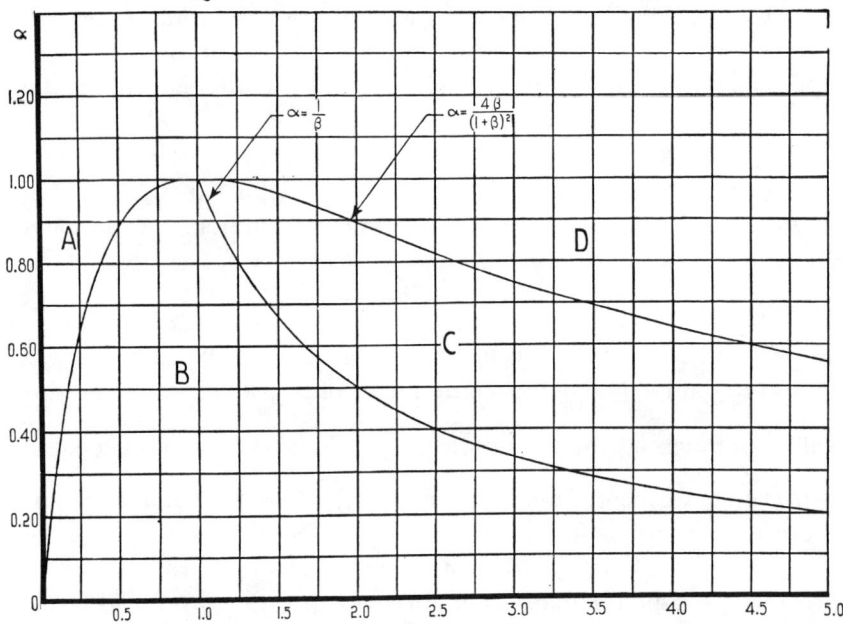

pound interest rate of growth. (Cf. column 4 of Table 2.) A single impulse of net investment will likewise send the system up to infinity at a compound interest rate of growth. On the other hand, a single infinitesimal unit of disinvestment will send the system ever downward at an increasing rate. This is a highly unstable situation, but corresponds most closely to the pure case of pump-priming, where the total increase in national income bears no finite ratio to the original stimulus.

The limitations inherent in so simplified a picture as that presented here should not be overlooked.[1] In particular, it assumes that the marginal propensity to consume and the *relation* are constants; actually these will change with the level of income, so that this representation is strictly a *marginal* analysis to be applied to the study of small oscillations. Nevertheless, it is more general than the usual analysis. Contrary to the impression commonly held, mathematical methods properly employed, far from making economic theory more abstract, actually serve as a powerful liberating device enabling the entertainment and analysis of ever more realistic and complicated hypotheses.

---

[1] It may be mentioned in passing that the formal structure of our problem is identical with the model sequences of Lundberg, and the dynamic theories of Tinbergen. The present problem is so simple that it provides a useful introduction to the mathematical theory of the latter's work.

13

DEFICIT SPENDING*

By John H. Williams‖

During the past decade of continuous deficits our thinking about fiscal policy has passed through a number of fairly definite phases. The early deficits were the automatic result of the depression. As the national income declined by one-half from 1929 to 1932, the federal revenue likewise declined one-half, while expenditures remained unchanged. The only fiscal attack upon the depression was not through "income creating" expenditures, so much discussed later on, but through what may be called "capital repair" expenditures by the Reconstruction Finance Corporation created in 1932. The Democratic party ran its campaign of that year on the issue of economy, attacking the budgetary deficits in general and the RFC expenditures in particular.

It is very difficult to say when the Roosevelt Administration began to think of deficit spending as a means to recovery. In this country it is always hard to define "the" Administration as distinguished from its personnel, which includes a large number of legislators, administrators, advisers, and research men all of whom, within the limits of their opportunities, are seeking to exert their influence but are by no means pulling in the same direction. And to all these must be added the numerous and diverse outside influences working upon and through them. In consequence, major changes of policy are likely to come slowly, and their origins are often difficult to trace. Undoubtedly many persons within the Administration favored deficit spending as a deliberate policy for recovery considerably before any such policy publicly emerged.

---

* *American Economic Review*, Volume XXX, Number 5, February 1941, pages 52–66. Reprinted by courtesy of The American Economic Association and the author.

‖ Harvard University.

In the early part of the first Roosevelt Administration, there was little or no evidence that public spending was to be a major policy of recovery. It is true that some early steps to cut expenditures were soon reversed, but the main emphasis for recovery in 1933 was on monetary policy and especially on raising the price of gold, with the repeatedly announced goal of raising commodity prices to the 1926 level. There was also the quite different approach through NRA, and much discussion of the contradictory character of these two major attacks upon the problem. The NRA policies had, in my opinion, an important bearing upon deficit spending. By raising costs they impaired its effects. They were related also in the sense that it was intended that the code activities under General Johnson should be accompanied by a public works program under Mr. Ickes, which gave rise to subsequent comment that the chief mistake may have been in not reversing their roles. But in this early public works program, which as it turned out amounted to very little, there seems to have been little or no emphasis on *deficit* spending as the means to recovery, and federal deficits were defended mainly on humanitarian grounds as necessary to provide temporary relief for unemployment until recovery could be achieved by other means.

Some date the beginnings of a conscious policy from Keynes's visit to this country in June, 1934, when he said that if we spent two hundred millions a month we would go back to the bottom of the depression, a net monthly deficit of three hundred millions would hold us even, and one of four hundred would bring full recovery. Keynes gave this formula, the precision of which I have always admired, to various meetings of economists and doubtless also to the Administration. There was no indication, however, then or for several years later that the government was deliberately pursuing a deficit policy as a major means to recovery, and the President's budget messages continued to promise an early balancing of the budget.

The fact seems to be that as interest in other recovery measures waned, while the deficits continued to be large, there was a growing disposition on the part of many persons, within and without the

Administration, to regard the deficits themselves as the major cause of the recovery. The first evidence that the Administration, as distinguished from a large and influential group within it, had adopted this view came during the new depression of 1937–38, when, after a protracted internal debate, a new spending program was hastily improvised in the spring of 1938, and passed by Congress. A similar program put before Congress in the spring of 1939 was defeated. Since then we have had the appropriations for the defense program, which has raised other issues than that of spending as a recovery measure and has had the support of the whole community regardless of attitude toward the earlier deficits.

I have begun with this reference to our experience because it helps me, at least, to see our problem in better perspective. There is an inevitable human tendency to rationalize experience, and as events have unfolded over the past decade there has been much shifting of positions as to theories and policies. I do not say this critically, but merely to remind us of the need for caution against overhasty conclusions that we have found in fiscal policy the key to the control of economic changes. It will help us all to recognize that in 1930 no advocates of deficit spending, if there were any, contemplated that by July, 1940, before the present defense program got underway, we would still have a deficit, that the expenditures of the fiscal years 1940 and 1939 would be the highest of the entire decade, exceeding even those of the year (1936) in which the soldiers' bonus was paid, or that for the entire decade the yearly revenue would average only 60 per cent of the expenditures; and this in spite of the fact that the revenue had been tripled since the bottom of the depression, with new taxes imposed and tax rates raised, and was about 50 per cent higher than in 1929.

I

It is encouraging, however, to realize that what I have called our rationalizations have been in accordance with a logical pattern. We have not had occasion to change our fundamental analysis of economic fluctuations so much as our ideas about the methods of controlling them. There have been, also, and quite naturally in view of the severity of the depression and the slowness of recovery, changes in emphasis upon the different elements in the analysis and upon the scope and gravity of the problem. The analysis itself is a logical unfolding of ideas prevalent in monetary and business cycle literature during the twenties and has its roots much farther back, in the writings of Wicksell and others. This is the analysis of the flow of income and of the dominant role played by investment in fluctuations of income, output, and employment.

During the twenties the emphasis was on central bank policy. The central bank, by its control of reserves, could control the quantity of money, which controlled the interest rate, which controlled investment, which controlled the business cycle. There was a shift of emphasis from the short-time rate to the long-time rate. There was a growing interest in the "natural rate," which equates saving and investment. There was a shift of emphasis from the rediscount rate to open-market operations. There was the controversy over federal reserve policy with relation to the stock market boom, with much discussion as to whether, by failing to raise rates soon enough and high enough, the Board had allowed the security boom to run to heights from which a general depression was bound to follow, or whether by attempting to pursue a restrictive policy toward security speculation, which was not its legitimate concern, it had through high money rates and contraction of the money supply brought on the very depression which it feared.

When the depression came, as already stated, the emphasis continued to be on central bank policy and the interest rate, with much insistence that open-market operations were not large enough, not begun soon enough, or not continued long enough. When these operations resulted in excess reserves, and the latter were greatly increased after 1933 by gold inflow, there was at first considerable interest in how much excess reserves it would take to break down the bankers' liquidity complex; but as the excess reserves continued to pile up and attain huge dimensions and interest rates sank to levels never previously reached, it was generally recognized that, whatever may have been the defects of central bank policy, the main trouble lay in the inadequacy of the interest rate, by itself, to control investment and the cycle.

I have not space to discuss in detail the reasons for the inadequacy. They were those cited by the reviewers of Keynes's *Treatise*, and expressly or tacitly accepted by him in his *General Theory* six years later: the fact that interest is but one of the costs of investment and unlikely to be controlling one, even though more important in long- than in short-time investment; the importance of expectations, which play so large a part in his later book but were minimized in the earlier one; the fact that there is not one rate of interest but many, variously affected by risk, marked organization, and other factors which not only set a bottom limit under most rates really pertinent to the control of investment (and leave some of them merely rigid at high levels) but also produce a perverse cyclical variation such that when the rates most subject to monetary control are falling in depression and rising in a boom in response to central bank policy, other rates are rising and falling in response to expectations of income affecting risk. In recent years the interest rate discussion has entered a new phase, with a growing recognition that rates may be both too high and too low at the same time, the low rates accomplishing nothing further to stimulate investment while causing injury to many institutions and individuals, while the high rates may still be retarding investment in some directions. And there has been growing recognition that this condition calls for other methods of attack than the traditional central bank methods.

II

Deficit spending is the logical sequel to central bank policy, and it was entirely logical that its first phase should be pump-priming, for the latter does not differ in purpose or in general analysis of the problem from central bank policy, but seeks to make more effective the methods of attack. The financing of deficits represents a further step toward making an easy money policy effective, for when combined with pressure through reserves, it affords an avenue for expansion of bank assets and deposits accompanied by a declining yield on government securities. In addition to the new money thus created, government borrowing provides an outlet for old deposits which might otherwise remain idle rather than assume the risks of investment in depression. Theoretically, the fall of the rate on government securities should spread to other investments and loans, attracting both bank and nonbank investors, until after a transition phase of refunding of old securities, the new issues market is affected and a stream of new investment set in motion. To some extent, this process has been discernible but when we review our experience as a whole, it is disappointing. The combination of deficit financing and excess reserve has accentuated the cleavage between interest rates too low and too high, and though there was some increase in activity in the market for new capital prior to the downturn of 1937, the entire period since 1933 has been characterized by a much smaller volume of new security issues than in the twenties, or in earlier periods on a comparable basis.

The main contribution, however, which pump-priming sought to make toward overcoming the inadequacy of central bank policy, was in the deficit spending itself rather than the method of its financing. If lowering the interest rate would not, by itself, sufficiently induce investment, this object could be achieved through the creation of new consumer income by means of deficits. Investment in producers goods would thus be induced through increased community spending on consumers goods. There was a presumption, at least at first, that under this combined stimulus of income creation and low interest rates, the deficits would not need to be large or long continued. The budget would have a diamond-shaped pattern corresponding to the business cycle, with deficits in depression and surpluses in boom periods both tapering from the turning points.

The main emphasis was laid on the multiplied and cumulative effects of the spending. It was in connection with pump-priming that the multiplier concept first came into our discussions. I do not pretend to have understood or even to have studied carefully the many ramifications and refinements of this concept as it has been applied, either alone or in combination with the acceleration principle, in this and later versions of fiscal theory. This has become one of the dialectical tilting grounds in economics, of which there are always several in each generation, and like so many others in the past it probably will not justify the time and ingenuity expended on it. I am similarly unimpressed with the attempts to find multipliers statistically for various countries. Perhaps the simplest version of the multiplier and the one most useful for the pump-priming analysis is that which considers the effects of an initial or primary deficit spending as a sequence through time, the secondary effects being the sum of the successive consumer incomes during the period, each multiplied by the percentage of income received which is spent, which in turn depends upon the percentage of leakage through saving. In the pump-priming theory, the combined primary and secondary spendings, with which alone the multiplier is concerned, would lead to tertiary spending, which is the induced investment; the investment would then have its own multiplied effect, and so on cumulatively, with deficits tapering, until the opposite phase of the cycle is reached and surpluses appear.

I do not think it is profitable to take time to discuss pump-priming in detail. Our own experience has not in general conformed to the expectations of its advocates as to the amount of induced investment or as to budget tapering, and certainly not to the expectation that there would presently be budget surpluses. I am inclined to side with those who hold that this kind of spending, in the form of relief to consumers, does not reach down far enough into the productive process to provide effective leverage, but soon dissipates its force in consumer transfers without much effect on investment, save possibly on short-run investment. Other comments I have to make seem equally applicable to later versions of fiscal theory and can be given later.

The vogue of pump-priming was prior to 1936–37. In 1936, Keynes, who had done most to stimulate the pump-priming discussion with the pamphlet on *The Means to Prosperity* (1933) and his disciple Kahn's article in the *Economic Journal* (1931) on the multiplier, published his *General Theory*, which dealt not with the business cycle but with a secular tendency toward underemployment. In this country, the recovery gave way in 1937 to a new depression at a time when the budget for a brief interval came into balance not through reduction of expenditures but owing partly to the mistaken policy of building a social security reserve, and even more to the fact that with rising national income the federal revenue substantially increased. The conviction grew that we were faced with something more than cyclical recovery from a major depression. The emphasis shifted from pump-priming to the need for deficits as compensation for long-run structural changes in the economy; deficits which might be permanent or at any rate should be continued so long as underemployment prevailed.

There is an interesting literature of the transition from pump-priming to long-run compensatory spending. Some of it is contained in the presidential messages after 1937 and in the discussions by senators and administration leaders of the spending act of 1938 and the spending bill of 1939. In the discussions of economists I have been interested and sometimes puzzled by the further treatment of the multiplier. The view has been expressed that deficit spending is not pump-priming in its effects because while it is self-multiplying it is not self-perpetuating. Standard models have been constructed which show that deficit expenditures have only a limited amount of leverage. It has been asserted that only investment and public spending have a multiplier.

In these views, it seems to me there is some confusion of thought. Every expenditure has a positive multiplier and every failure to spend a negative multiplier. What matters is the net change from period to period and not the character of the expenditure. Investment offset by saving has no net multiplier, and consumption beyond current income has such a multiplier, whether the consumption is financed by borrowing from the banking system or by previously accumulated saving. No expenditure of any kind has a self-perpetuating effect, and the multiplied effect of any expenditure is bound to be limited if there is any leakage at all through saving. But these facts tell us nothing as to whether deficit spending has pump-priming effects. What we need to know is its effects *outside* the multiplier, whether for example it does induce investment which induces further investment, or whether, if it does not, the fault lies in some other effects of deficit spending or in the character of the expenditure or in secular changes which have reduced the opportunities for investment, and so on. Not the least of our dangers is that of confusing this rather mechanical monetary concept with the deeper-seated forces with which we should be mainly concerned in our analysis of the economic effects of deficit spending.

III

Since 1936, as I have said, the emphasis in fiscal theory has been not on stimulating private investment, temporarily depressed, but on compensating for the lack of it. This is a fundamental change. It rests on the view that private capitalism is no longer capable of providing full employment. Two explanations of this defect have been offered: the oversaving theory and the underinvestment theory. It is important to recognize that these are two distinct explanations, though they can be combined and to a large extent have been in recent discussions.

Keynes's oversaving theory is derived from "psychological laws" operating in the institutional framework of modern private capitalism. Most important is the "propensity to consume," according to which as income rises a part of the increase is saved. Keynes believes an increasing fraction is saved, but this he says is not part of the law. To prevent reduction of income, output and employment, investment must increase equally with saving, but investment is limited by the "marginal efficiency of capital" (diminishing productivity as interpreted by "expectations"); and the cost of investment cannot be reduced sufficiently by lowering the rate of interest because at some minimum rate we prefer liquid funds to the risk of investment. Net idle saving forces income and employment down to some level at which, through the decline of saving, investment and saving become equal. To get more income and employment we must have deficit spending to offset idle saving or must tax away and spend the idle saving. This fiscal policy should be accompanied by monetary action to reduce interest rates and overcome, so far as possible, the effects of "liquidity preference."

This theory could never account for a depression without bringing in cumulative cyclical factors, which are not a part of the analysis. It merely tells us that as we progress to higher income levels, progress becomes harder; according to the "law" it is only as income rises that more is saved. What I have to say about employment, which is Keynes's chief criterion of progress, applies also to the underinvestment theory and will be given later.

Keynes's statement about the "propensity to consume" is a plausible hypothesis. Its application is limited by the fact that it cannot be applied to producers' saving, or at any rate to corporate saving which is an important part of the whole. It is further complicated by the fact that there is an opposite tendency in the business cycle, which Keynes had previously described as an excess of investment over saving in the boom and an excess of saving over investment in the depression. Though this is an inaccurate picture of the cycle, which I prefer to describe as a cycle of spending and not-spending, it illustrates the complication. Of course, both statements could be true, with the cyclical tendency riding on the surface of the more fundamental one.

In discussions of fiscal policy Keynes's hypothesis about saving has been too readily accepted as law or as fact. No one, so far as I know, has yet given us estimates of saving of a kind that really bear upon this argument. The data that have been most cited in discussions of fiscal policy—those of Kuznets and Terborgh for this country and Colin Clark for England—are estimates of realized investment. In the testimony at the TNEC hearing on saving and investment the data presented, which were called "offsets to saving," represented real investment. The most ambitious attempt to compare savings and investment is the SEC study by Goldsmith and Salant, but this deals mainly with real saving and investment. The same is true of the earlier Brookings studies. As Keynes pointed out in his book, real saving and investment must be equal. What is needed for his thesis is a study of *monetary* saving and investment. I appreciate the difficulty, perhaps the impossibility, of making such a study but until we have it we continue to deal with a hypothesis.

One kind of proof that has been offered seems to me no proof at all. The unprecedented growth of demand deposits in recent years has been accompanied by a great decline in velocity. This decline has been cited variously to prove "lack of confidence," lack of opportunities for investment, and the reality of the tendency toward oversaving. Taken alone it proves nothing but the failure of the increase in the money supply to induce spending. If in an effort to stimulate investment the money supply is doubled, but without effect, should we say that owing to the law of the propensity to consume the money has been saved? This kind of saving could readily be cured by reducing the money supply. We cannot identify saving with a decrease in velocity of money if the latter merely reflects an increase in money quantity. What other causes of reduced velocity there may have been is open to such interpretations as I have cited.

The underinvestment thesis has a better factual foundation than the oversaving theory, and presents a stronger case for long-run deficit spending. It is based on the view that as the capitalistic economy progresses it reaches a stage at which the opportunities for investment decline. This "mature economy" thesis is too familiar to require elaboration. It uses, in general, the same analytical apparatus as the oversaving theory, starting from the same truism that investment plus consumption equal income. It has the same criterion of prosperity: full employment. But the decline of opportunities for investment is not in the other theory, and the tendency toward oversaving is not necessarily a part of this one, though, as I have said, in much of the recent discussion the two have been combined.

The reasons why as an economy matures investment opportunities decline have been presented with great force and much statistical support. Some of them carry considerable conviction, particularly as regards their bearing on employment. This is especially true of the technological changes from capital-using to capital-saving devices. I am less convinced by the reference to declining rate of growth of population, not only because it relates to individuals rather than to families, but because it unduly subordinates, I believe, the possibilities of changes in quality (standard of living). The argument about the passing of the frontier seems to me not one of the strongest, largely because I am influenced by my earlier studies of international trade, which showed that trade was greatest not with the frontier countries but between the industrially developed countries having higher living standards and greater purchasing power. But as regards employment there may be no easy substitute for free land.

One of the most difficult and necessary tasks is to compare our experience of the past decade with the earlier great depressions, sifting out the elements of similarity and difference. Economic progress in the nineteenth century was very great but it came by jerks with recurring periods of unsettlement and stagnation. Each period had its special characteristics but economic maturity was not one of them. In how far is this latest experience ascribable to this new circumstance? Has this last experience been essentially different from the others or merely on a larger scale? The most difficult matter to square with the mature economy explanation is what happened in the rest of the world. This country stood virtually alone, except for France, in its failure to surpass substantially the level of output of the twenties. This difference cannot be accounted for by military expenditures except in a few cases, notably Germany and Japan. In England military expenditures were not an important influence before 1938 and in many other countries such expenditures were not a major factor in recovery. Yet many of them, especially England, are more mature than this country.

One plausible explanation that has been given of our virtually unique experience is the greater severity of our depression, following the greater expansion and the speculative boom of the twenties. The recovery from 1933 to 1937 was not only one of the longest in our history but compared very favorably in amplitude with any previous recovery. It began, however, from such a low level that the volume of output at its peak only slightly exceeded that of 1929. During the last year of the recovery the expansion consisted to a marked degree of inventory accumulation and forward buying. The ensuing decline, as always from an inventory boom, was sharp but not of long duration. I expected that the recovery would soon be resumed and would carry us well above the level of the twenties. There were clear indications that a new recovery was under way before the outbreak of the war and the defense program created a new situation.

IV

While the mature economy thesis does not seem to me a satisfactory explanation of our experience during the past decade, it remains an important concept for fiscal policy, and the future role of deficit spending will probably be strongly influenced by our understanding of its implications. I have felt for some time a need for clarification of this concept.

I entirely agree that as an economy matures investment tends to decline relative to total income, but what to conclude from this fact is less clear. As production has become more capitalistic, replacement has become the preponderant part of gross capital formation. The TNEC testimony showing that a number of our large corporations have relied increasingly upon depreciation allowances for capital improvement was corroborative of this trend. Kuznets has shown that in this country in 1919–35 replacement constituted 68 per cent (1929 prices) and new investment 32 per cent of the yearly average volume of gross capital formation. Leaving out public agencies his figures were 81 per cent replacement and 19 per cent net capital formation.[1] Colin Clark has shown that the yearly additions to British home capital have been declining since 1875. His figures of net investment as a percentage of national income show a decline from 12.2 per cent in 1907 to 8.1 per cent in 1924, 7.2 per cent in 1929, and 6.9 per cent in 1935.[2]

---

[1] *National Income and Capital Formation*, 1919–35, p. 49, and table 14.
[2] *National Income and Outlay*, p. 270.

But the British national income has continued to increase and perhaps never more notably than in the decade of the 1930's. What has changed is the character of the problem of economic progress, which has become increasingly that of taking advantage of opportunities to improve the capital we replace and the efficiency with which we use it. From this point of view, an increase in the obsolescence rate might well be of greater importance in determining real income and productivity per worker than the search for new outlets for further capital investment. And we should add, of course, that it is by no means certain that such outlets will not continue to be found, even in the mature economy. Colin Clark's own conclusion is:

> I believe the facts have destroyed the view up till now generally prevalent, that the rate of economic growth was primarily dependent upon the rate at which capital could be accumulated. The very rapid expansion at the present time [before the war] is taking place at a time of heavily diminishing capital accumulation. What is more remarkable, practically none of the capital which is being saved is being put into productive industry proper.

Economic progress involves an increase of income not only in relation to investment but also in relation to employment. In much of the monetary analysis of the past twenty years, income, output, and employment have been treated as counterparts which respond equally to changes in saving and investment. This may have had some advantages for short-run analysis, though it has led to much mechanical thinking in which employment has been regarded as an economic end in itself regardless of its character. It is the logical result of the savings-investment analysis that full employment should be the goal of fiscal policy. But the goal of economic progress is income, and the two do not have a fixed relation.

The rise of income relative to employment through the advance of technology has been one of the great economic phenomena of our times. It raises questions which thus far monetary and fiscal theory have refused to face. But we are making some progress. We have begun to stop identifying underemployment with depression. Now that under the stimulus of the defense program and

British war buying national income has risen substantially above any previous level while some seven million workers are still unemployed, it is beginning to seem inappropriate to describe a state of less than full employment as "stagnation," even in a technical monetary sense. But the lesson drawn is that we must spend more rather than less, for full employment remains the goal of fiscal policy.

Last summer Keynes published in the *New Republic*[1] a most significant article in which he referred to the failure of deficit spending to produce "anything like full employment in the United States." He ascribed this failure to the "gigantic powers of production" of a modern industrial economy. To quote:

> Coupled with institutional factors which tend to encourage accumulation and retard the growth of consumption when incomes increase, this means that an unprecedented output has to be reached before a state of full employment can be approached. The full industrial and agricultural capacity of the United States may well exceed 1929 by as much as, or even more than, 1929 exceeded 1914. . . . The conclusion is that at all recent times investment (and public) expenditure has been on a scale which was hopelessly inadequate to the problem. . . . It appears to be politically impossible for a capitalistic democracy to organize expenditure on the scale necessary to make the grand experiment which would prove my case . . . except in war conditions.

On similar reasoning, a number of American economists have recently said that our mistake in the thirties was in having annual deficits of some three billion dollars; they should have been ten to fifteen billions. My own view is that such a "grand experiment," besides being politically impossible in a democracy in peacetime and besides, incidentally, probably destroying democracy if it were tried, would not "prove the case," because the case as stated misconceives the nature of the problem. We have been accustomed to think of technological change as a temporary phenomenon temporarily displacing labor but through falling costs and widening market creating full employment once the state of technology has settled down. But the great question raised by modern experience is whether technology does settle down. Technological advance

---

[1] July 29, 1940.

was very great during the twenties, but Keynes says his public spending experiment failed because technological progress was much greater in the thirties. How ironical it would be if the ten-billions-a-year experiment should fail during the forties for the same reason.

I suggest that one important feature of an advanced capitalistic economy is that human labor becomes progressively the less efficient instrument of production compared with the alternative methods, which as I have already said, depend progressively less upon new investment in the quantitative sense and more upon new technique. The economic function of the producer is not to employ labor but to produce goods. At every step he faces anew the question whether to use more men or better machines and processes. Even in the present defense program the purpose will be to get maximum output rather than full employment. Even in England today there is complaint of unemployment. Even if we should attain full employment during a great burst of activity when we are taxing our economic capacity to the utmost and in our urgency cannot confine ourselves to the most efficient methods, it would not be permanent, even if that level of output should continue.

In monetary and fiscal theory unemployment is taken as a sign of waste. If it is pointed out that we can and in fact have increased income to new high levels without removing unemployment, the answer invariably given is that with full employment we would have still higher income. Keynes in the article I have quoted said: "The wealth producing capacity which is now going to waste in the United States is so far beyond our powers of measurement that it is useless to hazard a figure for it." But if we look at the problem as one in economics rather than simple arithmetic this is not so clear. There are always unutilized resources, material as well as human. Indeed, if this were the only question, why stop with the resources at hand? Why not count our unborn children among the unemployed? There is no other criterion of usability than the question does it pay in all the given circumstances. The question of waste of resources through unemployment can only be put to the test by increasing economically desirable output and if in such a test we find ourselves resorting to other means of production than human labor, the problem, whatever else it may be, is not one of economic waste.

I am not suggesting that unemployment is not our most serious human problem or that it is not the duty of government to provide for unemployment. The implications of what I have said for fiscal policy I will consider later.

A third important feature of a mature or advanced economy has been the growth of durable consumers goods. Terborgh has presented some striking figures for the United States from 1919 to 1939.[1] Of total expenditures (private and public) on all durable goods, producers and consumers, of 380 billion dollars, consumers durable goods amounted to 196 billions. The largest category—household goods—amounted to 91.3 billions or 24 per cent of the total. Residential housing amounted to 52.4 billions or 13.8 per cent. Manufacturing and mining expenditures for plant and equipment were 13.3 per cent, government expenditures for construction 12.1 per cent, passenger automobiles 11.8 per cent, and electric power and railroad expenditures combined 5.6 per cent.

Among the modern institutional changes which monetary and fiscal theorists have cited as preventing full employment have been those "retarding the growth of consumption," to quote again from Keynes's article. This is the other side of the oversavings thesis, but I have never seen the evidence to support it. I agree that a less unequal distribution of income would probably increase consumption, and that this is a legitimate concern of fiscal policy. I agree also that heavy taxes on consumption are undesirable when national income is depressed, or when there is less than full utilization of *economic* capacity (which is not to be confused with employment), though we cannot assume that there are not limits to taxes on higher and middle incomes beyond which not only consumption but economically desirable saving and investment will be impaired.

But to favor such policies is not to concede that in fact institutional changes have retarded the growth of consumption relative

---

[1] *Federal Reserve Bulletin*, September, 1939.

to income. It is doubtful whether in the more advanced countries the inequality of incomes has become greater during the last fifty years. Colin Clark in his latest book[1] presents evidence that consumption has been rising relative to income in Great Britain, Germany, and the United States. Certainly the growth of durable consumers goods, as Terborgh's figures indicate, has been one of the great phenomena of our times. It is a chief reason why I believe we have made too much of investment both in cyclical and in secular analysis. It bears also on the question of "outlets for saving," for while these are consumers goods their financing bears the same kind of relation to accumulated saving, and to credit from the banking system, as producers capital goods. Their bearing upon the multiplier I discussed in an earlier section. Since the first world war durable consumers goods have played a major role in economic fluctuations; nor is it possible to prove either from the data or by general reasoning that this type of expenditure has been the "passive" factor.

V

My purpose in this paper has not been to present a program for fiscal policy but to give some of my reflections about its theoretical foundations. I must, however, in concluding try to point out briefly some of the implications of what I have said for such a program.

The case for permanent deficits as compensation for oversaving and underinvestment tendencies seems to me unproved and based in considerable measure upon misconceptions of the nature and effects of the secular economic changes which are observable. I believe, further, and I think it follows from the logic, that if deficit spending were permanently carried on as compensation for tendencies toward contraction which would otherwise exist in the economy, and especially if we should take as our goal full employment, it would either eventually break down or would entirely transform our democratic, private capitalistic system; for its cost would become a constantly increasing fraction of the national

---

[1] *The Conditions of Economic Progress.*

income. I cannot stop to consider the banking and monetary aspects of such a policy, which are recognized by all students to be difficult. In so far as it is desirable to modify the flow of income it can be better done by taxation than by deficit spending. But the economic effects of different kinds of taxes constitute an intricate and difficult field which is even more in the pioneer stage today than deficit spending. We cannot proceed very fast or very far on a general formula about saving and consumption; and if we are seriously concerned about tendencies toward decline of investment, we must have due regard for the effects of tax measures upon risky investment. As a preliminary to a good tax structure, moreover, we must some day have a thorough overhauling of state and local in relation to federal taxation.

What I said earlier about the relation of income to employment points to the need for a permanent relief organization within a balanced budget. It is closely related also to old age security. One way to meet the problem may be by shortening the average work-span of the employed. Other questions are the flexibility of wages and the mobility of labor and enterprise. Another approach is through education for employment to help solve the problem of labor shortages existing side by side with unemployment. But I must leave this whole problem to others who know more about it. I can see no easy solution. Certainly I do not see it through deficit spending. As stated earlier it would clarify our thinking about fiscal policy to drop the criterion of full employment and think in terms of income.

It does not follow from what I have said about permanent deficits that governments should do no long-run borrowing for peacetime purposes. It has been desirable in the past, in this and many other countries, to do some of our investing collectively; and a moderate public works program for productive purposes, adjusted as much as possible to business cycle changes, is not inconsistent with the views I have expressed. There is a vast difference, both conceptually and quantitatively, between a policy of public betterment, based on what a country needs and can afford, and that of spending to get long-run full employment.

In the business cycle deficit spending can be of real assistance. For this purpose a large budget has advantages, for the automatic changes in it in response to economic changes can be large enough to have considerable effect, especially if we refrain on the decline from imposing new taxes or raising tax rates. Relief and unemployment insurance expenditures would add further flexibility and would probably have some pump-priming effect under conditions favorable to business confidence. One important requirement, I believe, would be to taper the deficits. It is in the tapering that the business cycle use of deficit spending comes most in conflict with the long-run view, for it involves a presumption that apart from the cycle the economy can be self-sustaining. Those who are convinced there are deeper seated contractive tendencies will want to spend sooner and will resist tapering on recovery. It has been my belief that if we could have begun to taper the deficits in 1935 when recovery was well under way, and could have avoided the labor difficulties of 1936-37, we might have avoided the new depression and carried the recovery to higher levels before the outbreak of the war.

One of the chief dangers in fiscal policy is the tendency toward exaggeration. We are behaving toward deficit spending as we behaved toward monetary policy in the twenties, expecting too much from it and defending partial failures by asking for larger applications of the treatment. With the recent requests for doubling or quadrupling the deficits we have reached about the same stage as in our insistence a decade ago upon larger and larger open-market operations.

Such overemphasis not only discredits fiscal policy but diverts attention from the need for other action. This has been particularly true as to price and cost behavior. Price and wage disturbances had more to do with the depression of 1937-38, I believe, than the sudden accidental balancing of the budget. One of the chief dangers in a spending program is that if not wisely applied it may raise prices and wage rates and interfere with its own success. One of the chief weaknesses of Keynes's analysis is his failure to see the importance of wages as a factor in cost of investment. In this country the confusion about wages and recovery, the failure to see that high wage rates are a result and not a cause of recovery, has done much to impair the effectiveness of deficit spending and other recovery measures.

Another consequence of exaggerated emphasis has been to make us think too much in terms of the aggregates of the income flow analysis. At the TNEC hearings already mentioned, the emphasis was on the contraction of investment in the thirties owing to oversaving and underinvestment and the consequent need for deficit spending; but the deficiency shown was mainly in housing, and to a smaller degree in business plant, and suggested the need for a housing program and an examination of conditions in the construction industry.

None of the comments I have made in this paper suggests that we should discard compensatory fiscal policy. On the contrary, nothing seems to me more important than that we should continue in the light of accumulating experience to study how to fit fiscal policy into a more rounded economic program. In so doing we must consider how fiscal policy can be used to preserve and improve rather than to destroy our present economic system and our democratic institutions.

14

AN APPRAISAL OF THE WORKABILITY OF COMPENSATORY DEVICES*

By John Maurice Clark‖

I have been told that no talk should include more than three ideas. Since the topic assigned me inevitably involves a larger number, it seems well to indicate at the start the points I shall stress the most. They lie in the field of expansion via deficit spending. The first point is that deficit spending can produce an industrial expansion, probably larger than itself, but tending to dwindle rapidly and disappear if the deficit spending stops. The second is that it is highly improbable that this form of stimulus can itself serve to initiate a revival that will endure after the stimulus is removed. And the third is that indefinite deficit spending is not an enduringly workable remedy for chronic, partial stagnation of an economic system like our own. I shall return to these points after dealing more briefly with other kinds of compensatory devices than deficit spending.

A preliminary question is: For what kinds of disturbances or dislocations are the measures aimed to compensate? It seems necessary to distinguish: (1) short cycles, (2) longer and more severe movements, and (3) a possible chronic state of partial stagnation which might be described as an underemployment-equilibrium, though not excluding cyclical fluctuations, (4) connected with these conditions, and especially with the third, secular changes in economic balance such as that resulting from a declining

---

* *American Economic Review*, Supplement, Volume XXIX, Number 1, March 1939. Reprinted by the courtesy of The American Economic Association and the author.
‖ Columbia University.

rate of growth of population or, possibly, of requirements for industrial capital. These distinctions will be kept in mind in the subsequent discussion of different compensatory devices.

I. Credit Controls

About credit controls I shall say little, deferring to those who are more expert. In general, they appear suitable to deal with the shorter cyclical movements. Also, since they have more power to restrain than to stimulate, they are appropriate to that theory which holds that the cause of depression is the preceding boom, and that the way to limit the depression is to restrict the boom. Further, if this type of policy succeeded in its immediate aim, its direct effect would seem to be an averaging of the rate of activity in booms and depressions, rather than a leveling-up to full-capacity rates of operation. If this averaging were accomplished, there might then be a further long-run tendency to bring unused resources into use and so gradually to level the rate of activity upward; but this is a debatable point, and the policy itself would seem to have no positive and direct effect in that direction.

If control were comprehensive, extending to all forms of credit, it could limit industrial expansion; but our existing machinery is not comprehensive to the necessary extent, and it seems to be unable wholly to stop "bootleg credit," as was illustrated in the stockmarket boom of 1929. It appears that for the purpose there is need of some qualitative control of the uses to which credit is put, and distinctions between different forms of credit do not at present seem a sufficient means of controlling the uses. Credit may be put to other uses than its form would naturally indicate. Consumer credit would need to be included in the system of control. And even granting comprehensive control, easy credit terms are not enough to make people use funds if prospective profits are a minus quantity. They can have some stimulative effect under favorable conditions, but they cannot of themselves bring the favorable conditions to pass, and their stimulative effect is limited. Credit control cannot by itself be expected to iron out major fluctuations by regularizing investment, and especially not to regularize it upward.

II. Taxed Money

Of systems of taxed money I am tempted not to speak at all, especially as they will be discussed later. As to the comprehensive system suggested by Mr. Dahlberg, I am impressed by the amazing complexity and ramification of the equipment of controls he finds necessary. Considering that any such new project of control regularly finds in practice that there are many additions necessary to stop up unforeseen gaps, one wonders what this system would grow into in application, if even the preliminary project is so complicated.

As to the form recently voted down in California, I am puzzled by the problem of the negative rate of interest implied in the present worth of a credit instrument yielding $100 at the end of a year and requiring weekly outlays amounting to more than $100 before the date of redemption. It also seems clear that the projected expansion of the flow of the circulating medium had no relation at all to any estimate of unused productive capacity which must be brought into use to supply the increase in real wealth which would be necessary if the money distribution were to produce any economic benefits. Further comment would perhaps be hardly useful. In any plans of this class, the uncertainties appear to baffle any attempt to predict results, including the uncertainty as to what the plan would turn into after it had failed to work precisely as first intended.

III. Unemployment Insurance as a Means of Regularizing Consumers' Buying Power

There is, of course, plenty of justification for this policy apart from its possible effect as a compensatory device. Considered solely from the latter standpoint, it is clearly suited to short cycles. In longer and larger movements, the "insurance" feature would presumably break down, and the system would become simply one form of deficit spending. In so far as it acts as insurance, benefits during depressions would be financed by the use of the accumulated reserves, in one way or another. But the liquidity of these reserves is a real problem; and it appears that for the purpose in hand this liquidity would be largely fictitious. Securities should not be dumped in large quantities on the markets at the times when large payments have to be made, these being precisely the times when the markets are least able to absorb them. Moreover,. these are just the times when the credit policy will point toward open-market purchases of public securities, rather than sales. Thus it seems that the reserves may more appropriately be used as collateral for borrowing. This consideration appears to strengthen the case for the proposition that reserves of the present type and amount are not called for in this variety of insurance. This question deserves serious consideration, together with the question whether a pay roll tax is the most rational method of stimulating employment.

How much effect can such a system have in stabilizing consumers' purchasing power? It seems hardly necessary to argue that it could not bring about complete stabilization, nor anything near it. The difficulties of financing such a burden are only too obvious. And it is also only too obvious that it is not practicable to guarantee workers, when they are not working, an income equal to what they earn when they are fully employed in a prosperous state of industry. This would mean that they would be guaranteed, for not working, more income per week than industry could possibly afford them when it is depressed and can offer only part-time employment. If the first movements of industry toward revival are not to be squelched, it must be possible for industry to hire workers who are receiving unemployment benefits, giving them something considerably short of full-time employment, and still affording them earnings which are larger than the unemployment benefits they have been receiving. In the nature of the case, the benefits cannot represent what we regard as a satisfactory "American standard of living." By benefits so limited, the shrinkage of purchasing power can be reduced, and depressions mitigated, but the major part of the problem will remain.

There is the further possibility of enabling individual industries or individual employers to secure lower premium rates by improving their unemployment record. This is sound in principle, but raises the question how much the individual industry or employer may be able to do in this direction. So far as the benefits cover seasonal unemployment, they are dealing with something which the individual employer can sometimes do a good deal to reduce, especially if cyclical fluctuations are absent or are not too severe. But cyclical fluctuations, except for minor and fairly regular ones, are too large and too uncertain for the individual employer to do much about by his own individual policy. And if they are violent, they carry with them a disruption of many kinds of schemes of seasonal stabilization.[1] This appears to have happened during the Great Depression. Here again, the possibilities of stabilization via unemployment insurance appear decidedly limited.

IV. Increased Wages as a Means of Increasing Consumers' Purchasing Power

First, we may assume that prices are raised enough to reimburse producers for increased wage outlays. This would not need to include at first any allowance for increased costs of inventory already on hand. The first effect would presumably be a temporary boom like that of the summer of 1933, occurring during the interval after the program was determined on and before it went into effect and due to producers stocking up in anticipation of increased costs and prices. Afterward, as the abnormally increased stocks were worked off, there would naturally be a reaction. If in the meantime nothing had happened to rouse expectations that some degree of revival would endure, the reaction would naturally carry the rate of activity as much below the initial rate as the boom had carried it above. However, while this was occurring, there would be another effect, arising from the fact that the initial increase in prices would not have to be as great as the increase of wage costs, due to the use of inventories bought or produced at earlier and lower prices or costs. This would lead to an increase

---

[1] On these points I am indebted to a study by Dr. Eli Ginzberg, of Columbia University, which is shortly to appear in book form.

in consumers' real purchasing power, which would tend to dwindle away as the old inventories were worked off, but would not be followed by a decline below previous levels. The total effect would be a compound of these two elements, plus the intangible element of business confidence. Whether any increase would be left after six months would depend on this intangible element.

In the second place, let us assume that prices are not raised by the full amount of increased wage costs, though some increases would presumably be necessary. In other words, let us assume the conditions contemplated by the early policy pronouncements of the NRA. Here the effects already considered would appear in diminished degree, together with an enduring increase in real wage disbursements, at the expense of profit margins per unit of sales. The net effect would depend on the relative magnitude, and also the timing, of the increase in purchases responding to the increased real-wage disbursements and any offsetting decreases resulting from the decreased profit margins per unit of sales. If both wages and profits were spent completely and with equal promptness, the two would offset one another. But since wages are disbursed and spent ahead of profits, there would naturally be a temporary stimulus to physical output, though since the total increase in consumers' spendings comes out of previous increases in wage-cost disbursements, it is hard to see how any increase in physical volume, from such a source, could bring a revival of profits. And the ultimate outcome would depend mainly on the effect on capital outlays.

We may fairly assume that at the time the program is initiated, capital outlays have been less than depreciation for some time and capital equipment has deteriorated. If the shrinkage in demand has not been too severe, and especially if confidence in natural recovery has not disappeared, there are likely to be capital outlays which would soon be made if wages were not increased. An increase in the rate of physical output, taken by itself, might tend to speed them up.[1] But taken in connection with a reduced profit

---

[1] Cf. Kuznets, "Relation Between Capital Goods and Finished Products in the Business Cycle," *Essays in Honor of Wesley Clair Mitchell*, pp. 209–67.

ratio and increased prices of capital goods, the net effect seems more likely to be a decrease in capital outlays below what they would have been if wages had not been increased. This is likely to outweigh the rather thin margin of increase in the wage earners' real spending power, and thus to have a retarding rather than a stimulating effect on recovery.

In 1933, however, the situation was different. There were then vast excesses of productive capacity, relative to the inordinately-shrunken demand, and there was little faith in natural recovery. Under these conditions there was little prospect of early revival of capital outlays if wages were undisturbed. In short, there was probably little to lose on the side of capital outlays, in the immediate future. In fact, one kind of capital outlay, namely, inventories, is closely enough related to current rate of output so that it might respond to this factor, even if profit margins were declining. Thus, in such a special situation, the net effect of wage increases might be stimulative to the rate of physical output at the bottom of a depression. Even here, however, if revival is to go very far, prospective earnings must be sufficient to justify capital outlays beyond the bare minimum which is virtually necessary if the current rate of output is to be handled at all.

It should perhaps not be necessary to note that the mere fact that wages have been raised does not tell us enough to enable us to predict the results at all definitely. The real question is whether they have been raised above what some workers are worth to an employer (in which case unemployment will result). As to rates of profit, the crucial question is the hope of early return to fairly normal levels.

Here, as in the first case, increased prices of capital goods are likely to prove a handicap to the revival of capital outlays. In the capital goods industries the way to recovery would seem to lie in reduced prices rather than in increased wage-cost disbursements. Other difficulties might be mentioned, perhaps especially the dilemma of sectional wage differentials in which the government necessarily becomes embroiled, and of which we have not heard the last.

To sum up, when conditions are as bad as they were in early 1933, increased wages may initiate the first steps of a revival, but the effect is likely to be soon spent unless other forces take up the burden and if other forces are to take up the burden, wage increases must not be carried too far. If they are carried too far they may effectually prevent anything more than a feeble and tentative revival.

V. Limitation of Hours, to Spread Work

This is hardly a means of stabilizing economic activity, but rather, in the main, a means of distributing the burden of unemployment. If combined with increased wage rates, it becomes a means of distributing the benefit of the increased wage rates so that instead of the same number of workers making increased weekly earnings, a larger number make the same weekly earnings as before. Any effect which the shortening of hours in a depression may have on total physical output is dependent on a balancing of factors too subtle to be assessed theoretically, and probably too obscure to be isolated statistically.

The chief danger is perhaps that of neglecting the distinction between a work-sharing standard of hours and a true optimum working week, which would be longer. The optimum may be taken as the length of working week needed to produce all the output that is worth producing, and work sharing, as a shorter week used to spread out a smaller amount of employment, at a time when we are unable for commercial reasons to produce up to the economic optimum. There is real danger that standards of hours of the work-sharing sort may persist into more normal times, when they will act to limit production to an undesirable extent. Even if the industrial system as a whole does not reach full capacity operation, such limitations of hours are likely to create bottlenecks which will limit total production.

It may perhaps be contended that our capacity to produce increases faster than we know how to assimilate the increase without experiencing the phenomenon spoken of as "overproduction," and lapsing into a depression; and that it is therefore desirable to prevent our productive power from growing too fast, even if this means stopping short of our inherent optimum capacity. This, however, is a doubtful point, and amounts to a confession of defeat which we are, I take it, not yet ready to make. Unless it is established as true, we may fairly assume that it is undesirable to do anything to set artificial limits on our power to produce.

VI. Anticyclical Deficit Spending Intended to Be Offset by Surplus Financing during Subsequent Prosperity

This is commonly spoken of as "pump-priming," but it seems that there is need to distinguish two types of possible effects, only one of which really deserves the name of pump-priming. First, such spending may be a stimulus to production, which may be self-multiplying to some extent but not to any significant extent self-perpetuating. In this aspect it may be useful to tide-over a depression until other forces initiate a self-sustaining revival. The much discussed "multiplier theory" implies this kind of an effect; and, strictly construed, it implies nothing more.

Secondly, there is the theory of pump-priming, properly so-called, if one may legitimately build a theory out of the implications of such a term. These implications include the idea that deficit spending can itself start a revival of such a sort that it can go on under its own power after the stimulus of deficit financing has been removed. This distinction seems important.

It is my present view that the multiplier theory contains a significant truth (though some formulations need considerable qualification) but that the pump-priming theory, as I have defined it, requires a combination of favorable conditions which are not likely to be found in practice. Our own experience in the Great Depression seems to indicate the power of deficit spending to produce a stimulus, probably greater than itself, and tending to stop when the deficit spending stops or shortly thereafter. But there seems to be no clear indication of enduring effects of the true pump-priming sort. We seem in danger of being committed to continued deficit financing in order to avoid an economic relapse. Let us examine the multiplier theory.

In the first place, its application is not confined to public spending. For the purpose in hand, private capital outlays are deficit spending, and carry all the stimulative effects without some of the

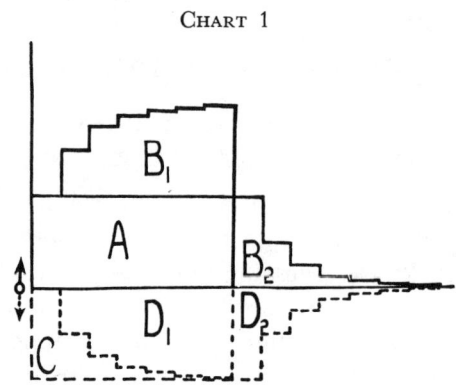

CHART 1

SIMPLIFIED MULTIPLIER DIAGRAM*

Vertical dimensions: dollar magnitudes. Horizontal dimension: time.
Area A = public deficit spending.
" B_1 = multiplier effect.
" B_2 = dwindling aftereffects.
" $C + D_1$ = public borrowing.
Areas, D_1, D_2 = deflationary uses of increased income.

drawbacks which apply to public deficit spending. My own first consideration of this theory was as an explanation of the expansion phase of a normal business cycle, and had nothing to do with public stimulative spending. It was not concerned to explain

---

* This chart is suggestive only. It is too neat and simple to represent accurately any probable facts, but exhibits to the eye (with no claims to accuracy) certain quantities which probably exist, and certain interrelations deserving investigation, to see if their existence is corroborated by the facts. (Further comment added on the occasion of reprinting, 1943: In terms of a balance between saving and investment, the chart traces the effect of an increase of "investment" in increasing income until increments of saving, represented under D_1, and increments of "investment," represented under A, are equal. Then a decrease in "investment" results in decreased income until savings, represented under D_2, decrease by an amount equal to the decrease in "investment." These income-movements are, of course, in money terms, not physical.)

cumulative increase so much as why it reaches a limit.[1] In the second place, the multiplier works downward as well as upward, and presumably at about the same rate. This is shown in the accompanying chart, representing orthodox multiplier theory in highly mechanical and simplified form. Vertical dimensions represent money quantities and horizontal dimensions represent time. The area A represents public stimulative spendings, continued for a long enough time—presumably more than one year—to allow practically the full "multiplier" effect to come into being. The area B_1 represents this multiplier effect (assuming constant "leakages" of $\frac{1}{2}$ and a multiplier of 2), and the area B_2 represents the dwindling aftereffects which continue after the public spending has stopped. They proceed on a downward curve which exactly reverses the upward curve of the multiplier. This represents what might be expected from a sudden stoppage of the public outlays, unless some stimulus from another source had occurred in the meantime. The recession of 1937–38 has by some been attributed, partly at least, to this kind of an effect, and the provision that the present public works program must be substantially completed by June 30, 1940, would appear calculated to produce what is from this standpoint precisely the wrong effect, when this deadline is reached.

This suggests the need of gradual tapering off of public spending. And this seems clearly desirable. But an examination of the geometry of the diagram will show that no mere tapering off will avoid a shrinkage of the total flow of income and spending. It may be mitigated if the leakages decline, and the multiplier correspondingly increases as the revival proceeds (and to some extent this is likely to happen). Or it may be counteracted if in the meantime some private investment spending comes into being, of a sort which is not closely tied to the current rate of consumer spending, and continues unabated after the tapering off of public spending begins. True pump-priming would seem to depend on the development of this kind of private investment. Let us look, then,

---

[1] This occurred about 1930, when Mr. R. F. Kahn must have been working out his formulation, first published in 1931.

at the effects of public deficit spending on private investment, this being the crucial factor from the standpoint of enduring effects. As Dr. Copeland has pointed out, public investment has not been able, with all the efforts we have made, to fill the gap created by shortage of private investment. A free flow of private investment remains a prime requisite of successful policy.

First, as to inventories. These apparently tend to follow the current rate of output fairly closely, increasing when it increases and decreasing when it decreases, being affected secondarily by the general state of business confidence. Thus the effect of changes in the amount of inventories would be to supplement and intensify the effect of the multiplier, both upward and downward, especially at times when the curve is rising or falling quite rapidly. No important enduring pump-priming effect is to be expected from this source.

The demand for durable capital equipment is affected by the obsolescence of existing units; and this is compounded with the effect of increasing demand for the final product, which may reduce or eliminate the amount of existing excess capacity of standard quality and efficiency. Equipment may be good enough to use for standby purposes or on a part-time basis, while if an increase of demand brought it into use for a larger percentage of the time, it would pay to replace or modernize it. Hence the demand for durable equipment does not remain at zero until all the existing excess capacity is in use, and then start up suddenly: it begins to rise with any significant increase in the demand for the product it manufactures. Thus public deficit spending, by increasing the demand for consumers goods, would naturally cause some increase in the demand for durable capital equipment; and this increase would come fairly promptly, without waiting for all the existing excess capacity to be called into use.

This effect would be complicated, however, by the effect of the policy on businessmen's expectations as to future demand and especially future net earnings. If they expect the pump to be primed successfully, they will be readier to make long-term investments, and that fact will of itself tend to bring the expectation to

APPRAISAL OF WORKABILITY OF COMPENSATORY DEVICES 303

pass. But if, on the contrary, they reckon that the current increase in demand for products is due to a temporary stimulus from public spending, and will disappear when this support is removed, this fact will make them slower to make long-term investments, except such as are physically necessary to meet the existing demand. Expectations of this sort will also tend to make themselves come true, and to cause the revival to be of a type which does depend on continuance of the governmental stimulus.

And if businessmen expect the public deficit spending to continue for a long time and in large volume, they will be affected by fear of ultimate impaired public credit, or of "inflation, or if not these, then at least by fear of burdensome taxes in the future. These are all retarding forces. The form of taxes will also have an effect, especially the question whether the system is so arranged that credits due to losses will or will not offset extra taxes due to high earnings. The present system is felt to have the quality of "heads I win, tails you lose," and this affects particularly the more speculative forms of investment. Recently a businessman, presented with opportunities of a speculative sort which would ordinarily appear as good risks, has said: "If we lose, we lose. And if we win, the government will get most of it. I guess we won't go into it." The revival since 1933 appears to have been marked by this kind of conservatism in private investment and to have been correspondingly limited.

One danger which has sometimes been mentioned is that of a progressive absorption of loanable funds, which if it did not lead to inflation might lead to a scarcity of funds for private borrowers when they did come into the market, thus tending to check revival. It has also been noted that this danger does not seem to have materialized in our recent experience. And on the whole it does not seem inherently likely to materialize; as may be illustrated by examining a neglected factor in the multiplier theory itself. The leakages which are responsible for the failure of the multiplier to go on expanding indefinitely themselves represent deflationary uses of income received from the public spendings, and these must, at least in a general way, tend to offset the inflationary effect of the public borrowings. They may not all come directly into the banks as loanable funds, but if they do not do that, they strengthen someone's credit position and thereby are likely to reduce the need of borrowing from the banks in the future.

Returning to the chart, the public borrowings and the deflationary effect of the leakages have been represented in dotted lines below the zero line. For simplicity, the deflationary uses of funds have been shown as offsets to the public borrowings, even though this may be subject to considerable qualification, since they may not all come into the same sectors of the credit market. Thus the rectangle C plus D_1 represents the total public borrowing, equal to the deficit spending. The area D_1 represents the deflationary uses of the resulting incomes, and the remaining area, C, may be taken (with qualifications already noted) as representing the net inflationary effect on the economic system as a whole. This is a finite quantity equal (in this figure) to twice the amount of deficit spending in one of the periods into which the figure is divided (and which represent the average time required for increased private income to lead to increased spending). So far as this representation can be taken as correct, this is the limit of the net absorption of credit (or of net inflation) for the whole economic system. The area D_2 represents the deflationary uses of what is left of the increased income after the public spending stops. It offsets the net absorption of credit, and leaves the system in an unexpanded state.

There has, however, been an important shift in credit relations. On the assumptions already made, the government owes more money and private individuals less. Whether this is beneficial or not I will not attempt to discuss. And whether this last bit of analysis is justified or not, the fact remains that there is nothing self-limiting about the debt the government is piling up. It goes on increasing without limit. It does not represent a net burden of this amount on the economic system as a whole, but it does represent an obligation on Americans as taxpayers to transfer ever increasing sums to Americans as bondholders; and this can easily reach a point at which it will retard business activity materially;

while even before that point is reached, the expectation of it can have a similar retarding effect.

Another retarding effect could occur in case the public spending program is so handled as to result in pegging the prices of construction and construction materials against a decline which might have proved attractive to private investors. Another can occur wherever the public investment which is being made enters into competition with private investment. Where this is the case, one dollar of public capital expenditure can easily scare away several dollars of private capital outlays. Dr. Copeland has shown that the amount of such competitive public investment has been very small, relative to the total; but the amount of private investment it has served to prevent may have been considerably larger.

One possibility seems particularly disquieting; namely, that the total deficit burden may reach a point at which it is doing more to hold business back than the current spending is doing to stimulate it, and still it may be true that the immediate effect of more spending will be a (temporary) stimulus, and the immediate effect of stopping will be a recession. When the total public debt has grown to threatening proportions, current additions will not quickly lift it to a new order of magnitude, and therefore may not make much immediate difference to the apprehensions which constitute the chief discouraging effect of the situation, while the immediate stimulative effect of further public outlays remains. Such a situation, if it comes about, would be almost exactly like that of the victim of a habit forming drug. The parallel is closer than one likes to contemplate.

Various other problems might be briefly mentioned. Sound and justified spending projects cannot be improvised, but must be planned and scrutinized long ahead. The planning which has been done since 1933 has accomplished much, but it probably remains true that public works cannot be gotten under way in large volume promptly enough to check the decline in a depression. Nor is it easy to taper them off promptly when the need for a stimulus decreases. If politically controlled, they are too tempting to those who could use them as political trading stamps or political bribes. And our experience has shown that it is easier for an administration to start Congress on this route than to stop it when it seems to have gone far enough. Our political shortcomings make it extraordinarily difficult for us to use such an anticyclical timing program with the necessary combination of skill, integrity, and backbone. Under these conditions, the fact that we have learned that deficit spending can really stimulate business may be one of the most dangerous results of the depression.

VII. Chronic Depression and Continued Deficit Spending

Most of the possible causes of chronic depression seem to act through a lack of disposition or capacity to spend the full amount of our national income as it is under conditions of reasonably full capacity operation. One way of expressing this is to say that under such conditions there is a tendency for savings out of income from immediate past production to exceed investment in the purchase of the products of current production. For this purpose, savings out of revaluation-income and investment in such things as securities already outstanding should be excluded. The effects of a declining rate of growth of population and of a possible declining rate of expansion of capital requirements register through this basic balance or unbalance.

Regardless of whether such an unbalanced tendency has existed in the past, it may exist in the future. The Brookings study has found it true of the post-War prosperity period; and while the figures are probably inconclusive, and the theory is to that extent unproved, one should be careful not to draw from this the unwarranted conclusion that it has been disproved.[1] The theory has also been criticized on the ground that, if it were true, there should have been a chronic depression during the twenties, instead of an unprecedented burst of prosperity. This criticism is worth examination, but seems on the whole unwarranted. Instead, it seems that, through the action of the investment markets, a discrepancy

---

[1] The Brookings study does not make the exclusions from savings which I have indicated above.

of the sort we are discussing could easily result in a temporary boom, leading to an ultimate reversal. Let us examine this possibility for a moment.

We may assume that four billion dollars flow into the securities markets seeking investment, while only three billions flow out through the issuance of new securities for the purchase of capital equipment. The natural result is a rise in the prices of outstanding securities. Some of the profits would be taken out to be spent for consumption and some would be reinvested, tending to a continued rise. If this were all, the process would presumably go on until one billion dollars had been taken out for consumption expenditures, after which prices and economic activity would be stabilized. And in the meantime, possibly five billions might have been added to the total market value of securities outstanding.

But this is not all, since people buy stocks on margins, and credit funds as well as savings flow into the markets, thus adding to the original one billion of excess funds seeking investment. Then prices of securities may not be stabilized until two or three billions instead of one billion have been taken out and used for consumption. In that case, an excess of savings would have been converted into an excess of spendings, and production, instead of being depressed or stabilized, would be stimulated. In the meantime, the prices of securities would have been raised to an irrationally high level in terms of prospective earnings, and this process would somewhere reach its limit, after which the whole structure would collapse. At this point I may take refuge in my rôle as a theorist, and leave it to the students of economic behavior whether this picture bears sufficient resemblance to the facts of the post-War boom and collapse to indicate the probability that it describes a significant causal element.

Immediate future conditions are different. With a market psychology not calculated to sustain a boom, and with margin trading limited by increased margin requirements, the same cause, if it operates, is perhaps more likely to result in chronic depression, possibly temporarily mitigated or neutralized by a more modest stock-market expansion. And this suggests the interesting theoretical query whether controls of the securities markets could be made so delicate as to have, at least temporarily, a neutralizing effect, if that were desired. Into that question I will not go.

If the basic tendency I am discussing exists, public deficit spending can be an offset, but not forever, and not in sufficient volume to neutralize any very large shortage of private investment; that is, not without disastrous consequences, defeating the end in view. We have not reached the limit of our debt-bearing power, but we do seem to have reached a point at which the piling up of public deficits is a deterrent to private capital outlays, and probably to a larger extent than further public spending can safely undertake to neutralize. Private investment has not vanished, but it has not fully recovered, especially investments involving considerable risk and looking to a long future. Fears of future deficits and exorbitant taxes awake easily and make revival an unduly sensitive plant. We can stand this for awhile more—preferably with some assurance that the treasury is not to be treated as a bottomless grab bag for pressure-group interests—and provided we are meanwhile making progress toward more enduring adjustments.

The problem might be formulated as one of stimulating investment, or limiting savings (and increasing consumer spendings) or both, the stimulative method being inherently the more promising. We might stimulate investment by methods which would increase profits and also increase savings; and we might limit savings by methods which would drastically reduce inequalities of income and also cripple the flow of investment. If they involved ill-judged increases of wages, they might thereby reduce the volume of employment. Neither of these is a solution, though the second is more clearly destructive than the first. What is needed is adequate incentive to invest, without such large rewards as would bring about a top-heavy scale of income distribution such as might result from high profits, or even from what business now regards as moderate profits on a rapidly increasing per capita investment (which is one of the postulates of our problem). Low interest rates are clearly indicated, but there is fairly wide agreement that this alone is not sufficient.

Wages should be as high as possible without actually reducing employment, and some added distribution of consumer-income out of public funds will probably be a necessity for some time to come, including assisted low-cost housing. Collective bargaining should increase. But business should not be given occasion to fear that government is fastening upon it a protected monopoly, more powerful and burdensome than any "capitalistic" monopoly; namely, a monopoly of organized labor. If grounds for such fears exist, they should be removed.

As to profits, after the lean years we have been through, capital will probably be content to invest on more moderate returns than prevailed before 1929; and it is my belief that it must do so if our system is to avoid shipwreck. But some prospective return is required. Taxes can without undue ill effects take enough to reduce materially the investor's remaining margin, but they must not treat gains and losses so unequally that risk-taking is penalized and turned into a virtual certainty of loss. Public utility capital will be forthcoming in adequate volume for lower returns than it has enjoyed in the past, if it knows what to expect—as at present it does not.[1] One thing which might lend important aid would be a reduction of the spread in costs between high-cost and low-cost producers, in order that business might be attractive to investors without the necessity of offering the low-cost producers unnecessarily high rewards, in order that the higher-cost producers may have enough to live on.

On the side of savings, the effects of the social security system on private savings should be studied, as well as the question of revising downwards the existing provisions for reserves, now financed out of pay roll taxes directly burdening the act of employing labor. We have here a powerful instrument for modifying the balance between saving and investment, if deliberately used with that purpose in mind. A tax system capable of raising large revenues from clear net income, without laying heavy burdens on

---

[1] Since the above was written the agreement of the TVA to purchase utility properties has reduced this uncertainty, but not wholly removed it.

small and smallish incomes, would be another powerful instrument in the right direction. At present, large volumes of tax-exempt securities seem to be an obstacle to a rational system.

Am I proposing a policy based on a stagnation theory which I have stated is unproved? I submit that, regardless of the truth or falsity of any such theory, the general measures I have suggested deserve to be either carried out or searchingly studied. If there is no truth in the stagnation theory, we could select from the proposed program simply those features favorable to liberal profits and optimistic business expectations, and be assured of the release of a flow of dammed up private investment greater than any deficit spending we could afford. The resulting recovery would, of course, end in another depression. And a more balanced policy has the better chances in the long run. In the meantime, we badly need statistics which may furnish better measures of savings, investment, and, so far as possible, potential investment.

To conclude, there is no simple formula, or set of formulas, guaranteed to cure all the irregularities and shortcomings of the system of private enterprise. If we are to keep the system at all, we must expect to put up with a good many of these shortcomings, including some business fluctuations. On the other hand, the operation of the system can be improved, and the fluctuations mitigated, by intelligent action. And it goes without saying that we shall be dissatisfied so long as there are serious shortages of employment, and that we shall be irresistibly moved to tinker with the system. Such tinkering is dangerous; granted. If crudely and impatiently done, we may very easily find that we have, without wishing it, tinkered the system out of existence. But doing nothing is dangerous, too. We live in dangerous times. What may reasonably be asked is that, when we tinker, we shall do it with a solemn sense of responsibility and with the utmost foresight humanly possible as to the consequences and their dangers.

15
A SURVEY OF MODERN MONETARY CONTROVERSY*

By Dennis H. Robertson‖

§ 1. There has occurred in recent years a vast orgy of debate in the fields of the theory of money, the theory of interest and the theory of trade fluctuation. Since the writers concerned have naturally tended to work out their own ideas in their own language, the debate has turned partly on questions of the meaning of words and of the inter-relation between different modes of thought and expression. Again, since some of them, animated by a sincere desire to impress the world with the importance of their message, have been at pains to emphasise their differences with older writers, the debate has turned partly on questions of *dogmengeschichte*, and tended at times to degenerate into a squabble about who said what first. Through the cloud of secondary disputation thus arising, it has not always been easy to see how far the parties are really at issue on matters of substance, or what the bearing of the whole discussion is on the problems of practical economic policy. To the lay public, and even to those professional economists whose main interest lies in other fields, the whole business must often have seemed, to quote from a characteristic letter of Edwin Cannan's which has recently been published, to resemble a number of Roman augurs disputing over the significance of the entrails of a

---

* This paper was read before the Manchester Statistical Society on Nov. 10, 1937, and was printed both in the Society's *Proceedings* and in *The Manchester School*, 1938, pages 133–153. It was reprinted as Chapter 17 of the author's book *Essays in Monetary Theory*, London, 1940, P. S. King. Reprinted here by the courtesy of the Manchester University Press, and the author.

‖ London School of Economics.

goose. Latterly several helpful attempts have been made to express precisely in mathematical terms some of the points at issue. Has a stage now been reached when it is possible to sum the whole position up broadly in more ordinary language, indicating in a general way what departments of the whole tangled controversy seem to be primarily concerned with words and methods, and what with more substantial issues? I do not know, but I should like in this paper to make the attempt.

The attempt, however, especially since it has to be made in cold print and not in informal talk, entails one grave risk which I must be prepared to run. The further one departs from meticulous argument, with quotation of chapter and verse, and the broader one attempts to paint the picture, the more one exposes oneself to the charge of distortion and misrepresentation. I do not know whether I shall enhance that risk or lessen it by abstaining from all quotations and from the mention of any living author by name: but that is the course which I have decided to pursue.

§ 2. I propose to begin by describing broadly in my own words the process of recovery from a depressed level of trade activity. An improved expectation of profit in the minds of entrepreneurs induces them to expand their expenditure on materials and labour, thus enlarging the total of money incomes. The monetary fuel for the expansion is provided partly by the creation of additional money by the banks, partly by the activation of money which has been lying idle in the hands of entrepreneurs themselves or of other people. It depends on circumstances whether the expansion starts in the trades making capital goods or in those making consumption goods: but in whichever it starts it will spread to the other. For the expansion of incomes in the capital trades leads to an increase of expenditure on consumption goods; and the increased profits made in the consumption trades constitute both a means and a motive for increased capital expenditure. And, of course, for similar reasons, expansion in one consumption trade spreads to other consumption trades, and expansion in one capital trade to other capital trades. The increase in expenditure tends to make prices rise, but the use of accumulated stocks, and the expansion of output, tend to prevent them from rising. Similarly the increased demand by entrepreneurs for the use of funds tends to make the rate of interest rise, but the creation of new money, and the withdrawal of old money from hoards, tend to prevent it from rising. In both cases, for whatever exact reasons, sooner or later the tendency to a rise in fact normally predominates.

I find it hard to believe that there will not be something like general agreement with this broad picture. Yet already, in filling in the details of this simple story, there is room for at least eight differences of opinion. I propose to classify these into differences of emphasis and differences of expression, and to deal first with the former.

§ 3. First, there is room for difference of emphasis as to the source of the stream of loanable funds which feeds the expansion. Some observers lay more stress on the creation of new money by the banks, others on the emergence of inactive money from its lair.

Secondly, with respect to each of these streams there is room for difference of emphasis as to how far the increased flow represents an automatic response to the increased demand, the mental disposition of the owners of the flow remaining unchanged; and how far it argues a changed mental disposition on their part—a revision of policy in the case of the banks, an improvement in the state of confidence in the case of the public. In geometrical language, are we to portray what has happened by a movement along an unchanged supply curve, or by a lowering of the whole curve? I am inclined to think that this is a matter in which mathematical habits of thought may have done some harm, by over-sharpening a distinction which in the world of human motive is apt to be somewhat blurred. Yet, so far as it goes, the issue is one about psychological facts, and not merely about words: and it has a bearing upon the course of interest-rates.

Thirdly, there is room for difference of emphasis as to whether, in the mutual impact of consumable goods and capital goods trades, the more active rôle is to be assigned to the former or to the latter.

Fourthly, there is the question whether the fertilising stream of loanable funds is to be regarded as flowing mainly through the credit market for short loans or through the capital market for long loans. This question is closely bound up with the third: for while expansion in the consumption goods trades involves recourse to the former market only, expansion in the capital goods trades involves recourse to the latter as well. It is also, for institutional reasons, somewhat closely bound up with the first question—that of the source of the funds. For while an entrepreneur may draw on his own inactive money either for the purchase of plant or for the purchase of materials and labour, the inactive money of other persons is more likely to be canalised, through the security and mortgage markets, into the former than the latter use: while *per contra* the money-creating banks have a traditional preference for lending, on short term, for working capital purposes.

There is however an institutional complication here on which some would lay much stress. The money-creating banks are not averse from intervention in one specialised department of the capital market, namely that concerned with Government debt. By relieving holders of their holdings, furnishing them instead with money which can be turned to other uses, the banks are thus able indirectly to propel a stream of long term loanable funds in the direction of those who wish to use them for the purchase of capital goods.

Fifthly, there is room for difference of emphasis as to the part played in the story by accumulated stocks of goods. On the one hand particular stress may be laid on the fact that it is on these stocks that the first impact of increased demand falls, and on the working of economic motive in the minds of the specialised merchants in whose hands they are largely concentrated; on the other hand, these things may be treated as complications of secondary importance.

In all these matters there is scope for difference of opinion as to what happens in the real world. There is room, therefore, not only for argument but for hope, within the well-known limitations of our unhappy science, that it may become increasingly possible to put argument to inductive test. But it would, I think, be very surprising if complete knowledge of the facts were to reveal that the sequence and balance of events were the same on each historical occasion. It may well prove that the views which find expression in these differences of emphasis are complementary rather than conflicting.

§ 4. I pass to the second class of differences, those which I have called differences of expression—though I am afraid there is no doubt that some of those who recognise here their own views will resent hearing them described in this way, since to themselves their own mode of language has quite naturally come to seem the ark of the covenant, essential to the exposition of the truth as they see it.

(i) First, a choice is open to us with regard to our treatment of the monetary fuel of expansion. We can analyse objectively, in terms of the flow of short term and long term loanable funds finding their way into and out of their respective markets in successive short arbitrarily delimited slices of time. Or we can analyse subjectively, in terms of the conditions which must exist, at successive arbitrarily selected points of time, if all the actors in the drama of the exchange of money for other assets are to be satisfied with their positions on the stage. So far as this paper goes, I have, as you will have observed, already made my choice; and for the purpose in hand, which is to give an account of events in language as nearly as possible approaching that of *Reading without Tears*, I am prepared to defend it. Against the alternative method it may, I think, be urged that psychological inferences from observed facts, valid enough in the still-life photography of stable situations, have their danger when introduced into the cinematography of processes of rapid and cumulative change. For at 5 p.m. on Wednesday, November 10, the moment we hit upon for our shot, it may be far from true that all the actors *are* satisfied with their positions on the stage. Things have turned out as they *have* turned out—there is nothing to be done about it at the moment—the banks are shut—the works manager is on leave—the cornfield has been laid down to grass. Considerations of this kind cannot, I think, be neglected if our economics is to be really dynamics and not simply comparative statics. Nevertheless, there is no need to be dogmatic or exclusive in this matter of verbal machinery. A Paretian analysis in terms of preferences equated at the margin does, provided it is duly qualified to allow for the occurrence of the unexpected and the undesigned, go deeper towards the heart of things than a mechanistic analysis in terms of money flows.

§ 5. (ii) Somewhat similar considerations arise in respect of the second matter to which I turn. We have a choice as to how we shall represent the causation of the rise in prices by which, as we have seen, expansion is normally accompanied. We can say that the rise is "due to" the impact of the swollen stream of money demand on to a volume of output initially unchanged; that the rise in prices in turn, since it is not accompanied by an equal rise in unit costs, stimulates an increase in the volume of output; and that the increase in output moderates the rise in prices which gave it birth. Alternatively we can say that the swollen stream of money demand stimulates an increase in the volume of output, and that the rise in prices is "due to" the fact that increased output can only be produced at rising marginal costs. The first method of approach leads naturally to the proposition "the greater the increase in output, the smaller the rise in prices," the second to the proposition "the greater the increase in output, the greater the rise in prices." Yet, paradoxically enough, these two propositions are not in conflict; each of them, in the sense in which it is intended, is true.

Against the first method of approach, that of the traditional quantity theory of money, it may be said that it is somewhat mechanical and also somewhat incomplete, since it fails to make explicit the underlying technical factors on which the outcome depends. The second method, the extension to "output as a whole" of the ordinary short period theory of value of individual commodities, fills in the gap. The danger of the second method, as an instrument for the analysis of a dynamic process, is to my mind that, unless expressed with extreme care, it leads to an overestimate of the extent to which, at any moment, the short-period equilibrium of the text-books is being attained. To say that price is determined by marginal cost is always bad theory; even to say that price at every moment is equal to marginal cost is a rash statement, unless the concept of marginal cost is defined with a sophistication which robs it of much of its instructiveness. We cannot, I think, in the analysis of a dynamic process, do without the supplementary Marshallian concept of *market* equilibrium, with price emerging from the mutual impact, at each moment, of the existing flows of money and of goods; and that is the concept of the quantity theory. Taking a longer viewpoint, price and output can be portrayed, if we like, as the joint determinees of the determining force of demand and supply, their respective levels being governed by the "elasticity of supply": though even so, the causal content of the concept of elasticity is the degree to which supply will "stretch itself out" under the impulse of a given change in price, not the degree to which price will "stretch itself up" in association with a given increase in supply.

I suggest therefore that here too a battle of words has been allowed to develop between two modes of thought each of which has something to contribute towards an understanding of the real world.

§ 6. (iii) Thirdly, I turn to a more complicated issue. There runs through much of the literature of this subject a suggestion that there is a peculiar connection between the rise in prices which occurs during an expansion and the contemporary formation of material capital—a connection of such a kind that those who suffer from the rising prices may be said in some sense to be bearing the burden involved in the formation of the material capital. Attempts have been made to give precision to this notion in various ways. Thus it has been said that throughout such a period capital-formation (sometimes nowadays called, rather confusingly, by the name "investment") is outrunning saving: or alternatively, that some of the saving which is being done is forced saving: or again, that a levy of real things is being extracted from certain sections of the population in the interests of capital-formation. Others, however, now denounce this whole order of ideas as nonsensical.

It is true, they say, that the rise in prices will raise the real incomes of entrepreneurs and lower those of dons and Members of Parliament, of *rentiers* and of the hired workers (of all grades) already in industrial employment. But the increased saving which will be done by the entrepreneurs is perfectly voluntary, and indistinguishable from any other saving. As for the dons and the *rentiers*, they are not of much account anyway; and as for the hired workers, they are getting the full value of their work to the entrepreneur (this part of the argument depends on the attainment of theoretical short period equilibrium); and in any case, since they are willing to continue at work for the lowered real wage, there is no foundation for the idea that any kind of constraint is being put upon them. To those rational arguments it is sometimes attempted to lend support by what appears to be a verbal trick. Definitions are so framed that the amount of money saved in any interval of time is identical with the amount of money devoted to the formation of material capital; and it is suggested that this *ex definitione* identity in itself somehow discredits the notion that there is anything worthy of special comment in the process by which the formation of capital is being carried on.

Thrown thus upon the defensive, the other party rake over again the entrails of the goose. They point out that the identity just mentioned would hold equally in a period of hyper-inflation in which prices were doubling every hour and output was not increasing at all; and they therefore decline to be impressed by it. They set themselves to excogitate alternatives to the offending definition—alternatives which turn on the parcelling of time into successive phases, or on a distinction between the saving, and the capital-formation, which is planned in advance and that which actually materialises. Attempts are made to analyse the concept of "levy" or "burden" into two parts, one associated instantaneously with each upward thrust of prices, the other enduringly with the raised state of prices. As regards the hired worker it is pointed out that in a period of rapid expansion the short-period marginal product of labour may well fall below its true or long-period marginal product; so that even if the worker is receiving the former he may in a sense be receiving less than his "due," even according to the rough canons of economic pseudo-justice. And it is suggested that the argument that his actions show him to be content to work for a lowered real wage is exposed to the same danger as other attempts to reason in terms of stable psychological preferences on the basis of the phenomena observed during periods of rapid change. So the debate goes on, and the end, I fancy, is not yet.

Now in all this there is, I believe, hardly any disagreement about what happens in the real world. In a sense therefore the controversy is, like the two preceding ones, one about words rather than about things. But it is also something more; for into the rival terminologies there enters an element of commentary or judgment. The party which seeks to give precision to the idea of a levy is anxious that we should understand that you cannot make an omelette without breaking eggs: the party which pours scorn on their efforts is anxious that we should understand that by breaking a few eggs you can make a most delicious omelette. This particular piece of verbal disputation, therefore, serves to introduce us to a more fundamental issue than any we have yet considered; and to that issue I now pass.

§ 7. Is there, or is there not, in considering the relation between monetary phenomena and general economic activity, anything in the notion that there is a certain state of affairs which is to be regarded as "normal," while every other state of affairs is to be regarded as a deviation from the normal, either by way of excess or defect? Until recently there has been, I think, something like general agreement that this *is* a valid and instructive notion; and a large number of attempts has been made to give it greater precision. Efforts have been made to define the policy which is required in order that money shall be "neutral" in its effect on economic life, not of course in the sense of failing to raise it above the low level which alone would be possible if there were no money, but in the sense of failing to introduce an incidental element of distortion or disturbance. The implications of this policy have been explored in terms of the behaviour of prices, of the rate of interest and of various types of incomes. A supplementary criterion of neutrality has been sought in the degree to which the banking system succeeds in acting as a true intermediary, that is in giving effect to the thrifty intentions of the public, without either outrunning them on the one hand or allowing them to go to waste on the other. Another has been sought in the degree to which "windfall" profits, or losses, accrue to the entrepreneur at the expense, or to the benefit, of the hired factors of production.

The difficulties which have been found in giving precision to this notion of normality or neutrality in the behaviour of money may be classified into three orders. The first arises already when we try to apply the notion to an imaginary static society. Even there the relation between the various criteria and subcriteria which have been proposed is not easy to establish. It would seem, for instance, that it must be conceivable that money should behave unneutrally (e.g. through a governmental inflation) even in a community of small independent farmers, craftsmen and traders, in which there is no question of distortion of contracts between entrepreneurs and hired factors; and this casts doubt on the adequacy of one of our suggested criteria. A second set of difficulties arises when we go on to examine the implications of neutrality in a society which is making steady progress in numbers, in technical skill, in capital equipment or in some combination of two or more of these three things. Some writers, for instance, have argued that under certain conditions neutrality will call for progressive reductions in the money rates of reward of the hired factors of production. Others would reply that it is satisfied *ex definitione* by the avoidance of entrepreneurial windfall profit or loss in the face of a money level of factor rewards which is to be regarded as one of the given conditions of the problem. Here the difficulty arises that we cannot take the money rates of reward of *all* the hired factors of production as fixed data if the particular type of progress under analysis entails an alteration in the relative abundance of the difference factors—as in the case, for instance, of a community whose capital equipment is growing faster than its population.

For these and similar difficulties it is not, I think, impossible to hope for reasonable, if somewhat rough and ready, solutions, and there has been, perhaps, some tendency to make too heavy weather about them. But a third and more formidable set of difficulties is encountered when we ask what there is left of the notion of monetary neutrality for a society which has once, for whatever reason, been thrown off the rails of steady advance, or for one which, like our own, has never really yet succeeded in adhering to them. Does it, under such conditions, imply the maintenance of the situation existing at the moment, or the restoration of some previously existing situation, or the attainment of some situation never hitherto attained? Or is it in fact not merely impossible to use it as a guide to policy but impossible even to believe that it means anything at all? And if it has no meaning in a fluctuating society, is it worth bothering about what it *would* mean in a steadily progressing one? Must not the whole line of thought be dismissed as a will-o'-the-wisp? It is this wave of scepticism as to the blessings of the golden mean, as to the validity of the Blondin[1] *motif* by which most monetary theory has been permeated, that lies behind the verbal sparrings about saving and investment and so forth, and is the real key to the controversies of the present day.

§ 8. In the light of this discussion, let us go back to the process of expansion with which we started. Penetrating as best we can behind the verbal smoke-screens, we shall find it possible, I think, to distinguish three attitudes of mind with which the expansory process is regarded. Since we have forbidden ourselves to mention names, we must find labels for these attitudes of mind; and we will call them the Optimistic, the Pessimistic and the Blondinian. But the matter is complicated, as we shall find, by the division of the Pessimists into two groups, united in little but their pessimism.

The thorough-going Optimist has cured himself of the Blondin complex, which he regards as an infantile obsession. To him the

---

[1] It appears, somewhat to my surprise, to be necessary to add a footnote to explain that Blondin was a famous tight-rope walker of the latter part of the nineteenth century.

expansion is a mere process of transition from one stable equilibrium to another, from stable equilibrium at a low level which should never have been allowed to exist to stable equilibrium at a much higher level; and he sees no reason why that higher level should not be the "normal" level in what he regards as the only respectable sense of that word, namely the level at which there is virtually full employment of all the human and material resources of the community. The Optimist is no doubt aware that the expansory process takes place in time and by stages; but he is not much interested in that fact, for his eyes are on the goal. So far as he meditates on the process at all, he pictures it as convergent and irreversible—or, to speak more simply, as a lift in which a wise community may voyage, almost timelessly and once for all, from the basement to the top floor.

The two Pessimists smell the seeds of trouble in the expansion from the start. To Pessimist A the processes by which it is being fuelled—the withdrawal of money from hoards, the creation of money by the banks—are sufficient evidence that it can come to no good. For in his eyes these are the very things which constitute unneutrality in the behaviour of money, bringing on to the markets for goods a one-sided stream of demand. True the output of goods is expanding; but it is expanding lopsidedly, with capital goods in alarming prominence. True also that profits are rising, furnishing entrepreneurs with the wherewithal to buy some of these capital goods, and mitigating to that extent the pressure on the banks and on the hoards; but that will come to an end by and by, as the classes who have been mulcted by the rise in prices gather strength to re-assert their claims. Then the inflated profits will shrink, the demand for capital goods fade away, and the expansion end, like all its predecessors, in collapse.

In the mind of Pessimist B the spectacle of expansion breeds a different fear. It is not the *means* for the purchase of capital goods whose drying up he foresees, but the *motive*. He resembles the Optimist in declining to be shocked at the methods by which the pump is being primed, and in laying great stress on current profits as a fertile source of funds for the purchase of capital goods; but he differs from the Optimist in seeing no secure platform ahead. For the size of these same profits gives him pause. Like Pessimist A he is concerned at their growth relatively to other incomes, but for a different reason; it is this relative growth itself, not the prospect of its reversal, which makes him uneasy. For rich people have less need to spend up to the hilt than poor people; hence sooner or later the rate of increase in the demand for consumption goods will decline, and with it will decline the incentive to purchase capital goods even on the existing scale. The entrepreneur profits which have been the sheet-anchor of revival will creep into funk-holes and so be revealed as the *fons et origo* of collapse.

The attitude of the unconverted Blondinian is more difficult to summarise; and it is easy to deride it as a ragbag of opposing views. Like Pessimist A he detects something *outré*, something worthy at least of special nomenclature, in the process by which the expansion is being fuelled. But he insists that climbing back on to a tight-rope is a different thing from falling off it on the other side, and that ostensibly similar measures are to be viewed with different eyes according as they contribute to the one proceeding or the other. To restore profits towards normality is not the same thing, though it may entail the same actions, as to inflate them beyond the normal; and a rise in the cost of living which, while thwarting the expectations of yesterday, restores those of the day before, is not necessarily either condemnable or certain to provoke resistance. Thus like the Optimist, the Blondinian has his gaze fixed, if I may mix the metaphor, upon a platform; but the platform is both less lofty than the Optimist's and less easily to be identified. For the business man will be in no hurry to admit that profits have been restored to normal; nor, with the best will in the world, is it easy for the Trade Union leader to distinguish between the windfall element in real wages which should be surrendered in the interests of higher employment, and the increment due to secular progress which can safely be retained. Above all, the state of employment of men and plant offers no certain test for the recognition of the platform; for the distribution of productive resources between the consumption and the capital-making trades is the result of the cyclical process from which we are seeking escape, and can neither be permanently taken for granted nor altered in the twinkling of an eye. Thus in respect of fullness of employment the "normal" now speedily attainable is inferior to the normal of our dreams—the normal of the society which has never lapsed from an even rate of progress. That higher normal, so the Blondinian fears, cannot be attained through the Optimist's recipe of aiming at it directly by letting the cumulative expansion rip—that would only be to court reaction and relapse. The only hope of attaining it lies in checking the cumulative expansion at some point selected with what judgment and wisdom we can command, and then letting the slow processes of occupational adjustment get to work. If, however, some such clean-up could once be effected, and a true Blondinian policy thereafter be pursued, we might indulge a reasonable hope for the future. For the disasters envisaged by the Pessimists—both the short sharp shortages of saving which are the bugbear of Pessimist A, and the longer, more debilitating gluts of saving which are the bugbear of Pessimist B—are alike the result of attempts to force unduly the pace of material progress.

§ 9. So far I have made little explicit mention of the rate of interest; for indeed, if I have a personal heresy in these matters, it is that in recent years, alike in academic financial and political circles, we have heard rather too much about that entity in connection with the processes of trade recovery and recession. But of course many of the discussions which I have passed in review can be, and have been, conducted in terms of the nature and behaviour of the rate of interest; and I must not let my personal heresy inhibit me from saying something more about it.

As I have already hinted (§ 4), and have argued at length elsewhere,[1] one of the controversies of which it has recently been the centre seems to me to be a shadow-fight. We may start by regarding the rate of interest ruling during any short period of time as the price which equates the flow of loanable funds, which some people are prepared to put on the market during that short period of time,

---

[1] *Economic Journal*, Sept. 1937, pp. 428 ff.

with the flow which other people are prepared to take off it. For this procedure it can be said that it accords well both with the ordinary language of the newspapers, and with the tendency of modern economic theory to exhibit the hire-prices of the several factors of production as special cases of a general law of pricing. Alternatively we may start by regarding the rate of interest ruling at a moment of time as registering a momentary contentment in the breasts of the members of the community with respect to the distribution of their resources between certain rival uses. For this more recondite approach there is also, on methodological grounds, a good deal to be said. But the two approaches are complementary, not conflicting: and both of them leave a great deal still to be added.

For the real issue lies deeper. In the broadest terms it can perhaps be put as follows. How close and fruitful an approach to reality do we attain by considering the rate of interest as the resultant of two main forces—man's ingenuity in dealing productively with the forces of nature on the one hand, and his reluctance to forgo the immediate consumption of the fruits of his efforts on the other? Of what order of magnitude is the difference made to the picture by taking account of two other factors—man's ability to control by means of specialised organs the supply of acceptable means of payment, and his readiness within limits to sacrifice income, whether present or future, in return for the advantages of avoiding trouble and of enjoying security against unforeseen contingencies?

The Blondinian answer to this question runs in terms of the divergence between a "natural" rate of interest, prescribed by the two major underlying forces specified just now, and an actual or market rate which is influenced also by the two minor or complicating ones. Like other Blondinian concepts, the natural rate of interest has encountered somewhat heavy weather in the course of its career. It was born entangled with probably fruitless speculations about what would happen in a world of barter, and with particular propositions about the behaviour of the price-level, from which it has had to be freed. It has tended to become entangled, too, with a different concept—that of an actually existing "profit-rate" received by the entrepreneur, and differing—whether through inclusion of a risk element or on account of imperfection in the market for loans—from the rate at which he can hire loanable funds from other people. Of the two forces deflecting the actual from the natural rate, which we may call for short monetary policy and liquidity preference, it is arguable that until recently too little attention has been paid by Blondinians to the latter; while in respect of the former it is possible to detect differences of emphasis as to the degree of its deflecting power, Wicksell, for instance (for I have not forbidden myself to mention the great dead) tending at times to represent it as almost absolute, and Marshall being concerned to stress its limitations. Above all, the concept of the natural rate of interest, like that of neutral money, has been explored rather from the point of view of a traveller who desires to keep to the straight path than from that of one who has lost it and desires to regain it. All things considered, it is not perhaps surprising that a movement should have developed to throw the natural rate of interest down the sink, and to pay scant heed to the cries of Blondinians to beware lest the bath-water may contain a precious baby.

§ 10. In the ruthless hands that grip the sides of the bath, we can perhaps recognise those of our old friends the Optimist and the Pessimist type B (§ 8). The Optimist is persuaded not only of the power of the monetary authority to make the short term rate of interest what it pleases, but of the existence of channels between the various parts of the capital market so wide and deep as to give that authority effective control over the long term rate of interest as well. He does not, I think, in essence deny, though he has his own way of re-phrasing, the Marshallian proposition that the same monetary action which tends to lower the rate of interest now will set in motion forces tending to raise it again later; but he believes that the monetary authority has it in its power to keep these forces indefinitely at bay through administering repeated doses of the same medicine. Nor again does he deny that, with a given level and a given distribution of output, a relation will be found existing between the rate of interest and the degree of the community's reluctance to postpone consumption. But he believes it to be within the power of the monetary authority to establish, without risk of reversal, such a level and distribution of output that this relation is satisfied, whatever rate of interest the authority chooses to prescribe.

On the other side of the bath stands the B Pessimist (who in this connection is sometimes the same natural person as the Optimist, in a different mood). In his eyes, as in those of the Optimist, the alleged extravagance of the human race presents no insuperable obstacle to the power of the monetary authority to keep down the rate of interest: that problem looks after itself through an appropriate adjustment of the distribution of real income in favour of those who are too rich to desire to be extravagant. His bugbear is a different trait of human nature—the debilitating caution which leads the owners of wealth to prefer safety to income and so to desire to withhold their saved wealth from productive uses. It is the business of the monetary authorities to indulge this craving for security to the best of their ability, and so to rob it of its sting, by providing the owners of wealth with plenty of nice safe money in exchange for their income-yielding assets. But it must be feared that there is a limit to their powers, and that after a point, so far as the long-term rate of interest goes, against the rock of "liquidity preference" the waves of monetary expansion will beat in vain.

In this field the shades of doctrine are so subtle, and still so much in a state of flux, that an attempt to paint a broad picture is especially risky; nevertheless I must take my life in my hands. It seems to me that between the Blondinian and the B Pessimist there are certain points of agreement and certain points of difference. Both would agree that at any moment the individual tends to hold his wealth so distributed between different uses that at the margin there is equality between the satisfaction which he derives directly from the inactive part and that which he derives, through the mediation of a flow of income, from the active part. Both would agree that a change in the individual's disposition towards the holding of inactive wealth, such as might be due for instance to an impairment or a restoration of political confidence, would lead to an attempt to transfer wealth from one use to the other; so that from a short period point of view the "state of liquidity preference," like the policy of the monetary authority, can be truly represented as exercising a *causal* influence upon the rate of interest. But in the mind of the Pessimist this causal influence of liquidity preference upon the rate of interest is a persistent and independent thing, overshadowing in importance every other force; while in the mind of the Blondinian, the longer the period of time under review, the more does this force recede into the background, yielding pride of place to the more fundamental influences of productivity and thrift. For this, in the mind of the Blondinian, there are two separate reasons. In the first place it does not seem to him likely that the rate of interest equated in the mind of the money-holder with the convenience and security derived from holding any nth unit of money is arrived at by some kind of intuition functioning *in vacuo*, which, apart from temporary fluctuations, gives an identical answer in all circumstances; it seems more likely that it will itself depend upon the rate of return obtainable from using resources in a more active manner. Thus (to use language departing a little, I am afraid, from that of *Reading without Tears*) the schedule connecting the holding of money with the rate of interest loses its status as an independent determining force, and becomes a kind of mobile satellite of the schedule connecting the rate of interest with the active employment of resources. But secondly, even if this were not so, and the "schedule of liquidity preference" remained unchanged in the face of growing wealth, what that schedule expresses is a desire not to hold so much money, but to hold, in the form of money, command over so many real things. Temporary fluctuations either way in the rate of interest will produce in the long run such movements in the level of prices and of money incomes as to destroy themselves, and to assign to the "liquidity preference schedule," as its permanent rôle, a share in the determination not of the rate of interest at all but of the price-level.

Thus the Blondinian, less sanguine than the Optimist about the power of the monetary authority to make the rate of interest what it pleases, is also less apprehensive than the Pessimist about the power of the hoarding instinct to oppose a chronic resistance to such a secular fall in the rate of interest as the forces of thrift and productivity may dictate. That is the nearest which I can get to putting in words of (approximately) one syllable the upshot of all this pother about the rate of interest.

§ 11. My purpose in this paper has been, first, to disentangle issues of words from issues of substance, and secondly, in respect of the latter, to set forth opposing viewpoints as fairly as possible without pronouncing between them. But I am aware that to many people I shall seem in my exposition to have done something more than justice to that general standpoint which I have called Blondinian. For to many people this standpoint seems outrageously timorous in its apprehensions that to aim always at the maximum level of activity immediately attainable is to court future trouble (§ 8); and at the same time outrageously complacent in its faith that through all the manifest evils of fluctuation there persists a long-period tendency of the system to right itself rather than, as some have argued, a chronic disposition to run down (§ 10). I would like therefore to end by making it plain that I think there is much even for the convinced Blondinian to keep turning over in his mind. How far has the resilience which he detects in the system been bound up with that rapid growth of population which for the western world has now become a thing of the past? Can the authoritarian State solve that problem of periodic painless transition from a higher to a lower level of fixed capital formation which liberalistic capitalism has failed to solve, and if so is the achievement worth the price? If it is not worth the price, would a drastic redistribution of income help towards keeping the system moving forward at a pace no greater than can be continuously maintained, and if so how is it to be achieved? To suspect that from a long-run point of view Cheap Money may prove a broken reed and Liquidity Preference a bogy man is not necessarily to suppose that all is for the best in the best of all possible worlds.

16

THE TRADE CYCLE*

By Ralph G. Hawtrey||

The output of literature on the subject of the trade cycle has increased beyond precedent since the war, but the numerous writers who have contributed to it have not always noticed that for the time being there *is* no trade cycle. The essential characteristic of the trade cycle is its periodicity. That of course is the meaning of the term, *cycle*. What struck the pre-war economists was that the alternation between good and bad trade was regularly spread over a period of from seven to eleven years, and that it was world-wide. Otherwise there would have been nothing to explain. That the state of trade should vary is what every one would expect. Were it always the same, like the temperature of the human body, that would have been at least as much in need of explanation as the trade cycle itself.

Since the war there have been ups and downs in trade, but they have not synchronised, or have only very partially synchronised, in different countries, and there has been no trace of regular periodicity. This change is significant, and ought to throw light on the explanation of the trade cycle. I shall return to it later on.

Clearly, in investigating the trade cycle, the first thing to consider is, what *are* the phenomena that vary periodically. The alternation is of good with bad trade, or of prosperity with depression. But these are vague terms. Students of the trade cycle are aware that the alternation is apparent at many different points.

---

* This article appeared originally in the Dutch "*De Economist*," 1926, and was reprinted as Chapter 5 of the author's book *Trade and Credit*, London, 1928, Longmans, Green and Company.

|| H. M. Treasury, London.

There is scarcely any field of economic activity which does not exhibit it.

But among the multifarious symptoms of the trade cycle, two tendencies stand out conspicuously and may well be treated as fundamental, a fluctuation in productive activity and a fluctuation in the price level. A fluctuation in productive *activity* is not to be confused with a fluctuation in *production*. The one is measured by the amount of effort put into production, the other by the amount of output resulting. Output depends partly on effort and partly on other factors, such as technical processes and natural conditions

Output may furnish a good measure of productive activity, when disturbing factors are absent or, if present, are allowed for. But employment is a better test. When the percentage of available workmen unemployed increases, productive activity is diminishing, and *vice versa*.

The trade cycle is composed of periods of good trade, characterised by rising prices and low unemployment percentages, alternating with periods of bad trade, characterised by falling prices and high unemployment percentages.

Since productive activity and the price level increase and decrease together, it necessarily follows that there is a corresponding fluctuation in the total *demand* for all products expressed in terms of money.

The money of which demand consists is provided directly or indirectly from people's incomes. The total of the incomes which people in any community have to spend I call the *consumers' income;* the total which they do spend I call the *consumers' outlay*. Consumers' income and consumers' outlay tend to be equal. The means of payment (comprising money and bank credit), which people have in hand, I call the *unspent margin*. Consumers' income and consumers' outlay can only differ in amount when the unspent margin changes.

The term "consumer" as here used must not be interpreted too narrowly. People spend their incomes not only on consumable products, but on investment. "Consumer" must be regarded as including "investor," and the consumers' outlay as including investment. For money invested is *spent*. It is spent on capital goods.

On the other hand, the consumers' outlay does not include the expenditure of traders on buying or producing goods to sell again. Such expenditure is not incurred out of a trader's income, but out of his turnover, the gross receipts of his business. All that comes out of his income is such additional capital as he puts into his business out of his own savings. This is expenditure from income on investment, whether the money be spent on an extension or improvement of fixed capital, or on a net addition to goods held in stock.

So understood, the consumers' outlay is the whole effective demand for everything that is produced, whether commodities or services. The trader who buys to sell again is merely an intermediary passing on a portion of this demand to one of his neighbours. The cyclical alternations in effective demand must therefore be alternations in the consumers' outlay.

Demand however is *relative*, and some economists have sought to explain the depression which marks the adverse phase of the trade cycle as due, not to an actual decrease in the consumers' outlay, but to an excess in the output of products.

The classical economists argued that general over-production was impossible, because no one produced except with a view to consuming, and therefore demand was necessarily equal to supply. Moreover, production was at its greatest during the active phase of the trade cycle, and fell off during the phase of depression, at the very time when the symptoms of over-production appeared. These difficulties could be met if the over-production were supposed to take the form of accumulation of excessive stocks of commodities. If production outstrips demand, it was said, a part of the products remains unsold, and traders, encumbered with unsold goods, become reluctant to produce more. Restricted production means restricted employment. Those conditions will continue so long as unsold stocks remain above normal. The redundant goods have to be sold off at a sacrifice of price. When that process is completed, traders' stocks will have been brought into relation with a reduced scale of production and consumption. The pressure on markets being then relieved, there is found to be a margin of unemployed capital and labour, anxious to start producing. When production revives, the existing stocks of commodities are found to be insufficient for the needs of markets, and the process of replenishing stocks makes for active production. Production in fact exceeds consumption, and will continue to do so till excessive stocks have again been accumulated, and the cycle is then started afresh.

This is a version of the over-production theory of the trade cycle. The theory by itself was incomplete, because it offered no explanation of why the accumulation and liquidation of stocks synchronised in different industries and different countries, or why the process should have a period of from seven to eleven years, or even why it should ever begin at all.

Accordingly the theory was further elaborated. To explain the length of the period, it was pointed out that, when output has to be increased in order to replenish stocks, the capacity of the industries concerned might have to be extended by the construction of new plant and fixed capital. That would take a considerable time. Not only does the construction of a piece of capital equipment often take months or even years, but the capacity of the constructional trades themselves is limited, and when they are con gested with orders they cannot undertake prompt completion.

At the end, therefore, of a time of depression, the period of recovery would be prolonged during the process of extending the equipment of industry. The climax would come when the fresh capital came into use, and the swollen output of consumable commodities would increase stocks up to normal and thereafter would exceed demand.

To explain why the movements synchronised in different industries, recourse was had to two arguments. In the first place, it was said, prosperity in one industry created demand for the products of others, and they in turn became prosperous and created further demand for one another's products. Secondly, the activity of an industry depended on psychological causes.

Producers become enterprising when they *expect* good markets; they become cautious when they *expect* markets to flag. Such expectations, it is said, are contagious; they are subject to the laws of crowd psychology. Optimism in one industry spreads to others; optimism in one country breeds optimism in all. In the same way pessimism when once it gets started tends to become universal.

The over-production theory thus elaborated represents, I think, fairly the explanation of the trade cycle prevalent among what I may call the classical school of economists. In many respects it fits the facts well. Experience shows that at a time of good trade the constructional trades are more active than the others, and when the tide turns they are more depressed. Stocks of commodities are redundant when trade is bad, and short when trade is good.

One thing, however, I have omitted. I have said nothing about monetary changes, or about the regulation of credit, upon which monetary changes usually depend. Economists of the classical school do not leave the monetary factor out altogether. But they regard it as subsidiary, and as merely modifying and perhaps intensifying tendencies otherwise accounted for.

But in the over-production theory, as I have just stated it, there are *presupposed* certain assumptions as regards money and credit.

The theory finds the explanation of trade activity in the replenishment of stocks depleted during the preceding depression, and of the depression in the liquidation of stocks accumulated during the preceding activity. The replenishment of stocks consists in an excess of traders' purchases over their sales. It is an addition to their physical capital, and must be paid for. The necessary funds can be provided either by savings out of income or by means of bank credit.

If they are provided by savings out of income, that means that a part of the consumers' outlay is diverted to the accumulation of stocks. If the consumers' outlay itself remains unchanged, what is left to provide the effective demand for commodities for consumption is correspondingly diminished. On that assumption there is nothing in the replenishment of stocks to make trade active.

If on the other hand traders increase their stocks with money borrowed from the banks, this is no longer so. The banks can *create* the necessary funds. The trader becomes indebted to the banker for the amount of his loan, and the banker becomes indebted to the trader for an equal amount on current account.

The trader can use the banker's obligation as a means of payment; he can assign it by cheque to those from whom he buys. He can thus add to his stocks of commodities without diminishing the amount of the consumers' outlay in other directions.

If the consumers' income and the consumers' outlay be supposed to balance at £1,000,000 a day, or £30,000,000 a month, and if traders set out to add £5,000,000 worth of commodities to their stocks in the course of three months, providing the necessary funds from their own savings, then the traders' demand for their own consumption will be diminished by that amount and the consumers' outlay as a whole for three months will be reduced from £90,000,000 to £85,000,000. If on the other hand the traders borrow the £5,000,000 from their bankers, the consumers' outlay will remain at £90,000,000, and the total demand experienced by producers will be increased to £95,000,000.

Here we have a definite addition to the consumers' outlay, a demand springing out of nothing. That does not however tell the whole story. It is important to trace as clearly as possible the ulterior effects of the creation of additional bank credit, and we shall return to the subject presently. Meanwhile it is enough to note that *without* the creation of additional bank credit, or some process equivalent to it, the desire of traders to add to their stocks will not on balance occasion any activity in trade at all.

Exactly the same line of argument applies to the creation of additional fixed capital. If the fixed capital is paid for from savings out of income, the amount of income available for other purposes is diminished by an equal amount. Professor Aftalion has maintained that the characteristic of the active phase of the trade cycle is a scarcity of consumable commodities relative to demand. In order to increase the supply, he contends, it is necessary in the first instance to extend the capital equipment of industry. That takes time, and while it is in progress the prices of consumable commodities are abnormally high, while the prices of capital goods, the products of the constructional and engineering trades and their materials, are also high, because they reflect the anticipations of ultimate profit from the sale of increased supplies of consumable goods. It would not be easy to establish the assumption here implicitly made, that at the end of the depression the capital equipment is not sufficient to give full employment to the population. But apart from that Professor Aftalion's argument really presupposes that the consumers' outlay provides an undiminished demand for consumable goods, while the additional supply of capital goods is paid for from some other source. In other words, whether by the creation of bank credit or some other means, the consumers' outlay is assumed to have been increased.

The same criticism is applicable once again to the supposed spread of prosperity from one industry to another. If the consumers' outlay is unchanged, then any increase in the amount spent on the products of one industry can only be at the cost of diminishing the amount spent on the products of others. So long as the consumers' outlay is supposed fixed, there is only one way in which it can be reconciled with an increase in economic activity, and that is by a general fall in prices. But this is the exact reverse of what experience of the trade cycle records; the active phase is invariably accompanied by rising prices, whereas falling prices are an outstanding characteristic of the phase of depression.

There remains the argument from the psychology of traders. Cannot trade become active because traders *expect* a good demand, even though their expectation is erroneous? And may not depression likewise be due to an expectation of a poor demand? An optimistic trader who gives orders for an additional supply of commodities need not pay for them till they are delivered. Meanwhile the producers will be the more fully employed on account of the additional orders. But the burden of financing the orders is not escaped. The producers must meet their outlay upon wages and other current costs from some source or other. Either they must borrow from their bankers, or they must meet these costs out of their own incomes. In the one case bank credits are created; in the other the consumers' outlay is encroached upon.

A speculative movement may lead to lucrative orders being given to producers for the delivery of goods at future dates. The prospective profit on such orders is part of a producer's income. If he refrains from anticipating the profit, and only borrows so much as is essential to pay current costs, he may be regarded as applying that part of his income to holding the goods in course of manufacture and in the interval before delivery. Here we have an increase in the consumers' income which does not depend on the creation of bank credits. But the addition so made to income is tied up with the goods in course of manufacture, and cannot come into the market for any other purpose till the order is completed and the goods are delivered. The purchaser must then pay for them, and he can only find the necessary means either from income or by borrowing.

If the speculator's expectation of a favourable market is mistaken, he will make a loss, or at any rate a smaller profit than he anticipated. This loss must be set against the producer's gain, and the consumers' income as a whole will not have been increased. Complicated as the effect of speculation may be, the amount of the consumers' income and the consumers' outlay remains the governing factor.

And at this point we may return to the question of their relation to the creation of bank credits. We saw that, if traders set out to increase their stocks of goods, and borrow the means of paying for them, there is an increase in the total effective demand. The traders' demand for additional stocks of goods, while it lasts, is *added* to the consumers' outlay, which comprised the pre-existing demand for goods for consumption.

The usual method of proceeding would be for a merchant or dealer in commodities to give orders to producers for fresh supplies, and it would be the producers in the first instance who would borrow. They might draw bills on the merchant and get them discounted by the banks, or they might obtain advances from the banks.

The sums credited to the producers are applied by them to pay the costs of production. But the costs of production are composed of the *incomes* of those who contribute to production, whether by their services or by the use of their property. The cost of materials used in production is similarly composed of the incomes of other producers. Thus the whole amount of the funds created by the banks is received as income, whether profits, wages, salaries, rent, or interest, by those engaged in producing the commodities.

The effect is to distribute the money advanced among them, and to increase their balances of cash by the amount distributed. There has in fact been an increase in the unspent margin, the total quantity of money and bank deposits. According to the quantity theory of money, that should tend, other things being unchanged, to raise prices.

We cannot assume without further consideration that other things will be unchanged. If the recipients of this extra money, both profit-makers and wage-earners, added it to their cash balances and kept it unspent, there would be no increase in the consumers' outlay, and no tendency for prices to rise. But this is extremely unlikely. Some of the recipients would be wage-earners newly brought into employment, who would spend their money on necessary consumption. Others would certainly spend some of their additional earnings on consumable goods. Others again would save part of the money, but saving would ordinarily take the form, not of hoarding money or of leaving it on current account at a bank, but of investing it. And money invested is spent on fixed capital.

A little of the money would remain behind in balances, for a man whose earnings are increased would hold on an average somewhat larger amounts of cash in hand than before; but probably much the greater part of the additional income is immediately in one way or another spent. It is spent on buying things from traders, who find their stocks of goods diminished, and are put in a position to pay off part of their indebtedness to their bankers with the cash received.

But we started by supposing that dealers in commodities desired to *increase* their stocks of commodities, and found it worth while to borrow from their bankers in order to hold additional stocks. Now we find that by doing so they bring into being a new consumers' demand, which tends to deplete their stocks almost as fast as they are replenished. What the traders have accomplished is limited to the excess of their purchases for stock over their sales to consumers, and the net increase in their indebtedness to the banks is so much as is required to finance this excess. The net increase in the unspent margin, the quantity of the means of payment, is equal to the same excess; seen from another point of view it is that part of their increased receipts which people leave in balances rather than spend or invest.

The traders' desire for increased stocks remains unsatisfied, and they continue giving increased orders to the producers. It may be pointed out that the consumers' outlay is increased as soon as the producers begin to borrow. The producers and their employees have more to spend while the orders are still uncompleted. The dealers find that the goods they have immediately in hand are actually diminished, though against the shortage they have command of a greater future supply. By the time an order is completed, the whole of its value will have become available to the producers as income. The net effect in increasing stocks will be limited to so much of this income as is kept in hand by the recipients in balances.[1]

In order to complete their programme of increasing stocks, the dealers in commodities must go on giving fresh orders, till the amount so kept in hand in cash balances is great enough to equal the additional stocks desired. But meanwhile the producers will be becoming more and more active, and there is a limit to their activity. As more and more producers become employed

---

[1] The recipients may spend this income not on commodities but on personal services. But those who are paid for rendering these services will in turn either spend the money or retain it in balances.

up to capacity,[1] they will tend to raise prices. And as the dealers experience more and more difficulty in placing orders and in securing early delivery of those placed, they will tend to defend their stocks against depletion by raising prices against the consumer. Here we have that rise of prices which the quantity theory of money tells us ought to occur. It comes about because people spend the money they receive, but only in so far as their expenditure cannot be met by increased production.

If we go back for a moment to the over-production theory, we can now see not merely that it presupposes an increase of bank credits as a pre-requisite condition of increased trade activity, but that the increase of bank credits gives rise to a complicated succession of reactions tending to intensify the activity far beyond its immediate effect.

It is equally true that when traders seek to diminish their stocks of commodities, there will be no flagging in the activity of trade unless they take steps to diminish their indebtedness to the banks. A dealer who reduces his stock, by restricting purchases or hastening sales, finds himself with more cash in hand. But if he spends the cash (whether on consumable commodities or on investments), it is paid away directly or indirectly to producers, and the adverse effect on markets is counteracted. The more normal course of events is that the dealers give less orders to the producers, the producers borrow less from the banks, they and their employees have less to spend, and the dealers consequently find that they sell less.

Here, as in the contrary case of the increase of orders, a *vicious circle* is set up. The dealers want to diminish their stocks of goods, but, when they restrict the orders they give to the producers, the consumers' outlay falls off, and their sales are so reduced that their stocks are little diminished.

The foregoing analysis of the effects of an acceleration or retardation of the creation of bank credit has been simplified

---

[1] The limit of capacity may be imposed by the available labour supply before all the available plant is active. This may occur in one locality or industry, or in industry as a whole.

by the omission of any reference to the investment market and the supply of fixed capital. The capital equipment of industry and transport for the most part differs essentially from those consumable goods which can be accumulated by merchants in stock. The effective demand for capital goods emanates from savings. These savings are a part of the consumers' outlay.

Nevertheless here also bank credit is a factor. It enters into the matter in at least three ways. A contractor who produces capital equipment may borrow from his banker for the interval before he receives payment. When the requisite funds have been raised in the investment market to pay for the capital equipment, a part of the shares or securities issued may be temporarily carried by underwriters or by dealers in the investment market with borrowed money. And finally an industrialist may avoid application to the investment market altogether, and may pay for an extension of his fixed capital by means of an advance from his banker, which he will hope to pay off out of profits in a short period of years. An increase or decrease of the bank credits created for these purposes has substantially just the same effect as an increase or decrease of those created to carry stocks of consumable commodities. The fundamental principle applicable to all cases is that no one borrows from a bank to hold the proceeds idle; he pays them away immediately, and they pass into circulation and swell the consumers' income and the consumers' outlay.

We have now shown that the variations of effective demand, which are the real substance of the trade cycle, must be traced to movements in bank credit. But we have still to explain why and how such movements in bank credit will occur.

Under pre-war conditions the creation of bank credit was governed by the supply of gold. If the lending operations of the banks were accelerated, and the consumers' outlay increased, we have seen that there would be an increase in people's cash balances. The balances of the well-to-do may be held in the form of bank credit, but those of the wage-earning classes must be in actual money, whether coin or paper. When the earnings of the working classes are increased, they begin to absorb cash, and the cash reserves of the banks are thereby weakened. Even in countries where paper money was used, the law did not allow of its indefinite increase without a prescribed backing of gold. Sooner or later therefore the restrictions on the supply of money would compel the banks to limit their lending.

That the transition from activity to depression was marked by a restriction of credit occasioned by a shortage of cash reserves in the banks is a fact proved by experience. But we still have to explain why the process by which the banks were led first to expand and then to contract credit was spread over a long period of years.

To a bank lending is the source of profit, and it will seek to lend as much as it can. But if any bank lends more freely than its neighbours, it will begin to lose cash at the clearing. This is a more immediate check upon it than the withdrawal of cash into circulation, and tends to make all the banks in a country keep pace with one another. It does not of itself prevent the whole community of banks from accelerating their lending operations together, but it prevents any sudden spurt except in concert. Such a simultaneous spurt may occasionally occur, when for example there is a reduction of bank rate, but in general the expansion of credit would be gradual.

And if the expansion of credit in one country with a gold standard outstrips the expansion of credit in the others, it will have to meet an adverse balance of payments. As we saw, an expansion of credit increases the consumers' outlay; it therefore makes the country a more favourable market to sell in. It attracts imports and diverts goods from export to the home market. The adverse trade balance thus occasioned has to be paid for in gold, and it can only be corrected, and the drain of gold stopped, by a contraction of credit.[1]

---

[1] When the balance of payments of any country is disturbed by any independent cause (e.g. external borrowing or lending, or good or bad crops) its credit position will diverge for the time being from that of its neighbours (see my *Currency and Credit*, pp. 110–16 and 163–74 (3rd edition).

Therefore just as one bank has to keep pace in lending with other banks in the same country, so one country must keep pace with the others. The desire for profit always points toward expansion, but, each bank and each country being imbued with caution lest it go too fast, the progress of the credit expansion is necessarily very gradual and slow. It is not merely like a procession keeping pace in response to a central command, which would no doubt move somewhat more slowly than a free individual. It is rather like a crowd moving without organisation towards an objective, under the condition that any individual who goes faster than the rest is immediately pulled back.

There is another factor which materially affects the rate of progress of the credit cycle. What ultimately limits the expansion of credit is the absorption of money into circulation, and we saw that it is absorbed mainly by the wage-earning classes, who receive and pay small sums, and have no banking accounts (excepting savings bank accounts which are really a form of investment). This absorption lags behind the credit expansion.

When employment improves and wages rise, the working classes spend the greater part of what they receive on consumable goods. The residue builds up their cash balances very slowly. The rise of wages lags some way behind the rise of prices and profits. In the course of revival after a depression, when the stage is reached at which industry is working approximately up to capacity, and prices are perhaps not far from normal, wages are still below normal. After an interval, when wages have reached normal, the cash holdings of the working classes have still not been brought up to their normal proportion to wages. There ensues a period when these cash holdings continue to increase. By the time they have increased not merely up to normal, but so far beyond it as to make a shortage in the cash reserves of the banks, considerable further progress will have been made with the credit expansion, and wages themselves will be well above normal. At that stage the banks will begin to restrict credit. By that time prices and profits will be swollen, and the consumers' outlay will be much above its normal amount. Producers will be working up to capacity under the pressure of an accumulation of forward orders. The restriction of credit will not be fully effective till these orders have been worked through; for so long as producers are engaged upon them they must borrow on any terms. There will therefore be an uncomfortable interval while producers remain busy, but the shadow of credit contraction is already upon trade. During that interval the workpeople will still be fully employed, wages cannot be reduced, and they will be absorbing cash. When at last the credit restriction becomes fully effective, and unemployment develops, the absorption of money into circulation will have reached a maximum.

The process of getting money back from circulation into the reserves of the banks is a slow and painful one. The pressure of unemployment and inadequate wages has to drive the working classes to draw upon their supplies of cash, or at any rate to prevent them increasing those supplies, while the new gold from the mines flows into the banks.

It would not be possible to calculate *a priori* what period the completion of a cycle of these processes would occupy. But at any rate it is not surprising that the period should extend over a considerable number of years.

The regulation of credit in an international system by reference to gold reserves supplies an adequate explanation of the rate of progress of the cycle and its periodic character, *once it is started*. But why does it start at all?

The answer to this question is that credit is *inherently unstable*. We have already referred to the "vicious circle" of expansion and contraction. Activity causes credit expansion, credit expansion increases demand, demand evokes greater activity. Depression damps down borrowing, diminished borrowing brings with it curtailed demand, curtailed demand means more depression.

It follows that a small or casual credit movement, whether expansion or contraction, tends to exaggerate itself. Once started, it grows, and will continue growing till the banks take active steps to stop it. Under the conditions we have assumed, they do not take these steps till the reserve position is affected, and by the time that occurs the movement will have gathered considerable momentum. The process of checking and reversing this momentum will be a fairly protracted one.

Therefore even if a state of perfect credit equilibrium could be established, it would give way at the first small disturbance, and a cyclical movement would develop. No other originating cause is called for than the endless fortuitous variations in the credit position and in traders' expectations, which are always occurring.

We have now travelled a long way from the over-production theory with which we started. In fact we have shown that trade depressions cannot be due to over-production; the disparity that arises between supply and demand cannot be due to an excess of supply, but must be due to a deficiency of demand. Demand, that is to say, the consumers' outlay, is curtailed owing to a restriction of credit. If the restriction of credit did not occur, the active phase of the trade cycle could be indefinitely prolonged, at the cost, no doubt, of an indefinite rise of prices and an abandonment of the gold standard. There is no over-production. Throughout the active phase production is at a high level, but that is because it can barely keep pace with consumption. Stocks of commodities are then below normal, and are still below normal when the restriction of credit brings the turning-point.

The standard of sufficiency in stocks is itself *relative*, and is dependent among other things upon the state of credit. It is usual for merchants to carry a part of their stocks with borrowed money, and any increase or decrease in stocks probably means an increase or decrease in their indebtedness. Interest on temporary advances is a small item to a manufacturer, whose main preoccupation is to keep his plant fully employed. But it is of considerable account to a merchant who makes a profit, often a very small percentage, on buying and selling large consignments of goods. To a merchant the inconvenience of letting his stocks fall a little below the usual amount is probably very slight. When the rate of interest rises, his idea of what is a reasonable amount to hold in stock is immediately modified; he begins to hasten his sales and restrict his orders.

The serious glut of goods which is so characteristic of a trade depression occurs at a later stage, when the contraction in the consumers' outlay has made itself felt in a decline of sales. Stocks then become actually greater than normal.

An expansion of credit is similarly started through the sensitiveness of merchants to the rate of interest. Merchants are tempted by cheap money to hasten their purchases.

It is obvious that much depends upon the psychology of the merchants and other traders, and particularly on their expectations as to the course of markets. One who expects demand to grow will hasten to buy. He anticipates the advantages of prompt sales or high prices or both. When prices are rising, the holding of goods in stock is itself profitable; when prices are falling, the holding of goods in stock is a source of loss. When prices are rising, a very high rate of interest may fail to deter merchants from borrowing; when they are falling, an apparently low rate of interest may fail to tempt them.

Here we find a new point of contact with the classical school of economists. They lay great stress on the state of business confidence and find one explanation of the trade cycle primarily in a rhythmical recurrence of errors of optimism and errors or pessimism.

It is taken for granted that the optimism and the pessimism are *mistaken*. But in reality this is not so. Optimism means the expectation that prices will rise or demand at a given price will expand. Pessimism means the expectation that prices will fall or demand at a given price will shrink. At a time of good trade, optimism is not mistaken at all, but is a perfectly correct view, and the same is true of pessimism at a time of bad trade. Each state of expectation tends to bring about its own fulfilment. The optimists borrow freely, and the spending power thus created brings about the rise of prices they hope for; the pessimists refrain from borrowing and the shortage of spending power brings about the fall of prices they fear. It is only at the turning-points, when the banks check borrowing, or succeed in reviving it, that the optimists and pessimists are respectively mistaken. And they may not be mistaken even there; they may have sufficient insight into the credit situation to anticipate the action of the banks. If this wisdom were general, the change from one phase of the cycle to the other would then be inaugurated without any initiative from the banks, by a spontaneous decrease or increase, as the case may be, in the borrowing operations of the traders. In practice, no doubt, there are invariably found some mistaken optimists when the decline starts, and some mistaken pessimists when the revival starts. But their existence is not essential to the credit theory of the trade cycle.

Traders' expectations, whether erroneous or correct, form one element in the problem of the regulation of credit. But under pre-war conditions the regulation of credit was guided by the state of gold reserves. If traders' expectations were of a kind to support and assist the action of the bankers in encouraging or discouraging borrowers, that facilitated their task. But if traders' expectations tended in the contrary direction, the bankers could not surrender their policy. They were bound to take whatever measures were necessary to make it prevail.

In fact *three* distinct influences have to be taken into account, and the state of trade depends upon their resultant. First, there is the rate of interest on the merchants' borrowings. Secondly, there is their expectation as to the course of prices. Thirdly, there is the actual extent of their sales. The first is within the control of the bankers. The second is psychological, but can be *influenced* by extraneous circumstances. The third depends on the net effect of the first two upon the consumers' outlay.

The inherent instability of credit, which becomes apparent in the vicious circle of expansion and the vicious circle of contraction, is due to the mutual relations of these three factors. Optimism encourages borrowing, borrowing accelerates sales, and sales accentuate optimism. Pessimism discourages borrowing, and the consequent decline in sales intensifies pessimism.

If merchants refused to be influenced in any way by expectations as to the future state of markets, the psychological factor would drop out, but the credit cycle would still persist. Borrowing would respond to the rate of interest, and the volume of sales would respond to the volume of borrowing. Therefore business psychology, though in practice a very important factor in the trade cycle, is not essential to it.

In general, traders' espectations conformed under pre-war conditions almost too easily to the state of credit. Difficulties in enforcing the control of credit occurred at the climax of trade activity, but that was chiefly on account of the heavy commitments which involved traders in further borrowing on any terms. A conflict between business sentiment and credit policy was more likely to occur in the depths of trade depression. After an overdose of credit contraction it was sometimes difficult to induce traders to embark on fresh enterprises, when everything seemed likely to end in a loss owing to falling prices.

A complication is introduced into the control of credit in that the psychology of the trader influences the velocity of circulation of money. When prices are expected to rise, people hasten to spend money, and hold smaller balances relatively to the extent of their transactions; when prices are expected to fall, they lose little by letting balances accumulate. The result is that a contraction of credit may have very little visible effect upon the amount of bank deposits. Borrowing is checked, but because balances are less quickly spent, existing indebtedness is not paid off.

In 1920 when bank rate in London was raised to 7 per cent, and the most intense deflation was set on foot, the total amount of bank deposits in England actually increased.

I started by saying that since the war there has been no trade cycle. This is in itself a valuable confirmation of the monetary explanation. For if the cause of the trade cycle is to be found in the gradual progress of a credit expansion in an international gold standard system, we should expect that when there is no such system there would be no cycle. In the United States there has been a gold standard since June, 1919, but the momentum of an international system has not been at work. In the interval of six and a half years trade in that country has risen to three successive maxima, in May, 1920, in March, 1923, and in February, 1925, with severe depressions in 1921 and in the early part of 1924.

Other countries have experienced similar short-period fluctuations, having little connection with those of the United States. Some in the throes of monetary collapse have become painfully familiar with the "catastrophe boom," the exaggerated activity associated with a rapid depreciation of the currency. Others, under the shadow of deflation, have suffered from chronic depression and unemployment. Thus the evils of fluctuations have not been avoided. This experience, however, has given us valuable assistance towards finding a remedy for the trade cycle. The Federal Reserve Banks have been confronted with the problem of how to avoid an undue expansion of credit and rise of prices, when exceptional gold imports have so swollen their reserves as to make the statutory proportions completely inoperative. They have been compelled to seek some other guide than the reserve proportions, and substantially they have adopted the policy of stabilising prices. The too ready acceptance of reserve proportions as the guide to credit policy was the real cause of the trade cycle before the war. Reserve proportions gave too tardy a warning of a credit expansion, and the credit expansion was allowed to gather impetus for years before the banks took effective steps to stop it. The trade depression was the accompaniment of the prolonged credit contraction which was thereafter necessary to restore the cash position of the banks. If the expansion is stopped before it goes too far, the need for anything more than a slight and transitory depression is avoided. American experience shows convincingly that for a single country this can be done. There is no reason in principle why the same remedy should not be applied to an international system, provided the authorities responsible for controlling credit are willing to co-operate. For Europe international co-operation with a view to preventing undue fluctuations in the purchasing power of gold was agreed on in principle at the Genoa Conference in 1922. Since then progress has been made towards that ideal not only in Europe but in America too, and we may hope that the trade cycle, the sinister cause of so much distress before the war, and particularly of periodical unemployment epidemics, will become a thing of purely historical interest.

17

PRICE EXPECTATIONS, MONETARY DISTURBANCES AND MALINVESTMENTS*

By Friedrich A. Hayek‖

I

The most characteristic feature of the work of our generation of economists is probably the general endeavour to apply the methods and results of the pure theory of equilibrium to the elucidation of more complicated "dynamic" phenomena. Perhaps one might have expected all generations of economists to have striven to approach nearer to reality by gradually relaxing the degree of abstraction of pure theory. Yet advance in this direction was not great during the fifty years preceding say 1920. The development of economics has not proceeded along the systematic lines of the textbook which advances step by step from the general to the particular. The answers to the pressing questions of real life could not wait till the slow progress of pure theory provided a scheme which would allow of immediate application in the more practical work.

It seems that as regards the attitude towards the applications of pure theory to the most complicated phenomena of economic dynamics, crises and industrial fluctuations, we can distinguish

---

* This essay reproduces the main argument of a lecture delivered on December 7th, 1933, in the *Sozialökonomisk Samfund* in Copenhagen and was first published (in German) in the *Nationalökonomisk Tidsskrift*, Vol. 73, No. 3, 1935, and later (in French) in the *Revue de Science Economique*, Liège, October, 1935. It was reprinted in English in *Profits, Interest and Investment*, London, 1939, George Routledge and Sons, Ltd.

‖ London School of Economics.

three main types. In many instances the men who most strongly felt the urgency of the problems existing in this field and attempted to solve them had little knowledge of the state of economic theory. This group includes, in addition to numberless cranks, several clear thinkers of rich experience to whom we are greatly indebted. A second group of men which is hardly less important consisted of scholars who, although well versed in current theoretical speculation, regarded it as of little use for the task in which they were mainly interested. Both groups have considerable achievements to their credit and I shall later have occasion to mention some important contributions from about 1850 onwards which we owe to them. It is by no means clear that this debt is smaller than that which we owe in this field to the third group, namely to those scholars who attempted—as it may appear to us, prematurely—to apply an over-simplified and defective theory to these complicated phenomena. Although their endeavour to justify in this way their concentration on pure theory and to demonstrate its usefulness was undoubtedly right, and although their instinct that only this path would ultimately lead to a really satisfactory explanation was right, the result of these early attempts, from the celebrated *Théorie des Débouchés* onwards, was frequently to press the problems into the strait-jacket of a scheme which did not really help to solve them.

II

It was only the modern development of equilibrium analysis together with the increasing awareness of the conditions and limitations of the applicability of the equilibrium concept which has taught us to recognise the nature of the problems existing in this field and which has indicated the paths towards their solution. And even if the different students of these problems proceed along different routes, it is probably true to-day to say that in all countries with a great theoretical tradition the efforts of the younger men in our subject is directed towards bridging the gulf between "statics" and "dynamics." To some the differences which exist here between different "schools" may appear very large. Yet whether the different individuals, in their zeal to advance, stress the deficiencies of the existing "static" theory more or less strongly appears to me to be based much more on differences of temperament than on differences in the aims or in the methods used. I believe that the great majority of the younger economists share the belief that the continuity of the development can be preserved and that only this will help us to reach our goal.

What we all seek is therefore not a jump into something entirely new and different but a development of our fundamental theoretical apparatus which will enable us to explain dynamic phenomena. Not very long ago I myself still believed that the best way to express this was to say that the theory of the trade cycle at which we were aiming ought to be organically superimposed upon the existing theory of equilibrium. I am now more inclined to say that general theory itself ought to be developed so as to enable us to use it directly in the explanation of particular industrial fluctuations. As has recently been shown very convincingly by Dr. Lutz,[1] our task is not to construct a separate theory of the trade cycle, that is of a construction of a detailed scheme which will fit all actual trade cycles, but rather a development of those sections of general theory which we need in the analysis of particular cycles—which often differ from one another very considerably.

A great part of this work will certainly consist in the elaboration of particular chapters of general theory, especially of the theory of capital and the theory of money, in the direction of a more careful analysis of the processes resulting from any change in the data. It is, however, the common peculiarity of all such attempts to make the theory more realistic that they soon bring us back to the fundamental problem of all economic theory, that is to the question of the significance of the concept of equilibrium and its relevance to the explanation of a process which takes place in time. There can be no doubt that here some of the formulations of the theory of equilibrium prove to be of little use and that not only their particular content but also the idea of equilibrium as such which they use will require a certain amount of revision.

---

[1] F. Lutz, *Das Konjunkturproblem in der Nationalökonomie.* Jena, 1932.

That this concept of equilibrium has in the past not always had the same meaning and that this meaning has often not been very clear can hardly be denied. This is at least true of the application of the concept of equilibrium to the phenomena of a competitive society, while if applied to the economic activities of an isolated person or of a centrally directed communist system it probably has a definite meaning. While in this latter case we can legitimately speak of a necessary equilibrium between the decisions which a person will make at a given moment, it is much less clear in what sense we can apply the same concept to the actions of a great number of persons, whose successive responses to the actions of their fellow-beings necessarily take place in time, and which can be represented as a timeless equilibrium relationship only by means of unrealistic special constructions.

Equilibrium analysis certainly needs, if we want to apply it to a changing competitive system, much more exact definitions of its basic assumptions than are commonly given. The realistic significance of the tendencies towards a state of equilibrium, traditionally described by pure theory, can be shown only when we know what the conditions are under which it is at least conceivable that a position of equilibrium will actually be reached.

The main difficulty of the traditional approach is its complete abstraction from time. A concept of equilibrium which essentially was applicable only to an economic system conceived as timeless could not be of great value. Fortunately in recent times there have been considerable changes on this very point. It has become clear that, instead of completely disregarding the time element, we must make very definite assumptions about the attitude of persons towards the future. The assumptions of this kind which are implied in the concept of equilibrium are essentially that everybody foresees the future correctly and that this foresight includes not only the changes in the objective data but also the behaviour of all the other people with whom he expects to perform economic transactions.[1]

---

[1] Since the above was written I have further elaborated and partly revised this discussion of the relationship between equilibrium and foresight in a paper on "Economics and Knowledge," published in *Economica* for February, 1937.

It is not my intention to enter here more fully into these recent developments of equilibrium analysis and I hope what I have said will suffice to explain certain conclusions which I want to draw from them as to the study of dynamic phenomena. It appears to me that from this new angle it should at last become possible to give somewhat more definite meaning to certain concepts which most of us have been using somewhat loosely. I am thinking in particular of the statement frequently made that a whole economic system (or a particular price, as e.g., the rate of interest) either is or is not in equilibrium.

It is evident that the various expectations on which different individuals base their decisions at a particular moment either will or will not be mutually compatible; and that if these expectations are not compatible those of some people at least must be disappointed. It is probably clear also that expectations existing at a particular moment will to a large extent be based on prices existing at that moment and that we can conceive of constellations of such prices which will create expectations inevitably doomed to disappointment, and of other constellations which do not bear the germ of such disappointments and which create expectations which—at least if there are no unforeseen changes in external circumstances—may be in harmony with the actual course of events. This consideration appears to me to provide a useful starting point for further developments of the theory of industrial fluctuations.

III

Every explanation of economic crises must include the assumption that entrepreneurs have committed errors. But the mere fact that entrepreneurs do make errors can hardly be regarded as a sufficient explanation of crises. Erroneous dispositions which lead to losses all round will appear probable only if we can show why entrepreneurs should all simultaneously make mistakes in the same direction. The explanation that this is just due to a kind of psychological infection or that for any other reason most entrepreneurs should commit the same avoidable errors of judgment does not carry much conviction. It seems, however, more likely that they may all be equally misled by following guides or symptoms which as a rule prove reliable. Or, speaking more concretely, it may be that the prices existing when they made their decisions and on which they had to base their views about the future have created expectations which must necessarily be disappointed. In this case we might have to distinguish between what we may call justified errors, caused by the price system, and sheer errors about the course of external events. Although I have no time to discuss this further, I may mention that there is probably a close connection between this distinction and the traditional distinction between "endogenous" and "exogenous" theories of the trade cycle.

The most interesting case, for our present purpose, of such decisions of entrepreneurs where the outcome depends entirely on the correctness of the views *generally* held about future developments, is, of course, the case of investments in so far as these are affected by the situation of the capital market in general and not by the special position of particular industries. Here the same cause may bring about malinvestments not only in one or a few but in all industries at the same time. The success of almost any investment made for a considerable period of time will depend on the future development of the capital market and of the rate of interest. If at any moment people begin to add to the productive equipment this will as a rule represent only a part of a new process which will be completed only by further investments spread over a period of time; and the first investment will therefore prove to have been successful only if the supply of capital makes the expected further developments at later dates possible. In general it is probably true to say that most investments are made in the expectation that the supply of capital will for some time continue at the present level. Or, in other words, entrepreneurs regard the present supply of capital and the present rate of interest as a symptom that approximately the same situation will continue to exist for some time. And it is only some such assumption that will justify the use of any additional capital to begin new round-about methods of production which, if they are to be completed, will require continued investment over a further period of time. (These further investments which are necessary if the present investments are going to be successful may be either investments by the same entrepreneurs who made the first investment, or—much more frequently—investments in the products produced by the first group by a second group of entrepreneurs.) If these expectations are to be realised it is necessary not that the supply of capital during the relevant period remains absolutely unchanged, but, as I have tried to show on another occasion,[1] that during no interval of time should it fall by more than has before been utilised to start new processes (as distinguished from continuing uncompleted ones).

Very large and unforeseen fluctuations of saving would therefore be sufficient to cause extensive losses on investments made during the period preceding them and therefore to create the characteristic situation of an economic crisis. The cause of such a crisis would be that entrepreneurs had mistakenly regarded a temporary increase in the supply of capital as permanent and acted in this expectation. The only reason why we cannot regard this as a sufficient explanation of economic crises as we know them is that experience provides no ground for assuming that such violent fluctuations in the rate of saving will occur otherwise than in consequence of crises. If it were not for the crises, which therefore we shall have to explain in a different way, the assumption of the entrepreneurs that the supply of saving will continue at about the present level for some time would probably prove to be justified. The decisions of the entrepreneurs as to the dates and quantities of consumers' goods for which they provide by their present investments would coincide with the intention of the consumers as to the parts of their incomes which they want to consume at the various dates.

IV

It is, of course, a well-known fact that the current supply of money-capital is not necessarily identical with the amount of

---

[1] Cf. the article on "Capital and Industrial Fluctuations," *Econometrica*, Vol. 2, No. 2, April, 1934 (now reprinted as appendix to the second edition of *Prices and Production*) where I have also somewhat more fully explained the distinction between complete and incomplete processes of production alluded to in the text.

current savings. All sorts of monetary disturbances, shortly described as changes in the quantity of money and changes in the velocity of circulation of money but in fact much more variegated in nature than these terms at first suggest, may change the supply of money capital independently of the supply of savings. This means, however, that entrepreneurs will often base their decisions about their investment plans on a symptom which in no way indicates even the current willingness of the consumers to save, and therefore provides no guide whatever for a forecast of how they will distribute their income in the future between consuming and saving. Entrepreneurs will make their decisions about the volume of their investments, i.e., about the quantities of consumers' goods they will produce at various dates, as if the present distribution of monetary demand between consumers' goods and investments corresponded to the way in which the consumers divide their income between consuming and saving. The result of this must be that the proportion in which entrepreneurs will divide their resources between production for the near future and production for the distant future will be different from the proportion in which consumers' in general want to divide their current income between current consumption and provision for consumption at a later date.

In such a situation there exists evidently a conflict between the intentions of the consumers and the intentions of entrepreneurs which earlier or later must manifest itself and frustrate the expectations of at least one of these two groups. The situation is certainly not one of equilibrium in the sense defined before. A condition of equilibrium would require that the intentions of the two groups are at least compatible. It precludes a situation in which current prices, and particularly current rates of interest, create expectations concerning the future behaviour of some members of the society which are entirely unfounded. An equilibrium rate of interest would then be one which assured correspondence between the intentions of the consumers and the intentions of the entrepreneurs. And with a constant rate of saving this would be the rate of interest arrived at on a market where the supply of money capital was of exactly the same amount as current savings.

If the supply of money capital is increased, by monetary changes, beyond this amount, the result will be that the rate of interest will be lowered below the equilibrium rate and entrepreneurs will be induced to devote a larger part of the existing resources to production for the more distant future than corresponds to the way in which consumers divide their income between saving and current consumption. At the time when the entrepreneurs make this decision the consumers have no possibility of expressing their wishes with sufficient emphasis since their money incomes are as yet unchanged while the expansion of credit has increased the fund available for investment. The investment of these funds, however, must in the course of time increase total income by nearly the full amount of these funds, either because wages are raised in order to attract people away from producing consumers' goods towards producing capital goods, or because the funds are used to employ formerly unemployed workers. This will certainly tend to increase the intensity of the demand for consumers' goods—how far will depend on how consumers distribute their additional money income between consuming and saving.

The first point which we must keep in mind here is that this increase in aggregate money incomes cannot mean an increase of real incomes and is much more likely to mean a decrease of real incomes to many individual consumers. However great the amount of money at the disposal of the consumers, they can never consume more than the current supply of consumers' goods—and if the new investments have led to a diversion of already employed factors into longer processes of production, this must lead, to that extent, to an actual decrease of the current output of consumers' goods. The increase in the returns from the existing permanent resources in consequence of the new investments will not come until much later. But even when the first results of the new investments begin to come on the market, this increase in the output will amount to only a fraction of the additional incomes and, as will appear in a moment, it is this relation between the increase in incomes and the increase in the output of consumers' goods which is relevant to our problem.

There is little reason to assume that, in the circumstances we are considering, the share of the increased money incomes spent on current consumption will be diminished. The willingness to save on the part of the consumers will have been little affected by these changes; and their capacity to save will, if anything, have decreased. Only in so far as redistributions of income have taken place during the whole process, favouring those more inclined to save at the expense of those less inclined to save, a certain increase in the proportion of the income actually saved may be expected. But whether the consumers divide their additional money income in the old proportion between current consumption and saving, or whether the proportion is slightly more favourable to saving, the increase in money incomes will in any case lead to an increase in the monetary demand for consumers' goods and therefore to an increase in the prices of consumers' goods.

This increased intensity of the demand for consumers' goods need have no unfavourable effect on investment activity so long as the funds available for investment purposes are sufficiently increased by further credit expansion to claim, in the face of the increasing competition from the consumers' goods industries, such increasing shares of the total available resources as are required to complete the new processes already under way. That this requires a continued expansion of credit proceeding at a progressive rate and that this, even apart from all legal or traditional obstacles, cannot be continued indefinitely, even if it were only because it would inevitably lead to a cumulative rise in prices which earlier or later would exceed any limit, is not difficult to see.[1] What is mainly of interest for our present purpose is, however, what will happen when the inevitable moment comes when the demand for consumers' goods begins to rise not only absolutely but also relatively to the funds available for investment.

V

We have now reached the point where the conflict between the intentions of the consumers and the intentions of the investors begins

---

[1] See in this connection my article in *Econometrica*, already quoted, particularly pp. 161 f.

to manifest itself—the conflict caused by the distortion of the capital market by credit expansion. The entrepreneurs who have begun to increase their productive equipment in the expectation that the low rate of interest and the ample supply of money capital would enable them to continue and to utilise these investments under the same favourable conditions, find these expectations disappointed. The increase of the prices of all those factors of production that can be used also in the late stages of production will raise the costs of, and at the same time the rise in the rate of interest will decrease the demand for, the capital goods which they produce. And a considerable part of the newly created equipment designed to produce other capital goods will stand idle because the expected further investment in these other capital goods does not materialise.

This phenomenon of a scarcity of capital making it impossible to use the existing capital equipment appears to me the central point of the true explanation of crises; and at the same time it is no doubt the one that rouses most objections and appears most improbable to the lay mind. That a scarcity of capital should lead to the existing capital goods remaining partly unused, that the abundance of capital goods should be a symptom of a shortage of capital, and that the cause of this should be not an insufficient but an excessive demand for consumers' goods, is apparently more than a theoretically untrained mind is readily persuaded to accept. Yet the truth of these apparent paradoxes appears to me to be established beyond doubt. Before I proceed to explain them further it is perhaps not inappropriate to show that some of the most experienced observers of the crises of the mid-nineteenth century had been constrained to accept them.

Their explanations of these crises were usually expressed in terms of an excessive conversion of circulating capital into fixed capital, induced by the creation of "fictitious capital,"[1] and leading in the end to a scarcity of "disposable" or "floating" capital which

---

[1] On the origin of this term see now J. Viner, *Studies in the Theory of International Trade*, 1937, p. 196 note.

made a completion of many of the newly started ventures impossible. The author who mainly developed and popularised this doctrine in connection with the great railway booms and the following crises in the middle of the nineteenth century was the first editor of the *Economist*, James Wilson. It was later taken up by a group of Manchester economists and finally introduced into academic economics by Bonnamy Price in England and Courcelle-Seneuil and V. Bonnet in France. And Yves Guyot even summed up the fundamental idea in the following characteristic sentence (I quote from the English translation of his *La Science Economique*): "Commercial and Financial Crises are produced, not by over-production, but by over-consumption."[1]

Perhaps it may be claimed that a doctrine which gained such wide acceptance right at the beginning of the systematic study of industrial fluctuations cannot be as much opposed to sound common sense as it seems to appear to many to-day after a century of propaganda in favour of under-consumptionist explanations. That these early attempts did not have a more lasting success was probably due to the vague meaning of the various capital concepts which they had taken from the City jargon of the time. It is not difficult to see that with this very imperfect conceptual apparatus the adherents of this theory must have found it difficult to explain convincingly what they had rightly seen and to defend their accounts against criticisms. Even to-day we have not yet quite outgrown the stage in which the ambiguity—or rather lack—of meaning of the various concepts of capital which we still employ is a constant obstacle to real understanding. This is not least true of the term of "scarcity of capital" itself, and of the closely related concept of "free capital" to which it refers. Even if we connect fairly clear ideas with the term "scarcity of free capital," and even if the term is often used with advantage, nevertheless it is in a sense misleading and will easily lead one to ask meaningless questions. The difficulty is that the term appears to refer to some single,

---

[1] Yves Guyot, *Principles of Social Economy*, London, 1884, p. 249. For a slightly fuller account of these theories of the middle of the nineteenth century see the appendix to the third chapter of the second edition of *Prices and Production*, 1934.

measurable entity, some amount of money or "subsistence fund" which represents the "free capital" and which in real life simply does not exist. What we actually mean when we speak of scarcity or abundance of free capital is simply that the distribution of demand between consumers' goods and capital goods compared with the supply of these two kinds of goods is either relatively favourable or relatively unfavourable to the former.

VI

More important, however, is another difficulty connected with the traditional concepts of capital. It is this difficulty which seems to me to necessitate a restatement of the Wicksell-Mises theory of industrial fluctuations in the form which I have tried to sketch in this lecture. Prevailing ideas about how capital would normally be kept quantitatively intact in changing circumstances suggested the notion that a period of intense investment activity followed by a period when the value of much of the capital so created was destroyed might be treated as periods of alternating accumulation and decumulation of capital. For most practical purposes this may indeed represent a fairly adequate description of the real facts. Theoretically this way of approach appeared particularly attractive because it seemed to make it possible to describe the conditions of a stable equilibrium in the way which at the present moment is very fashionable; in terms of the correspondence between (net) saving and (net) investment. Yet the first serious attempts exactly to define these two magnitudes, which are supposed to correspond in some quantitative sense, proved that these concepts had by no means a very clear meaning. Both concepts depend, as can be easily shown, on a vague idea that capital is "normally" kept or preserved constant in some quantitative sense: savings being that part of income which is not consumed we have to know first what income is, that is, we have to determine what part of total (gross) receipts has to be deducted for the amortisation of capital; and similarly we can determine the magnitude of new investments only if we first decide what amount of investment activity is required in order merely to maintain old capital. Whether we are able to decide what savings and what investment are depends therefore on whether we can give the idea of maintaining capital intact a clear and realistic meaning.

That this can be easily done is usually taken for granted; in fact it seems to be regarded as so obvious, that a more careful study of the question has mostly been regarded as unnecessary and has hardly ever been attempted. As soon, however, as one makes any serious attempt to answer this question, one finds not only that the concept of the maintenance of capital has no definite meaning, but also that there is no reason to assume that even the most rational and intelligent entrepreneur will ever in dynamic conditions be either willing or able to keep his capital constant in any quantitative sense, that is with respect to any of the measurable properties of capital itself. How entrepreneurs will behave in particular circumstances and whether the value of the capital under their control will experience unexpected increases or decreases in value will, of course, depend on the wisdom and foresight of the entrepreneurs. But, as I hope to show more fully on another occasion,[1] even if we could assume that entrepreneurs possessed full knowledge of all the relevant future events there would be no reason to expect that they would act in such a manner as to keep the value of their capital (or any other measurable dimension of this capital itself—as distinguished from the income derived from it) at any particular figure.

If the "Wicksellian" theory of crises were really as dependent on the traditional concepts of saving and investment as would seem to appear from the extensive use of these terms in the current expositions of it, the considerations just advanced would constitute a grave objection to it. Fortunately, however, there is no such necessary connection between that theory and these concepts. In the form in which it has, tentatively and very sketchily, been restated in the earlier part of this lecture, it appears to me to be quite independent of any idea of absolute changes in the quantity of capital and therefore of the concepts of saving and investment in

---

[1] Cf. now the article on "The Maintenance of Capital," *Economica*, August 1935, pp. 247 ff.

their traditional sense. The starting point for a fully developed theory of this kind would be (*a*) the intentions of all the consumers with respect to the way in which they wish to distribute at all the relevant dates all their resources (not merely their "income") between current consumption and provision for future consumption, and (*b*) the separate and independent decisions of the entrepreneurs with respect to the amounts of consumers' goods which they plan to provide at these various dates. Correspondence between these two groups of decisions would be characteristic of the kind of equilibrium which we now usually describe as a state where savings are equal to investments and with which the idea of an equilibrium rate of interest is connected. A rate of interest below that equilibrium rate would then induce entrepreneurs to devote a smaller share of the available resources to production for current consumption than the share of the income earned by these resources actually spent on consumption. This may mean that entrepreneurs lengthen the investment period by more than is justified by the voluntary "saving" of the entrepreneurs in the usual (net) sense of the term, or that they do not shorten the existing processes of production sufficiently to take full account of the "impatience" of the consumers (that is, in the usual terminology, of their desire to consume capital). It need not therefore be capital consumption in the absolute sense of the term, which is the essential characteristic of a crisis (as I have myself suggested on earlier occasions) but merely that the consumers demand a more rapid supply of consumers' goods than is possible in view of the decisions of the entrepreneurs as to the form and volume of their investments. Practically this correction probably makes little difference, but theoretically the statement of the theory can be made unobjectionable only if we free it from any reference to the absolute quantity of capital.

VII

It is scarcely possible to give in a short lecture more than a mere sketch of the developments taking place at the moment in trade cycle theory. And I need hardly add that in my view this development is still very far from complete and that what we can say to-day must necessarily be tentative and will probably undergo much further revision as time goes on. But even when at last we are able to state this particular argument in a more unobjectionable and convincing form than we can to-day, this will not mean an end but only a beginning. Even when we have answered the question how entrepreneurs will react to the expectations of particular price changes there will remain the much more difficult and important question of what determines the expectations of entrepreneurs and particularly of how such expectations will be affected by any given change of present prices. All these questions are still a more or less unworked field in which the first pioneer work has been done by one or two Scandinavian economists. And while I cannot quite agree with Professor Myrdal when he alleges that in my theory there is no room for the role played by expectations[1]—to show how important a place they do play was in fact one of the purposes of this lecture—I am on the other hand in complete agreement with him when he stresses the great importance of this element in the further development of the theory of industrial fluctuations. I have no doubt that in this field the whole complex of the theory of uncertainty and risk, to which Scandinavian economists have recently given so much attention, will become increasingly important.[2]

---

[1] Cf. G. Myrdal, Der Gleichgewichtsbegriff als Instrument der geldtheoretischen Analyse, *Beiträge zur Geldtheorie*, Ed. by F. A. Hayek, Vienna, 1933, p. 385.

[2] See in this connection J. R. Hicks, "Gleichgewicht und Konjunktur," *Zeitschrift für Nationalökonomie*, Vol. IV, No. 4, 1933, and A Suggestion for Simplifying the Theory of Money, *Economica*, February, 1935.

18

ECONOMIC PROGRESS AND DECLINING POPULATION GROWTH*

By Alvin H. Hansen‖

The main papers and the round tables in this year's program, like those of a year ago, concern a single, though broadly inclusive, subject. A year ago we considered the various factors which influence *fluctuations* in the rate of investment, income and employment. In selecting the topic for this year we have turned away in large measure from the ever-present and all-absorbing problem of cyclical fluctuations and have set ourselves the task of probing the problems of structural change in our economy, involving among other things also how these structural changes in various countries have affected the cycle itself. In the main sessions and in the round-table discussions various aspects of "The Changing American Economy" are considered—changes in the structure and functioning of our economic institutions. The topic is, however, so vast that even in a meeting as large as ours it is quite impossible to include all aspects pertinent to the subject; and doubtless many members will feel that important segments of the problem have been overlooked by our program committee.

One may ask: "Is there any special reason why in the year 1938 we should devote our attention as economists to the general subject 'The Changing Character of the American Economy'"? Through-

---

* Presidential address delivered at the Fifty-first Annual Meeting of the American Economic Association, Detroit, Michigan, December 28, 1938. Printed in *The American Economic Review*, Volume XXIX, Number 1, Part 1, March 1939. Reprinted by the courtesy of the American Economic Association and the author.

‖ Harvard University.

out the modern era, ceaseless change has been the law of economic life. Every period is in some sense a period of transition. The swift stream of events in the last quarter century offers, however, overwhelming testimony in support of the thesis that the economic order of the western world is undergoing in this generation a structural change no less basic and profound in character than that transformation of economic life and institutions which we are wont to designate loosely by the phrase "the Industrial Revolution." We are passing, so to speak, over a divide which separates the great era of growth and expansion of the nineteenth century from an era which no man, unwilling to embark on pure conjecture, can as yet characterize with clarity or precision. We are moving swiftly out of the order in which those of our generation were brought up, into no one knows what.

Overwhelmingly significant, but as yet all too little considered by economists, is the profound change which we are currently undergoing in the rate of population growth. In the decade of the nineteen-twenties the population of the United States increased by 16,000,000—an absolute growth equal to that of the pre-war decade and in excess of any other decade in our history. In the current decade we are adding only half this number to our population, and the best forecasts indicate a decline to a third in the decade which we are about to enter.

Inadequate as the data are, it appears that the prodigious growth of population in the nineteenth century was something unique in history. Gathering momentum with the progress of modern science and transportation, the absolute growth in western Europe mounted decade by decade until the great World War; and in the United States it reached the highest level, as I have just noted, in the post-war decade. The upward surge began with relatively small accretions which rapidly swelled into a flood. But the advancing tide has come to a sudden halt and the accretions are dwindling toward zero.

Thus, with the prospect of actual contraction confronting us, already we are in the midst of a drastic decline in the rate of population growth. Whatever the future decades may bring, this present fact is already upon us; and it behooves us as economists to take cognizance of the significance of this revolutionary change in our economic life.

Schooled in the traditions of the Malthusian theory, economists, thinking in terms of static economics, have typically placed an optimistic interpretation upon the cessation of population growth. This indeed is also the interpretation suggested by the National Resources Committee which recently has issued an exhaustive statistical inquiry into current and prospective changes in population growth. In a fundamental sense this conclusion is, I think, thoroughly sound; for it can scarcely be questioned that a continued growth of population at the rate experienced in the nineteenth century would rapidly present insoluble problems. But it would be an unwarranted optimism to deny that there are implicit in the current drastic shift from rapid expansion to cessation of population growth, serious structural maladjustments which can be avoided or mitigated only if economic policies, appropriate to the changed situation, are applied. Indeed in this shift must be sought a basic cause of not a few of the developments in our changing economy.

Adam Smith regarded growth of population as at once a consequence and a cause of economic progress. Increasing division of labor would, he argued, bring about greater productivity, and this would furnish an enlarged revenue and stock, from which would flow an enlarged wages fund, an increased demand for labor, higher wages, and so economic conditions favorable for population growth. Now a growing population, by widening the market and by fostering inventiveness, in turn facilitated, he thought, division of labor and so the production of wealth. Thus he arrived at an optimistic conclusion. Population growth, he held, stimulated progress and this in turn stimulated further growth and expansion. In contrast, the pessimistic analyses of Malthus and Ricardo stressed the limitation of natural resources and the danger of an increasing population's pressing down the margin of cultivation to a point at which real income would be reduced to a bare subsistence level. In this static analysis the more dynamic approach of Adam Smith was quite forgotten. If we wish to get a clear insight into the economic consequences of the current decline in population growth, it is necessary to return to the suggestion of Adam Smith and to explore more fully the causal interconnection between economic progress, capital formation and population growth.

Economic analysis from the earliest development of our science has been concerned with the rôle played by economic progress. Various writers have included under this caption different things; but for our purpose we may say that the constituent elements of economic progress are (a) inventions, (b) the discovery and development of new territory and new resources, and (c) the growth of population. Each of these in turn, severally and in combination, has opened investment outlets and caused a rapid growth of capital formation.

The earlier economists were concerned chiefly with the effect of economic progress upon the volume of output, or in other words, upon the level of real income. For them economic progress affected the economic life mainly, if not exclusively, in terms of rising productivity and higher real income per capita.

Not until the very end of the nineteenth century did an extensive literature arise which stressed the rôle of economic progress as a leading, if not the main, factor causing fluctuations in employment, output, and income. Ricardo had indeed seen that there was some relation between economic progress and economic instability; but it was left for Wicksell, Spiethoff, Schumpeter, Cassel, and Robertson to elaborate the thesis that economic fluctuations are essentially a function of economic progress.

More recently the rôle of economic progress in the maintenance of full employment of the productive resources has come under consideration. The earlier economists assumed that the economic system tended automatically to produce full employment of resources. Some unemployment there was periodically, owing to the fluctuations incident to the business cycle; but in the upswing phase of the cyclical movement the economy was believed to function in a manner tending to bring about full recovery—maximum output and employment. This view was inspired by a century in which the forces of economic progress were powerful and strong, in which investment outlets were numerous and alluring. Spiethoff saw clearly that technological progress, the development of new industries, the discovery of new resources, the opening of new territory were the basic causes of the boom, which in turn was the progenitor of depression. Indeed he believed that once the main resources of the globe had been discovered and exploited, once the whole world had been brought under the sway of the machine technique, the leading disturbing factors which underlie the fluctuations of the cycle would have spent their force and an era of relative economic stability would ensue. But he did not raise the question whether such stability would be achieved at a full-employment and full-income level.

The business cycle was *par excellence* the problem of the nineteenth century. But the main problem of our times, and particularly in the United States, is the problem of full employment. Yet paradoxical as it may seem, the nineteenth century was little concerned with, and understood but dimly, the character of the business cycle. Indeed, so long as the problem of full employment was not pressing, it was not necessary to worry unduly about the temporary unemployment incident to the swings of the cycle. Not until the problem of full employment of our productive resources from the long-run, secular standpoint was upon us, were we compelled to give serious consideration to those factors and forces in our economy which tend to make business recoveries weak and anaemic and which tend to prolong and deepen the course of depressions. This is the essence of secular stagnation—sick recoveries which die in their infancy and depressions which feed on themselves and leave a hard and seemingly immovable core of unemployment.

In every great crisis the struggle of contending groups maneuvering for an advantageous position amidst rapid change whips up the froth and fury of political and social controversy. Always there is present the temptation to explain the course of events in terms of the more superficial phenomena which are frequently manifestations rather than causes of change. It is the peculiar function of the economist however to look deeper into the underlying economic realities and to discover in these, if possible, the causes of the most obstinate problem of our time—the problem of under-employment. Fundamental to an understanding of this problem are the changes in the "external" forces, if I may so describe them, which underlie economic progress—changes in the character of technological innovations, in the availability of new territory, and in the growth of population.

The expanding economy of the last century called forth a prodigious growth of capital formation. So much was this the case, that this era in history has by common consent been called the capitalistic period. No one disputes the thesis that without this vast accumulation of capital we should never have witnessed the great rise in the standard of living achieved since the beginning of the Industrial Revolution. But it is not the effect of capital formation upon real income to which I wish especially to direct attention. What I wish to stress in this paper is rather the rôle played by the process of capital formation in securing at each point in this ascending income scale fairly full employment of the productive resources and therefore the maximum income possible under the then prevailing level of technological development. For it is an indisputable fact that the prevailing economic system has never been able to reach reasonably full employment or the attainment of its currently realizable real income without making large investment expenditures. The basis for this imperious economic necessity has been thoroughly explored in the last half century in the great literature beginning with Tougan-Baranowsky and Wicksell on saving and investment. I shall not attempt any summary statement of this analysis. Nor is this necessary; for I take it that it is accepted by all schools of current economic thought that full employment and the maximum currently attainable income level cannot be reached in the modern free enterprise economy without a volume of investment expenditures adequate to fill the gap between consumption expenditures and that level of income which could be achieved were all the factors employed. In this somewhat truistic statement I hope I have succeeded in escaping a hornets' nest of economic controversy.

Thus we may postulate a consensus on the thesis that in the absence of a positive program designed to stimulate consumption, full employment of the productive resources is essentially a function of the vigor of investment activity. Less agreement can be claimed for the rôle played by the rate of interest on the volume of investment. Yet few there are who believe that in a period of invesment stagnation an abundance of loanable funds at low rates of interest is alone adequate to produce a vigorous flow of real investment. I am increasingly impressed with the analysis made by Wicksell who stressed the prospective rate of profit on new investment as the active, dominant, and controlling factor, and who viewed the rate of interest as a passive factor, lagging behind the profit rate. This view is moreover in accord with competent business judgment.[1] It is true that it is necessary to look beyond the mere *cost* of interest charges to the indirect effect of the interest rate structure upon business expectations. Yet all in all, I venture to assert that the rôle of the rate of interest as a determinant of investment has occupied a place larger than it deserves in our thinking. If this be granted, we are forced to regard the factors which underlie economic progress as the dominant determinants of investment and employment.

A growth in real investment may take the form either of a deepening of capital or of a widening of capital, as Hawtrey has aptly put it. The deepening process means that more capital is used per unit of output, while the widening process means that capital formation grows *pari passu* with the increase in the output of final goods. If the ratio of real capital to real income remains constant, there is no deepening of capital; but if this ratio is constant and real income rises, then there is a widening of capital.

According to Douglas[2] the growth of real capital formation in England from 1875 to 1909 proceeded at an average rate of two

---

[1] *Cf.* J. E. Meade and P. W. S. Andrews, "Summary of Replies to Questions on Effects of Interest Rates," *Oxford Econ. Papers*, no. 1; also J. Franklin Ebersole, "The Influence of Interest Rates upon Entrepreneurial Decisions in Business—A Case Study," *Harvard Bus. Rev.*, vol. xvii, pp. 35–39. The indirect effect on valuation is perhaps overlooked.

[2] Paul H. Douglas, *The Theory of Wages*, Macmillan, 1934, pp. 464–5.

per cent per annum; and the rate of growth of capital formation in the United States from 1890 to 1922 was four per cent per annum. The former is less than the probable rate of increase of output in England, while the latter is somewhat in excess of the annual rise of production in the United States. Thus, during the last fifty years or more, capital formation for each economy as a whole has apparently consisted mainly of a widening of capital. Surprising as it may seem, as far as we may judge from such data as are available, there has been little, if any, deepening of capital. The capital stock has increased approximately in proportion to real income. This is also the conclusion of Gustav Cassel;[1] while Keynes[2] thinks that real capital formation in England may have very slightly exceeded the rise in real income in the period from 1860 to the World War. If this be true, it follows that, in terms of the time element in production, which is the very essence of the capital concept, our system of production is little more capitalistic now than fifty or seventy-five years ago. It requires, in other words, a period of employment of our productive resources no longer than formerly to reproduce the total capital stock. The "waiting," so to speak, embodied in our capital accumulations is no greater today than half a century or more ago. Capital has indeed grown relative to labor. Thus the technical coefficient of production, with respect to capital, has increased. While this indicates a more intensive application of capital relative to the other factors, it does not necessarily imply any deepening of capital.

In important areas the capital stock has not increased significantly even in relation to population. This is notably true in the service industries. Moreover, in the field of housing real capital has little more than kept pace with population growth. In manufacturing as a whole it is certainly true that real capital formation has not only far outstripped population but has also risen more rapidly than physical product. The studies of Douglas for the United States and Australia show that real fixed capital invested

---

[1] Gustav Cassel, *On Quantitative Thinking in Economics*, Oxford, 1935, chapter 6.
[2] J. M. Keynes, "Some Economic Consequences of a Declining Population," *Eugenics Review*, April, 1937.

in manufacturing increased more rapidly than physical output of manufactured goods. On the other hand, Carl Snyder's[1] data, which run in terms of value of invested capital and value of product, indicate that for important separate industries, such as textiles, iron and steel, and petroleum, capital has grown little or no faster than output since about 1890. With respect to the automobile industry, according to his findings, capital investment has risen no more rapidly than value of product, while in the electrical industries, invested capital increased at a slower rate than output after 1907. Considering the economy as a whole, including fields of economic activity other than manufacturing, there is no good evidence that the advance of technique has resulted in recent decades, certainly not in any significant measure, in any deepening of capital. Apparently, once the machine technique has been developed in any field, further mechanization is likely to result in an increase in output at least proportional to and often in excess of the net additions to real capital. Though the deepening process is all the while going on in certain areas, elsewhere capital-saving inventions are reducing the ratio of capital to output.

In order to get some insight into the effect of population growth upon capital formation, it is necessary to consider the rôle it plays in conjunction with other factors in the widening and deepening process. The widening of capital is a function of an increase in final output, which in turn is due partly to an increase in population and partly to an increase in per capita productivity, arising from causes other than a larger use of capital per unit of output. On the other hand, the deepening of capital results partly from cost-reducing changes in technique, partly (though this is probably a much less significant factor) from a reduction in the rate of interest, and partly from changes in the character of the output as a whole, with special reference to the amount of capital required to produce it.

Now the rate of population growth must necessarily play an important rôle in determining the character of the output; in other

---

[1] Carl Snyder, "Capital Supply and National Well-Being," *Am. Econ. Rev.*, June, 1936.

words, the composition of the flow of final goods. Thus a rapidly growing population will demand a much larger per capita volume of new residential building construction than will a stationary population. A stationary population with its larger proportion of old people may perhaps demand more personal services; and the composition of consumer demand will have an important influence on the quantity of capital required. The demand for housing calls for large capital outlays, while the demand for personal services can be met without making large investment expenditures. It is therefore not unlikely that a shift from a rapidly growing population to a stationary or declining one may so alter the composition of the final flow of consumption goods that the ratio of capital to output as a whole will tend to decline.

In the beginning stages of modern capitalism both the deepening and the widening processes of capital formation were developing side by side. But in its later stages the deepening process, taking the economy as a whole, rapidly diminished. And now with the rapid cessation of population growth, even the widening process may slow down. Moreover it is possible that capital-saving inventions may cause capital formation in many industries to lag behind the increase in output.

An interesting problem for statistical research would be to determine the proportion of investment in the nineteenth century which could be attributed (a) to population growth, (b) to the opening up of new territory and the discovery of new resources, and (c) to technical innovations. Such an analysis it has not been possible for me to make, and I shall venture only a few rough estimates together with some qualitative judgments. With respect to population growth some insight into the problem may perhaps be gained by considering first the rôle of population growth in the rise of aggregate real income. The various estimates agree that the annual rate of growth of physical output up to the World War was roughly three per cent in western Europe and nearly four per cent in the United States. Of this average annual increase something less than half of the three per cent increase in western Europe can be attributed to population growth, while something more than half of the annual increase in the United States can be assigned to the increase in the labor supply. Thus it appears that per capita output has increased both in western Europe and in the United States at approximately one and one-half per cent per annum. This increase can be attributed mainly to changes in technique and to the exploitation of new natural resources.

We have already noted that capital formation has progressed at about the same rate as the rise in aggregate output. Thus, as a first approximation, we may say that the growth of population in the last half of the nineteenth century was responsible for about forty per cent of the total volume of capital formation in western Europe and about sixty per cent of the capital formation in the United States. If this is even approximately correct, it will be seen what an important outlet for investment is being closed by reason of the current rapid decline in population growth.

Obviously the growth of population affects capital formation most directly in the field of construction, especially residential building. From decade to decade the increase in the number of dwellings had maintained a close relation to the increase in population. In the decade of the twenties, however, the increase in houses ran about twenty-five per cent in excess of previous decennial increases in relation to population. According to Kuznets, during the seven prosperous years 1923 to 1929, a quarter of the net capital formation was residential building. But the effect of population growth on capital formation is, of course, felt in other spheres as well. This is notably true of all the various municipal and public utilities, and also of the manufacture of essential consumers' goods.

An interesting excursus would lead us into a consideration of the problem how far an increase in population itself contributed to a more efficient technique and so was in part responsible for the rise in per capita real income. According to the older Malthusian view, the growth of population would act counter to the effect of technological progress upon per capita productivity, and would thus slow down the rise in per capita real income. If this were correct, population growth considered by itself alone would tend to check the rise in per capita consumption, and this in turn, *via* the so-called *Relation*, would affect the volume of capital formation. According to the optimum population theory, however, it may not infrequently be the case, and indeed probably was during the greater part of the nineteenth century, that population growth itself facilitated mass production methods and accelerated the progress of technique. If this be correct, population growth was itself responsible for a part of the rise in per capita real income, and this, *via* the influence of a rising consumption upon investment, stimulated capital formation. Thus it is quite possible that population growth may have acted both directly and indirectly to stimulate the volume of capital formation.

It is not possible, I think, to make even an approximate estimate of the proportion of the new capital created in the nineteenth century which was a direct consequence of the opening up of new territory. The development of new countries was indeed so closely intertwined with the growth of population that it would be difficult to avoid double counting. What proportion of new capital formation in the United States went each year into the western frontier we do not know, but it must have been very considerable. Apparently about one-fourth of the total capital accumulations of England were invested abroad by 1914, and one-seventh of those of France.

These figures, while only suggestive, point unmistakably to the conclusion that the opening of new territory and the growth of population were together responsible for a very large fraction—possibly somewhere near one-half—of the total volume of new capital formation in the nineteenth century. These outlets for new investment are rapidly being closed. The report on *Limits of Land Settlement* by President Isaiah Bowman and others may be regarded as conclusive in its findings that there are no important areas left for exploitation and settlement. So far as population is concerned, that of western Europe has already virtually reached a standstill; but that in eastern Europe, notably in Russia, is still growing, and so also is that in the Orient. And much of this area will probably experience a considerable industrialization. But it is not yet clear how far the mature industrial countries will participate in this development through capital export. Russia still has a long way to go before she becomes completely industrialized; but foreign capital is not likely to play any significant rôle in this process. India will offer some opportunity for British investment, but the total is likely to be small relative to the volume of British foreign investments in the nineteenth century. China and the Orient generally offer, in view of the present and prospective turmoil in that area, relatively meager investment opportunities. At all events, no one is likely to challenge the statement that foreign investment will in the next fifty years play an incomparably smaller rôle than was the case in the nineteenth century.

Thus the outlets for new investment are rapidly narrowing down to those created by the progress of technology. To be sure, the progress of technology itself played in the nineteenth century a decisive rôle in the opening of new territory and as a stimulus to population growth. But while technology can facilitate the opening of new territory, it cannot create a new world or make the old one bigger than it is. And while the advance of science, by reducing the death rate, was a major cause of the vast nineteenth-century increase in population, no important further gains in this direction can possibly offset the prevailing low birth rate. Thus the further progress of science can operate to open investment outlets only through its direct influence on the technique of production.

We are thus rapidly entering a world in which we must fall back upon a more rapid advance of technology than in the past if we are to find private investment opportunities adequate to maintain full employment. Should we accept the advice of those who would declare a moratorium on invention and technical progress, this one remaining avenue for private investment would also be closed. There can be no greater error in the analysis of the economic trends of our times than that which finds in the advance of technology, broadly conceived, a major cause of unemployment. It is true that we cannot discount the problem of technological unemployment, a problem which may be intensified by the apparently growing importance of capital-saving inventions. But, on the other side, we cannot afford to neglect the type of innovation which creates new industries and which thereby opens new outlets for real investment. The problem of our generation is, above all, the problem of inadequate private investment outlets. What we need is not a slowing down in the progress of science and technology, but rather an acceleration of that rate.

Of first-rate importance is the development of new industries. There is certainly no basis for the assumption that these are a thing of the past. But there is equally no basis for the assumption that we can take for granted the rapid emergence of new industries as rich in investment opportunities as the railroad, or more recently the automobile, together with all the related developments, including the construction of public roads, to which it gave rise. Nor is there any basis, either in history or in theory, for the assumption that the rise of new industries proceeds inevitably at a uniform pace. The growth of modern industry has not come in terms of millions of small increments of change giving rise to a smooth and even development. Characteristically it has come by gigantic leaps and bounds. Very often the change can best be described as discontinuous, lumpy, and jerky, as indeed D. H. Robertson has so vividly done. And when a revolutionary new industry like the railroad or the automobile, after having initiated in its youth a powerful upward surge of investment activity, reaches maturity and ceases to grow, as all industries finally must, the whole economy must experience a profound stagnation, unless indeed new developments take its place. It is not enough that a mature industry continues its activity at a high level on a horizontal plane. The fact that new railroad mileage continued to be built at about the same rate through the seventies, eighties and nineties was not sufficient. It is the *cessation of growth* which is disastrous. It is in connection with the growth, maturity and decline of great industries that the principle of acceleration operates with peculiar force. And when giant new industries have spent their force, it *may* take a long time before something else of equal magnitude emerges. In fact nothing has emerged in the decade in which we are now living. This basic fact, together with the virtual cessation of public investment by state and local governmental bodies, as indicated by a decline of $2,000,000,000 in their net public debt since 1932, explains in large measure the necessary rise in federal expenditures.[1]

Spiethoff was quite right when he argued that a vigorous recovery is not just spontaneously born from the womb of the preceding depression. Some small recovery must indeed arise sooner or later merely because of the growing need for capital replacement. But a full-fledged recovery calls for something more than the mere expenditure of depreciation allowances. It requires a large outlay on new investment, and this awaits the development of great new industries and new techniques. But such new developments are not currently available in adequate volume. It is my growing conviction that the combined effect of the decline in population growth, together with the failure of any really important innovations of a magnitude sufficient to absorb large capital outlays, weighs very heavily as an explanation for the failure of the recent recovery to reach full employment. Other factors are certainly significant and important, particularly our failure to control the cost structure and to grapple effectively with specific situations, such as those presented by the railroads and by building construction.

We have noted that the approaching cessation of population growth and the disappearance of new territory for settlement and exploitation may cut off a half or more of the investment outlets which we were wont to make in the past. We are thus compelled to fall back upon that measure of capital formation which is associated with the advance of technique and the rise in per capita output. But current institutional developments are restricting even this outlet. The growing power of trade unions and trade associations, the development of monopolistic competition, of rivalry for the market through expensive persuasion and advertising, instead of through price competition, are factors which have rightly of late commanded much attention among economists.

---

[1] *Debts and Recovery 1929 to 1937*, The Twentieth Century Fund, 1938, p. 230.

There is, moreover, the tendency to block the advance of technical progress by the shelving of patents.

Under vigorous price competition, new cost-reducing techniques were compulsorily introduced even though the scrapping of obsolete but undepreciated machinery entailed a capital loss. But under the monopoly principle of obsolescence new machines will not be introduced until the undepreciated value of the old machine will at least be covered by the economies of the new technique. Thus progress is slowed down, and outlets for new capital formation, available under a more ruthless competitive society, are cut off. Capital losses which could not be avoided under rigorous price competition can be and are avoided under an economic system more closely integrated by intercorporate association and imperfect competition. If we are to save the one remaining outlet for private capital formation, deliberate action of a far bolder character than hitherto envisaged must be undertaken in order to make the price system and free enterprise sufficiently responsive to permit at least that measure of capital formation to which the rate of technological progress had accustomed us in the past.

Yet even though this much were achieved, it is necessary to recognize that such a rate of progress would not provide sufficient investment outlets to give us full employment of our resources. With a stationary population we could maintain as rapid a rise in per capita real income as that experienced in the past, by making annually only half the volume of new investment to which we have been accustomed. A volume of investment adequate to provide full employment could give us an annual percentage increase in per capita output greatly in excess of any hitherto attained.

Various measures have been offered to maintain full employment in the absence of an adequate rate of technological progress and of the development of new industries. Consumption may be strengthened by the relief from taxes which drain off a stream of income which otherwise would flow into consumption channels. Public investment may usefully be made in human and natural resources and in consumers' capital goods of a collective character designed to serve the physical, recreational and cultural needs of the community as a whole. But we cannot afford to be blind to the unmistakable fact that a solution along these lines raises serious problems of economic workability and political administration.

How far such a program, whether financed by taxation or by borrowing, can be carried out without adversely affecting the system of free enterprise is a problem with which economists, I predict, will have to wrestle in the future far more intensely than in the past. Can a rising public debt owned internally be serviced by a scheme of taxation which will not adversely affect the marginal return on new investment or the marginal cost of borrowing? Can any tax system, designed to increase the propensity to consume by means of a drastic change in income distribution, be devised which will not progressively encroach on private investment?[1]

As so often in economic life, we are confronted by a dilemma. Continued unemployment on a vast scale, resulting from inadequate private investment outlets, could be expected sooner or later to lead straight into an all-round regimented economy. But so also, by an indirect route and a slower process, might a greatly extended program of public expenditures. And from the standpoint of economic workability the question needs to be raised how far such a program can be carried out in a democratic society without raising the cost structure to a level which prevents full employment. Thus a challenge is presented to all those countries which have not as yet submitted to the yoke of political dictatorship. In one of our round tables we are discussing divergencies in the success of governmental spending in democratic countries and in totalitarian states. Totalitarian states have the great advantage that they can rigorously check the advance of costs, including wage rates, while engaging in an expansionist program of public investment. Democratic countries cannot in modern times escape from the influence exerted by organized groups upon the operation of the price system. From the standpoint of the workability of the system of free enterprise, there emerges the problem of sovereignty in democratic countries confronted in their internal economies with

---

[1] Joseph J. Spengler, "Population Movements, Employment, and Income," *Southern Econ. Jour.*, Oct., 1938.

powerful groups—entrepreneurial and wage-earning—which have robbed the price system of that impersonal and non-political character idealized in the doctrine of laissez-faire. It remains still to be seen whether political democracy can in the end survive the disappearance of the automatic price system.

Thus we are confronted with various alternatives. On the one side, there is the proposal to risk a negative governmental policy in the expectation that the recuperative forces to which we have long been accustomed will, in the absence of political interference, re-assert themselves. On the other side, there is the proposal to go forward under full steam with unrestrained governmental expansion until full employment has been reached. Those who have no doubts whatever about the correctness of their economic analyses will not hesitate to make a bold choice of policy. But others, impressed with the stubborn economic realities of a rapidly changing world, on the one side, and the frailties of human nature in its power to make the appropriate adaptation to change, on the other, will not be so sure, and may prefer to take a course that risks neither a negative policy nor a breakdown of collective management.*

I suggest that the net income-creating governmental expenditures ought to be tapered off as we approach a full-employment income level. The economic situation at this point becomes increasingly explosive. Bottle-necks begin to appear. Costs rise. Labor aggressively demands wage increases. Rising costs lead to inventory speculation. We encounter the familiar vicious spiral of rising costs and rising prices with growing inefficiency. At this level the spending program becomes relatively ineffective as a means to raise the real income of the community. This danger point is clearly reached sooner in a democratic country than in a totalitarian state. At what precise point it is reached depends upon the degree of discipline and self-restraint which the various economic groups have achieved or can achieve under democratic institutions.

---

* In the subsequent paragraphs the author has made certain revisions in 1943.

The objection will almost certainly be raised that the argument which I have directed against continued governmental spending to the point of full employment, could equally well be directed against private investment, once the upper danger zone has been reached. I should doubt the validity of this criticism. Moreover, at full employment, the volume of savings is so great that this acts as a restraint upon inflation. If, however, the government continues to pour out funds at a lavish rate, wage-earners and employers alike are prone to take the easy course which leads to higher costs and higher prices. But if reliance could not be placed upon a stream of purchasing power external to business itself, we could expect, I think, a more vigorous resistance to uneconomic cost-raising demands. Public spending is the easiest of all recovery methods, and therein lies its danger. If it is carried too far, we neglect to attack those specific maladjustments without the removal of which we cannot attain a workable cost-price structure, and therefore we fail to achieve the otherwise available flow of private investment.

There are no easy answers to the problems that confront us. And because this is true, economists will not perform their function if they fail to illuminate the rapidly shifting course of economic development, and through such neglect unwittingly contribute to a dangerous lag in adjustments to change. Equally they will not perform their function if they fail to disclose the possible dangers which lurk in the wake of vastly enlarged governmental activities. Choices indeed must be made, and scientific analysis and painstaking research can aid by exploring the probable consequences of alternative choices. The problems which I have raised offer a challenge to our profession. The great transition, incident to a rapid decline in population growth and its impact upon capital formation and the workability of a system of free enterprise, calls for high scientific adventure along all the fronts represented by the social science disciplines.

19

GENERAL OVERPRODUCTION*
A Study of Say's Law of Markets
By Hans Neisser‖

I. The Monetary Basis of Say's Law of Markets

A. The Two Classical Principles

Until recently, J. B. Say's Law of Markets has been widely accepted by economic theorists,[1] even though Say's contention of the impossibility of general overproduction[2] seemed contradicted by the recurring experiences of severe crises. The presence of general overproduction, however, so impressed Say that he felt compelled to introduce modifications of his theory, which destroyed its consistency.[3] This he did by defining "production," not in the usual sense of physical output of goods and services but only as the production of goods of which the sales receipts cover the costs. Thus Say reduced his Law of Markets to a meaningless tautology.[4]

---

* Revised and abridged version of an article published under the same title in *The Journal of Political Economy*, Volume XLII, 1934, pages 433–465.
  Reprinted by the Courtesy of the University of Chicago Press and the author.
  ‖ Graduate Faculty, New School for Social Research; Formerly University of Pennsylvania.

[1] See, for example, Spiethoff's "Crises" in the *Handwörterbuch der Staatswissenschaften*, VI, 78.

[2] As stated in his *Traité d'economie politique* (Brussels, 1827), I, 171: "Certain produits surabondent, parce que d'autres sont venus manquer."

[3] Cf. the description of the development of Say's Law of Markets in Bergmann's *Geschichte der nationalökonomischen Krisentheorien* (Stuttgart, 1895), pp. 67 ff. Also Miksch, *Gibt es eine allgemeine Überproduktion?* (Jena, 1929), pp. 11 ff.

[4] Cf. Say, *Cours complet d'economie politique pratique* (3d ed.: Brussels, 1837), Trois. partie, Div. 1, chap. iii: "Au fait, on ne produit véritablement que lorsque tous les services productifs étant payes, le produit vaut ses frais de production."

These modifications must be omitted from the account of the theory if it is to be utilized as a theory of business cycles: It will have to be called "overproduction" if goods cannot be sold at cost. Our problem is to reconcile such a state of affairs with the Law of Markets. With this purpose in mind, it is useful to reexamine the famous statement of Say's Law—"Products are given in exchange for products"—by emphasizing its monetary implications, thus following the line of thought suggested by Say himself.

We shall attempt to elucidate the working of Say's Law in both a stationary and a growing economy. Let us begin with a stationary economy. One commodity suddenly finds itself deprived of a market; there is partial overproduction because of a change in the tastes of consumers. In this case consumers will spend a smaller share of their income for this commodity and a larger share will remain for other products. As Say has thus formulated it (cf. footnote 3), partial overproduction in one industry implies underproduction in others, with a consequent increase in prices and profits. The premise of this argument, which may also be called the first principle of classical theory, is that purchasing power, expressed as a quantity of money, cannot be lost in circulation.

The second fundamental principle of classical theory is arrived at by dropping the assumption that the volume of production is constant. If we assume an increase in production in one field of activity, output of other industries being maintained at the usual level, it is possible that the expanding industry will absorb a greater share of total purchasing power than before, and yet the increase in aggregate sales might be less than expected by the producer and fall short of the actual increase in aggregate cost of production. In this case the industry would encounter difficulties in selling the additional product, and there would be a deficit in the expanded industry as well as in the other stationary ones, which, as a result of the smaller share of purchasing power devoted to them, are unable to earn their customary returns. But it is obvious that although we have here general overproduction, it is an overproduction due to monetary causes. The money flow has not increased in proportion to the quantity of commodities. In contrast to the first case, the general price level will be lowered. Accordingly the second principle of the traditional classical theory (which, even today, has adherents) states the absolute position of the general price level is a matter of indifference; only *price ratios* or *exchange values* are of importance. As soon as the price level has adjusted itself to the new volume of production, the apparent general overproduction will again become only partial, according to the Law of Markets.

Say, himself, in order to overcome the difficulties suggested in our second illustration, adopted a procedure other than the one indicated by the second principle. According to Say, there are no obstacles to making the quantity of money proportionate to the quantity of goods; indeed, this increase is supposed to take place automatically.[1] It is obvious that the practicability of this theoretical solution for any particular economy depends first on its system of currency and credit. Second, even if such a proportional increase of purchasing power would encounter no institutional difficulties, it is still questionable whether it would not find obstacles inherent in the structure of the capitalistic economy, dependent as the increase is on the demand for bank credit. Even the first principle of the classical theory—the principle of the indestructibility of nominal purchasing power—cannot claim unconditional validity; for it is clear that purchasing power, in this connection, can only refer to that portion of it which is circulating. Hoarding, in particular, may cause a reduction in the flow of purchasing power. The analysis of the theory of underconsumption will take us further into a consideration of this problem.

B. *Indifference of the Price Level?*

The discussion of the second principle maintaining the irrelevance of the absolute price level can be brief, despite the many

---

[1] *Traité*, p. 167: "La marchandise intermédiaire, qui facilite tous les échanges (la monnaie), se remplace aisément dans ce cas-là par des moyens connus aux négociants, et bientôt la monnaie afflue, par la raison que la monnaie est une marchandise, et que toute espèce de marchandise se rend aux lieux où l'on en a besoin." These "moyens" are described by Say as follows: "Des effets au porteur, des billets de banque, des crédits ouverts, des compensations de créances, comme à Amsterdam et à Londres."

existing controversies, since there are a number of recent discussions which clarify this problem.[1]

Opponents of the modern idea of price stabilization have argued that every increase in output attributable to a rise in productivity would allow a frictionless lowering of prices, since a proportional reduction in unit cost would be achieved.[2] According to these opponents, the principle of keeping the money-stock constant must be strictly adhered to, in order to avoid credit inflation and consequent collapse. An increase in the quantity of money would be permissible only to compensate for a change in the velocity of circulation of money or for the growing differentiation[3] in the production process.

For our purposes, it is only essential that the classicists, by allowing in some cases for an increase in the volume of money, surrender their position of the irrelevance of the general price level; for, if it were irrelevant, not even such changes of the current money-flow would make necessary an increase in the quantity of money. This concession of the classicists implies the general thesis of the adherents of stabilization[4] that, regardless of the conditions under which commodity prices may fall, the prices of the factors of production can be lowered only by a long drawn-out depression. Wages are difficult to change, debt contracts cannot be changed at all or only under the imminent threat of bankruptcy. If one accepts this thesis, then the idea that all increases in output resulting from so-called "changes in productivity" would exercise a harmless price-lowering influence in a nonsequitur. "Increased productivity" is an indefinite concept. We can reasonably speak

---

[1] See my remarks in "Kreislauf des Geldes" (*Weltwirtschaftliches Archiv*, Vol. XXXIII, Part IV, April 1931). Especially note Haberler's "Die Kaufkraft des Geldes und die Stabilisierung der Wirtschaft," (*Schmoller's Jahrbuch*, Vol. LV., 1932); W: Egle's *Neutrales Geld* (Jena: Gustav Fischer, 1933).

[2] Hayek is the principal exponent of this thought, in "Production and Prices" (London, 1931).

[3] This means an increase in the number of "middlemen" without any change in technique or amount of factors of production.

[4] This is expressly stated by Hayek, *op. cit.*, p. 91.

only of the productivity (or "efficiency") of a single factor of production, which is measured by the ratio of output to the input of the specific factor. In increasing output, the "productivity" of one factor—the amount of which remains constant—can rise, while that of the other, which is increased, can decline; thus we find that with the successive application of doses of fertilizer upon a given plot, the productivity of the capital (here represented by the fertilizer) becomes less, while that of the soil increases. And we can only speak of an *average* change in productivity of all the factors when their quantitative relation remains the same.

For this reason the writers referred to in footnote 1 on page 388 distinguish[1] between genuine "technological progress" and "intensive growth," although both are changes in the technique of production. Intensive growth occurs when one single factor is increased while the other factors remain unchanged, for example, when the amount of capital per worker is increased. These technical changes were dormant within the reach of management but had not been applied for lack of one factor of production or, what is the same thing, because of the high price of this factor. On the other hand, we call it "technological progress" if, without any increase in the amount of the factors of production, output is increased as a result of improved methods of production. In this case, the total monetary outlay remains constant, despite increased production, so long as the prices of the factors of production do not vary; hence the price of the product can be lowered in proportion to the increase of output without any loss.[2] In contrast to technological progress proper, the case of intensive growth is characterized by an increase in the total of real costs; given the prices for

---

[1] I retain this terminology used by me already in 1931. Mr. Hawtrey's term "deepening of capital" is synonymous with my "capital intensive growth."

[2] This is, of course, not correct where the elasticity of demand is less than unity. No doubt, if technological progress should occur in industries with a low elasticity of demand, withdrawal of factors of production from these industries and a rearrangement of the whole economic system would be necessary. But that could not be prevented by price stabilization; and what the industry with $\eta < 1$ loses, other industries would gain.

the factors of production,[1] a rise in the total of monetary cost follows.

It is here unnecessary to discuss the case of "extensive growth" in which capital and labor (or more exactly, all factors of production) increase proportionately. The new labor force and the additional capital are combined in the customary fashion. Theoretically, intensive and extensive growth are closer related than intensive growth and technological progress.

The foregoing considerations, which have thus far taken us along well-worn paths, have led to a valuable result. The second principle of the classical theory, which stresses the indifference of the price level, can be upheld only with important qualifications. We may say that all those cases of depression are caused by "relative deflation" in which the system "grows" faster than the money flow. No particular business-cycle theory would be necessary to explain this phenomenon. Relative deflation acts exactly the same as an absolute decrease in the money flow. Deflation of any kind creates aggregate losses and invalidates Say's Law.

On the other hand, we may treat cases of technological progress under the assumption that the flow of purchasing power is constant. Considered from a practical viewpoint, this means that we are sponsoring the stabilization of average income rates; or, expressed in other words, to avoid the difficulties in the average concept, we consider such an increase of the money-flow as "appropriate" as will permit the different income rates to be changed in strict correspondence to the changes in the relative marginal productivity of the respective factors. Stating the issue in this manner makes possible also an answer to the theoretical question: How shall we judge all the "mixed" cases in which technological progress proper is linked with an increase in capital per worker, and this not only in a single enterprise but also in the whole economic system?

---

[1] Strictly speaking, this condition cannot be fulfilled since, according to the law of decreasing returns, the return on capital must decline. Nevertheless, the total outlay for interest payments, and, thus, total money costs may rise. If not, we have a complicated situation which may be disregarded here, since it does not bear on our results.

Constancy of the money-flow would induce deflation; on the other hand, an increase in the money-flow that is proportionate to the increase in the current output would produce inflationary effects, as in the case of pure technological progress. Here, also, by stabilizing the income rates, both dangers are avoided.

We have used the term "money-flow," as distinguished from the money stock, to stress the fact that hoarding and liquidating brings about monetary deflation in the same manner as the physical destruction of money. It must be pointed out, however, that we can distinguish two branches of the money flow not always varying at the same rate, viz, the income flow and the business flow. From the first, consumers' goods are paid for, and in a progressive economy, also additional capital goods. The business flow is the source of the demand for producers' goods, as far as they serve replacement. In cases of growth, both branches are assumed to be increased. This is self-evident in the cases of extensive growth, but true also for intensive growth, because the larger the capital, the larger also the turnover on the higher stages of production. Moreover, in the latter case the business flow must be increased to a greater extent than the income flow, because the rate of increase will be smaller for the net output than for the capital stock.

If, on the one hand, one of the basic principles of the Law of Markets had to be qualified, on the other hand, Say's doctrine is in some ways confirmed, considering it from the viewpoint of business-cycle theory, as distinguished from monetary theory. We can venture the opinion that general overproduction, which would create aggregate losses in the system is essentially a deflationary phenomenon, whether it be absolute or relative deflation. This does not mean, however, that it has only a monetary cause. This point of view will be taken when we examine the two most important nonmonetary theories of crises—the theory of underconsumption and the theory of overcapitalization.

Our problem is the following: Assuming that the monetary institutions do *not* offer any obstacle to an appropriate increase in the money flow, how can underconsumption or overcapitalization bring about *general* overproduction and *aggregate* losses?

II. UNDERCONSUMPTION

A. *The Monetary Basis of the Theory of Underconsumption*

We may distinguish between two distinct types of underconsumption theory. There is, on the one hand, the school that follows the classical formulation of Rodbertus;[1] in this group are included R. Luxemburg, Sternberg, and Loewe (Marx's attitude was doubtful), and, independent of Rodbertus' followers, the English economist, J. A. Hobson. On the other hand, there is a school of popular writers, represented, for example, by Foster and Catchings[2] and by A. E. Powell.[3] These writers use more primitive arguments, which can be dealt with briefly.[4] If we assume, for example, as Powell does, that the quantity of goods and the quantity of money do not grow simultaneously but that there is a lag between them, the quantity of money growing less rapidly than the quantity of goods, deflation follows necessarily. Foster and Catchings even hold that every profit-making transaction necessitates an increase in the quantity of money over that which existed at the beginning of the production processes, because otherwise the entrepreneur could not take in more money than he had paid out as costs. Obviously, they have confused the outcome of a single act in production with the total transactions of a whole economic system, in which usually profit need not be hoarded in the form of money but may be consumed or invested. In the case of a growing economy, Foster and Catchings endeavor to eliminate the time-honored solution to the problem (which suggests a proportionate increase in the flow of money), by contending that the

---

[1] Sismondi and Malthus may be disregarded here.

[2] *Primarily Profits* (Boston and New York, 1925).

[3] *The Flow Theory of Economics* (London, 1931). The writings of C. H. Douglas follow the same line of thought, although on a lower intellectual level.

[4] For a criticism of Foster and Catchings, see my article "Zur Theorie des wirtschaftlichen Gleichgewichts" in *Kölner Sozialpolitische Vierteljahrsschrift*, July 6, 1927, pp. 105 ff. Hayek's article "The Paradox of Saving" (*Economica*, 1931) deals with these authors primarily from the point of view of the indifference of the price level.

money newly created by expansion of bank credit does not reach in time the sphere of income and does not function as additional demand for the increased supply of goods.[1] However, this thesis can be easily disproved by a closer analysis of the circulation of money. Since a considerable part of the additional money created by credit is paid out immediately as wage fund, whereas the additional production usually takes time to reach the stage of definitely finished goods (available output), it is much more probable that additional supply lags behind additional demand than the other way round.

The classical type of underconsumption theory rejects from the outset all purely monetary considerations based on the quantity theory of money. Not the quantity of money, but the value of money is presumed to be constant: the quantity of money is supposed to increase in proportion to the growth of the economy. But, according to this theory, such an increase cannot prevent a discrepancy from arising between the structure of production and the distribution of demand among the various produced goods. According to Rodbertus, the iron law of wages, with its unvarying real wage, reduces the share of the working-class in national income, while the proportion of consumables in the increasing net output of the system remains the same. The purchasing power of those income receivers who utilize their incomes primarily for the acquisition of consumers' goods increases at a diminished rate so that the supply of consumers goods cannot be purchased at its cost price. The ideas of Luxemburg and Sternberg are basically the same. Thus, according to their theories, even in case of slow changes, the adjustment of production to demand is impossible. We find the essentially dynamic element of the theory of underconsumption first in the writings of Loewe,[2] in which the possibility of such an adjustment is not denied. However, technological progress which occurs during periods of revival is made responsible

---

[1] See *Profits*, p. 317.
[2] "Wie ist Konjunkturtheorie überhaupt möglich?" *Weltwirtschaftliches Archiv*, October 1926, pp. 185 ff.

for sharply reducing the demand for specific consumers' goods, by displacing labor and thereby shutting off its demand for wage goods.

In the following section we shall examine more closely the relationship between production and demand. Here we are, first of all, interested in the main question of the relation of the theory of underconsumption to the Law of Markets. Granted that discrepancies occur between the structures of production and demand, how do we explain the sudden disappearance of purchasing power? Does not that portion of purchasing power which is denied to the workers accrue to the entrepreneur, so that total purchasing power and value of output in terms of current prices remain in balance? And does not the effect of this accrued purchasing power in the hands of the entrepreneur in some industries increase profit, improve business, and produce all the symptoms of "underproduction"? Following the lead of Rodbertus, theorists of the underconsumption school have answered this question with the thesis that this profit increase cannot be "realized"; for profits are derived from the sale of goods and goods cannot be sold at a profitable price when the bulk of consumers lacks purchasing power. This answer is, however, inadequate because it does not explain the phenomenon of the destruction of purchasing power. Purchasing power can be destroyed only by monetary processes like hoarding, discharging of bank debt, etc. This becomes clear if we suppose a stationary economy with a constant volume of production and a given amount of Government paper money as the only medium of exchange. Then suppose that we subject this economy to a sudden rise in savings and a corresponding contraction in consumption. Undoubtedly, the producers of consumers' goods will only be able to sell them at a loss. They cannot "realize profits." But since the nominal amount of purchasing power remains the same, only two alternative explanations are possible: Either the income recipients hoard, for some reason, the amount not spent on consumables, in which case we have a deflation-crisis proper, or they use it for the purchase of producers' goods, in which case they create a prosperity for other industries. In the second case, overproduction remains partial.[1]

The essential assumption of the underconsumption theory is, therefore, that funds not spent on consumers' goods will not be invested. If the demand for cigars changes over to that for cigarettes, the overproduction in the cigar industry must correspond to an underproduction in the cigarette industry. The relation in this case is a horizontal one in parallel branches of industry. It is different if we consider the case of vertically related branches of economy, such as the relation between producers' goods and consumers' goods industries. If all consumers' goods industries should suddenly be deprived of markets, owing to a sharp decrease in demand for consumers' goods, current investment would decline too.

The current losses in consumers goods industries hamper not only the investment in consumers goods industries but also in capital goods industries, although the latter would not experience actual losses at the same time as the former. In other words, in times of partial overproduction in the consumers goods industries, there will be a sharp rise in the *risk* premium which is one determinant of the demand price for capital.

This falling-off of total investment, however, is predicated on monetary events which have been overlooked by the theories of underconsumption. In this connection, what does the "failure to invest" mean? It must mean either hoarding or liquidation,[2] or

---

[1] Under the customary system of wage payments at the end of the work-week, even the discharged workers will possess an amount of purchasing power over a certain period of time, the expenditure of which may permit the entrepreneur to realize profits. In case of advance wage payments, it is the entrepreneur who, when workers are discharged and the wage bill is reduced, will find a surplus amount of purchasing power in his hands, which means that the profit has already been realized.

[2] It seems useful to distinguish between hoarding of income (which, in times of depression, is bound to be compensated, sooner or later, by dishoarding) and liquidation of capital, which is not necessarily offset by similar processes of compensation. In the latter case the entrepreneur stops disbursing a part of his receipts and accumulates bank deposits.

the repayment of bank loans. The latter obviously could happen only in our modern credit economy. Recognition of this fact not only constitutes a theoretically indispensable addition to the explanation of crises by the theory of underconsumption but it is also of significance in understanding the course of modern depressions. After the crisis the expansion of bank credit is suddenly discontinued, whereas the supply of goods continues to be increased because the momentum of production requires time to slow down. The credit mechanism is thus responsible for the pressure of a relative deflation, as well as of the absolute deflation due to hoarding, liquidation, and the repayment of bank debts. This fact explains the severity and duration of the modern depression, as contrasted with earlier epochs, during which the destruction of purchasing power was primarily caused by hoarding and liquidation, and terminated rapidly when the coffers of the rich began to overflow with coins. The working of the credit mechanism explains, also, why the crisis initiated by underconsumption must terminate sooner or later. Emergency compels the activation of savings deposits, thus creating new purchasing power by way of credit; and hoarding, liquidation (in the form of bank deposits), and the payment of bank loans leads eventually to a condition of liquidity that facilitates the granting of new credit to those industries which have readjusted their cost or make profits for other reasons.

Hitherto we have assumed the correctness of the investment theory expounded by the underconsumption school. But this correctness is in fact very much disputed by the "orthodox" theorists. According to this orthodox opinion, investment does not depend on the profit earned at the lowest stage of production, but on the rate of interest alone. In our opinion, the orthodox theorists neglect the importance of the level of the demand function for capital, whereas the underconsumption school neglects the significance of the form. On the whole, however, the former neglect is more serious because shifts in the demand curve could easily wipe out all advantages from a declining interest-rate level. This proposition needs a further explanation.

According to the orthodox opinion, the opposite is true: On the higher stages of production, the losses arising out of a declining demand for consumers' goods are more and more compensated and ultimately wiped out by the accumulating advantages from lower interest rates. But if we consider, for the sake of the argument, the different stages as combined in one vertical concern, we see at once that the intake of this concern easily could fall below the amount of the wage bill alone (assuming a deflationary process going on), so that even a decline of interest rates to zero would not be an adequate compensation.

Our analysis has confirmed the central idea of the underconsumption theory, if rewritten in monetary terms.

To state it briefly: We apply the concept of partial overproduction to the two spheres of consumers goods industries and capital goods industries. Let us suppose, for the sake of simplicity, that at the outset the system is in a state of monetary "pseudo-equilibrium," in which (1) no cost items are accounted for which are not accompanied by simultaneous disbursements to income receivers or for replacement purposes; (2) the money stock is increased appropriately; and (3) there is no spontaneous tendency to increase the volume of hoards; then net income equals the *cost* value of net output, and if net income were immediately expended in full for goods and services, no general overproduction could arise. Partial overproduction, however, in consumers goods industries would be generated if the share of income spent for consumers goods is smaller than the share of consumers goods in net output, valued at costs. Such a partial overproduction in the consumers goods industries must, according to Say's Law, be *initially* accompanied by an overproduction in capital goods industries. The very fact, however, of losses in the consumers goods industries will generalize overproduction by discouraging investment and reducing the money flow below its appropriate level. The cumulative shrinkage of activities is discontinued at the latest if the inclination to invest increases again or if net saving is reduced to zero.

The following question remains: What are the typical events which throw the initial equilibrium out of gear, which, in other words, cause the saving quota in national income (the "structure of demand") to differ from the share of the net output of capital goods (deducting replacements) in total net output (the "structure of production"), the outputs being valued at costs? The origin of the discrepancy between the structure can lie either in events affecting the structure of production or in events affecting the structure of demand.

B. *Spontaneous Changes in the Structure of Production*

Spontaneous changes in the structure of production are such changes as not caused by a change in demand, but, on the contrary, requiring an adjustment of demand. Investment and technological progress are the two main types to be discussed, since extensive growth is a limiting case pertaining to the economy as a whole, and not affecting the relations between aggregate demand and aggregate supply. It is our contention that intensive growth by itself only in exceptional cases is able to create any substantial partial overproduction; technological progress will cause such partial overproduction in consumers goods industries if certain additional conditions are satisfied; and the combination of intensive growth and technological progress will bring about this effect most frequently.

1. As to intensive growth, we must remember that if spending habits remain unchanged, underconsumption would be possible only if the increase in productive capacity is one-sidedly concentrated in the consumers goods industries. In equilibrium, however, the marginal productivity of capital, in terms of value, is the same at all points of the system; thus, investment is, under perfect competition at least, spread over the whole economy. It is true, experience would divert investment from consumers goods industries in which the marginal productivity of capital in terms of value declines relatively sharply (on account of a sharp decline in physical productivity or a low income elasticity of the good produced), and investment will be concentrated in industries more favored by the conditions of production or by demand. But that does not mean that investment is restricted to *consumers goods industries;* it will materialize as well in those capital goods industries which produce the equipment and material for the favored consumers goods industries. Surely, since the concentration of investment, just described, repre-

sents an *adjustment* to demand, no discrepancy between the structure of production and the structure of demand can develop.

The situation is more complicated, however, if we assume that with increasing income as it arises from the operation of more equipment, the spending quota changes itself.[1] Suppose that people try to save the whole additional income created by the use of more equipment, then any investment in consumers goods industries, wherever materializing, will prove unprofitable; and eventually also investment in capital goods industries will be discontinued. In view of the fact, however, that the current annual increment to the stock of capital is small if compared with the stock itself, and that both the annual change in the capital stock per worker and the change in the ensuing output per worker are even smaller, the process just described will not take the nature of a crisis in the sense of business cycle theory, but of a secular slump from underconsumption. It is doubtful that it ever has materialized. On the other hand, as long as income receivers are willing to consume a part of their additional income, adjustment of the structure of production is possible.

2. Technological progress is a much more rapid process rendering timely adjustment difficult. In its pure form, however, it increases only the physical volume of output, leaving its cost value unaffected. As long as the total expenditure for consumables remains the same, no *aggregate losses* in consumers goods industries would be possible, regardless of the demand elasticities of the individual consumers goods. This condition is, however, not likely to be satisfied despite the structure of demand, according to our present assumption, being unchanged; for if the real income (in terms of consumables) increases, people are inclined to spend a smaller fraction than before and to save more, regardless of the fact that the real costs of the output have not increased.

3. The danger of underconsumption is enhanced by the means through which technological progress usually materializes. In principle, it could be carried out without any net investment, whenever in the existing plants the need for replacement arises. If the new methods of production require plants of a larger size, a merger of the old plants would allow the application of the new methods without requiring net investment. In actual fact, however, existing plants are likely to be expanded without merger and new plants will be established. In other words, technological progress is likely to bring about a sudden concentration of investment, the ensuing increase in the cost value of output rendering a timely adjustment of supply to demand more difficult. If technological progress is largely concentrated in consumers goods industries, underconsumption is bound to arise.

---

[1] This change must not be confused with the change in the structure of demand discussed as cause of underconsumption in the subsequent subsection. In the latter case, the spending habits change for a *given* income; here the spending quota changes with rising income.

C. *Spontaneous Changes in the Structure of Demand*

Changes in tastes in the sense that, at a given income, income receivers save more than before are not infrequent with individuals; for the system as a whole, they are much rarer, mostly averaged out according to the law of large numbers. There exist, however, secular and cyclical changes in the inclination to save. Secular changes are sufficiently slow to allow an adjustment of the structure of production to the new demand situation; cyclical changes, which are the *consequence* of a preceding crisis or upswing, cannot be used as explanation of underconsumption. There remain, at given tastes and size of national income (1) the sudden changes brought about by the development of what has not quite correctly been called *capital consumption* and (2) sudden changes in the *income distribution*, which would reduce the inclination to spend. It is rather generally accepted that a decline in the share of the lower income classes reduces the spending quota.

As to the sudden changes in "capital consumption," it suffices to refer to the increase and termination of in instalment buying and the large speculative gains on the stock exchange, partly consumed, which characterized the boom of the twenties.

As to sudden changes in the income distribution, three typical cases require comment.

1. Any sudden shift of demand destroys capital, in the economic sense of the word, by making some industries or parts of them unprofitable (partial overproduction); and though the rising profits in some other industries will cause there an expansion of output and employment, the elasticity of the existing stock of equipment will scarcely be large enough to secure full reemployment of the workers dismissed. Since the reduction of the physical volume of production may pertain exclusively or predominantly to capital goods industries, the lowering of the share of labor in the constant national income may create underconsumption, especially if wage rates are pressed down swiftly by rising unemployment. Ordinarily, it is doubtful whether the size and rapidity of the changes in demand, which appear here as the prime mover, are large enough to bring about the effect of underconsumption.

2. "Uncompensated" technological progress that displaces laborers is certainly of greater significance than the preceding case. Again, underconsumption is caused only if the technological progress is concentrated in capital goods indus-

tries. In this case, the cost value of output in consumers goods industries would remain the same (in contrast to the cost value of output in capital goods industries which would decline), while consumers buying power would be lowered. It must be noted that technological progress by no means always displaces labor (there are "capital saving" inventions) and that, if it does, the effect is frequently compensated by a timely increase in the stock of equipment, which attracts labor.

3. The third typical instance is that of *inflation* in which wage rates lag behind the commodity price rise. The term includes not only the typical cases of credit expansion, faster than current output during period of prosperity, and governmental paper money inflation, but as pointed out in Section I-B, inflationary effects are produced also by keeping the price level constant during periods of technological progress, since in this way the profit margin is rapidly increased.

The prices of some cost elements (materials, machines, etc.) used in the production of wage goods would rise, increasing the unit costs of production of these goods above the limited purchasing power of the lower income classes. It is, therefore, in the form of a sudden decline in the *share* of these income classes in national income that underconsumption appears here, spelling the end of investment in general and converting inflation into deflation.

III. Overcapitalization

The theory of underconsumption assumes that overproduction exists in the entire range of consumers' goods. The theory of overcapitalization on the contrary, emphasizes overproduction in the sphere of producers' goods.

As to the causes of this glut, we may expect a far reaching symmetry with the causes of underconsumption; there will be changes in the structure of production or in the structure of demand in such a way that the savings quota of national income tends to become smaller than the share of the net output of capital goods in total net output, both taken at cost value. Over-capitalization could also be called "overconsumption" or "under-saving."

On the other hand, partial overproduction in the sphere of capital goods industries cannot by itself be *generalized*. Losses in the capital goods industries do not discourage investment in consumers goods industries, while losses in the consumers goods industries discourage investment in both, consumers goods industries and capital goods industries. As theory of crisis and depressions, the over-capitalization theory is inadequate and needs supplementation.

As to the causes of "under-saving," we can follow the pattern of Sections II-B and II-C. First, the changes in the structure of production! The case of technological progress causing an increase in real income and, thus, with given spending habits, a decline in the spending quota, obviously cannot have a parallel here. But to the instance of technological progress concentrating investment in consumers goods industries and creating underconsumption, there is the parallel of technological progress concentrating investment in capital goods industries, creating undersaving. Likewise, as to the changes in the structure of demand, there is no perfect parallelism. In practice, capital saving inventions which would raise the workers' share in national income and reduce saving are too rare to affect the whole sphere of capital goods industries. Besides sudden increases in the wage level created "institutionally," we have to mention here again the case of *inflation*. We pointed out in II-B that underconsumption might arise if wage rates lagged behind the general rise in the price-level. Obviously, also the opposite development is possible. Wage rates might rise so sharply that, instead of underconsumption, undersaving might occur. And, thirdly, there is an intermediate rate of wage increase, which is just sufficient to prevent underconsumption, yet not so high as to create undersaving.

It has been argued that "undersaving" in the sense used here, could always be relieved by sufficient bank credit expansion, so-called "forced saving." However, in our model, bank credit expansion cannot proceed unlimited but is oriented on the income standard. Too, the expansion of bank credit has always found institutional limits strengthened by the desire of banks and corporations to liquidate a proper part of bank loans by selling securities to the public. Above all, forced saving is restricted by the desire of wage earners to maintain, if not to improve the standard of living. It is easy to see that this desire itself, coupled with the attempts to prevent undersaving from materializing, might lead to boundless inflation.

Undersaving in the sense used here is sometimes also called "capital scarcity." This term is misleading because it could be interpreted as pointing to the scarcity in the existing *stock of capital goods*, while undersaving describes a peculiar disposition about the current *flow of income*. Moreover, one should not talk about "scarcity" of anything without indicating the standard relative to which the thing is scarce. . Let us examine the concept of capital scarcity from these viewpoints:

1. Savings may be scarce relative to the cost value of the net output of capital goods. This is "undersaving."
2. Savings may be scarce relative to the demand for capital funds at the prevailing interest rate: then the interest rate will rise and the funds will be allotted to the highest bidder, a competitive process which does not by itself create a partial, let alone a general overproduction.
3. Savings may be scarce relative to the needs of completing large investment projects already started and financed in instalments. This is Cassel's model; like undersaving it requires supplementation to serve as theory of general overproduction or crisis.
4. The stock of capital may not be sufficient to employ the available supply of labor at the prevailing wage rate.

While underconsumption and undersaving cannot exist at the same time, capital scarcity in the sense of No. 4, is, of course, compatible with underconsumption. As pointed out, failure to achieve full re-employment of displaced workers—i.e., capital scarcity, No. 4—may *create* underconsumption; thus undersaving in one period may be responsible for underconsumption in a subsequent one.

The relation of No. 3 to undersaving and underconsumption is more complicated. In principle, No. 3 is neutral. But "capital scarcity" in the sense of No. 3 permits an interpretation which relates it closely to undersaving. To a lack of saving there corresponds something in the realm of real commodities, to wit, a lack of intermediate goods on certain so-called higher stages of production, especially, although by no means exclusively, a lack of "capital goods in process"; the so-called "structure of production" is not "completed."

Conclusions

Our analysis has shown that Say's Law of Markets, denying the possibility of general overproduction, is only valid if a general lowering of the price level is regarded as immaterial. This is rarely maintained today. Our second result is therefore more important, that the profit principle which governs capitalistic economy, might compel a contraction of purchasing power under certain conditions, and thus lead to a general glut of markets. In other words, the law of the indestructibility of purchasing power, which is merely a different statement of the Law of Markets, is subjected to severe qualifications as soon as we consider the vertical interrelations between the spheres of producers' goods and consumers' goods. Thus we find ourselves closer to a synthesis of the monetary and non-monetary theories of business cycles—more so than appears possible when reviewing the heated arguments between the two schools of thought. Moreover, a closer connection is established between the theory of underconsumption and the theory of overcapitalization, although these two theories were based originally on different concepts: sudden changes in the structure of expenditure cause either underconsumption or overcapitalization, according to the direction of the change; technological progress acts in the same way by concentrating investments either in consumers' goods or producers' goods industries. It would be too pretentious, however, if we regarded the doctrines of underconsumption and overcapitalization, developed and modified above, as adequately explaining two types of business cycles. They represent no more than fragments of these types. In order to present a complete explanation and to convert a set of abstract partial mechanisms into typical sequences of real events, further concrete development in various directions is necessary, primarily with reference to international relations, and the peculiarities of the credit system.

20

MONETARY POLICY AND INVESTMENT*

By Howard S. Ellis‖

"A society . . . which saves, can escape a progressive fall in income and investment only through the continuous development of new investment outlets, such as are created by technological progress, the rise of new industries, the discovery of new resources, the opening up of new territory, and the growth of population": thus writes Professor Hansen.[1] In diametrical opposition Professor King believes that "whenever . . . new equipment for producing direct goods is much needed, interest and profit rates rise, and, as a result, we invest more and spend less. Thus adjustments in the direction of equilibrium are always being made. The process is automatic, hence economists have no occasion to worry either about lack of opportunities for investment or about a surplus of funds awaiting investment."[2] It is my conviction that the truth lies between the extremes of these two views, that it is possible to indicate in a general way the resolution of this great divergence, and finally that the solution is essential for any reasonable monetary and economic policy.

Let us consider first saving—I use both this term and investment in an *ex ante* sense. Now the first step in saving—even in saving by institutions such as life insurance companies, building and loan

---

* *American Economic Review*, Supplement, Volume XXX, Number 1, March 1940, pages 27–38. Reprinted by the courtesy of The American Economic Association and the author.

‖ University of California, Berkeley.

[1] Alvin Hansen, *Full Recovery or Stagnation?* (New York, 1938), p. 296.

[2] Willford I. King, "Are We Suffering from Economic Maturity," *Journal of Political Economy*, 48 (October, 1939), 5, 616.

societies, corporations, savings banks, and authorities—is the accumulation of money. As matters stand, part of the savings get no farther: they are absorbed into hoards or dissipated by "attempts to hoard" for the time being. The fruition of saving in investment is not "automatic." But this is not to agree with the Keynesian tenet that *any* net saving automatically decreases investment and income,[1] nor to agree with Lange that saving over an "optimum rate" has these effects.[2] The original Keynesian version of the impasse, as a number of critics have pointed out,[3] rests upon the assumption of an absolutely elastic schedule of liquidity preference—people are willing to hoard unlimited amounts of money.

Even Lange's more moderate version, whereby the desire to hold money increases with higher incomes and lower interest rates, does not give us an automatic impasse from either cyclical or secular angles through exceeding an optimum propensity to save. The optimum is said to rest upon a counterbalancing of two forces: the expansive force given by a fall of interest rates when people do not spend but instead make a part of the active circulation available for liquidity reserves, and a depressive force given to entrepreneur expectations when the demand for consumption goods falls off. For a theory in which all of the variables are operating simultaneously, the expansive force of lower interest rates involves a paradox: output is being expanded through the accumulation of funds being used neither for consumption nor investment. A truly dynamic theory, which dates its variables, conceives of low interest rates as an "expansionary tendency likely to arise during the contraction," in Haberler's phrase, and exercising its actual expansive force later in recovery. The same flaw of simultaneity or timeless variables appears in the supposed depres-

---

[1] J. M. Keynes, *The General Theory of Employment, Interest, and Money* (London, 1936), p. 84.

[2] Oskar Lange, "The Rate of Interest and the Optimum Propensity to Consume," *Economica*, 5 N.S. (February, 1938), 17, 12–32. See above pp. 169–192.

[3] *Ibid.*, p. 19: J. R. Hicks, "Mr. Keynes and the Classics," *Econometrica*, 5 (April, 1937), 147–160: Gottfried Haberler, *Prosperity and Depression*, revised ed. (Geneva, 1939), pp. 218, 246.

sive force: current investment falls or remains low because current consumption is restricted. But it has been justly observed by Hansen that "former recoveries have typically been carried forward on a wave of new investment which was *not* narrowly gauged by the current and immediate level of consumption purchases. Large, bold projects, looking far into the future, have typically been undertaken in the upswing period."[1] Thus though Lange correctly holds that the demand for capital goods derives from consumers goods, the derivation need not be from contemporary consumption.

While the allegedly orthodox view that savings pass automatically into investment cannot be maintained, neither can the doctrinaire oversaving view be supported that saving (either any saving or that exceeding an imagined optimum) automatically fails to arrive at investment or even reduces it. There is nothing automatic, mechanical, or functional about it either way. The more attention comes to be centered upon technical, psychological, and institutional factors which either facilitate or impede the movement of savings into investment, the more rapidly will the theoretical cleavage disappear. A frank, nonpartisan observer readily recognizes that, under sufficiently adverse circumstances, saving not only results in no investment but actually induces contraction through hoards, attempts to hoard, or adverse entrepreneur expectations, but that if these obstacles can be reduced or removed, saving adds to the complement of capital goods.

In the acute phases of cyclical depression the strong increase of liquidity preference results in a failure of savings to pass into investment. Looking aside for the time being from measures directed toward encouraging investment, it may be good public policy in protracted depressions to penalize not only that hoarding which springs from the conversion of non-monetary to monetary assets (liquidation) but even that hoarding which comes from current income (saving). To generalize from the cyclical to the secular situation as to fact and policy would, however, be perilous.

---

[1] Hansen, *Full Recovery or Stagnation?* p. 279; the italics are the author's.

A progressive and persistent increase of the desire for liquidity, as something subjective, spontaneous, endogenous, and separable from the objective facts adverse to investment, is difficult to conceive for either private or institutional savers.[1] Furthermore, secular increase of hoarding of this character would be easy to offset by an even secular increase in money.[2] Measures designed to reduce saving in what is called "secular stagnation" seem to ignore that, even with a certain leakage or loss, savings do pass into investment, and that investment raises incomes. Keynesians agree with orthodox theorists that the greater the complement of capital instruments the higher are real wages. Suppose that a portion of national savings slips persistently into hoards or that persons and institutions constantly attempt to hoard a portion of their savings. Even so, would not a permanent policy of reducing savings spell the perpetuation of supply-reduction measures appropriate only to the short run, and an attempt to achieve prosperity through scarcity?

One characteristic of cyclical periods of increasing production, quite aside from mechanical reactions envisaged by the older quantity theories, is rising prices from improved anticipations. Voluntary saving has this superiority over expansion solely through credit creation, that it liberates factors without causing their prices to rise; or, alternatively, a given amount of credit expansion will go farther in carrying forward employment with the accompaniment of voluntary saving than without it. The driving force of increased production is certainly not saving but factors on the demand side, to which we come in a moment; but voluntary saving supplies the wherewithal for expanding output in the most salutary way.

One final observation upon savings. Recent statistical enquiries of Colin Clark and others establish clearly the validity of the emphasis upon income and not interest rates as the chief variable

---

[1] Jacob Viner, "Mr. Keynes on the Causes of Unemployment," *Quarterly Journal of Economics*, 51 (November, 1936), 1, 152–160.
[2] Gottfried Haberler, "The Interest Rate and Capital Formation," *Capital Formation and its Elements* (New York: National Industrial Conference Board, 1939), pp. 126–127.

upon which the magnitude of savings depends.[1] This signifies by necessary counter-implication that for a given amount of income, savings are fairly inflexibly determined—by corporation practices, the distribution of income, social mores, and private habits. Public policies directed toward saving itself therefore impinge against particularly stubborn and resistant forces. Consider the present[2] situation with its lethargy of investment, but with its lurking danger of an ultimate war boom of disastrous proportions. If the state introduces measures to alter the deep-seated social, economic, and political determinants of saving, may it not have to reverse its policy and attempt to teach corporations and private persons new habits again in a twelvemonth? Has not Keynes himself illustrated this absurdity in his pronouncements since the outbreak of war?[3] Any so-called "secular" situation is apt to see something happen; long-run or persistent inactivity may be suddenly terminated by cyclical developments. Savings itself is something too inflexible for successful manipulation.

The middle-ground position with respect to saving would run somewhat as follows. Savings are neither automatically transferred to investment nor automatically diverted from investment. The transfer process is conditioned by technical, psychological, and institutional factors of great complexity, probably defying any functional expression. In periods of acute cyclical depression when saving means hoarding, it may, in particular cases, seem advisable to encourage consumption through doles and other measures. Over longer periods showing a lagging pace of investment, increasing the funds available for liquidity reserves would suffice to offset an indigenous increase of desire for liquidity per se; but if, as seems more probable, the obstacles inhere in the demand side, penalizing hoarding would be curing symptoms. Measures to reduce voluntary saving have been supported upon the argument that in less-than-full employment, the potential supply of

---

[1] Colin Clark, *National Income and Outlay* (London, 1937).
[2] The time reference of the present article is to the Autumn of 1939.
[3] J. M. Keynes, *New York Times*, November 14, 1939, p. 5.

capital cannot be the limiting factor.[1] But in this situation the supplies of *all* factors appear redundant; and since the historical evidence seems to indicate that revivals have not been based upon rates of current consumption, saving cannot be charged with this redundance. Voluntary saving itself appears as a normal economic function, carrying advantages over alternative provisions for expansion; and, unless the state abrogates this function to itself, saving does not lend itself well to manipulation. Finally, nothing in this philosophy affords any apology for inequality merely for the sake of saving.

Before we pass from the supply side of the problem in saving to the demand side in investment, it is necessary to be sure that we have in mind the precise character of the ailment envisaged in current discussions as economic maturity, stagnation, or a contracting economy. We may fall victim to pressing various physical or biological analogies too far, or we may simply be coining new synonyms for depression, bad times, crises, or the "dearth" of Elizabethan times. What specifically is the complaint? Is it chronic under-utilization of physical plant, persisting unemployment of labor, low interest rates, low wages and profits, low incomes generally? The question would, of course, not be worth asking if there were not confusion on the subject. Sometimes, for example, the prevalence of very low rates in certain segments of the money market is taken as the earmark of stagnation, and yet it is fairly clear that without unemployment and idle plant we would feel no especial concern over low interest rates. Indeed in theories of equilibrium with less than full employment, low interest rates are the necessary requisite to reaching full employment. Again, are low incomes in general the complaint? Such an answer would be suggested by the term chronic depression, for in cyclical depression incomes are low. But in fact we discover stagnation attributed primarily to societies with large incomes, and the contemporary scene in America is thought to be characterized by a reasonably good level of national income. If low income rates do not con-

---

[1] Colin Clark, *op. cit.*, p. 273.

stitute stagnation, what does? Economists of all persuasions would agree, I believe, that the current malady is chiefly the underutilization of factors. This directs the enquiry to the demand side, and in a society based upon private enterprise, particularly to the demand for capital, or investment.

Obstacles to investment fall into three broad categories—institutional, psychological, and technical.[1] Subsequent analysis will indicate that the technical obstacles are partly unreal and partly pure guesses as to the future; some of the psychological obstacles are unimportant, and those which are serious derive for the most part from institutional factors. We discover the very core of stagnation in rigid prices, monopoly restriction of output, inequality in the distribution of income, difficulties in changing the direction of production including adaptation to certain new, more "social" wants, relatively high levels of interest in some segments of the money market, and, finally, certain political factors—taxes which bear upon enterprise, tariffs and quotas, embargoes on capital movements, expropriation of property, and the like. It is the essence of a synthesizing theory, such as that advanced in these pages, to dispense with analytical elements upon which there prevails complete disagreement, and to utilize elements upon which there is fair accord. Upon this basis, the general oversaving thesis and the doctrine of lacking technological uses of capital will have to go by the boards, but the institutional elements remain as common ground. The term institutional must, however, be conceived broadly, for some of these obstacles reach deep into the foundations of the system of private enterprise or even, according to one school of thought, inevitably characterize the system. Anticipating some subsequent conclusions upon policy, I may say that the synthesizing analysis almost necessarily implies for the present situation a relatively large volume of government investment, though the conservative may wish to insist upon its transitional character.

---

[1] A somewhat similar classification is employed by Gottfried Haberler, "Interest Rate and Capital Formation," *loc. cit.*, pp. 123–125. Of course the classification is not "hard and fast."

Certain marginalia seem to be in order concerning the nature of institutional obstacles to full employment and the investment of savings. Rigid wages have often been said to be the very foundation of the Keynesian system.[1] This is indeed true in one sense: Keynes believes it easier as a matter of policy in a society with increasing productivity to allow money wage rates to rise and to prevent commodity prices from falling, than to stabilize money wages and force commodity prices down. Critics have generally missed the point, however, that in his analysis of equilibrium with less than full employment, rigid wages do not appear in the enumeration of factors responsible for the situation. For this reason the Keynesian theory is psychological and technological, but not, at least explicitly, institutional. It is only necessary to work the explanation of Keynesian policy back into the analysis of unemployment, however, to discover its common ground with traditional theory. The inflexibility of wages downward when other prices generally are falling, or the tendency of strongly organized labor to a successive racheting of wage rates upward in "normal" times, is quite consonant with the orthodox position that, however much a lessening of inequality may be desired, an advance of wages unaccompanied by a parallel increase of productivity will result in unemployment.

The analysis of underemployment must incorporate not only wage rigidity, but it must take full account of monopoly and other price rigidities throughout the system. To have done this in systematic fashion constitutes the great superiority of Myrdal's work on *Monetary Equilibrium* over the Keynesian systems.[2] As a cause of equilibrium with less than full employment, monopoly and monopolistic price policy figure less significantly for their levy upon consumer real income than for their restriction of the field of investment. Labor, capital, and all hired resources tend to be used in the restricted quantities determined by marginal-revenue

---

[1] Haberler, *Prosperity and Depression*, 2nd ed., p. 235, n. 1, pp. 238–239; W. W. Leontief, "The Fundamental Assumption of Mr. Keynes' Monetary Theory of Unemployment," *Quarterly Journal of Economics*, 51 (November, 1936), 1, 192–198.

[2] Gunnar Myrdal, *Monetary Equilibrium* (London, 1939), especially Chap. VI.

product and not marginal product.[1] In view of the complete agreement of traditional equilibrium economics, of the older theories of cyclical variation, and of the Keynesian-Stockholm school as to the disequilibrating effect of monopolistic and other rigid prices, I think it safe to ignore the contrary proposition that price rigidities act as "stabilizers." Mr. Hicks succeeds in demonstrating only that if a commodity is initially overpriced, a rise of other prices may reduce disequilibrium and stay the advance of those other prices. He does not consider the case in which an administered price is too high but other prices fall,[2] though it is precisely in depression or stagnation that monopoly influences are most nefarious! Professor Hansen, the leading proponent of the stagnation thesis in this country, develops the argument with great care against a background of inflexible prices and costs.[3]

The second set of institutional obstacles to investment turns upon extreme inequalities in the distribution of wealth and income. Inequality of wealth permits to only a few the entry into productive enterprises requiring large blocks of capital; it restricts to a few the development of personal capacities of high technical order. Consequently inequality not only springs from but also fosters monopoly. Inequality of income increases the amount of voluntary savings; if institutional obstacles interfere with the flow of savings into investment this aggravates difficulties. It may be noted that this does not constitute savings or inequality per se into the cause of unemployment after the fashion of Rodbertus or Keynes. Without monopoly and other institutional interferences to the transfer process, a competitive system endowed with a non-deflationary monetary policy would apparently utilize savings—perhaps not without cyclical interruptions—whether or not they sprang from a humane distribution of income.

I touch briefly upon other institutional obstacles, although the potency of the aggregate, including price rigidities and inequality,

---

[1] E. H. Chamberlin, "Monopolistic Competition and the Productivity Theory of Distribution," in *Explorations in Economics* (New York, 1936), pp. 237–250.
[2] J. R. Hicks, *Value and Capital* (Oxford, 1939), pp. 265–268.
[3] Hansen, *Full Recovery or Stagnation?* pp. 299–301.

could account adequately for the existing lethargy of investment. A society enjoying a growth of national income naturally desires to consume in new ways. Being comfortably ensconced in sheltered positions, monopolies do not in general reveal much concern about catering to new wants. This very immobility would tempt the innovator, the true entrepreneur in Schumpeter's sense; but often the way is blocked by the necessity of formidable initial outlays upon the "selling costs" of monopolistic competition. The process of changing over to new types of production works against heavy costs, friction, and uncertainties. Furthermore, many fields which seem to be indicated as genuinely corresponding to consumer or public demand have so social or communal a character—hospitals, or slum clearance conjoined with housing projects—that private enterprise has found the conditions of production and demand too complex and unusual. Many of these applications of capital may in the end cover the competitive "opportunity costs," though the state itself for the present has to play the innovator. Much the same appears to be true of certain more risky channels of production already served by private enterprise but suffering under disproportionately high money costs in comparison with safer investments.[1] Moody's triple A rating may be an institution weighing heavily on unorthodox but necessary economic experimenters.

Finally it may be asked whether saving itself and the technical potentialities of investment can be charged with the ruthless thwarting of enterprise which prevails in the fields of foreign investments and international trade? Even an exponent of "Beggar-my-Neighbour Remedies for Unemployment" emphasizes that the conditions necessary for short-run advantages are complex, and that such "remedies" defeat themselves in the long run by provoking retaliation.[2] I do not need to expatiate upon the lets and hindrances to investment involved in some of our domestic policies

---

[1] Robert A. Gordon, "Fiscal Policy as a Factor in Stability," *The Annals of the American Academy of Political and Social Science* (November, 1939), p. 112.

[2] Joan Robinson, "Beggar-my-Neighbour Remedies for Unemployment," *Essays in the Theory of Unemployment* (New York, 1937), pp. 210–231.

since these have been sufficiently exposed, frequently with suspicious zeal.

In addition to objective or institutional, there exist also psychological impediments to real capital formation, but few of them arise spontaneously or persist independently. Particularly is this true of liquidity preference. Most hoarding springs not from miserliness but from insufficiently attractive alternatives. If, indeed, accumulation outstrips improvement, there may be a psychological resistance to low interest rates. But if there is no prospect of a reversal of the situation, few potential investors will continue the hunger strike; as Haberler remarks, "After a while even John Bull will become accustomed to 2 per cent or 1 per cent."[1] The same observation holds regarding a possible general abatement in the venturesomeness of entrepreneurs, particularly in large corporations through the spread of professional entrepreneur-manager control divorced from ownership. Eventually the investor would be forced to a recognition of realities: that he cannot eat his cake in the form of conservatism and security and also have it in the form of the high returns to be expected only from assumption of marked risks. For the rest, the so-called "psychological impediments" are not distinguishable from objective conditions. There is no native instinct not to invest, though there is the subjective reflection of difficulties engendered by rigid costs and prices, monopoly, and other "real" factors.

The third set of obstacles envisaged by the theory of equilibrium with less-than-full employment is supposed to stem from inelasticity or lack of sufficient magnitude in the underlying technological schedule of capital productivity or efficiency. This I believe to be the weakest paragraph in the brief, the least eligible for a synthesizing analysis. In the first place productivity or efficiency pertains only to actual investment—not to saving which bogs down in abortive lacking, losses, hoards or attempts to hoard. There can be no obstacle to investment from the shape or position of the demand function itself; at most it would mean that, if there existed

---

[1] Haberler, *Capital Formation, op. cit.*, p. 128.

an institutional or psychological floor to interest rates, we should reach equilibrium with less employment than we should with greater elasticity or magnitude in the demand for capital. Eliminating such a floor on the basis of the improbability of continuous absorptions into liquidity reserves,[1] we are bound to conclude that inelasticity or small extent in the capital demand function signifies only low interest rates—not idle men and machines. Some persons in lower income brackets would suffer through reductions in insurance and annuity benefits and the shrinkage of income from endowments; but in general low interest would mean a welcome reduction of inequality and living by owning.

But the alleged inelasticity or limited demand from a technological angle is itself subject to grave doubts. Looking forward, the stagnation theorists have felt gloomy at the prospect of capital-saving inventions. At most this is merely a possibility. Why should it be a gloomy one? Laborsaving inventions like the linotype have sometimes resulted in a greater demand for labor; by the same token, capital-saving improvements may actually increase the demand for capital at given rates of interest. But if demand for capital and interest rates fall, would not the relative and absolute incomes of labor be increased and inequality diminished by its increased relative importance in production? Looking backward, the pessimists have observed, as in the Temporary National Economic Committee hearings on saving and investment,[2] a close correlation of national income and new expenditures upon mining and manufacturing equipment. Since the World War, it is pointed out, capital outlays have gone heavily into "nonbusiness" lines of production—houses, roads, and public works; but because investment has not gone precisely into the narrow category of "mining and manufacturing equipment," even the halcyon twenties fall under the baleful characterization of stagnation pre-

---

[1] This point is made with great clarity by Haberler, *ibid.*, pp. 125–127.

[2] Cf. *Tables and Charts for Use in Hearings on Savings and Investment before the Temporary National Economic Committee*, Securities and Exchange Commission (lithoprinted, 1939); and the testimony of Hansen and Currie on May 16, 1939, as given in Releases No. S10 and S12.

vented only by special circumstances. If we include these non-business capital goods under investment, then the secular stagnation of investment is a matter of one decade, scarcely to be distinguished, so far as we can perceive thus far, from an unusually severe or prolonged cyclical movement.

Why should umbrage fall upon nonbusiness lines of production? Man shall not live by blast furnaces alone. Is there anything more natural than that society should take its increased income in more of durable consumers goods, or eventually also in more non-durable consumers goods and leisure? Is an increase of demand for non-durable consumers goods—an increase in the "propensity to consume"—a way out of stagnation, but an increase in demand for durable consumers goods not? The plain answer is, of course, that employment of labor need not depend upon investment in mining and manufacture. As Professor King insists, "As long as the modal family income in the United States is under $1,000 per year, there certainly is no need to conjure up wants for new and unknown products or to establish new industries in order to find a market for far more goods than our present industries can produce."[1] Residential real estate has shown negative net investment for nearly a decade, according to Kuznets' figures, and there were even minuses in the years 1935 on.[2] If we include durable consumers goods within the pale of investment, potential increases in the demand schedule for capital would appear to be very great. And if we include as possible destinations for increased national income also nondurable consumers goods and personal services, the bogey of lacking technical applications for capital disappears.[3]

The inevitable objection to this sort of argument will be that existing plant, having been constructed upon expectations of continued expansion along the old lines of population growth, etc., now suffers under a dearth of demand. What does it avail to point to the possibilities of profitable production with a totally

---

[1] King, *loc. cit.*, p. 617.

[2] Simon Kuznets, *National Income and Capital Formation* (New York, 1937), p. 48; National Bureau of Economic Research, Bul. 74 (July, 1939), Table I.

[3] According to Keynesian terminology, anyone who employs labor invests!

recast orientation of outlets and physical equipment, when it is the obvious necessity that existing plant be profitably employed? I should heartily welcome such a response for actually it contributes to the middle-ground theory, to the truth between extremes, being sought for. The objection makes its contribution in abandoning the thesis of an ultimate or underlying lack of demand for capital goods, and by stressing the inappropriateness of the present supply or stock of instruments. This inappropriateness of present supply is a horse of considerably different color from the Keynesian lack or inelasticity of demand for capital. Actually the situation may be further resolved into its components. Part of existing instruments of a specific sort are worthless—not capital at all; whereas another part of less specific sort has a high potential productivity, because the recasting of production makes heavy demands for new equipment. The realization of this potentiality encounters institutional obstacles in the narrower sense: rigid costs, monopoly inertia and restriction of the field of investment, disproportionate risk-loadings outside the gilt-edge security market, and the like. Antitrust measures and plans to increase the availability of credit help, no doubt; but government investment appears to be the most powerful weapon against monopoly prices and wages, and against institutional inertia in general. Whether the system of private enterprise is inherently impotent in the contemporary scene, whether it is itself an institutional obstacle, and whether the entry of government into investment spells socialism—these are questions which will ultimately find their own answers.

In concluding upon the supposed technological obstacles or lack of demand for capital, let us return to a passage quoted at the outset of these remarks: "A society . . . . which saves, can escape a progressive fall in income and employment only through the continuous development of new investment outlets, such as are created by technological progress, the rise of new industries, the discovery of new resources, the opening up of new territory, and the growth of population." I disagree. A society which saves can escape a fall in employment and income if it can successfully cope with institutional obstacles; new investment outlets exist in adequate volume in known but unexploited techniques without the necessity of the various creations in the list; and I do not believe that we want those created outlets particularly—in some cases not at all. Technological progress! Is the crying need of economic society today our ineptness in making things? Is agriculture archaic, our commerce unprogressive? Granted that we generically desire to reduce production costs, here, too, we encounter frictions and institutional obstacles. Have we, for example, entirely forgotten about technological unemployment? New industries! Is the variety and quality of our wares sadly limited? New resources! Do we in the United States chiefly suffer from an inadequacy of natural resources? Territory! Do we too need a Manchuria, Abyssinia, or Czechoslovakia? Growth of population! Do we propose to cure unemployment by encouraging the birth rate? So much emphasis has been laid upon the retardation of population growth rate that some lines written by Hicks deserve repetition: "One cannot repress the thought that perhaps the whole Industrial Revolution of the last two hundred years has been nothing else but a vast secular boom, largely induced by the unparalleled rise in population. If this is so, it would help to explain why, as the wisest hold, it has been such a disappointing episode in human history."[1] I do not think it can be gainsaid that technological improvement or population growth eases the savings-investment process, given the institutional obstacles. But the main question is: how do we want to mend matters?

The economic policy based upon the present attempt at finding a middle-ground truth takes up the positive contributions and rejects the extravagances in both the oversaving and classical positions. Such a policy is not directed toward the reduction of saving nor the conjuring up of created investment outlets; it is directed against those factors which both wings of theoretical opinion envisage as impeding the flow of saving to investment—price rigidities, monopoly, inequality, political obstacles to free private enterprise and initiative. The philosophy is liberal in that it

---

[1] Hicks, *Value and Capital*, p. 302, n. 1.

seeks to rehabilitate and perpetuate private enterprise and competition; but it is also radical. In the first place, it accepts extensive government expansion into the field of investment as a means of breaking industrial and labor union monopolies and price rigidities, and as a means of launching production to correspond with the social wants of a relatively high-income country—into slum clearance, hospitals, recreational opportunities, free public education, and the like. In doing so, the state must seek to compete with private, competitive industry directly as little as possible, and it must avoid a ruinous indirect competition through failure to charge to its projects their full opportunity costs in labor, land, and capital.[1] The creation of a separate capital budget for public investments would eliminate the anomaly of charging capital expenditures to current income;[2] on the other hand, since the breaking into monopoly profits might show some handsome returns upon the public ventures, it might be wise to record that fact also. In the second place, inequality of wealth and income must be vastly decreased. Investment opportunities for capital and careers open to the talents must be widely distributed if a system is to be competitive. If business interests adopt an attitude of irreconcilableness, they prolong and intensify unemployment and sew the seed of crack-pot schemes for "30-Thursday," "share the wealth," or social revolution.

The role of monetary policy in the indicated direction of public policy is modest but an integral part of the whole. Schemes for curing symptoms by penalizing the holding of cash balances will be rejected, while a policy of easy money is continued so long as investment lags. Since we have the curious combination of idle men and machines as a heritage from the Great Depression and at the same time the possibility of a war boom of large proportions, constant alertness to price-level movements, price differentials, security values, inventories, physical production, and other indices

---

[1] In this respect the plan of A. A. Berle falls short; cf. "A Banking System for Capital and Capital Credit," TNEC Release No. S11 (May 23, 1939), p. 14.

[2] Cf. Gordon, *loc. cit.*, p. 113.

of cyclical variation will continue to be requisite. So far as contributing to the solution of continued unemployment is concerned, the functions of monetary policy, outside the avoidance of a runaway prosperity fever, are two. The banking system can continue and even increase its activity in putting idle savings at the disposal of government investment, assuming that this investment is animated by the purpose of breaking monopoly, cost rigidities, and the inertia of enterprise in directions of public demand. Action by the banking system in this respect is, however, clearly limited by its responsibility for cyclical developments, especially currently in view of the volume of excess reserves. In the second place, carefully articulated plans are not wanting for increasing the availability of credit without heavy risk premia to small enterprises and second- and third-rate credit ratings.[1] The success of such plans depends, of course, upon a rational articulation with monetary policy in general, and with the investment, taxation, relief, and labor policies of the government. Promising lines of attack upon the persistence of unemployment and the lethargy of investment are, however, for the most part beyond the province of the banking system and the monetary authority.

---

[1] Cf. L. L. Watkins, *Commercial Banking Reform in the United States* (Ann Arbor, Michigan: Michigan Business Studies, 1938) 8, 5, pp. 56–70; Guy Greer, "America's Greatest Need Today," *Harper's Magazine* (December, 1939), pp. 1–13; Berle, *loc. cit.*

21

THE COBWEB THEOREM*

By Mordecai Ezekiel‖

History of the "Cobweb Theorem"

Regularly recurring cycles in the production and prices of particular commodities have been recognized by students of prices for more than fifty years.[1] Many economists have been disturbed by the apparent inconsistency between the persistence of these observed cycles and the tendency towards an equilibrium posited by economic theory. Descriptions of the mechanism of these self-perpetuating commodity cycles were well developed a decade or more ago, but despite various partial explanations, a definite theoretical explanation for them had not been established. Finally three economists, in Italy, Holland, and the United States, apparently independently, worked out the theoretical explanation which has since come to be known as the "cob-web theorem."[2] As it happened, all three papers were published in German, two in the same issue of the same publication. Only recently has the theory begun to be generally recognized in English-speaking countries.

---

* *Quarterly Journal of Economics*, February 1938, pages 255–280. Reprinted by the courtesy of the Quarterly Journal of Economics and the author.

‖ Department of Agriculture, Washington.

[1] S. Benner, Benner's Prophecies of Future Ups and Downs in Prices, Cincinnati, 1876.

For a bibliography of other early studies of the corn-hog price cycle, see "Factors Affecting the Price of Hogs," by G. C. Haas and Mordecai Ezekiel, U. S. Dept. Agr. Bul. 1440, 1926, pp. 67–68.

[2] This name was apparently first suggested by Nicholas Kaldor in his article "A Classificatory Note on the Determinateness of Equilibrium," Rev. of Econ. Studies, Vol. 1, p. 122. February 1934.

All three originators of the theory followed the same basic idea of carrying successive production, price, and production readjustments back and forth between the supply and demand curves. Schultz's demonstration[1] was the simplest, presenting merely one example, of the convergent type; but also plotting the resulting time-series of prices and quantities. Tinbergen's analysis was more complete, presenting both the convergent and divergent types,[2] and referring to Hanau's statistical analysis of hog prices in Germany[3] as a realistic illustration. Ricci's analysis, published in the same issue with Tinbergen's, presented diagrams of all three basic types, convergent, divergent, and continuous.[4] In each case, these first statements of the cobweb analysis were introduced only incidentally. Schultz used it as an illustration of the difference between simultaneous readjustment of supply to demand and lagging readjustment; Tinbergen as showing that where the production response lags behind the price change "instead of equilibrium being reached . . . a continuing movement of price and production is possible"; and Ricci as a basis for showing (in a review of Moore's work) how important were the precise values of the elasticities of supply and demand, since such greatly different economic consequences might follow from slight differences in their numerical values. No one of the three, however, considered the broader significance of the cobweb theory in its relation to economic theory as such.

Subsequently, in the article cited above, Kaldor called attention to the cobweb analysis as bearing on the determinateness of equilibrium in those cases "where the adjustments are completely

---

[1] Henry Schultz, Der Sinn der Statistischen Nachfragen, Heft 10, Veröffentlichungen der Frankfurter Gesellschaft für Konjunkturforschung, Kurt Schroeder Verlag, Bonn. 1930. See especially page 34.

[2] J. Tinbergen, Bestimmung und Deutung von Angebotskurven, Ein Beispiel, Zeitschrift für Nationalökonomie, Wien, Band 1, Heft 5, 1930, p. 671.

[3] Arthur Hanau, Die Prognose der Schweinepreise, Sonderheft 7 and 18, Vierteljahrshefte zur Konjunkturforschung, Institut für Konjunkturforschung, Berlin, 1928 and 1930.

[4] Umberto Ricci, Die "Synthetische Ökonomie" von Henry Ludwell Moore, Zeitschrift für Nationalökonomie, Wien, Band 1, Heft 5, 1930, p. 656.

discontinuous"; and Leontief showed that where the supply or demand curves are of an erratic shape, the same set of curves might produce either a convergent or a divergent series.[1] The cobweb theory has also been discussed as a theoretical explanation for the hog cycle in England.[2] More recently, it has been incorporated in an American elementary text on economic theory.[3] Despite this increasing attention to it, however, the theory has remained substantially in the form first stated by its originators. This article attempts to develop the theory more generally, and to clarify its relation both to neo-classical economic theory and to statistical price analysis.

Restatement of the Theory of Market Price

The price on a current market, under conditions of pure competition,[4] over a given limited period of time tends to be determined by the interaction of the supply and demand on that market. Demand (indicated by the curve DD' in section A of Figure 1) represents the schedule of the number of units of the commodity (Q) which purchasers stand willing to buy within the period specified at varying prices (P); supply (indicated by the curve SS') represents the number of units of the commodity which holders (or producers) of the product stand willing to sell within the specified period at varying prices. Since for every purchase there must be a sale, the quantity sold must equal the quantity bought. Under pure competition the equilibrium price for the

---

[1] Wassily Leontief, Verzögerte Angebotsanpassung und Partielles Gleichgewicht, Zeitschrift für Nationalökonomie, 1934.

[2] R. H. Coase and R. F. Fowler, Bacon Production and the Pig-Cycle in Great Britain, Economica, Vol. II, No. 6, p. 143; also reply by Ruth Cohen and J. D. Barker, and rejoinder by Coase and Fowler, in Vol. II, No. 8, pp. 408–428. 1935.

[3] Archibald MacDonald McIsaac and James G. Smith, Introduction to Economic Analysis, pp. 430–435. 1936.

[4] Here "pure" is used in the same sense as that given by Chamberlin; the market may be imperfect, but if competition is pure, i.e., not monopolistic, the supply and demand curves define the condition of equilibrium. See Edward Chamberlin, The Theory of Monopolistic Competition, pp. 12–29. 1936.

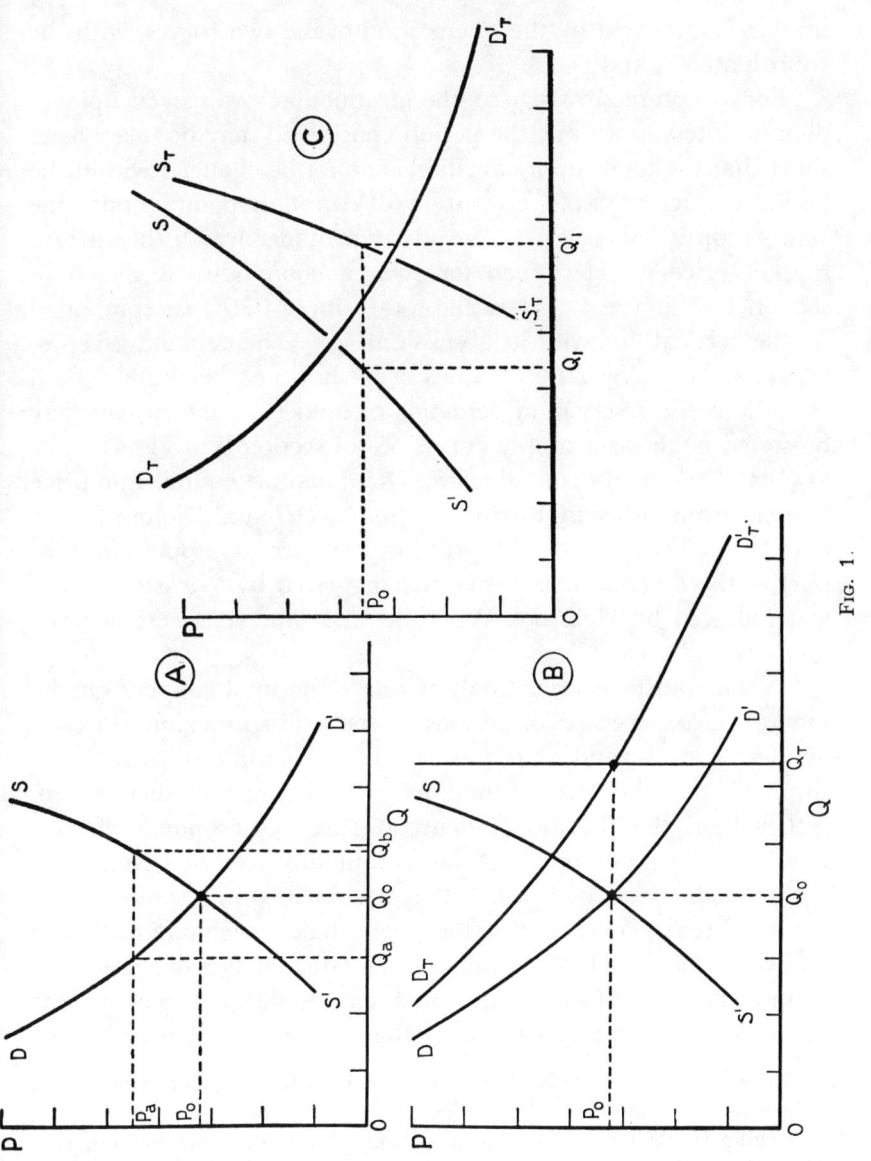

Fig. 1.

market is indicated by the intersection of the two curves, with the coördinates P_o and Q_o.

For a commodity where the production process occupies a definite interval of time, the period considered may be taken as so short that the total supply available cannot be changed within the period (as, for example, the supply of cotton or potatoes once the year's crop is harvested). The situation under which the current market price is determined for such a commodity is shown in section B of Figure 1. Here the total supply (OQ_t) is represented by the vertical line with its abscissa at Q_t. The demand is represented as before by DD'. As has been shown earlier,[1] under such conditions the reservation demands of holders of the supply may be stated either as a supply curve, SS' of section B of Figure 1, or as part of the total demand curve, D_tD_t'; and the equilibrium price is then given either by the intersection of DD' and SS', or of D_tD_t' and Q_t. This method of expressing the current supply curve as part of the demand curve was first suggested by Wicksteed,[2] and was followed by Holbrook Working[3] and other pioneers of price analysis.

When statistical price analysts relate the total supplies on the market in a succession of periods to the prices prevailing in each of those periods, and determine a curve describing that relationship, it is thus the curve of total demand, D_tD_t', which they obtain, rather than the traditional demand curve of economic theory, DD'. If the total supply of the commodity cannot be changed within each period with which they are dealing, in response to the prices of that period, and if they have made adequate statistical allowance for price level, population growth, changes in consumers' income, and other factors which may tend to shift the level or slope of the total demand curve, then their analyses will reveal quite

---

[1] Mordecai Ezekiel, Statistical Analyses and Laws of Price, Quarterly Journal of Economics, 43, pp. 199–214. 1928.

[2] Philip H. Wicksteed, The Common Sense of Political Economy, pp. 498–544. 1910.

[3] Holbrook Working, Factors Determining the Price of Potatoes in St. Paul and Minneapolis, University of Minnesota, Agricultural Experiment Station, Tech. Bul. 10, p. 17. 1922.

accurately the slope and position of the curve $D_tD'_t$. It is possible to measure the curve DD' separately, or the curve SS', but the determination of each requires a separate study, with a different series of quantity data instead of the total quantity. In the subsequent portions of this paper, the term "demand curve" will be used to refer to the total demand curve, $D_tD'_t$, rather than to the purchasers' demand curve, DD'.

Where a commodity is non-perishable (such as cotton or wheat), a large part of the reservation demand may be for storage rather than for other disposition. In such cases, a low price will tend to reduce the supply for sale in the current period, but to increase the total supply on hand in the next period. At the same time, the price paid in one period may influence the quantity that will be produced in the next succeeding period. These two relations are shown in section C of Figure 1. Here $D_tD'_t$ is the demand curve for the current period, as before. SS', however, is the supply curve for quantity produced in the *next succeeding* period in response to price in the previous period. The horizontal distance from SS' to $S_tS'_t$ represents the carryover of stored supply from the current period to the succeeding period, in response to the price of the current period. Thus, for a price of OP_0, new production will supply the quantity OQ_1 in the next period, while the quantity $Q_1Q'_1$ will be carried over in storage, giving a total supply of OQ'_1. This total supply in the subsequent season, in response to the prevailing price in the current season, is given by the total supply curve $S_tS'_t$. Where the negative variation in carryover in response to price is larger than the positive variation in production in response to price, the total supply curve may even be negative in slope, rather than positive as usually assumed. Even when this occurs, however, the total demand curve, composed of the two negative elements of buyers' demand and sellers' reservation demands, will always be more elastic than the total supply curve, composed of the negative element of carryover and the positive element of newly-produced supply. When the term "supply curve" is used hereafter in this paper, it will be the curve of total supply, $S_tS'_t$, which is thus designated.

Restatement of the Theory of Normal Price

The normal price is that price at which the market price would tend to settle over a period of time long enough to bring quantities demanded (by purchasers) and quantities produced into an equilibrium. Traditional theory assumes that under static conditions (and under pure competition) this equilibrium would tend to be reëstablished, following any accidental disturbance. For those commodities where there is an appreciable time interval between a change in price and the change in production in response to that change in price, the cobweb theorem shows that the series of reactions may be quite complex.

The upper portion of Fig. 2 shows the relations between demand and subsequent supply for the special case of a commodity where a change in price in one period does not affect production until the next period but does completely determine supply in that period. The (total) demand curve is represented by D_tD_t'; it shows the schedule of prices received in period 1 for varying supplies available in period 1. The (total) supply curve is represented by S_tS_t'; it shows the schedule of quantities available in period 2 for varying prices paid in period 1.

Altho this figure is drawn in two dimensions—prices and quantities—it sets forth the relations of three variables. In the case of a current market, quantity bought must equal the quantity sold, for both quantities relate to the same period and are identical. In Figure 2, however, this identity no longer holds. OQ_1 is the quantity which sets the price in period 1; OQ_2 is the quantity (in period 2) called forth by that price. Altho only one price—P_1—is involved, two distinct and different quantities are represented—OQ_1 and OQ_2—and there is no *mathematical* reason why they must be identical. Instead, the cobweb theory reveals the series of reactions which may result from such situations, and demonstrates how and under what conditions equilibrium may be established. Since the two curves of Figure 2 exist in different time dimensions, they are not drawn intersecting, but rather lapping over one another without real contact.

The "Cobweb Theory"

The phases of the cobweb theory which have already been stated by others may first be briefly summarized:

Case 1, Continuous Fluctuation

In the lower portion of Figure 2, the series of reactions is portrayed for the curves shown in the upper portion of the figure. The quantity in the initial period (Q_1) is large, producing a relatively low price where it intersects the demand curve, at P_1. This low price, intersecting the supply curve, calls forth in the next period a relatively short supply, Q_2. This short supply gives a high price, P_2, where it intersects the supply curve. This high price calls forth a corresponding increased production, Q_3, in the third period, with a corresponding low price, P_3. Since this low price in the third period is identical with that in the first, the production and price in the fourth, fifth, and subsequent periods will continue to rotate around the path Q_2, P_2, Q_3, P_3, etc. As long as price is completely determined by the current supply, and supply is completely determined by the preceding price, fluctuation in price and production will continue in this unchanging pattern indefinitely, without an equilibrium being approached or reached. This is true in this particular case because the demand curve is the exact reverse of the supply curve, so that at their overlap each has the same elasticity. This case has been designated the "case of continuous fluctuations."

Case 2, Divergent Fluctuation

Where the elasticity of supply is greater than the elasticity of demand, the series of reactions works out as shown in the upper portion of Fig. 3. Starting with the moderately large supply, Q_1, and the corresponding price, P_1, the series of reactions is traced by the dotted line. In the second period, there is a moderately reduced supply, Q_2, with the corresponding higher price, P_2. This high price calls forth a considerable increase in supply, Q_3, in the third period, with a resulting material reduction in price, to

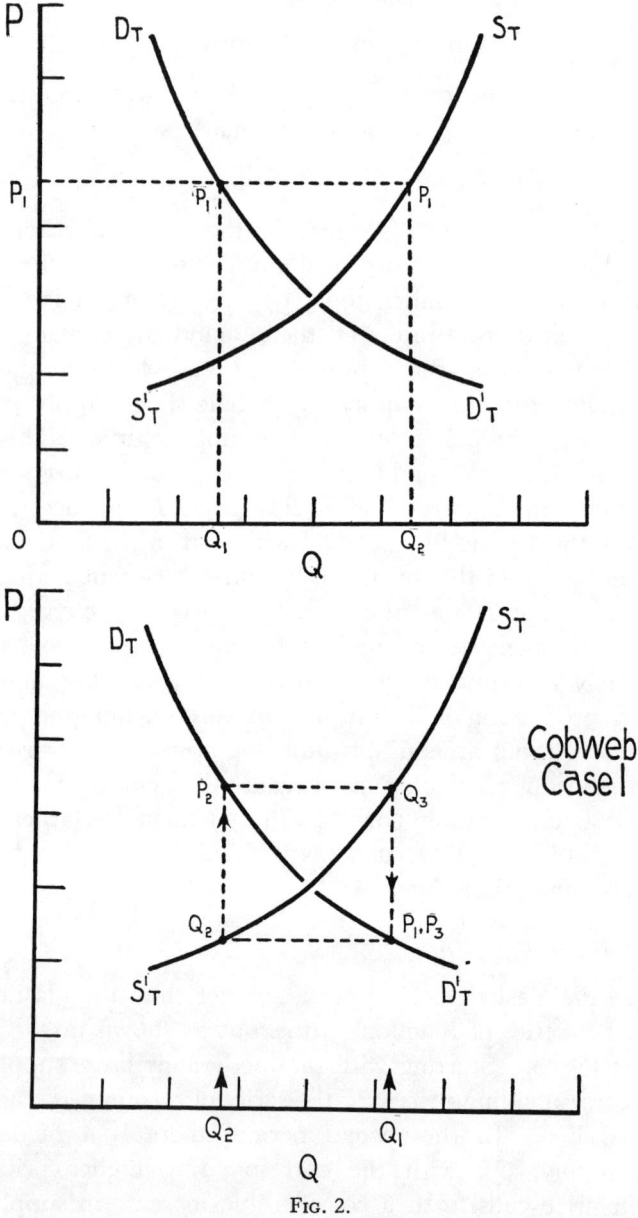

Fig. 2.

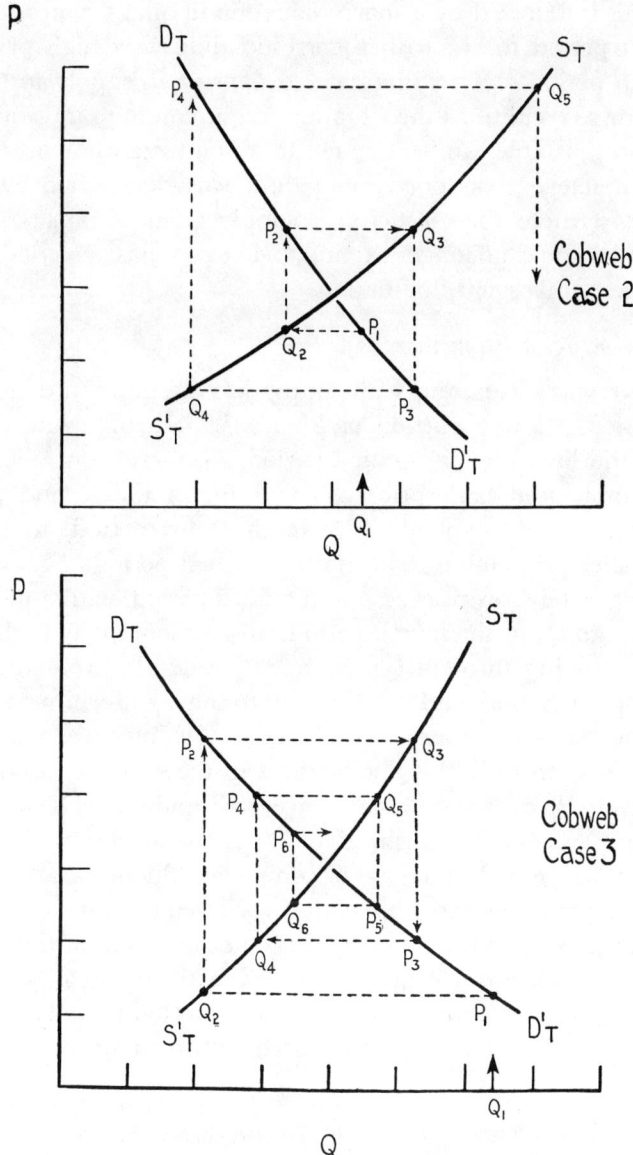

Fig. 3.

P_3. This is followed by a sharp reduction in quantity produced in the next period to Q_4, with a corresponding very high price, P_4. The fifth period sees a still greater expansion in supply to Q_5, etc. Under these conditions the situation might continue to grow more and more unstable, until price fell to absolute zero, or production was completely abandoned, or a limit was reached to available resources (where the elasticity of supply would change) so that production could no longer expand. The case has been designated the "case of divergent fluctuation."

Case 3, Convergent Fluctuation

The reverse situation, with supply less elastic than demand, is shown in the lower portion of Figure 3. Starting with a large supply and low price in the first period, P_1, there would be a very short supply and high price, Q_2 and P_2, in the second period. Production would expand again in the third period, to Q_3, but to a smaller production than that in the first period. This would set a moderately low price, P_3, in the third period, with a moderate reduction to Q_4 in the fourth period; and a moderately high price, P_4. Continuing through Q_5, P_5, and Q_6 and P_6, production and price approach more and more closely to the equilibrium condition where no further changes would occur. Of the three cases considered thus far, only this one behaves in the manner assumed by equilibrium theory; and even it converges rapidly only if the supply curve is markedly less elastic than the demand curve. The case has been designated "the case of convergent fluctuation."

To this point this paper has merely reviewed the points developed in earlier papers on the theory of price analysis and on the cobweb theory.[1] As thus developed, the cobweb theory explains swings in production and price in successive production periods, but does not fully explain the long cycles observed in many commodities.

---

[1] Leontief, loc. cit., has shown that in cases where the supply curve and the demand curve are of erratic shape, with marked changes in elasticity along one or both curves, the cobweb reaction may be convergent at some points on the curves, and divergent at others. Such cases are a mixture of the three simple types summarized here.

THE COBWEB THEOREM

The following portions of this paper present a further extension of the cobweb analysis that may be useful as a theoretical framework for the investigation of such long cycles.

Case 1a, Two-period Lag in Supply, Continuous Fluctuation

In the cases considered thus far, it has been assumed that a change of price in one period was reflected in a corresponding change in production in the next succeeding period. In some commodities (such as hogs, beef cattle, apples, etc.) two or more seasons may be required for the production process, so that two or more periods may elapse before the effect of price upon production becomes apparent. If we assume that the effect of price upon production appears entirely in the second succeeding period, how will the "cobweb" work out? This further condition may be examined for any one of the three cases shown. The upper portion of Fig. 4 shows it for Case 1, as Case 1a.

Since two years are required for the result of the first year to appear, the supplies for the first two years, Q_1 and Q_2, must be assumed, with the resulting prices P_1 and P_2. In response to the initial low price, production two years later, in the third period, is reduced to Q_3, with the resulting high price, P_3. This is followed in the fifth year by a corresponding increase to Q_5, with a corresponding low price, P_5. Since this is a subclass of Case 1, the reaction continues in alternate years around the same pathway, P_5, Q_7; P_7, Q_9; etc. Likewise, the price and supply of the second year, Q_2 and P_2, are followed two years later by reduced supply, Q_4, and increased price, P_4; four years later by Q_6 and P_6, and so on *ad infinitum*.

Case 3b, Three-year Lag in Supply, Convergent Fluctuation

A further illustration of delayed response may be developed by assuming a production period three years in length. This also may be combined with any of the three original cases. Applying it to the third case, results are secured as shown in the lower portion of Figure 4, as Case 3b.

Here three initial supplies are assumed: Q_1, very small; Q_2, moderately small; and Q_3, just equal to the normal supply. The

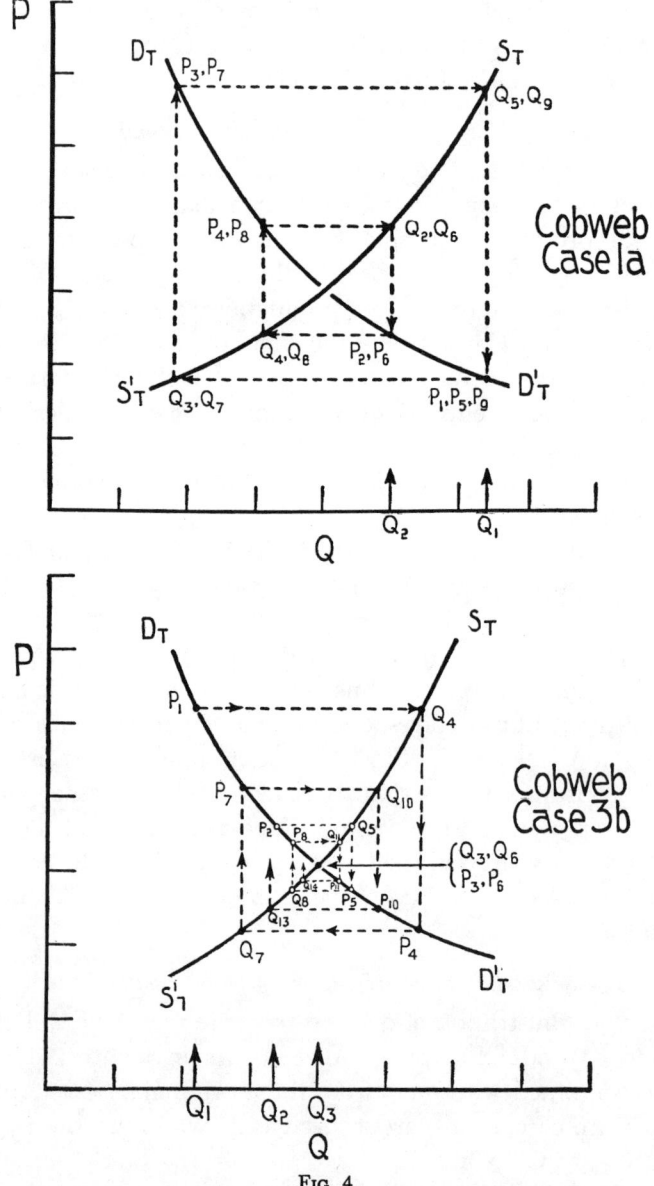

Fig. 4.

corresponding prices, P_1, P_2, and P_3, produce reactions in production three years later as shown: Q_4, a great expansion; Q_5, a moder-

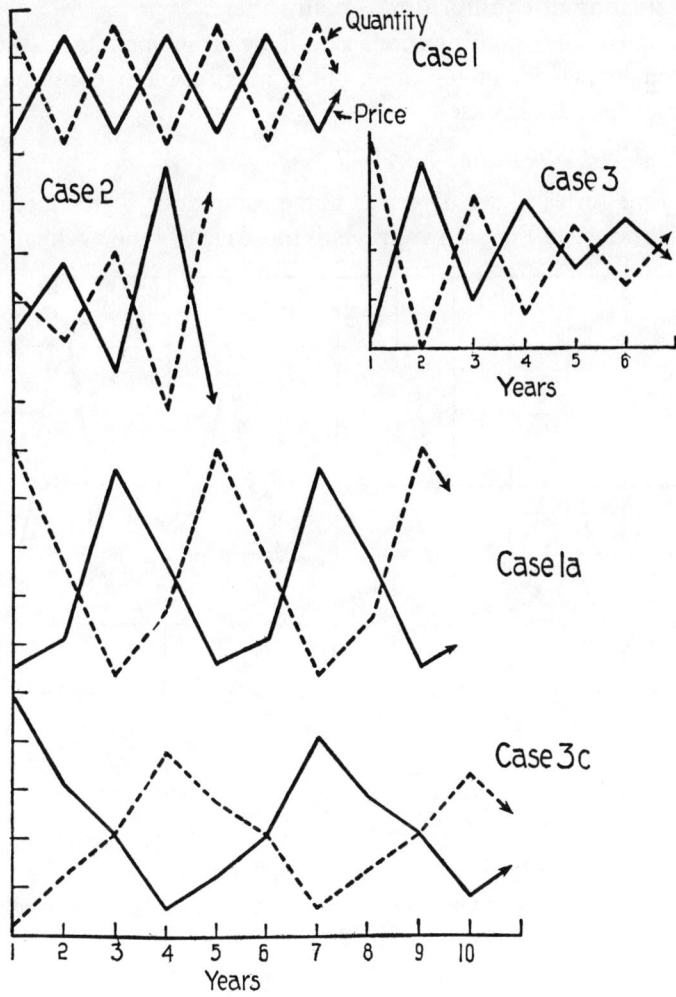

FIG. 5.
Time series of price and quantity.

ate expansion; and Q_6, no expansion. The resulting prices, P_4, P_5, and P_6, produce corresponding effects on production three years further on, at Q_7, Q_8, and Q_9; and so on. Since the case is of the convergent type, the "cobwebs" traced by the 1, 4, 7, 10 series and the 2, 5, 8, 11 series converge slowly, while the 3, 6, 9 series, starting at equilibrium, remains there.

Various other combinations could be developed by assuming even longer periods of response, or by making other combinations with the three basic cases.

The Time Series Traced by Price and Production

A time-series chart of prices and production in the successive periods shown in Figs. 2 to 4, reveals more clearly the cyclical char-

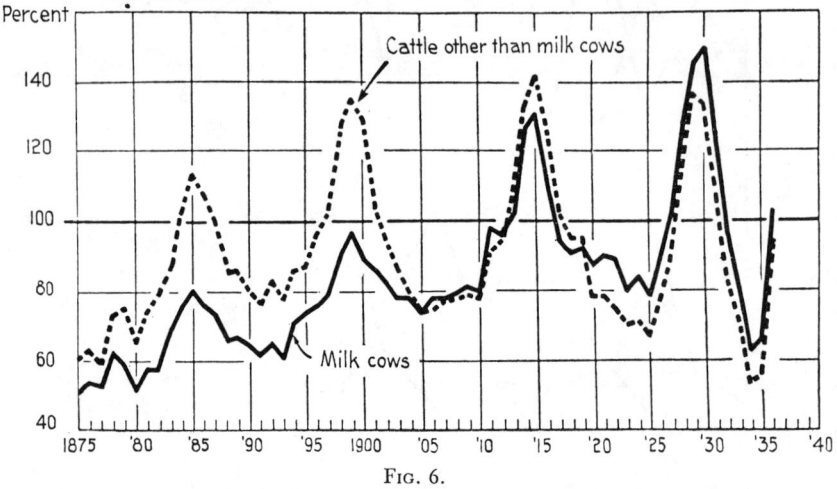

Fig. 6.

Purchasing power per head of milk cows and cattle other than milk cows, 1875 to date. (Index numbers (1910–14 = 100).)

acter of the resulting processes, as shown in Fig. 5. Cases 1, 2, and 3, with a one-year lag in response, all produce two-year cycles. The continuous, divergent, and convergent character of the three cases is clearly evident, both in production and in price. Case 1a, with a two-year lag in production, has a four-year period from peak to peak; and Case 3c, with a three-year lag, a six-year period. The continuous character of the cycle in Case 1a, and the slow convergence of the cycle in Case 3c, are also apparent.

While it is evident that these synthetic time series have been constructed under highly rigid assumptions, it is interesting to compare them with some actual price and production cycles, as shown in Fig. [6 and] 7. [Fig. 6 shows the prices of cows and cattle corrected for changes in wholesale prices;] Fig. 7, hog prices stated as a ratio to the price of corn, that is, the number of bushels of corn that can be bought with a hundred pounds of hogs. The changes in the adjusted prices of cattle and milk cows both reflect the underlying cycle in cattle numbers. The similarities are evident; it is also apparent that the actual cycles are more irregular, both in length and in shape, than are the cycles based upon the fixed periods of the theory.

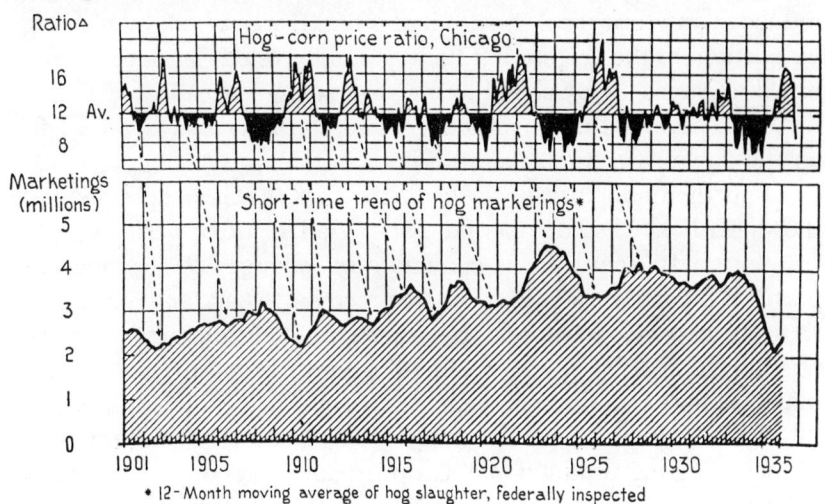

FIG. 7.
Hog-corn price ratios and hog marketings.

LIMITATIONS OF THE COBWEB THEORY

The cobweb theory can apply exactly only to commodities which fulfill three conditions: (1) where production is completely determined by the producers' response to price, under conditions of pure competition (where the producer bases plans for future production on the assumption present prices will continue, and that his own production plans will not affect the market); (2) where the time needed for production requires at least one full period before production can be changed, once the plans are made;

and (3) where the price is set by the supply available. Obviously commodities where either price or production is set by administrative decisions (i.e., where monopolistic competition prevails), or where production can respond almost immediately to changed demands, cannot be expected to show the cobweb reaction.

Even for the commodities which approximately fulfill the assumptions, however, the theory must be limited. In many commodities farmers can do little to increase their future production, once they have made their initial commitment in acres seeded or in animals bred. But altho they cannot increase, they can reduce at any time until the product is finally marketed, by plowing up portions of the crop or letting it go unharvested, by slaughtering breeding stock, or by slaughtering pigs young instead of fattening them. There is thus in practice some elasticity of response left, on the downward side at least.

A further difficulty arises from the fact that few commodities show clearly marked one-period, two-period, or three-period supply reactions. In many farm commodities, changes in acreage are partly influenced by prices of the preceding year, and partly by those of two years before. In other commodities, such as hogs, not only the price of the commodity itself, but the price of raw materials for its production, such as corn, may be equally important.[1]

An even more serious limitation is that imposed by natural conditions affecting production. Crop production is dependent upon yield per acre as well as acreage; and yields are greatly influenced by the weather. In the past, yields and acreage have been about equally important in influencing cotton production, but yield changes have been far more important than acreage changes in corn. In other crops, such as tobacco, acreage varies much more than yield.[2] Variability in yield may result in a very large crop when acreage has been sharply reduced, or vice versa.

---

[1] Louis H. Bean, "The Farmers' Response to Price," Jour. Farm Econ., XI, pp. 368–385, especially page 385. July, 1929.

[2] Louis H. Bean, "Some Limitations to the Control of Agricultural Production in the United States," American Coöperation, American Institute of Coöperation, 1932, pp. 461–465.

Unusual weather may occasionally change what would otherwise be a large crop to a normal one, and so restore prices to a point where subsequent variation will be slight—until another abnormal yield is secured. Most of the time, however, natural variations may tend to result in unduly high or unduly low production, and thus set a new cycle of response in reaction. Even in commodities which follow the convergent pattern, the actual cycles may be quite similar to those of either of the other types, if abnormally large or small crops occur frequently enough to cause a marked departure from normal and to start again a long series of convergent cycles before stability is again approached. The combination of "cobweb" reactions with occasional crop disasters or gluts may be sufficient to produce recurring cyclical changes in production and prices, rather than stability, as the normal situation over a considerable number of commodities.

Another difficulty arises from the fact that actually production may not swing from very high to very low, even with a one-year response. Analyses of acreage response for various crops show that there is a limit to the per cent farmers will increase their acreage in any single year, so that even with a one-year response period, several years of successive increase in acreage may be required before very high prices are reflected in very high production. A very large contraction in acreage can be made in a single year, however, so that on the down side a single year of very low prices may be followed by a great contraction in acreage. Similarly, in industries producing products with a long life, such as ships or houses, price is not set by the current production, but by current production added to the existing stock, and the current production may be quite small compared to that existing supply. In such cases price affects subsequent *additions to* supply, but *total supply* affects the price. The cobweb theory would need to be further extended and modified to apply to such cases.

Finally, there is no commodity for which the third condition—that the supply alone sets the price—is completely fulfilled. There are many commodities, especially farm products, whose prices ordinarily show larger variations due to changes in supply than to all other influences combined; yet their prices are also influenced by changes in the supply of competing products, changes in the prosperity or income of consumers, and changes in institutional factors affecting their market, such as tariff quotas, freight rates, weather conditions, and even style changes. Under unusual conditions, as during the years from 1931 to 1934, these forces which shift the position of the demand curve may far outweigh changes in supply as determinants of commodity prices, even for articles such as potatoes where a slight change in supply produces a disproportionately large change in price. In between periods of great economic upheaval, as from 1900 to 1913, or from 1922 to 1929, these shifts in demand may be relatively slight or regular, and it is during such periods that any underlying tendencies to cyclical reactions in individual products would be most clearly revealed.

Not All Commodity Cycles are "Cobwebs"

Not all cyclical phenomena in individual industries are traceable to the "cobweb reaction." In durable or semidurable goods, the average length of service of the equipment, and the bunching of replacements in recurring periods, may give rise to a separate cyclical phenomenon which has been called "the replacement cycle." In producers' goods, especially in producers' goods several steps removed from the final product, such as in machine tools or die making, the demand for the producers' goods may appear only when production of consumers' goods is increasing, and may disappear entirely when demand for the final product is stable. Similarly, demand for machinery to make the machines to make the final product may appear only when the demand for the final product is increasing at an increasing rate.[1] The derived character of the demand for producers' goods may thus give rise to cyclical phenomena in producers' goods' industries of a quite different

---

[1] J. M. Clark, "Business Acceleration and the Law of Demand; a technical factor in economic cycles," Journal of Political Economy March 1917; Ragnar Frisch, "The Inter-relation between Capital Production and Consumer-Taking," Jour. of Pol. Econ., October 1931, also replies by J. M. Clark in December 1931 and October 1932 issues.

character. Many recurring cycles in commodity prices may thus be found to be due to causes other than the cobweb reaction. The cobweb theorem as summarized here should be used as an hypothesis in studying the interactions of supply and demand only for those commodities whose conditions of pricing and production satisfy the special assumptions on which it is based, not as a blanket explanation of all industrial cycles.

Equilibrium Economics in the Light of the Cobweb Theory

The limitations just discussed apply, not to the cobweb theory as theory, but to the range within which it is a valid hypothesis. If we assume that, despite these limitations, the cobweb explanation will prove to be significant for many commodities, we may then ask how this theory affects economic theory as a whole.

Classical economic theory rests upon the assumption that price and production, if disturbed from their equilibrium, tend to gravitate back toward that normal. The cobweb theory demonstrates that, even under static conditions, this result will not necessarily follow. On the contrary, prices and production of some commodities might tend to fluctuate indefinitely, or even to diverge further and further from equilibrium.

The equilibrium concept lies at the heart of classic theory. If prices and production do not converge rapidly to an equilibrium, then each industry may recurringly attract to it more labor and investment than it can use to advantage, and may leave that labor and equipment only partly utilized much of the time. In a series of industries, all showing individual cycles of the "cobweb" type, at any one time some will be operating at full capacity, or above the equilibrium point; others will be operating below the equilibrium point, at far below capacity; while others will be operating near the equilibrium point, but below the capacity installed at their recurring periods of over-expansion. For the whole series of industries combined, the installed capacity will materially exceed the portion that is in use at any one time; and the workers, trained for service in individual industries and prevented by various frictions from shifting readily into other industries, will always be partly unemployed. If many industries thus tend to develop—for occasional use—more labor and equipment than they need for normal output, labor and capital as a whole will never be fully utilized. If many commodities are chronically varying *above* and *below* their individual equilibria, then the economic system will never organize all its resources for the most effective use, but will always be operating below the total installed capacity and with more or less unemployment. Even under the conditions of pure competition and static demand and supply, there is thus no "automatic self-regulating mechanism," which can provide full utilization of resources. Unemployment, excess capacity, and the wasteful use of resources may occur even when all the competitive assumptions are fulfilled. If enough commodities follow the cobweb form of reaction, competitive readjustments may fail notably to reach the most productive employment of resources.[1]

In seeking to explain the persistent existence of unemployment and excess capacities, modern economists have laid increasing emphasis on the failure of our economic society to provide the competition assumed in traditional theory, and have turned to the new theory of imperfect or monopolistic competition, or to examination of the balance between savings and the need for new investment,[2] as theoretical explanations of the existing situation. From the foregoing discussion, however, it appears that even in those areas of the economic system where reasonably effective pure competition still prevails, cobweb cycles may prevent the system from reaching its most effective utilization of resources. Where competition is absent or monopolistic, we must study the other ways in which production and price are controlled; where pure competition is present, we must examine the mechanism and sequence of price and production reactions to determine whether they do work effectively toward an optimum adjustment.

---

[1] For a different approach to under-utilization of resources, note Alvin H. Hansen, Mr. Keynes on Underemployment Equilibrium, Jour. Pol. Econ., XLIV, p. 667. 1936.

[2] John Maynard Keynes, General Theory of Employment, Interest and Money.

CLASSIFIED BIBLIOGRAPHY OF ARTICLES ON BUSINESS CYCLE THEORY

Compiled by
HAROLD M. SOMERS
University of Buffalo

The dynamic behavior of business-cycle theory during the past decade has placed an increasingly heavy burden of responsibility and work on the teacher, the student and the research worker in the field. Altered points of emphasis and refined methods of analysis have led to a thoroughgoing re-examination of older concepts, methods, analyses, conclusions and recommendations for policy. It is becoming more and more difficult to do justice to any topic, new or old. This classified bibliography is intended to ease the burden somewhat by providing a guide to the articles dealing with the major subjects discussed in a course on business-cycle theory.

The complex multiple-oneness of the subject of business cycles makes any classification, however broad, extremely dangerous. The groups and sub-groups adopted here break the field down rather finely and somewhat artificially. The divisions mark off various *aspects* of business-cycle theory and not various business cycle theories. The categories can obviously not be mutually exclusive and their only justification is that they provide a nucleus of articles around which any one using the bibliography can construct a more complete picture. The subject of monetary interest-theory, for instance, appears almost everywhere in business-cycle literature, regardless of the title of the particular piece.

Nevertheless it is felt desirable to provide a list of some sixty items—which should be sufficient as an introduction. It is hoped that the notes at the beginning of each division will serve to increase the usefulness of the bibliography. But any user who still feels that the classification is more dangerous than useful is urged to disregard the headings and sub-headings. The items are listed chronologically under each division, except that an attempt is made to avoid breaking into a particular controversy or train of thought.

Articles originally published in periodicals or multi-author books are included. Reviews of books appear only when they are of peculiar interest to the development or present state of the subject. Numerous foreign-language items have been admitted but the coverage in that sphere is not so great as in the English language. The past twenty years have been treated intensively and some items appear for earlier years. Statistical and historical studies are included only where they have a direct bearing on some important question in the theoretical field. Discussions of current wartime and postwar economic problems are excluded unless techniques of permanent value are involved. Above all, it must be emphasized that the coverage is by no means complete, so that the omission of any item does not imply any judgment regarding the quality of the item.

I am greatly indebted to Professor Fritz Machlup for his constant assistance and advice in the preparation of this bibliography and to Professor Howard S. Ellis and Professor Gottfried Haberler for valuable consultations. I have also been aided greatly by the bibliographies appearing in the *American Economic Review*, the *Quarterly Journal of Economics*, the *Economic Journal*, the *Review of Economic Statistics* (R. A. Gordon), *Contemporary Monetary Theory* by R. J. Saulnier, *German Monetary Theory* by H. S. Ellis, *Theory of Prices* (Vol. II) by A. W. Marget; by the references contained in *Prosperity and Depression* (3rd edition) by G. Haberler; and by a preliminary list drawn up by the late Dr. Horace G. White, Jr. My wife, Claire Somers, bore the major share of the heavy burden of clerical work connected with the preparation of this bibliography. None of the individuals mentioned should be held responsible for the topical arrangement or for the inclusion, omission or classification of any item. Indeed, it is hoped that the difficult nature of the task will relieve even the compiler of some of the responsibility for the many defects of this undertaking.

H. M. S.

Buffalo, N. Y.
January, 1944.

CLASSIFIED BIBLIOGRAPHY

	PAGE
I. Overall Discussions and Development of Business-Cycle Theory	446
II. Dynamic and Econometric Business-Cycle Analysis	448
III. Savings and Investment; Underemployment Equilibrium and Underconsumption	451
A. Savings and Investment	451
B. Concepts of Employment, Income and Capacity	453
C. Underemployment Equilibrium	454
D. Underconsumption and Purchasing Power	456
IV. Multiplier and Acceleration Principles; Fiscal Policy	458
A. The Multiplier Principle and the Consumption Function	458
B. The Acceleration Principle and the Demand for Durable Goods	460
C. Interaction of the Multiplier and Acceleration Principles	461
D. Fiscal Policy and National Income	462
V. Monetary and Capital Aspects of Business-Cycle Theory; Monetary Policy	465
A. Monetary and Capital Theories	465
B. Monetary Interest Theories	471
C. Effectiveness of Monetary Policy	474
VI. Psychological Influences, Expectations and Investment Decisions	475
VII. Technology, Innovations, Reinvestment and Inventory Cycles	477
A. Technology and Innovations	477
B. Reinvestment and Depreciation	478
C. Inventories	478
VIII. Wages, Costs and Prices in Relation to Output and Employment	478
A. Wages and Employee Compensation	478
B. Price Rigidity, Monopolistic Factors, Costs	481
IX. Special Industry Cycles: Agriculture and Building	482
A. Agricultural, Weather and Cosmic Cycles	482
B. Building Cycles	482
X. Secular Tendencies: Long Waves and the Stagnation Thesis	483
A. Long Waves; Wars	483
B. Stagnation Thesis; Population Growth	484
XI. International Aspects	485
XII. Discussions of Business-Cycle Control	486
INDEX OF AUTHORS	489

I. OVERALL DISCUSSIONS AND DEVELOPMENT OF BUSINESS-CYCLE THEORY

Includes historical articles which throw light on various types of theories. See, for instance, Slichter (1938). Historical articles emphasizing a particular type of theory are in the respective divisions. See, for instance, Hansen (1938) in IV-D. Articles on the development of business-cycle theory which fit into one of the subsequent divisions are placed there. See, for instance, Burchardt (1928) in V-A. Overall discussions dealing primarily with business-cycle control are in XII.

*MITCHELL, W. C., Business cycles, *Business Cycles and Unemployment*, 5–18. New York: National Bureau of Economic Research, 1923.

SPIETHOFF, A., Krisen, *Handwörterbuch der Staatswissenschaften*, VI (1925) 8–91.

MILLS, F. C., An hypothesis concerning the duration of the business cycle, *Journal of the American Statistical Association*, XXI (1926) 447–457.

AFTALION, A., The theory of economic cycles based on the capitalistic technique of production, *Review of Economic Statistics*, IX (1927) 165–170.

SCHUMPETER, J. A., The explanation of the business cycle, *Economica*, VII, old series (1927) 286–311.

ROHTLIEB, C., Ur den nyaste konjunkturforskningen, *Ekonomisk Tidskrift*, XXXII (1930) 1–21.

SCHUMPETER, J. A., Mitchell's business cycles, *Quarterly Journal of Economics*, XLV (1930–31) 150–172.

FOA, B., Recenti teorie monetarie del ciclo, *Giornale degli Economisti*, LXXI (1931) 847–873.

BAARS, A., De crisis theorie van den heer S. de Wolff, *De Economist*, LXXX (1931) 399–444.

SPRAGUE, O. M. W., Major and minor trade fluctuations, *Journal of the Royal Statistical Society*, XCIV (1931) 540–549. Discussion, 549–563.

CLAY, H., in *The World's Economic Crisis and the Way of Escape*, 105–147. New York: The Century Co., 1932.

AFTALION, A., Les crises économiques et financières, Académie de Droit International, *Recueil des Cours*, XXXIX (1932) 277–350.

CLARK, J. M., Business cycles: the problem of diagnosis, *Journal of the American Statistical Association*, XXVII (1932, supplement) 212–217.

ROBERTSON, D. H., The future of trade cycle theory, *Der Stand und die nächste Zukunft der Konjunkturforschung* (Festschrift für Arthur Spiethoff) 238–242. Munich: Duncker & Humblot, 1933. Reprinted in *Essays in Monetary Theory*, 98–103. London: King, 1940.

SCHUMPETER, J. A., Depressions, *Economics of the Recovery Program*, 3–21. New York and London: McGraw-Hill, 1934.

WISNIEWSKI, J., Interdependence of cyclical and seasonal variation, *Econometrica*, II (1934) 176–184.

VINCI, F., Significant developments in business cycle theory, *Econometrica*, II (1934) 125–139.

---

*Reprinted in the present volume.

CLARK, J. M., Factors making for instability, *Journal of the American Statistical Association*, XXIX (1934, supplement) 72–74.

BOUNIATIAN, M., Economic depression and its causes, *International Labour Review*, XXX (1934) 1–22.

HANEY, L. H., The processes of business revival in the light of 1933 conditions, *Journal of the American Statistical Association*, XXIX (1934, supplement) 75–80.

*SCHUMPETER, J. A., The analysis of economic change, *Review of Economic Statistics*, XVII (1935) 2–10.

SCHUMPETER, J. A., A theorist's comment on the current business cycle, *Journal of the American Statistical Association* XXX (1935, supplement) 167–168.

WERNETTE, J. P., Business cycles, *Carver Essays* (N. E. Hines, ed.) 208–225. Cambridge: Harvard University Press, 1935.

LEDERER, E., Developments in economic theory, *American Economic Review*, XXVI (1936, supplement) 151–160.

HABERLER, G., Some reflections on the present situation of business cycle theory, *Review of Economic Statistics*, XVIII (1936) 1–7.

CLARK, J. M., Wesley C. Mitchell's contribution to the theory of business cycles, *Methods in the Social Sciences* (S. A. Rice, ed.) 662–680. Chicago: University of Chicago Press, 1931. Reprinted in *Preface to Social Economics*, 390–406. New York: Farrar & Rinehart, 1936.

HANSEN, A. H., BODDY, F. M. and LANGUM, J. K., Recent trends in business cycle literature, *Review of Economic Statistics*, XVIII (1936) 53–61. Reprinted in *Full Recovery or Stagnation?*, 111–133. New York: W. W. Norton, 1938.

SMITH, H., Marx and the trade cycle, *Review of Economic Studies*, IV (1936–37) 192–204.

WILSON, J. D., Marx and the trade cycle, *Review of Economic Studies*, V (1937–38) 107–113.

SMITH, H., Marx and the trade cycle: a reply, *Review of Economic Studies*, VI (1938–39) 76–77.

OHLIN, B., Employment stabilization and price stabilization, *The Lessons of Monetary Experience* (A. D. Gayer, ed.) 318–328. New York: Farrar & Rinehart, 1937.

PRIBRAM, K., How to ascertain the definition of some notions which are fundamental to business cycle analysis, *Revue de l'Institut International de Statistique*, IV (1936) 212–231; and *Bulletin de l'Institut International de Statistique*, XXIX (1937) 186–200.

PRIBRAM, K., The notion of 'economic system' underlying business-cycle analysis, *Review of Economic Statistics*, XIX (1937) 92–99.

DOBB, M., Economic crises, *Political Economy and Capitalism*, 79–129. London: Routledge, 1937.

MEHTA, J. K., The theory of employment and industrial depression, *Indian Journal of Economics*, XVIII (1937) 143–154.

WAGEMANN, E. (editor), Zum Problem der Vollbeschäftigung, *Vierteljahrshefte zur Wirtschaftsforschung*, 12 Jg. (1937–38) Heft 3, Neue Folge, 259–324.

SLICHTER, S. H., The period 1919–1936 in the United States: its significance for business-cycle theory, *Review of Economic Statistics*, XIX (1937) 1–19.

BODE, K., Prosperität und Depression, *Zeitschrift für Nationalökonomie*, VIII (1937) 597–614.

STEINDL, J., Prosperität und Depression, *Österreichische Zeitschrift für Bankwesen*, (1937).

KAHN, R. F., The League of Nations enquiry into the trade cycle, *Economic Journal*, XLVII (1937) 670–679.
HABERLER, G., Mr. Kahn's review of "Prosperity and Depression," *Economic Journal*, XLVIII (1938) 322–333.
KAHN, R. F., Rejoinder, *Economic Journal*, XLVIII (1938) 333–336.
HAWTREY, R. G., Prof. Haberler on the trade cycle, *Economica*, V, new series (1938) 93–97.
MUNISWAMY, M. K., Recent trends in trade cycle theory, *Indian Journal of Economics*, XVIII (1938) 399–406.
SCHWEITER, A., Synthese in der Konjunkturtheorie?, *Zeitschrift für Schweizerische Statistik und Volkswirtschaft*, III (1938) 316–332.
ELLIS, H. S., Notes on recent business cycle literature, *Review of Economic Statistics*, XX (1938) 111–119.
MUKHERJEE, B., (1) Trade cycle and its remedies. (2) The nature and causes of trade cycles. *Indian Journal of Economics*, XVIII (1938) 407–417, 419–432.
PETER, H., Kreislauftheorie, *Archiv für Mathematische Wirtschafts- und Sozialforschung*, IV (1938) Heft 3, 251–259.
SLICHTER, S. H., The downturn of 1937, *Review of Economic Statistics*, XX (1938) 97–110.
ANGELL, J. W., Factors making for change in the character of the business cycle, *American Economic Review*, XXIX (1939, supplement) 217–223.
RÖPKE, W., Streifzüge durch die neuere konjunkturtheoretische Literatur, *Zeitschrift für Schweizerische Statistik und Volkswirtschaft*, 76 Jhrg (1940) 38–50.
BARNETT, P., Business-cycle theory in the United States, 1860–1900. *Journal of Business*, University of Chicago, XIV (1941) pp. 124.
KNIGHT, F. H., The business cycle, interest and money: a methodological approach, *Review of Economic Statistics*, XXIII (1941) 53–67.
SOMERS, H. M., The performance of the American economy, *The Growth of the American Economy* (H. F. Williamson, ed.), 319–341, 751–781. New York: Prentice-Hall, 1944.

II. DYNAMIC AND ECONOMETRIC BUSINESS CYCLE ANALYSIS

Includes descriptions of dynamic and econometric methods, and overall applications of these methods. Specific applications are placed in the respective sections. See, for instance, Samuelson (1939) in IV-C.

Aggregative models which assist in an understanding of business-cycle problems are included. See, for instance, Leontief (1937).

CLARK, J. M., The relation between statics and dynamics, *Economic Essays* (Jacob H Hollander, ed.) 46–70. New York: Macmillan, 1927.
KUZNETS, S. S., Equilibrium economics and business-cycle theory, *Quarterly Journal of Economics*, XLIV (1929–30) 381–415.
SOUTER, R. W., Equilibrium economics and business-cycle theory: a commentary, *Quarterly Journal of Economics*, XLV (1930–31) 40–93.
ÅKERMAN, J., Dynamische Wertprobleme, *Zeitschrift für Nationalökonomie*, II (1930–31) 579–616.

CLASSIFIED BIBLIOGRAPHY OF ARTICLES

DEMARIA, G., Saggio sugli studi di dinamica economica, *Rivista Internazionale di Scienze Sociali e Discipline Ausiliarie*, XXXVIII (1930) 107–130, 222–257.

OPARIN, D. I., Das theoretische Schema der gleichmässig fortschreitenden Wirtschaft als Grundlage einer Analyse ökonomischer Entwicklungsprozesse, *Weltwirtschaftliches Archiv*, XXXII (1930) 105–134, 406–445.

ALTSCHUL, E., Die Mathematik in der Wirtschaftsdynamik, *Archiv für Sozialwissenschaft und Sozialpolitik*, LXIII (1930) 523–538.

CARELL, E., Über Gegenstand und Methode der 'Dynamik,' *Jahrbücher für Nationalökonomie und Statistik*, CXXXV (1931) 192–208.

JÉRAMEC, P., Une théorie dynamique de la production et son illustration par l'étude de l'activité industrielle dans la région parisienne (1927–31), *Journal de la Société de Statistique de Paris*, LXXII (1931) 232–267.

ROOS, C. F., A mathematical theory of price and production fluctuations and economic crises, *Journal of Political Economy*, XXXVIII (1930) 501–522.

AMOROSO, L., Equazione differenziale della domanda e teoria matematica delle crisi economiche, *Giornale degli Economisti*, LXXI (1931) 39–40.

HAMBURGER, L., Een nieuwe weg voor conjunctuur-onderzoek, een nieuwe richtlijn voor conjunctuur-politiek, *De Economist*, LXXIX (1930) 1–39; and, Analogie des fluctuations économiques et des oscillations de relaxation, *Indices du Mouvement des Affaires*, IX (1931, supplement).

HAMMARSKJÖLD, D., Utkast till en algebraisk metod för dynamisk prisanalys, *Ekonomisk Tidskrift*, XXXIV (1932) 157–176.

ÅKERMAN, J., Quantitative economics, *Weltwirtschaftliches Archiv*, XXXV (1932) 34–65.

THEISS, E., A quantitative theory of industrial fluctuations caused by the capitalistic technique of production, *Journal of Political Economy*, XLI (1933) 334–349.

CREEDY, F., On equations of motion of business activity, *Econometrica*, II (1934) 363–380.

HALDANE, J. B. S., A contribution to the theory of price fluctuations, *Review of Economic Studies*, I (1933–34) 186–195.

AMOROSO, L., La dynamique de la circulation, *Econometrica*, III (1935) 400–410.

BORDIN, A., Il significato di alcune moderne teorie matematiche della dinamica economica, *Giornale degli Economisti*, L (1935) 161–210, 369–421, 580–611.

KALECKI, M., Essai d'une théorie du mouvement cyclique des affaires, *Revue d'Economie Politique*, XLIX (1935) 285–305.

KALECKI, M., A theory of the business cycle, *Review of Economic Studies*, IV (1936–37) 77–97.

KALECKI, M., A macrodynamic theory of business cycles, *Econometrica*, III (1935) 327–344; and, Comments on the macrodynamic theory of business cycles, *Eçonometrica*, IV (1936) 356–360.

JAMES, R. W. and BELZ, M. H., The influence of distributed lags on Kalecki's theory of the trade cycle, *Econometrica*, VI (1938) 159–162.

FRISCH, R., and HOLME, H., The characteristic solutions of a mixed difference and differential equation occurring in economic dynamics, *Econometrica*, III (1935) 225–239.

LEDERER, E., The problem of development and growth in the economic system, *Social Research*, II (1935) 20–38.

TINBERGEN, J., Annual survey: suggestions on quantitative business cycle theory, *Econometrica*, III (1935) 241–308.

BRATT, E. C., Relations of institutional factors to economic equilibrium and long-time trend, *Econometrica*, IV (1936) 161–183.

FRISCH, R., On the notion of equilibrium and disequilibrium, *Review of Economic Studies*, III (1935–36) 100–105.

ANDERSON, O. N., The statistical technique of business cycle investigations, *Publication of the Statistical Institute for Economic Research*, State University of Sofia, (1936) 55–78.

SLUTZKY, E., The summation of random causes as the source of cyclic processes. *Econometrica*, V (1937) 105–146.

TINBERGEN, J., Einige Grundfragen der mathematischen Konjunkturtheorie, *Archiv für mathematische Wirtschafts- und Sozialforschung*, III (1937) 1–14, 83–97.

LEONTIEF, W. W., Interrelation of prices, output, savings, and investment, *Review of Economic Statistics*, XIX (1937) 109–132.

FORBANO, J., Ciclo e svolgimento dinamico, *Giornale degli Economisti*, LIII (1938) 845–886.

VIANELLI, S., Sullo studio delle distribuzioni statistische nella dinamica economica, *Giornale degli Economisti*, LIII (1938) 773–787.

GIBSON, A. H., No evidence of a cycle in trade conditions, *Bankers', Insurance Managers' and Agents' Magazine*, CXLVI (1938) 337–359.

SNOW, E. C., Is the trade cycle a myth?, *Journal of the Royal Statistical Society*, CI (1938) 565–591.

RADICE, E. A., A dynamic scheme for the British trade cycle, 1929–1937, *Econometrica*, VII (1939) 47–56.

FIRTH, G. G., An excursion in dynamic theory, *Economic Record*, XV (1939) 68–73.

KÄHLER, A., Forecasting the business cycle, *Social Research*, VI (1939) 341–360.

KEYNES, J. M., Professor Tinbergen's method—a method and its application to investment activity, *Economic Journal*, XLIX (1939) 558–568.

TINBERGEN, J., On a method of statistical business-cycle research: a reply, *Economic Journal*, L (1940) 141–154. Comment by J. M. Keynes, 154–156.

*TINBERGEN, J., Econometric business cycle research, *Review of Economic Studies*, VII (1939–40) 73–90.

HAAVELMO, T., The inadequacy of testing dynamic theory by comparing theoretical solutions and observed cycles, *Econometrica*, VIII (1940) 312–321.

CHAIT, B., Les fluctuations économiques et l'interdépendence des marches: a reply (with a rejoinder by Susanne E. Hotelling), *Journal of Political Economy*, XLVIII (1940) 740–744.

KOOPMANS, T., The degree of damping in business cycles, *Econometrica*, VIII (1940) 79–89.

KOOPMANS, T., Distributed lags in dynamic economics, *Econometrica*, IX (1941) 128–134.

KOOPMANS, T., The logic of econometric business-cycle research, *Journal of Political Economy*, XLIX (1941) 157–181.

KEESING, F. A. G., Econometrie, *De Economist*, (1941).

TINBERGEN, J., Critical remarks on some business-cycle theories, *Econometrica*, X (1942) 129–146.

HAAVELMO, T., Statistical testing of business-cycle theories, *Review of Economic Statistics*, XXV (1943) 13–18.

FLOOD, M. M., Recursive methods in business-cycle analysis, *Econometrica*, VIII (1940) 333–353.

LERNER, A. P., Professor Hicks' dynamics, *Quarterly Journal of Economics*, LIV (1939–40) 298–306.
MORGENSTERN, O., Professor Hicks on value and capital, *Journal of Political Economy*, XLIX (1941) 361–393.
ANDERSON, M. D., Dynamic theory of employment, *Southern Economic Journal*, VII (1940) 37–50.
LINDAHL, E., Professor Ohlin om dynamisk teori, *Ekonomisk Tidskrift*, LXIII (1941) 236–247.
OHLIN, B., Professor Lindahl om dynamisk teori, *Ekonomisk Tidskrift*, XLIII (1941) 170–181.
HEFLEBOWER, R. B., The effect of dynamic forces on the elasticity of revenue curves, *Quarterly Journal of Economics*, LV (1940–41) 652–666.
SAMUELSON, P. A., The stability of equilibrium: comparative statics and dynamics, *Econometrica*, IX (1941) 97–120.
SAMUELSON, P. A., The stability of equilibrium: linear and non-linear systems, *Econometrica*, X (1942) 1–25.
SMITHIES, A., Process analysis and equilibrium analysis, *Econometrica*, X (1942) 26–38.
TINTNER, G., A "simple" theory of business fluctuations, *Econometrica*, X (1942) 317–320.
GILBERT, R. V. and PERLO, V., The investment-factor method of forecasting business activity, *Econometrica*, X (1942) 311–316.
BODE, K., Plan analysis and process analysis, *American Economic Review*, XXXIII (1943) 348–354.
SAMUELSON, P. A., Dynamics, statics and the stationary state, *Review of Economic Statistics*, XXV (1943) 58–68.
KEIRSTEAD, B. S., A note on "equilibrium in process," *Canadian Journal of Economics and Political Science*, IX (1943) 235–242.

III. SAVINGS AND INVESTMENT; UNDEREMPLOYMENT EQUILIBRIUM AND UNDERCONSUMPTION

Includes definitions of the concepts and a statement of equilibrium conditions.

The more dynamic aspects of employment theory are reserved mainly for IV but many of the articles in the present section (particularly reviews of Keynes) cover many topics in business-cycle theory.

III-A. SAVINGS AND INVESTMENT

This is confined to what has become known as the "savings-investment" controversy. Many references to this subject will also be found in III-C, IV-A and V-A.

MONROE, A. E., Investment and saving: a genetic analysis, *Quarterly Journal of Economics*, XLIII (1928–29) 567–603.
HAYEK, F. A., Gibt es einen Widersinn des Sparens?, *Zeitschrift für Nationalökonomie*, I (1929–30) 387–429.
LEDERER, E., Erwiderung auf den Aufsatz von Friedrich A. Hayek, Wien: 'Gibt es einen Widersinn des Sparens?', *Zeitschrift für Nationalökonomie*, I (1929–30) 751–754.
HAYEK, F. A., Reply, *Zeitschrift für Nationalökonomie*, I (1929–30) 755–761.
HAYEK, F. A., The "paradox" of saving, *Economica*, XI (1931) 125–169. Translation of Hayek (1929–30) above. Reprinted in *Profits, Interest and Investment*, 199–263. London: Routledge, 1939.

HAYEK, F. A., A note on the development of the doctrine of forced saving, *Quarterly Journal of Economics*, XLVII (1932–33) 123–133. Reprinted in *Profits, Interest and Investment*, 183–197. London: Routledge, 1939.

HARDY, C. O., Savings, investment and the control of business cycles, *Journal of Political Economy*, XXXIX (1931) 390–400.

HANSEN, A. H., and TOUT, H., Annual survey of business cycle theory: investment and saving in business cycle theory, *Econometrica*, I (1933) 119–147. Reprinted in *Full Recovery or Stagnation?*, 331–343. New York: W. W. Norton, 1938.

ROBERTSON, D. H., Saving and hoarding, *Economic Journal*, XLIII (1933) 399–413. Reprinted in *Essays in Monetary Theory*, 65–82. London: King, 1940.

KEYNES, J. M., Mr. Robertson on "saving and hoarding," *Economic Journal*, XLIII (1933) 699–701.

HAWTREY, R. G., Mr Robertson on "saving and hoarding," *Economic Journal*, XLIII (1933) 701–708.

ROBERTSON, D. H., A rejoinder, *Economic Journal*, XLIII (1933) 709–712.

WALKER, E. R., Saving and investment in monetary theory, *Economic Record*, IX (1933) 185–201.

ROBINSON, J., A parable on savings and investment, *Economica*, XIII (1933) 75–84.

VITO, F., Il risparmio forzato e la teoria di cicli economici, *Rivista Internazionale de Scienze Sociali*, V (1934) 3–46.

THEISS, E., Dynamics of saving and investment, *Econometrica*, III (1935) 213–224.

BODE, K. and HABERLER, G., Monetary equilibrium and the price level in a progressive economy, *Economica*, II, new series (1935), 75–81. Rejoinder by R. F. Harrod, 82–84.

EGLE, W., Saving, investment, and crisis, *Journal of Political Economy*, XLIII (1935) 721–742.

VILLARD, H. H., Dr. Moulton's estimates of saving and investment, *American Economic Review*, XXVII (1937) 479–489.

*OHLIN, B., Some notes on the Stockholm theory of saving and investment, *Economic Journal*, XLVII (1937) 53–69, 221–240.

CURTIS, M., Is money saving equal to investment? *Quarterly Journal of Economics*, LI (1936–37) 604–625.

LERNER, A. P., Saving equals investment, *Quarterly Journal of Economics*, LII (1937–38) 297–309.

*LUTZ, F. A., Outcome of the saving-investment discussion, *Quarterly Journal of Economics*, LII (1937–38) 588–614.

*LERNER, A. P., Saving and investment: definitions, assumptions, objectives, *Quarterly Journal of Economics*, LIII (1938–39) 611–619.

LANGE, O., Savings in process analysis, *Quarterly Journal of Economics*, LIII (1938–39) 620–622.

CURTIS, M., Saving and savings, *Quarterly Journal of Economics*, LIII (1938–39) 623–626.

LUTZ, F., Final comment, *Quarterly Journal of Economics*, LIII (1938–39) 627–631.

HABERLER, G., National income, savings and investment, *Studies in Income and Wealth*, Vol. II, 139–188. New York: National Bureau of Economic Research, 1938.

FELLNER, W., Savings, investment and the problem of neutral money, *Review of Economic Statistics*, XX (1938) 185–192.

ANDERSON, M. D., Dynamic theory of savings and investment, *Southern Economic Journal*, V (1938–39) 27–44.
BRONFENBRENNER, M., The Keynesian equations and the balance of payments, *Review of Economic Studies*, VII (1939–40) 180–184.
DE VEGH, I., Savings, investment, and consumption, *American Economic Review*, XXXI (1941, supplement) 237–247.
WRIGHT, D., Internal inconsistency in D. H. Robertson's 'saving and hoarding concepts', *Economic Journal*, LI (1941) 334–337. Comment by Robertson, 337–338.
MARSCHAK, J., Identity and stability in economics: a survey, *Econometrica*, X (1942) 61–74.
MACHLUP, F., Forced or induced saving: an exploration into its synonyms and homonyms, *Review of Economic Statistics*, XXV (1943) 26–39.

III-B. CONCEPTS OF EMPLOYMENT, INCOME AND CAPACITY

Includes only a small part of the discussion of the concepts of national income, employment and capacity and does not attempt to cover the field of statistical determination.
This subject is also discussed in III-A and IV-A.

BRISSENDEN, P. F., Under-employment, *Business Cycles and Unemployment*, 67–77. New York: McGraw-Hill, 1923.
NATHAN, R. R., Estimates of unemployment in the United States, 1929–1935, *International Labour Review*, XXXIII (1936) 49–73.
CLARK, J. M., Productive capacity and effective demand, *Economic Reconstruction*, 105–126. New York: Columbia University Press, 1934. Reprinted in *Preface to Social Economics*, 355–378. New York: Farrar & Rinehart, 1940.
THORP, W. L., The problem of overcapacity, *Economic Essays in Honor of Wesley Clair Mitchell*, 477–496. New York: Columbia University Press, 1935.
TAUSSIG, F. W., Employment and the national dividend, *Quarterly Journal of Economics*, LI (1936-37) 198–203.
ROBINSON, J., Disguised unemployment, *Economic Journal*, XLVI (1936) 225–237.
BARGER, H., Disguised unemployment: a comment, *Economic Journal*, XLVI (1936) 756–759.
ROBINSON, J., A rejoinder, *Economic Journal*, XLVI (1936) 759–760.
COPELAND, M. A., Concepts of national income, *Studies in Income and Wealth*, Vol. I, 3–63. New York: National Bureau of Economic Research, 1937.
COMMONS, J. R., Capacity to produce, capacity to consume, capacity to pay debts, *American Economic Review*, XXVII (1937) 680–697.
KUZNETS, S. S., National income and capital formation—a comment (rejoinder by C. Warburton), *Journal of the American Statistical Association*, XXXIII (1938) 714–721.
VILLARD, H. H., Some aspects of the concept of capacity to produce, *Review of Economic Statistics*, XXI (1939) 13–20.
WARBURTON, C., Three estimates of the value of the nation's output of commodities and services: A comparison. *Studies in Income and Wealth*. Vol. III, 320–397. New York: National Bureau of Economic Research, 1939.

KEYNES, J. M., The concept of national income: a supplementary note, *Economic Journal*, L (1940) 60–65.
MEANS, G. C., Basic structural characteristics and the problem of full employment, *The Structure of the American Economy: Towards Full Use of Resources*, 3–9. Washington, D. C.: Government Printing Office, June, 1940.
BOWLEY, A. L., and KEYNES, J. M., The measurement of real income, *Economic Journal*, L (1940) 340–342.
NIXON, R. A. and SAMUELSON, P. A., Estimate of unemployment in the United States, *Review of Economic Statistics*, XXII (1940) 101–111.
WOLFE, A. B., "Full utilization," equilibrium, and the expansion of production, *Quarterly Journal of Economics*, LIV (1939–40) 539–565. Reprinted in *Readings in the Social Control of Industry*, 418–451. Philadelphia: Blakiston, 1943.
MAY, G. C., Gross income, *Quarterly Journal of Economics*, LV (1940–41) 521–525.
FRANKEL, H., Quantitative and qualitative full employment, *Bulletin of the Institute of Statistics*, Oxford, III (1941) 342–346.
LONG, C. D., JR., The concept of unemployment, *Quarterly Journal of Economics*, LVII (1942) 1–30.

III-C. UNDEREMPLOYMENT EQUILIBRIUM

Is confined to the description of the conditions of underemployment equilibrium and parts of the problem, and includes discussions of earlier writers who dealt with this subject.

Further discussion of particular aspects of this question may be found in III-D, IV-A, IV-C, IV-D, V-B, VI, VIII, and X-B.

LEONTIEF, W. W., Implicit theorizing: a methodological criticism of the neo-Cambridge school, *Quarterly Journal of Economics*, LI (1936–7) 337–351.
HANSEN, A. H., Mr. Keynes on underemployment equilibrium, *Journal of Political Economy*, XLIV (1936) 667–686. Reprinted in *Full Recovery or Stagnation?* 13–34. New York: W. W. Norton, 1938.
GREIDANUS, T., "De ontwikkeling van Keynes' economische theorieën," *De Economist*, LXXXV (1936), 697–738.
HICKS, J. R., Mr. Keynes' theory of employment, *Economic Journal*, XLVI (1936) 238–253.
LERNER, A. P., Mr. Keynes' general theory of employment, interest and money, *International Labour Review*, XXXIV (1936) 435–454.
CASSEL, G., Keynes' "General theory," *International Labour Review*, XXXVI (1937) 437–445.
LERNER, A. P., Keynes' "General theory"; a rejoinder to Professor Cassel, *International Labour Review*, XXXVI (1937) 585–590.
NEISSER, H., Commentary on Keynes, *Social Research*, III (1936) 459–478.
LEDERER, E., Commentary on Keynes, *Social Research*, III (1936) 478–487.
REDDAWAY, W. B., The general theory of employment, interest and money, by J. M. Keynes, *Economic Record*, XII (1936) 28–36.
PIGOU, A. C., Mr. J. M. Keynes' general theory of employment, interest and money, *Economica*, III, new series (1936) 115–132.

ROBINSON, J., The long-period theory of employment, *Zeitschrift für Nationalökonomie*, VII (1936) 74–93. Reprinted in *Essays in the Theory of Employment*, 105–138. New York: Macmillan Company, 1937.

SCHÜLLER, R., Keynes' Theorie der Nachfrage nach Arbeit, *Zeitschrift für Nationalökonomie*, VII (1936) 475–482.

CHAMPERNOWNE, D. G., Unemployment, basic and monetary: the classical analysis and the Keynesian, *Review of Economic Studies*, III (1935–36) 201–216.

HARDY, C. O., The general theory of employment, interest and money, by J. M. Keynes, *American Economic Review*, XXVI (1936) 490–493.

VINER, J., Mr. Keynes on the causes of unemployment, *Quarterly Journal of Economics*, LI (1936–37) 147–167.

ROBERTSON, D. H., Some notes on Mr. Keynes' general theory of employment, *Quarterly Journal of Economics*, LI (1936–37) 168–191. Largely reprinted in *Essays in Monetary Theory*, 114–121. London: King, 1940.

LEONTIEF, W. W., The fundamental assumption of Mr. Keynes' monetary theory of unemployment, *Quarterly Journal of Economics*, LI (1936–37) 192–197.

KEYNES, J. M., The general theory of employment, *Quarterly Journal of Economics*, LI (1936–37) 209–223.

DAVIDSON, D., Nationalekonomien i stöpsleven, *Ekonomisk Tidskrift*, XXXVIII (1936) 87–102, 103–124; XXXIX (1937) 1–12.

MEADE, J. E., A simplified model of Mr. Keynes' system, *Review of Economic Studies*, IV (1936–37) 98–107.

KNIGHT, F. H., Underemployment: and Mr. Keynes' revolution in economic theory, *Canadian Journal of Economics and Political Science*, III (1937) 100–123.

HICKS, J. R., Mr. Keynes and the "classics"; a suggested interpretation, *Economometrica*, V (1937) 147–159.

MANTOUX, E., La "théorie generale" de M. Keynes, *Revue d'Economie Politique*, LI (1937) 1559–1590.

HAWTREY, R. G., Essays in the theory of employment, *Economica*, IV (1937) 455–460.

SCOTT, H. R., Mr. J. M. Keynes, C. B., in the London Times, *Indian Journal of Economics*, XVIII (1937) 199–203.

VINING, R., Suggestions of Keynes in the writings of Veblen, *Journal of Political Economy*, XLVII (1939) 692–704.

MERWIN, C. L., Jr., American studies of the distribution of wealth and income by size, *Studies in Income and Wealth*, Vol. III, 3–77. New York: National Bureau of Economic Research, 1939.

WARD, E. E., Marx and Keynes's general theory, *Economic Record*, XV (1939) 152–167

ALEXANDER, S., Mr. Keynes and Mr. Marx, *Review of Economic Studies*, VII (1939–40). 123–135.

ROBINSON, J., Marx on unemployment, *Economic Journal*, LI (1941) 234–248.

CLARK, J. M., The attack on the problem of full use, *The Structure of the American Economy: Towards Full Use of Resources*, 20–26. Washington, D. C.: Government Printing Office, 1940.

HORNEDO, E., Keynes, el ahorro y la inversion, *Trimestre Economico*, VII, Jan.-Mar., 1941, 635–657.

DILLARD, D., Keynes and Proudhon, *Journal of Economic History*, II (1942) 63–76.

DILLARD, D., Gesell's monetary theory of social reform, XXXII *American Economic Review*, (1942) 348–352.
O'LEARY, J. J., Malthus and Keynes, *Journal of Political Economy*, L (1942) 901–919.
O'LEARY, J. J., Malthus' General theory of employment and the post-Napoleonic depressions, *Journal of Economic History*, III (1943) 185–200.
SHIBATA, K., Some questions on Mr. Keynes' General theory of employment, interest and money, *Kyoto University Economic Review*, XII (1937) 83–96.
HARROD, R. F., Mr. Keynes and traditional theory, *Econometrica*, V (1937) 74–86.
JÖHR, W. A., "Verbrauchsneigung" und "Liquiditätsvorliebe." Eine Auseinandersetzung mit J. M. Keynes, *Jahrbücher für Nationalökonomie und Statistik*, CXLVI (1937) 641–662.
REDDAWAY, W. B., Special obstacles to full employment in a wealthy community, *Economic Journal*, XLVII (1937) 297–307.
CHAND, G., J. M. Keynes and the trade cycle, *Indian Journal of Economics*, XVIII (1938) 501–513.
MÜHLENFELS, A. von, Allgemeine "Theorie der Beschäftigung, des Zinses und des Geldes, *Schmollers Jahrbuch*, LXII (1938) 221–229.
AMMON, A., Keynes' "Allgemeine Theorie der Beschäftigung," *Jahrbücher für Nationalökonomie und Statistik*, CXLVII (1938) 1–27.
KALDOR, N., Stability and full employment, *Economic Journal*, XLVIII (1938), 642–657.
*LANGE, O., The rate of interest and the optimum propensity to consume, *Economica*, V, new series (1938) 12–32.
SMITH, H., Full employment with a nonhomogeneous labour force, *Econometrica*, VII (1939) 64–76.
SHIBATA, K., Further comments on Mr. Keynes' general theory, *Kyoto University Economic Review*, XIV (1939) 45–72.
DELIVANIS, J., L'opinion de J. M. Keynes sur l'emploi, l'intérêt et la monnaie, *Revue des Sciences Economiques et Financières*, (1939). Also *Epitheoresis Koinonikes kai Demosias Oikonomikes*, (1939).
BERGSON, A., Prices, wages and income theory, *Econometrica*, X (1942) 275–289
BENNION, E. G., Unemployment in the theories of Schumpeter and Keynes, *American Economic Review*, XXXIII (1943) 336–347.
LERNER, A. P., Some Swedish stepping stones in economic theory, *Canadian Journal of Economics and Political Science*, VI (1940) 574–591.
CAPLAN, B., Some Swedish stepping stones in economic theory; a comment, *Canadian Journal of Economics and Political Science*, VII (1941) 559–562.
PLIMSOLL, J., An Australian anticipator of Mr. Keynes, *Economic Record*, XV (1939) 108–110.

III-D. UNDERCONSUMPTION AND PURCHASING POWER

Includes several items on the "underconsumption theory" and also includes discussion of purchasing power relevant to an appreciation of the theory. Some discussions of income distribution are also included.
Closely related items are in III-A, III-C, IV-A and VIII.

ANGELL, J. W., Consumers' demand, *Quarterly Journal of Economics*, XXXIX (1925) 584–611.
FOSTER, W. T., and CATCHINGS, W., Comments, *Essays on Foster and Catchings: "Profits,"* 5–18. Newton, Mass.: Pollak Foundation for Economic Research, 1927.
SOUTER, R. W., Essay I, *Essays on Foster and Catchings: "Profits,"* 19–55. Newton, Mass.: Pollak Foundation for Economic Research, 1927.
OLMSTED, F. L., Essay II, *Essays on Foster and Catchings: "Profits,"* 56–71. Newton, Mass.: Pollak Foundation for Economic Research, 1927.
BICKERDIKE, C. F., Essay III, *Essays on Foster and Catchings: "Profits,"* 72–88. Newton, Mass.: Pollak Foundation for Economic Research, 1927.
NOVOGILOV, V. V., Essay IV, *Essays on Foster and Catchings: "Profits,"* 89–131. Newton. Mass.: Pollak Foundation for Economic Research, 1927.
ROBERTSON, D. H., The monetary doctrines of Messrs. Foster and Catchings, *Quarterly Journal of Economics*, XLIII (1928–29) 473–499. Reprinted in *Economic Essays and Addresses*, 139–162. London: King, 1931.
BERRIDGE, W. A., Employment and the buying power of consumers, *Review of Economic Statistics*, XII (1930) 186–192.
ANSIAUX, M., Under-consumption as a factor in the economic cycle, *International Labour Review*, XXVI (1932) 8–25.
HOBSON, J. A., Underconsumption. An exposition and a reply, *Economica*, XIII (1933) 402–417.
DURBIN, E. F. M., A reply, *Economica*, XIII (1933) 417–425.
HOBSON, J. A., A rejoinder, *Economica*, XIII (1933) 425–427.
CHAMBERLIN, E., Purchasing power, *Economics of the Recovery Program*, 22–37. New York and London: McGraw-Hill, 1934.
*NEISSER, H., General overproduction, *Journal of Political Economy*, XLII (1934) 433–465.
HANSEN, A. H., The flow of purchasing power, *Economic Reconstruction*, 210–238. New York: Columbia University Press, 1934. Reprinted in *Full Recovery or Stagnation?* 141–160. New York: W. W. Norton, 1938.
DOUGLAS, P. H., Purchasing power of the masses and business depression, *Economic Essays*, 105–130. New York: Columbia University Press, 1935.
BACHMANN H., Kaufkraft und Arbeitslosigkeit. Eine kritische Untersuchung der "Kaufkrafttheorie," *Zeitschrift für Schweizerische Statistik und Volkswirtschaft*, LXXIII (1937) 416–423.
HUMPHREY, D. D., Analysis of capital supply and national well-being, *American Economic Review*, XXVII (1937) 705–710.
MCCRACKEN, H. L. and others, Rate of consumption, *American Economic Review*, XXVIII (1938, supplement) 146–148.
CRUM, W. L., The creation and function of purchasing power, *Bulletin of the Harvard Business School Alumni Association*, (1938).
CLARK, J. M., John A. Hobson: heretic and pioneer (1858–1940), *Journal of Social Philosophy*, V (1939–40) 356–359.
KREPS, T. J., Consumption a vast underdeveloped economic frontier, *American Economic Review*, XXXI (1941, supplement) 177–199.
MIRKOWICH, N., The economics of John A. Hobson, *Indian Journal of Economics*, XXIII (1942) 175–185.

IV. MULTIPLIER AND ACCELERATION PRINCIPLES; FISCAL POLICY

Items are placed in A, B or C where they deal primarily with technical aspects of multiplier and acceleration principles and their interactions, respectively. They are placed in D when they involve fiscal applications of these principles or deal with fiscal policy generally.

See also III-C and X-B.

IV-A. THE MULTIPLIER PRINCIPLE AND THE CONSUMPTION FUNCTION

Includes technical expositions of the multiplier principle and those discussions of consumption and the consumption-income pattern which are applicable to the multiplier principle.

See also III-C and III-D.

Discussions of the foreign-trade multiplier are also found in XI.

KAHN, R. F., The relation of home investment to unemployment, *Economic Journal*, XLI (1931) 173–198.

MITNITZKY, M., The effects of a public works policy on business activity and employment, *International Labour Review*, XXX (1934) 435–456.

MITNITZKY, M., Economic effects of changes in consumers' demand, *Social Research*, I (1934) 199–218.

CLARK, J. M., Cumulative effects of changes in aggregate spending as illustrated by public works, *American Economic Review*, XXV (1935) 14–20. Reprinted in *Preface to Social Economics*, 379–389. New York: Farrar & Rinehart, 1936.

*HABERLER, G. VON, Mr. Keynes' theory of the "Multiplier": a methodological criticism, *Zeitschrift für Nationalökonomie*, VII (1936) 299–305.

NEISSER, H., Secondary employment: some comments on R. F. Kahn's formula, *Review of Economic Statistics*, XVIII (1936) 24–30.

KAHN, R. F., Dr. Neisser on secondary employment: a note, *Review of Economic Statistics*, XVIII (1936) 144–147.

NEISSER, H., A rejoinder, *Review of Economic Statistics*, XVIII (1936) 147–148.

KEYNES, J. M., Fluctuations in net investment in the United States, *Economic Journal*, XLVI (1936) 540–47.

SMITHIES, A., The propensity to consume, *Economic Record*, XIII (1937) 97–100.

COOMBS, H. C., The propensity to consume; a comment on the note by Dr. Smithies, *Economic Record*, XIII (1937) 250–255.

SMITHIES, A., A further comment, *Economic Record*, XIII (1937) 256.

DIRKS, F. C., Retail sales and labor income, *Review of Economic Statistics*, XX (1938) 128–134.

STAEHLE, H., Retail sales and labor income, *Review of Economic Statistics*, XX (1938) 135–141.

CLARK, C., Determination of the multiplier from national income statistics, *Economic Journal*, XLVIII (1938) 435–448.

JASTRAM, R. W., and SHAW, E. S., Mr. Clark's statistical determination of the multiplier, *Economic Journal*, XLIX (1939) 358–365.
HOLDEN, G. R., Mr. Keynes' consumption function and the time-preference postulate, *Quarterly Journal of Economics*, LII (1937–38) 281–296.
KEYNES, J. M., Mr. Keynes' consumption function, *Quarterly Journal of Economics*, LII (1937–38) 708–709.
HOLDEN, G. R., Mr. Keynes' consumption function, a rejoinder, *Quarterly Journal of Economics*, LII (1937–38) 709–712.
KEYNES, J. M., Mr. KEYNES' consumption function, *Quarterly Journal of Economics*, LIII (1938–39) 160.
STAEHLE, H., Short-period variations in the distribution of incomes, *Review of Economic Statistics*, XIX (1937) 133–143.
KEYNES, J. M., Mr. Keynes on the distribution of incomes and "propensity to consume": a reply, *Review of Economic Statistics*, XXI (1939) 129.
STAEHLE, H., A rejoinder, *Review of Economic Statistics*, XXI (1939) 129–130.
STONE, R. and STONE, W. M., The marginal propensity to consume and the multiplier, a statistical investigation, *Review of Economic Studies*, VI (1938) 1–21.
SHAW, E. S., A note on the multiplier, *Review of Economic Studies*, VI (1938) 60–64.
GILBOY, E. W., The propensity to consume, *Quarterly Journal of Economics*, LIII (1938–39) 120–140.
DUNCAN, A. J., The propensity to consume; a comment, *Quarterly Journal of Economics*, LIII (1938–39) 632.
GILBOY, E. W., The propensity to consume: a reply, *Quarterly Journal of Economics*, LIII (1938–39) 633–638.
SHACKLE, G. L. S., The multiplier in closed and open systems, *Oxford Economic Papers*, II (1939) 135–144.
MARSCHAK, J., Family budgets and the so-called multiplier, *Canadian Journal of Economics and Political Science*, V (1939) 358–362.
POLAK, J. J., Fluctuations in United States consumption, 1919–1932, *Review of Economic Statistics*, XXI (1939) 1–12.
PLUMPTRE, A. F. W., The distribution of outlay and the "multiplier" in the British Dominions, *Canadian Journal of Economics and Political Science*, V (1939) 363–372.
*CLARK, J. M., An appraisal of the workability of compensatory devices, *American Economic Review*, XXIX (1939, supplement) 194–208.
*MACHLUP, F. Period analysis and multiplier theory, *Quarterly Journal of Economics*, LIV (1939–40) 1–27.
ANDERSON, M. D., Employment, investment, and the multiplier, *Econometrica*, VIII (1940) 240–252.
GILBOY, E. W., Income-expenditure relations, *Review of Economic Statistics*, XXII (1940) 115–121.
ROMBOUTS, A. L. G. M., Statistische meting van Keynes' begrippen "Propensity to consume" "Propensity to save" en "Investment multiplier" voor Nederland, *De Economist*, LXXXIX (1940) 659–672.
DOWDELL, E. G., The multiplier, *Oxford Economic Papers*, IV (1940) 23–38.
DALY, M. C., An approximation to a geographical multiplier, *Economic Journal*, L (1940) 248–258.

IYENGAR, S. K., The investment multiplier, *Indian Journal of Economics*, XXIII (1942) 80–82.
TINBERGEN, J., Does consumption lag behind incomes? *Review of Economic Statistics*, XXIV (1942) 1–8.
RHODES, E. C., The distribution of incomes, *Economica*, IX (1942) 245–256.
TUCKER, R. S., Distribution of income in 1935–36, *Journal of the American Statistical Association*, XXXVII (1942) 489–495.
EZEKIEL, M., Statistical investigations of saving, consumption, and investment, I and II, *American Economic Review*, XXXII (1942) 22–49 and 272–307.
FRIEND, I., Ezekiel's analysis of saving, consumption and investment, *American Economic Review*, XXXII (1942) 829–835.
HANSON, A. C., CORNFIELD, J., and EPSTEIN, L. A., Income and spending and saving of city families in wartime, *Monthly Labor Review*, LV (1942) 419–434.
HANSON, A. C., and CORNFIELD, J., Spending and saving of the nation's families in wartime, *Monthly Labor Review*, LV (1942) 700–713.
WALLIS, W. A., The temporal stability of consumption patterns, *Review of Economic Statistics*, XXIV (1942) 177–182.
FULCHER, G. S., Saving of individuals in relation to income, *American Economic Review*, XXXII (1942) 835–840.
BANGS, R. B., The changing relation of consumer income and expenditure, *Survey of Current Business*, XXII (1942) 8–12.
METZLER, L. A., Effects of income redistribution, *Review of Economic Statistics*, XXV (1943) 49–57.
SAMUELSON, P. A., A fundamental multiplier identity, *Econometrica*, XI (1943) 221–226.
LANGE, O., The theory of the multiplier, *Econometrica*, XI (1943) 227–245.
KLEIN, L. R., Pitfalls in the statistical determination of the investment schedule, *Econometrica*, XI (1943) 246–258.

IV-B. THE ACCELERATION PRINCIPLE AND THE DEMAND FOR DURABLE GOODS

Includes technical expositions of the acceleration principle and those discussions of the "investment function" and the demand for durable goods which are directly pertinent to the acceleration principle.

See also IV-C and VI.

CARVER, T. N., A suggestion for a theory of industrial depressions, *Quarterly Journal of Economics*, XVII (1902–1903) 497–500.
BICKERDIKE, C. F., A non-monetary cause of fluctuations in employment, *Economic Journal*, XXIV (1914) 357–370.
*CLARK, J. M., Business acceleration and the law of demand; a technical factor in economic cycles, *Journal of Political Economy*, XXV (1917) 217–235. Reprinted with additional note in *Preface to Social Economics*, 327–354. New York: Farrar & Rinehart, 1936.
FRANK, L. K., A theory of business cycles, *Quarterly Journal of Economics*, XXXVII (1922–23) 625–642.
FRISCH, R., The interrelation between capital production and consumer-taking, *Journal of Political Economy*, XXXIX (1931) 646–654.

CLARK, J. M., Capital production and consumer-taking, *Journal of Political Economy*, XXXIX (1931) 814–816.
FRISCH, R., Capital production and consumer-taking—a rejoinder, *Journal of Political Economy*, XL (1932) 253–255.
CLARK, J. M., Capital production and consumer-taking—a further word, *Journal of Political Economy*, XL (1932) 691–693.
FRISCH, R., Capital production and consumer-taking—a final word, *Journal of Political Economy*, XL (1932) 694.
HAWTREY, R. G., review of *Les Crises Economiques* by M. Bouniatian, *Economic Journal*, XLII (1932) 435–438.
KUZNETS, S. S., Relation between capital goods and finished products in the business cycle, in *Economic Essays in Honor of Wesley Clair Mitchell*, 209–267. New York: Columbia University Press, 1935.
TINBERGEN, J., Statistical evidence on the acceleration principle, *Economica*, V, new series (1938) 164–176.
HART, A. G., Consumption markets, *American Economic Review*, XXVIII (1938 supplement) 113–125.
HARING, A., and others, Durable consumers goods, *American Economic Review*, XXVIII (1938, supplement) 149–154.
SILBERLING, N. J., Some aspects of durable consumer goods financing and investment fluctuations, *American Economic Review*, XXVIII (1938) 439–446.
TIPPETTS, C. S., Postponable purchasing of durable consumers' goods and the business cycle, *Journal of the American Statistical Association*, XXXIV (1939) 27–31.
WELINDER, C., Hayek och Ricardoeffekten, *Ekonomisk Tidskrift*, XLII (1940) 33–39.
WRIGHT, D. McC., A neglected approach to the acceleration principle, *Review of Economic Statistics*, XXIII (1941) 100–101.
Roos, C. F. and SZELISKI, V. v., The demand for durable goods, *Econometrica*, XI (1943) 97–122.

IV-C. INTERACTION OF THE MULTIPLIER AND ACCELERATION PRINCIPLES

Includes discussions of Harrod's comprehensive interaction schema and comments on various parts of the latter (even if not directly concerned with the interaction) as well as more restricted discussions of the interaction of the multiplier and acceleration principles (such as Samuelson's) or of the interaction between the multiplier principle and the "investment function" (such as Kaldor's).

HANSEN, A. H., Harrod on the trade cycle, *Quarterly Journal of Economics*, LI (1936–37) 509–531. Reprinted in *Full Recovery or Stagnation?*, 35–58. New York: W. W. Norton, 1938.
ROBERTSON, D. H., review of *The Trade Cycle* by R. F. Harrod, *Canadian Journal of Economics and Political Science*, III (1937) 124–127.
NEISSER, H., Investment fluctuations as cause of the business cycle (review of *The Trade Cycle* by R. F. Harrod), *Social Research*, IV (1937) 440–460.
LOKANATHAN, P. S., Mr. Harrod on the trade cycle, *Indian Journal of Economics*, XVIII (1938) 515–521.
MAKOWER, H., Elasticity of demand and stabilization, *Review of Economic Studies*, VI (1938–39) 25–32.

SUMNER, J. D., A note on cyclical changes in demand elasticity, *American Economic Review*, XXX (1940) 300–308.
HARROD, R. F., An essay in dynamic theory, *Economic Journal*, XLIX (1939) 14–33.
HAWTREY, R. G., Mr. Harrod's essay in dynamic theory, *Economic Journal*, XLIX (1939) 468–475.
NOGARO, B., "The trade cycle," d'après R. F. Harrod, *Revue d'Economie Politique*, LIV (1940) 107–112.
*SAMUELSON, P. A., Interactions between the multiplier analysis and the principle of acceleration, *Review of Economic Statistics*, XXI (1939) 75–78.
SAMUELSON, P. A., A synthesis of the principle of acceleration and the multiplier, *Journal of Political Economy*, XLVII (1939) 786–797.
TOWLE, H. L., The new type of business cycle: an industrial interpretation, *Journal of Business of the University of Chicago*, Vol. XIII (1940) 360–386.
KALDOR, N., A model of the trade cycle, *Economic Journal*, L (1940) 78–92.
HUBBARD, J. C., A model of the forty-month or trade cycle, *Journal of Political Economy*, L (1942) 197–225.
PODUVAL, R. N., "Multiplier," "pump-priming" and "acceleration," *Indian Journal of Economics*, XXIII (1943) 271–276.

IV-D. FISCAL POLICY AND NATIONAL INCOME

Technical expositions of the multiplier principle are found in IV-A.

Applications to fiscal policy, and directly pertinent discussions of government finance, are included here.

HAWTREY, R. G., Public expenditure and the demand for labour, *Economica*, V (1925) 38–48.
DICKINSON, F. G., Public construction and capital unemployment, *Annals of American Academy of Political Science*, 139 (1928) 175–209.
BIELSCHOWSKY, G., Business fluctuations and public works, *Quarterly Journal of Economics*, XLIV (1929–30) 286–319.
WARMING, J., International difficulties arising out of the financing of public works during depression, *Economic Journal*, XLII (1932) 211–224.
KAHN, R. F., The financing of public works—a note, *Economic Journal*, XLII (1932) 492–495.
SLICHTER, S. H., Making booms bear the burden of relief—some financial implications of unemployment reserves, *Harvard Business Review*, XI (1932–33) 327–335.
MACHLUP, F., Zur Frage der Ankurbelung durch Kreditausweitung, *Zeitschrift für Nationalökonomie*, IV (1933) 398–404.
HARRINGTON, J. L., Self-liquidating public works as a factor in equalizing employment in times of depression, *Stabilization of Employment*, 108–116. Bloomington, Indiana: Principia Press, 1933.
KAHN, R. F., Public works and inflation, *Journal of the American Statistical Association*, XXVIII (1933, supplement) 168–173.
LOUCKS, W. N., Municipal public works as a stabilizer of employment, *Stabilization of Employment* (C. F. Roos, ed.) 98–107. Bloomington, Indiana: Principia Press, 1933.

CLASSIFIED BIBLIOGRAPHY OF ARTICLES 463

HAWTREY, R. G., Public expenditure and trade depression, *Journal of the Royal Statistical Society*, XCVI (1933) 438–458. Discussion, 459–477.
WOLMAN, L., Employment stabilization through public works, *Stabilization of Employment*, 85–97. Bloomington, Indiana: Principia Press, 1933.
SLICHTER, S. H., The economics of public works, *American Economic Review*, XXIV (1934, supplement) 174–185.
GAYER, A. D., Monetary policy and public works, *Economic Reconstruction*, 160–169. New York: Columbia University Press, 1934.
WALKER, E. R., Public works as a recovery measure, *Economic Record*, XI (1935) 187–201.
COLM, G., and LEHMANN, F., Public spending and recovery in the United States, *Social Research*, III (1936) 129–166.
HEINIG, K., The state budget and public works, *International Labour Review*, XXXIV (1936) 153–176.
GAYER, A. D., The effectiveness of public works as a recovery expedient, *Index, Svenska Handelsbanken*, XI (1936) 91–105.
HANSEN, A. H., The consequences of reducing expenditures, *Academy of Political Science Proceedings*, XVII (1936–38) 466–478. Reprinted in *Full Recovery or Stagnation?* 275–289. New York: W. W. Norton, 1938.
BRETHERTON, R. F., The sensitivity of taxes to fluctuations of trade, *Econometrica*, V (1937) 171–183.
RUNEMARK, Den Föreslagna Omläggningen av Riksstatens Uppställning, *Föredrag Hållna Inför Svenska Ekonomföreningen*, No. 2, 1937; Kungl. Maj:ts proposition No. 225, Bihang till riksdagens protokoll, 1937; Kungl. Maj:ts proposition No. 199, Bihang till riksdagens protokoll, 1938.
BRESCIANI-TURRONI, C., The "multiplier" in practice: some results of recent German experience, *Review of Economic Statistics*, XX (1938) 76–88.
SMITH, D. T., An analysis of changes in federal finances, July 1930 to June 1938, *Review of Economic Statistics*, XX (1938) 149–160.
KAZAKEVICH, V. D., Public works in two depressions, *Science and Society*, II (1937–38) 471–488.
SHAW, H. F. R., The economics of public spending, *American Federationist*, XLV (1938) 1080–1084.
Public works as a factor in economic stabilization, *International Labour Review*, XXXVIII (1938) 727–757.
HANSEN, A. H., Pump-priming, new and old, *Barron's*, April 11, 1938. Reprinted in *Full Recovery or Stagnation?* 290–302. New York: W. W. Norton, 1938.
GAYER, A. D., Fiscal policies, *American Economic Review*, XXVIII (1938, supplement) 90–112.
LUTZ, H. L., Federal depression financing and its consequences, *Harvard Business Review*, XVI (1938) 129–140.
RICHTER-ALTSCHAEFFER, H., A note on the "economics of public investment," *Journal of Political Economy*, XLVI (1938) 414–416.
COLM, G., Reply, *Journal of Political Economy*, XLVI (1938) 416.
HERRING, E. P., The politics of fiscal policy, *Yale Law Review*, XLVII (1938) 724–745.
HAIG, R. M., and others, Fiscal policies, *American Economic Review*, XXVIII (1938) 132–135.

SCHUMPETER, E. B., English prices and public finance, 1660–1822, *Review of Economic Statistics*, XX (1938) 21–37.
BECKHART, B. H., The banking and fiscal system in its relation to the current business downturn, *Conference Board Survey* (January 20, 1938, supplement) pp. 4.
COOMBS, H. C., General theory and Swedish economic practice, *Economic Record*, XV (1939) 135–149.
COPELAND, M. A., Public investment in the United States, *American Economic Review*, XXIX (1939, supplement) 33–41.
GALBRAITH, J. K., Fiscal policy and the employment-investment controversy, *Harvard Business Review*, XVIII (1939) 24–34.
FREUND, G., Budgetary deficits as an aid to business, *Bankers Magazine*, CXXXVIII (1939) 13–16.
POOLE, K. E., Tax remission as a means of influencing cyclical fluctuations, *Quarterly Journal of Economics*, LIII (1938–39) 261–274.
GORDON, R. A., Fiscal policy as a factor in stability, *American Academy of Political and Social Science, Annals*, CCVI (1939) 106–113.
CADMAN, P. F., National income and deficit financing, *American Bankers Association, Lectures* (1939) 5–41.
MYRDAL, G., Fiscal policy in the business cycle, *American Economic Review*, XXIX (1939, supplement) 183–193.
MUSGRAVE, R. A., The nature of budgetary balance and the case for the capital budget, *American Economic Review*, XXIX (1939) 260–271.
SALANT, W. S., A note on the effects of a changing deficit, *Quarterly Journal of Economics*, LIII (1938–39) 298–304.
HICKS, J. R. and HICKS, U. K., Public finance in the national income, *Review of Economic Studies*, VI (1938–39) 147–155.
WOOLFSON, A. P., The unbalanced budget and the national income, *Bankers Magazine*, CXXXVIII (1939) 287–290.
SMITH, D. T., Is deficit spending practical? *Harvard Business Review*, XVIII (1939) 35–43. .
KÖHLER, A, Government spending, its tasks and limits, *Social Research*, VI (1939) 194–206.
SAMUELSON, P. A., Theory of pump-priming reëxamined, *American Economic Review*, XXX (1940) 492–506.
HIGGINS, B., and MUSGRAVE, R. A., Deficit finance—the case examined, *Public Policy* (C. I. Friedrich and E. S. Mason, ed.). II, 136–207. Cambridge, Mass.: Grad. School of Public Administration, 1941.
STAUFFACHER, C., The effect of governmental expenditures and tax withdrawals upon income distribution 1930–1939, *Public Policy*, II, 232–261. Cambridge, Mass.: Grad. School of Public Administration, 1941.
ROSA, R. V., A multiplier analysis of armament expenditure, *American Economic Review*, XXXI (1941) 249–265.
ROBINSON, J., Review of R. F. Bretherton, et. al., *Public Investment and the Trade Cycle in Great Britain*, *Economic Journal*, LI (1941) 127–129.
FRANKEL, S. H., Consumption, investment and war expenditure in relation to the South African national income, *South African Journal of Economics*, (1941).

*Williams, J. H., Deficit spending, *American Economic Review*, XXX (1941, supplement) 52–66.
Bratt, E. C., Timing pump-priming expenditure, *American Economic Review*, XXXI (1941) 97–98.
Altman, O. L., Private investment, full employment, and public funds, *American Economic Review*, XXXI (1941, supplement) 228–236.
Copeland, M. A., The defense effort and the national income response pattern, *Journal of Political Economy*, L (1942) 415–426.
Hardy, C. O., Fiscal policy and the national income: a review, *American Economic Review*, XXXII (1942) 103–110.
Simons, H. C., Hansen on fiscal policy, *Journal of Political Economy*, L (1942) 161–196.
Samuelson, P. A., Fiscal policy and income determination, *Quarterly Journal of Economics*, LVI (1941–42) 575–605.
Somers, H. M., The impact of fiscal policy on national income, *Canadian Journal of Economics and Political Science*, VIII (1942) 364–385.
Smithies, A., The behavior of money national income under inflationary conditions *Quarterly Journal of Economics*, LVII (1942–43) 113–128.
Kuznets, S. S., National income and taxable capacity, *American Economic Review*, XXXII (1942, supplement) 37–75.
Gilbert, D. W., Taxation and economic stability, *Quarterly Journal of Economics*, LVI (1941–42) 406–429.
MacGibbon, D. A., Fiscal policy and business cycles, *Canadian Journal of Economics and Political Science*, IX (1943) 77–82.
Stern, E. H., Public expenditure in the national income, *Economica*, X, new series (1943) 166–175.
Wright, D. McC., Moulton's *The New Philosophy of Public Debt*, *American Economic Review*, XXXIII (1943) 573–590.
Higgins, B., Postwar tax policy, *Canadian Journal of Economics and Political Science*, IX (1943) 532–556.

V. MONETARY AND CAPITAL ASPECTS OF BUSINESS-CYCLE THEORY; MONETARY POLICY

The theoretical contributions on monetary and capital aspects are in A, items dealing primarily with monetary interest theory are discussed in B, and articles which deal primarily with monetary policy (as distinguished from the development of a monetary cycle theory) are listed in C.

Technical discussions of money and banking and of monetary or banking reforms, such as the 100% plan, are not included.

V-A. Monetary and Capital Theories

Includes both "purely monetary" and "overinvestment" aspects except that technology and innovations are placed in VII-A. Discussions of monetary policy as such are found in V-C.

Spiethoff, A., Vorbemerkungen zu einer Theorie der Überproduktion, *Schmollers Jahrbuch*, XXVI (1902) 721–759.

WICKSELL, K., The influence of the rate of interest on prices, *Economic Journal*, XVII (1907) 213–220.
KEYNES, J. M., review of *Theorie des Geldes* by L. von Mises, *Economic Journal*, XXIV (1914) 417–419.
YOUNG, A. A., review of *Currency and Credit* by R. G. Hawtrey and *Stabilizing the Dollar* by I. Fisher, *Quarterly Journal of Economics*, XXXIV (1919–20) 520–532.
ROBERTSON, D. H., review of *Monetary Reconstruction* by R. G. Hawtrey, *Economic Journal*, XXXIII (1923) 204–207.
HAWTREY, R. G., review of *Monetary Reform* by J. M. Keynes, *Economic Journal*, XXXIV (1924) 227–235.
HAWTREY, R. G., Mr. Robertson on banking policy, *Economic Journal*, XXXVI (1926) 417–433.
HARROD, R. F., Mr. Robertson's views on banking policy, *Economica*, VII, old series (1927) 224–232.
TAPPAN, M., Mr. Robertson's views on banking policy: a reply to Mr. Harrod, *Economica*, VIII, new series (1928) 95–109.
HAWTREY, R. G., The monetary theory of the trade cycle and its statistical test, *Quarterly Journal of Economics*, XLI (1926–27) 471–486.
BOUNIATIAN, M., Industrielle Schwankungen, Bankkredit und Warenpreise, *Archiv für Sozialwissenschaft und Sozialpolitik*, LVIII (1927) 449–477.
BOUNIATIAN, M., The theory of economic cycles based on the tendency toward excessive capitalization, *Review of Economic Statistics*, X (1928) 67–79.
SHAFER, J. E., An explanation of the business cycle, *American Economic Review*, XVIII (1928) 617–628.
BURCHARDT, F., Entwicklungsgeschichte der monetären Konjunkturtheorie, *Weltwirtschaftliches Archiv*, XXVIII (1928) 77–143.
STRIGL, R., Die Produktion unter dem Einfluss einer Kreditexpansion, *Schriften des Vereins für Sozialpolitik*, CLXXIII (1928) 185–211.
*HAWTREY, R. G., The trade cycle, *De Economist*, LXXV (1926) 169–185. Reprinted in *Trade and Credit*, 82–104. London: Longmans, Green & Co., 1928.
COPELAND, M. A., Money, trade and prices—a test of causal primacy, *Quarterly Journal of Economics*, XLIII (1928–29) 648–666.
MACHLUP, F., Geldtheorie und Konjunkturtheorie, *Mitteilungen des Verbandes österreichischer Banken und Bankiers*, XI (1929) 166–174.
HABERLER, G., review of *Geldtheorie und Konjunkturtheorie* by F. A. von Hayek, *Journal of Political Economy*, XXXIX (1931) 404–407.
PIGOU, A. C., review of *Trade and Credit* by R. G. Hawtrey, *Economic Journal*, XXXIX (1929) 183–194.
KUZNETS, S. S., Monetary business cycle theory in Germany, *Journal of Political Economy*, XXXVIII (1930) 125–163.
NEISSER, H., Notenbankfreiheit? *Weltwirtschaftliches Archiv*, XXXII (1930) 446–461.
WILLIAMS, J. H., The monetary doctrines of J. M. Keynes, *Quarterly Journal of Economics*, XLV (1930–31) 547–587.
KEYNES, J. M., An economic analysis of unemployment, *Unemployment as a World Problem* (Q. Wright, ed.) 3–42. Chicago: University of Chicago Press, 1931.
FELLNER, W., Zum Problem der universellen Überproduktion, *Archiv für Sozialwissenschaft und Sozialpolitik*, LXVI (1931) 522–556.

HABERLER, G., Die Kaufkraft des Geldes und die Stabilisierung der Wirtschaft, *Schmollers Jahrbuch*, LV (1931) 33–63.
HAYEK, F. A., Reflections on the pure theory of money of Mr. J. M. Keynes, *Economica*, XI (1931) 270–295, XII (1932) 22–44.
KEYNES, J. M., The pure theory of money: a reply to Dr. Hayek, *Economica*, XI (1931) 387–397.
HAYEK, F. A., A rejoinder to Mr. Keynes, *Economica*, XI (1931) 398–403.
ROBERTSON, D. H., Mr. Keynes' theory of money, *Economic Journal*, XLI (1931) 395–411.
KEYNES, J M., A rejoinder, *Economic Journal*, XLI (1931) 412–423.
LORIA, A., Keynes sulla moneta, *La Riforma Sociale*, XLII (1931) 113–120.
HABERLER, G., Money and the business cycle, *Gold and Monetary Stabilization*, (Q. Wright, ed.) 43–74. Chicago: University of Chicago Press, 1932.
HANSEN, A. H., A fundamental error in Keynes' "Treatise on Money," *American Economic Review*, XXII (1932) 462.
BOUNIATIAN, M., Die vermeintlichen Kreditkreierungen und die Konjunkturschwankungen, *Jahrbücher für Nationalökonomie und Statistik*, LXXI, new series (1932) 337–364.
KEYNES, J. M., Keynes' fundamental equations: a note, *American Economic Review*, XXII (1932) 691–692.
HAWTREY, R. G., Consumers' income and outlay, *Manchester School*, II (1931) 45–64.
FISHER, I., The debt deflation theory of great depressions, *Econometrica*, I (1933), 337–57.
JEVONS, H. S., Banking and the price level, *Manchester School*, II (1931) 10–17.
KEYNES, J. M., in *The World's Economic Crisis and the Way of Escape*, 27–55. New York: The Century Co., 1932.
SRAFFA, P., Dr. Hayek on money and capital, *Economic Journal*, XLII (1932) 42–53.
HAYEK, F. A., Money and capital: a reply, *Economic Journal*, XLII (1932) 237–249.
SRAFFA, P., A rejoinder, *Economic Journal*, XLII (1932) 249–251.
HANSEN, A. H., Hayek's *Monetary Theory and the Trade Cycle*, *The Nation*, CXXXVII (1933) 329–331. Reprinted in *Full Recovery or Stagnation?* 82–87. New York: W. W. Norton, 1938.
MACHLUP, F., The liquidity of short-term capital, *Economica*, XII (1932) 271–284.
BROCK, F., Zur Theorie der Konjunkturschwankungen, *Weltwirtschaftliches Archiv*, XXXV (1932) 419–443.
ROBBINS, L., Consumption and the trade cycle, *Economica*, XII (1932) 413–430.
FRASER, L. M., The significance of the stock exchange boom, *American Economic Review*, XXII (1932) 193–202.
STAFFORD, J., The relation of banking technique to economic equilibria, *Manchester School*, III (1932) 113–143.
HAWTREY, R. G., review of *Prices and Production* by F. A. von Hayek, *Economica*, XII (1932) 119–125.
BILIMOVIC, A., Zum Problem des "neutralen Geldes," *Zeitschrift für Nationalökonomie*, IV (1932–33) 53–84.
HAYEK, F. A. Über "neutrales Geld," *Zeitschrift für Nationalökonomie*, IV (1932–33) 659–661.

HAWTREY, R. G., review of *Monetary Theory and the Trade Cycle* by F. A. von Hayek, *Economic Journal*, XLIII (1933) 669–672.

FISHER, I., The relation of employment and the price level, *Stabilization of Employment*, (C. F. Roos, ed.) 152–159. Bloomington, Indiana: Principia Press, 1933.

MYRDAL, G., Der Gleichgewichtsbegriff als Instrument der geldtheoretischen Analyse, *Beiträge zur Geldtheorie* (F. A. Hayek, ed.) 361–487. Vienna: Julius Springer, 1933.

DANIELS, G. W., The circulation of money in relation to production and employment, *Manchester School*, IV (1933) 15–29.

PEDERSEN, J., Wicksells Theorie des Zusammenhangs zwischen Zinssatz und Geldwertschwankungen, *Archiv für Sozialwissenschaft*, LXIX (1933) 129–150.

ANGELL, J. W., and FICEK, K. F., The expansion of bank credit, *Journal of Political Economy*, XLI (1933) 1–32, 152–193.

ADARKAR, B. P., The "fundamental error" in Keynes' treatise, *American Economic Review*, XXIII (1933) 87.

SIMMONS, E. C., Mr. Keynes' control scheme, *American Economic Review*, XXIII (1933) 264–273.

KEYNES, J. M., Reply, *American Economic Review*, XXIII (1933) 675.

RÜBNER-PETERSEN, K., The error in the fundamental equations: a new interpretation, *American Economic Review*, XXIV (1934) 595–602.

HILL, M., The period of production and industrial fluctuations, *Economic Journal*, XLIII (1933) 599–610.

HAYEK, F. A., Capital and industrial fluctuations, *Econometrica*, II (1934) 152–167.

NEISSER, H., Monetary expansion and the structure of production, *Social Research*, I (1934) 434–457.

ROBERTSON, D. H., Industrial fluctuation and the natural rate of interest, *Economic Journal*, XLIV (1934) 650–656. Reprinted in *Essays in Monetary Theory*, 83–91. London: King, 1940.

HAWTREY, R. G., review of *Des Crises Générales et Périodiques de Surproduction* by J. Lescure, *Economic Journal*, XLIV (1934) 104–111.

HARROD, R. F., review of *Trade Depression and the Way Out* by R. G. Hawtrey, *Economic Journal*, XLIV (1934) 279–282.

HANSEN, A. H., The flow of purchasing power, *Economic Reconstruction* 210–238. New York: Columbia University Press, 1934. Reprinted in *Full Recovery or Stagnation?* 141–160. New York: W. W. Norton, 1938.

MITCHELL, W. C., review of *The Great Depression* by L. Robbins, *Quarterly Journal of Economics*, XLIX (1934–35) 503–507.

SHACKLE, G. L. S., Some notes on monetary theories of the trade cycle, *Review of Economic Studies*, I (1933–34) 27–38.

DANIELS, G. W., Spending and investing, *Manchester School*, V (1934) 102–117.

HARROD, R. F., The expansion of credit in an advancing community, *Economica*, I, new series (1934) 287–299.

ROBERTSON, D. H., Mr. Harrod and the expansion of credit, *Economica*, I, new series (1934) 473–475.

HARROD, R. F., Rejoinder to Mr. Robertson, *Economica*, I, new series (1934) 476–478.

CLASSIFIED BIBLIOGRAPHY OF ARTICLES 469

SNYDER, C., The problem of monetary and economic stability, *Quarterly Journal of Economics*, XLIX (1934–35) 173–205.

REED, H. L., The stabilization doctrines of Carl Snyder, *Quarterly Journal of Economics*, XLIX (1934–35) 600–620.

ROBERTSON, D. H., review of *The Great Depression* by L. Robbins, *Economica*, II, new series (1935) 103–106. Reprinted in *Essays in Monetary Theory*, 168–172. London: King, 1940.

HICKS, J. R., A suggestion for simplifying the theory of money, *Economica*, II, new series. (1935) 1–19.

ELLIS, H. S., Die Bedeutung der Produktionsperiode für die Krisentheorie, *Zeitschrift für Nationalökonomie*, VI (1935) 145–169.

*HAYEK, F. A., Price expectations, monetary disturbances and maladjustments, *Nationalökonomisk Tidsskrift*, LXXIII (1935) 171–191. Reprinted in *Profits, Interest and Investment* 135–157. London: Routledge, 1939.

HAYEK, F. A., The maintenance of capital, *Economica*, II, new series (1935) 241–276. Reprinted in *Profits, Interest and Investment*, 83–134. London: Routledge, 1939.

HAYEK, F. A., Investment that raises the demand for capital, *Review of Economic Statistics*, XIX (1937) 174–177. Reprinted in *Profits, Interest and Investment*, 73–82. London: Routledge, 1939.

BARGER, H., The banks and the stock market, *Journal of Political Economy*, XLIII (1935) 763–777.

BARGER, H., Neutral money and the trade cycle, *Economica*, II, new series (1935) 429–447.

THOMAS, W., Use of credit in security speculation, *American Economic Review*, XXV (1935) 21–30.

TUCKER, R. S., Government control of investments and speculation, *American Economic Review*, XXV (1935, supplement) 140–150.

EGLE, W., Money and production, *Journal of Political Economy*, XLIII (1935) 306–330.

THOMAS, B., The monetary doctrines of Professor Davidson, *Economic Journal*, XLV (1935) 36–50.

STAFFORD, J., A note on the equilibrium rate of interest, *Economic Journal*, XLV (1935) 259–268.

ROSENSTEIN-RODAN, P. N., The coordination of the general theories of money and price, *Economica*, III, new series (1936) 257–280.

ROBERTSON, D. H., Röpke: crises and cycles, *Economica*, III, new series (1936) 476–478. Reprinted in *Essays in Monetary Theory*, 173–176. London: King, 1940.

EDDY, G. A., Security issues and real investment in 1929, *Review of Economic Statistics*, XIX (1937) 79–91.

SIMMONS, E. C., Die Bedeutung starrer Preise für die Geldtheorie, *Weltwirtschaftliches Archiv*, XLVI (1937) 526–542.

REYNAUD, P.-L., Essais sur la monnaie neutre: I. Monnaie neutre et économie réelle; II. Monnaie neutre et échanges internationaux, *Revue d'Economie Politique*, LI (1937) 1192–1216, 1367–1393.

REISCH, R., Die neue Geld- und Kreditpolitik, *Zeitschrift für Nationalökonomie*, VIII (1937) 409–443.

KÄHLER, A., Scarcity and abundance of capital as cause of crisis, *Social Research*, IV (1937) 74–90.
ALBRECHT, G., Bemerkungen zum Problem der Überproduktion, *Jahrbücher für Nationalökonomie und Statistik*, CXLVI (1937) 285–308.
HAWTREY, R. G., The credit deadlock, *The Lessons of Monetary Experience* (A. D. Gayer, ed.) 129–144. New York: Farrar & Rinehart, 1937.
ARACKIE, R., Industrial fluctuations, *Economica*, IV, new series (1937) 143–167.
LEDERER, W., The volume of money and the business cycle, *Social Research*, IV (1937) 209–224.
KAMITZ, R., Über die Wirkungen des Hortens, *Zeitschrift für Nationalökonomie*, VIII (1937) 469–493.
FORSTMANN, A., Über produktive und nichtinflatorische Kreditgewährung, *Weltwirtschaftliches Archiv*, XLV (1937) 543–597.
ESPINOSA, A. DEGLI, Appunti di teoria della moneta, *Rivista di Politica Economica*, XXVII (1937) 292–312.
BRAEUTIGAM, H., Automatische Deflation, neutrales Geld und Kapitalbildung, *Weltwirtschaftliches Archiv*, XLV (1937) 598–611.
KROLL, G., Das Problem der organischen Wirtschaftserweiterung—Replik, *Weltwirtschaftliches Archiv*, XLV (1937) 612–616.
ANGELL, J. W., The general dynamics of money, *Journal of Political Economy*, XLV (1937) 289–346.
BROCK, F., Kapital, Kapitalzins und Investitionsspanne, *Weltwirtschaftliches Archiv*, XLVII (1938) 472–496.
BOER, A., Kapitaltheorie und Kapitalbildung, *Jahrbücher für Nationalökonomie und Statistik*, CXLVII (1938) 28–54.
WAGEMANN, E., Moderne Methoden der Kreditpolitik, *Vierteljahrshefte zur Konjunkturforschung*, XII (1937–38) 138–153.
EGLE, W., "Monetary" conditions of economic stability, *American Economic Review*, XXVIII (1938) 482–487.
WATTLES, G., Wicksell's business cycle analysis, *Carleton College Current Economic Issues*, May 31, 1938.
*ROBERTSON, D. H., A survey of modern monetary controversy, *Manchester School*, IX (1938) 1–19. Reprinted in *Essays in Monetary Theory*, 133–153. London: King, 1940.
KALDOR, N., Mr. Hawtrey on short and long term investment, *Economica*, V, new series (1938) 461–467.
ROSTOW, W. W., Investment and the great depression, *Economic History Review*, VIII (1938) 136–158.
ROSTOW, W. W., Explanation of "The Great Depression" (1873–1896): an historian's view of modern monetary theory, *Economic History*, IV (1940) 356–370.
TANAKA, K., On Prof. Hayek's theory of trade cycle, *Journal of the Kobe University of Commerce*, I (1939) 1–30.
KALDOR, N., Capital intensity and the trade cycle, *Economica*, VI, new series (1939) 40–66.
LACHMANN, L. M., On crisis and adjustment, *Review of Economic Statistics*, XXI (1939) 62–68.

HAWTREY, R. G., The trade cycle and capital intensity, *Economica*, VII, new series (1940) 1–15.
KALDOR, N., Reply, *Economica*, VII, new series (1940) 16–22.
ANGELL, J. W., Bank deposits and the business cycle, *American Economic Review*, XXX (1940, supplement) 80–82.
MACHLUP, F., Bank deposits and the stock market in the cycle, *American Economic Review*, XXX (1940, supplement) 83–91.
WILSON, T., Capital theory and the trade cycle, *Review of Economic Studies*, VII (1939–40) 169–179.
VAN DER VALK, H. M. H. A., Kapitaalmarkt- en conjunctuurproblemen, *De Economist*, LXXXIX (1940) 629–658.
LACHMANN, L. M., A reconsideration of the Austrian theory of industrial fluctuations, *Economica*, VII (1940) 179–196.
ROBERTSON, D. H., A Spanish contribution to the theory of fluctuations, *Economica*, VII (1940) 50–65.
PALANDER, I., "Om Stockholmsskolans" begrepp och metoder: metodologiska reflexioner kring (G.) Myrdals "monetary equilibrium," *Ekonomisk Tidskrift*, (1941) 88–143.
SMITHIES, A., Professor Hayek on "The Pure Theory of Capital," *American Economic Review*, XXXI (1941) 767–779.
KIRTY, V. S. R., The classical theory of equilibrium and the monetary theory of the trade cycle, *Indian Journal of Economics*, XXII (1941) 177–188.
NEISSER, H., Monetary equilibrium and the natural rate of interest, *Social Research*, VIII (1941) 454–68.
HICKS, J. R., The monetary theory of D. H. Robertson, *Economica*, IX, new series (1942) 53–57.
MARSCHAK, J., Wicksell's two interest rates, *Social Research*, VIII (1941) 469–478.
BRONFENBRENNER, M., The role of money in equilibrium capital theory, *Econometrica*, XI (1943) 35–60.
STOLPER, W. F., Monetary equilibrium and business-cycle theory, *Review of Economic Statistics*, XXV (1943) 88–92.
MISES, L. VON, "Elastic expectations" and the Austrian theory of the trade cycle, *Economica*, X, new series (1943) 251–252.

V-B. MONETARY INTEREST THEORIES

Includes discussions of the loanable-funds and the liquidity-preference theories of interest and those analyses of money and liquidity directly pertinent to an evaluation of these theories.
See also III-C, V-A and V-C.

HALM, G., Das Zinsproblem am Geld- und Kapitalmarkt, *Jahrbücher für Nationalökonomie und Statistik*, LXX, new series (1926) 97–121.
NEUMAN, A. M., The doctrine of liquidity, *Review of Economic Studies*, III (1935–36) 81–99.
ELLSWORTH, P. T., Mr. Keynes on the rate of interest and the marginal efficiency of capital, *Journal of Political Economy*, XLIV (1936) 767–790.

KEYNES, J. M., The theory of the rate of interest, *The Lessons of Monetary Experience* (in Honor of Irving Fisher) (A. D. Gayer, ed.) 145–152. New York: Farrar & Rinehart, 1937.
LACHMANN, L. M., Uncertainty and liquidity preference, *Economica*, IV, new series (1937) 295–308.
GRAZIANI, A., Vecchie e nuove teorie sull' interesse, *Rivista di Politica Economica*, XVI (1937) 945.
TAKATA, Y., Determination of the rate of interest, *Kyoto University Economic Review*, XII (1937) 1–20.
ELLIS, H. S., Some fundamentals in the theory of velocity, *Quarterly Journal of Economics*, LII (1937–38) 431–472.
KEYNES, J. M., Alternative theories of the rate of interest, *Economic Journal*, XLVII (1937) 241–252.
OHLIN, B., Alternative theories of the rate of interest, *Economic Journal* XLVII (1937) 423–428.
ROBERTSON, D. H., Alternative theories of the rate of interest, *Economic Journal*, XLVII (1937) 428–436.
HAWTREY, R. G., Alternative theories of the rate of interest, *Economic Journal*, XLVII (1937) 436–443.
KEYNES, J. M., The "ex-ante" theory of the rate of interest, *Economic Journal*, XLVII (1937) 663–669.
ROBERTSON, D. H., Mr. Keynes and finance, *Economic Journal*, XLVIII (1938) 314–318.
KEYNES, J. M., Comment, *Economic Journal*, XLVIII (1938) 318–322.
ROBERTSON, D. H., Mr. Keynes and 'finance': a note, *Economic Journal*, XLVIII (1938) 555–556.
LAUTENBACH, W., Zur Zinstheorie von John Maynard Keynes, *Weltwirtschaftliches Archiv*, XLV (1937) 493–525.
LANDAUER, C., A break in Keynes' theory of interest, *American Economic Review*, XXVII (1937) 260–266.
RILEY, R. H., Note on "A break in Keynes' theory of interest," *American Economic Review*, XXVIII (1938) 312–314. (With a reply and rejoinder) 314–319.
MILLIKAN, M. F., and others, General interest theory, *American Economic Review*, XXVIII (1938, supplement) 69–72.
CANNING, J. B. and others, Rate of interest, *American Economic Review*, XXVIII (1938, supplement) 73–76.
MILLIKAN, M., Liquidity-preference theory of interest, *American Economic Review*, XXVIII (1938) 247–260.
BISSELL, R. M. Jr., The rate of interest, *American Economic Review*, XXVIII (1938, supplement) 23–40.
SHAW, E. S., False issues in the interest theory controversy, *Journal of Political Economy*, XLVI (1938) 838–856.
FLEMING, J. M., The determination of the rate of interest, *Economica*, V, new series (1938) 333–341.
ROBINSON, J., The concept of hoarding, *Economic Journal*, XLVIII (1938) 231–236.
LERNER, A. P., Alternative formulations of the theory of interest, *Economic Journal*, XLVIII (1938) 211–230.
BROWN, A. J., The liquidity-preference schedules of the London clearing banks, *Oxford Economic Papers*, I (1938) 49–82.

MEHTA, J. K., Coördination of the theories of interest, *Indian Journal of Economics*, XIX (1938) 251–263.
MELVILLE, L. G., The theory of interest, *Economic Record*, XIV (1938) 1–13.
CONSIGLIO, V., Impiego, interesse e moneta nella teoria generale del Keynes, *Economia*, XXII (1938) 100–142.
MAKOWER, H., and MARSCHAK, J., Assets, prices and monetary theory, *Economica*, V, new series (1938) 261–288.
MARSCHAK, J., Money and the theory of assets, *Econometrica*, VI (1938) 311–325.
KEYNES, J. M., The process of capital formation, *Economic Journal*, XLIX (1939) 569–574.
THIRLBY, G. F., The rate of interest, *South African Journal of Economics*, VII (1939) 1–17.
D'SOUZA, V. L., Theory of interest reconsidered, *Indian Journal of Economics*, XIX (1939) 473–481.
DATTA, B., Interest and the complex of preferences, *Indian Journal of Economics*, XIX (1939) 491–499.
BROWN, A. J., Interest, prices, and the demand schedule for idle money, *Oxford Economic Papers*, II (1939) 46–69.
REDDAWAY, W. B. and DOWNING, R. I., Zero rates of interest, *Economic Record*, XV (1939) 94–98.
DE SCITOVSZKY, T., A study of interest and capital, *Economica*, VII, new series (1940) 293–317.
MORTON, W. A., A zero deposit rate, *American Economic Review*, XXX (1940) 536–553.
KALECKI, M., The short-term and the long-term rate, *Oxford Economic Papers*, IV (1940) 15–22.
ADARKAR, B. P. and GHOSH, D., Mr. Keynes' theory of interest, *Indian Journal of Economics*, XXI (1941) 285–300.
MEHTA, J. K., The negative rate of interest, *Indian Journal of Economics*, XXI (1941) 301–306.
HART, A. G., Peculiarities of indifference maps involving money, *Review of Economic Studies*, VIII (1940–41) 126–128.
FELLNER, W., and SOMERS, H. M., Alternative monetary approaches to interest theory, *Review of Economic Statistics*, XXIII (1941) 43–48.
SOMERS, H. M., Monetary policy and the theory of interest, *Quarterly Journal of Economics*, LV (1940–41) 488–507.
KALECKI, M., The short-term rate of interest and velocity of cash circulation, *Review of Economic Statistics*, XXIII (1941) 97–99.
SALANT, W. S., The demand for money and the concept of income velocity, *Journal of Political Economy*, XLIX (1941) 395–421.
HIGGINS, B., A diagrammatic analysis of the supply of loan funds, *Econometrica*, IX (1941) 231–240.
KAFKA, A., Professor Hicks' theory of money interest, *American Economic Review*, XXXI (1941) 327–329.
SWAN, T. W., Some notes on the interest controversy, *Economic Record*, XVII (1941) 153–165.

LUTZ, F. A., The structure of interest rates, *Quarterly Journal of Economics*, LV (1940–41) 36–63.
MARX, D. JR., The structure of interest rates: comment, *Quarterly Journal of Economics*, LVI (1941–42) 152–156.
LUSHER, D. W., The structure of interest rates and the Keynesian theory of interest, *Journal of Political Economy*, L (1942) 272–279.
ROOS, C. F. and SZELISKI, V. v., The determination of interest rates, *Journal of Political Economy*, L (1942) 501–535.
GOODWIN, R. M., Keynesian and other interest theories, *Review of Economic Statistics*, XXV (1943) 6–12.
SMITHIES, A., The quantity of money and the rate of interest, *Review of Economic Statistics*, XXV (1943) 69–76.
TUCKER, D. S., The interest rate and saving, *Journal of the American Statistical Association*, XXXVIII (1943) 101–104.
LESER, C. E. V., The consumer's demand for money, *Econometrica*, XI (1943) 123–140

V-C. EFFECTIVENESS OF MONETARY POLICY

Includes discussions of the aims of monetary policy, recommendations on the use of monetary policy, practical surveys of the influence of the rate of interest and some historical discussions of the use of monetary policy.

See particularly V-A and also III-C and V-B.

MOULTON, H. G., Commercial banking and capital formation, *Journal of Political Economy*, XXVI (1918) 714–723.
ADAMS, T. S., Financial devices for controlling or mitigating the severity of business cycles, *Business Cycles and Unemployment*, 262–271. New York: McGraw-Hill, 1923.
ANGELL, J. W., Monetary theory and monetary policy: some recent discussions, *Quarterly Journal of Economics*, XXXIX (1924–25) 267–299.
SNYDER, C., The influence of the interest rate on the business cycle, *American Economic Review*, XV (1925) 684–699.
CASSEL, G., The rate of interest, the bank rate and the stabilization of prices, *Quarterly Journal of Economics*, XLII (1927–28) 511–529.
ROBERTSON, D. H., Theories of banking policy, *Economica*, VIII (1928) 131–146. Reprinted in *Essays in Monetary Theory*, 39–59. London: King, 1940.
MITCHELL, W. F., **Interest** rates as factors in the business cycle, *American Economic Review*, XVIII (1928 supplement) 217–233.
SPRAGUE, O. M. W., Money and credit and their effect on business, *Recent Economic Changes in the United States*, 657–708. New York: McGraw-Hill, 1929.
WILLIS, H. P., Federal Reserve policy in depression, *Gold and Monetary Stabilization* (Q. Wright, ed.), 77–108. Chicago: University of Chicago Press, 1932.
ANGELL, J. W., Monetary prerequisites for employment stabilization, *Stabilization of Employment* (C. F. Roos, ed.), 206–226. Bloomington, Indiana: Principia Press, 1933.
HARRIS, S. E., Higher prices, *Economics of the Recovery Program*, 90–138. New York and London: McGraw-Hill, 1934.

CURRIE, L., The failure of monetary policy to prevent the depression of 1929–32, *Journal of Political Economy*, XLII (1934) 145–177.
MELVILLE, L. G., The schedule of interest rates and investment, *Economic Record*, X (1934) 167–181.
MACHLUP, F., The rate of interest as cost factor and as capitalization factor, *American Economic Review*, XXV (1935) 459–465.
HANSEN, A. H., Monetary policy in the upswing, *The Lessons of Monetary Experience* (A. D. Gayer, ed.), 89–98. New York: Farrar & Rinehart, 1937.
ECCLES, M. S., Controlling booms and depressions, *The Lessons of Monetary Experience* (A. D. Gayer, ed.), 3–22. New York: Farrar & Rinehart, 1937.
PEDERSEN, J., Monetary policy and economic stability, *The Lessons of Monetary Experience* (A. D. Gayer, ed.), 179–201. New York: Farrar & Rinehart, 1937.
ANGELL, J. W., The general objectives of monetary policy, *The Lessons of Monetary Experience* (A. D. Gayer, ed.), 50–88. New York: Farrar & Rinehart, 1937.
VILLARD, H. H., The federal reserve system's monetary policy in 1931 and 1932, *Journal of Political Economy*, XLV (1937) 721–739.
NICHOLSON, J. L., The fallacy of easy money for the small business, *Harvard Business Review*, XVII (1938) 31–34.
EBERSOLE, J. F., The influence of interest rates upon entrepreneurial decisions in business—a case study, *Harvard Business Review*, XVII (1938) 35–39.
HENDERSON, H. D., The significance of the rate of interest, *Oxford Economic Papers*, I (1938) 1–13.
HABERLER, G., The interest rate and capital formation, *Capital Formation and its Elements*, 119–133. New York: National Industrial Conference Board, 1938.
MEADE, J. E. and ANDREWS, P. W. S., Summary of replies to questions on effects of interest rates, *Oxford Economic Papers*, I (1938) 14–31.
ROBERTSON, D. H., Hawtrey: A century of bank rate, *Economic Journal*, XLIX (1939) 94–96. Reprinted in *Essays in Monetary Theory*, 184–196. London: King, 1940.
LOKANATHAN, P. S., Interest and investment, *Indian Journal of Economics*, XIX (1939) 483–490.
PLUMPTRE, A. F. W., The role of interest rates and bank credit in the economies of the British Dominions, *Economic Journal*, XLIX (1939) 222–236.
ANDREWS, P. W. S., A further inquiry into the effects of rates of interest, *Oxford Economic Papers*, III (1940) 33–73.
HAAVELMO, T., The effect of the rate of interest on investment: a note, *Review of Economic Statistics*, XXIII (1941) 49–52.

VI. PSYCHOLOGICAL INFLUENCES, EXPECTATIONS AND INVESTMENT DECISIONS

See also III-C, IV-B and V-C.

LAVINGTON, F., Uncertainty and its relation to the rate of interest, *Economic Journal*, XXII (1912) 398–409.
DENNISON, H. S., Management and the business cycle, *Journal of the American Statistical Association*, XVIII (1922), 20–31.
MITCHELL, T. W., Competitive illusion as a cause of business cycles, *Quarterly Journal of Economics*, XXXVIII (1923–24) 631–652.

HART, A. G., Anticipations, business planning, and the cycle, *Quarterly Journal of Economics*, LI (1936–37) 273–297.

SHACKLE, G. L. S., Dynamics of the crisis: a suggestion, *Review of Economic Studies*, IV (1936–37) 108–122.

HUTCHISON, T. W., Expectation and rational conduct, *Zeitschrift für Nationalökonomie*, VIII (1937) 636–653.

HART, A. G., Failure and fulfillment of expectations in business fluctuations, *Review of Economic Statistics*, XIX (1937) 69–78.

LACHMANN, L. M., Preiserwartungen und intertemporales Gleichgewicht, *Zeitschrift für Nationalökonomie*, VIII (1937) 33–46.

HUTCHISON, T. W., Note on uncertainty and planning, *Review of Economic Studies*, V (1937–38) 72–74.

KALECKI, M., The principle of increasing risk, *Economica*, IV, new series (1937) 440–447

BUCHANAN, N. S. and CALKINS, R. D., A comment on Mr. Kalecki's "Principle of increasing risk," *Economica*, V, new series (1938) 455–460. (With a reply by Mr. Kalecki.)

SWEEZY, P. M., Expectations and the scope of economics, *Review of Economic Studies*, V (1937–38) 234–237.

MELVILLE, L. G., The place of expectations in economic theory, *Economic Record*, XV (1939) 1–16.

SHACKLE, G. L. S., Expectations and employment, *Economic Journal*, XLIX (1939) 442–452.

KALDOR, N., Speculation and economic stability, *Review of Economic Studies*, VII (1939–40) 1–27.

DOW, J. C. R., A theoretical account of futures markets, *Review of Economic Studies*, VII (1939–40) 185–195.

KALDOR, N., A note on the theory of the forward market, *Review of Economic Studies*, VII (1939–40) 196–201. Comments by Dow and Kaldor, 201–205.

SHACKLE, G. L. S., The nature of the inducement to invest, *Review of Economic Studies*, VIII (1940) 44–48.

HART, A. G., Uncertainty and inducement to invest, *Review of Economic Studies*, VIII (1940) 49–57. (With a reply by G. L. S. Shackle.)

BUCHANAN, N. S., Toward a theory of fluctuations in business profits, *American Economic Review*, XXXI (1941) 731–753.

CHENAULT, L. R., Buchanan's theory of fluctuations in business profits, *American Economic Review*, XXXII (1942) 840–842.

SHACKLE, G. L. S., A means of promoting investment, *Economic Journal*, LI (1941) 249–260.

MARSCHAK, J., Lack of confidence, *Social Research*, VIII (1941) 41–62.

BUCHANAN, N. S., Anticipations and industrial investment decisions, *American Economic Review*, XXXII (1942, supplement) 141–155.

SHACKLE, G. L. S., A theory of investment-decisions, *Oxford Economic Papers*, VI (1942) 77–94.

LACHMANN, L. M., The rôle of expectations in economics as a social science, *Economica*, X, new series (1943) 12–23.

SHACKLE, G. L. S., The expectational dynamics of the individual, *Economica*, X, new series (1943) 99–129.

VII. TECHNOLOGY, INNOVATIONS, REINVESTMENT AND INVENTORY CYCLES

Includes investment aspects of business-cycle theory not primarily of a monetary nature. Some discussions of Schumpeter's theory of economic development are also included here.

See also IV-A, IV-B and V-A.

VII-A. TECHNOLOGY AND INNOVATIONS

ENGLAND, M. T., Promotion as the cause of crises, *Quarterly Journal of Economics*, XXIX (1914–15) 748–767.

GREGORY, T. E., Rationalization and technological unemployment, *Economic Journal*, XL (1930) 551–567.

HANSEN A. H., Institutional frictions and technological unemployment, *Quarterly Journal of Economics*, XLV (1930–31) 684–697.

KALDOR, N., A case against technical progress?, *Economica*, XII (1932) 180–196.

BOUNIATIAN, M., Technical progress and unemployment, *International Labour Review*, XXVII (1933) 327–348.

LEDERER, E., Technical progress and unemployment, *International Labour Review*, XXVIII (1933) 1–25.

JACKSON, D. C., Machinery and unemployment, *Stabilization of Employment* (Charles F. Roos, ed.) 33–51. Bloomington, Indiana: Principia Press, 1933.

KIMBALL, D. S., Social effects of mass production, *Stabilization of Employment* (Charles F. Roos, ed.) 52–69. Bloomington, Indiana: Principia Press, 1933.

KÄHLER, A., The problem of verifying the theory of technological unemployment, *Social Research*, II (1935) 439–460.

FLAMM, I. H., The problem of technological unemployment in the United States, *International Labour Review*, XXXI (1935) 344–363.

WARBURTON, C., Plateaus of prosperity and plains of depression, *Economic Essays* (in Honor of W. C. Mitchell) 497–516. New York: Columbia University Press, 1935.

STERNBERG, F., Prolonged unemployment, technical progress and the conquest of new markets, *International Labour Review*, XXXVI (1937) 446–485.

FISHER, A. G. B., Technical improvements, unemployment and reduction of working hours, *Economica*, IV, new series (1937) 371–385.

MCCRACKEN, H. L., Technological unemployment, *Journal of Business of the University of Iowa*, (1937).

LUGLI, L., La funzione dinamica del credito in Schumpeter e Hahn, *Giornale degli Economisti*, XVIII (1939) 862–873.

KUZNETS, S. S., Schumpeter's business cycles, *American Economic Review*, XXX (1940) 257–271.

MIRKOWICH, N., Schumpeter's theory of economic development, *American Economic Review*, XXX (1940) 580.

KALECKI, M., A theorem on technical progress, *Review of Economic Studies*, VIII (1941) 178–184.

NEISSER, H., "Permanent" technological unemployment, *American Economic Review*, XXXII (1942) 50–71.
HAGEN, E. E., Savings, investment and technological unemployment, *American Economic Review*, XXXII (1942) 553–555.
NEISSER, H., The concept of technological unemployment: a reply to Mr. Hagen's criticism, *American Economic Review*, XXXII (1942) 555–557.
SWEEZY, P. M., Professor Schumpeter's theory of innovation, *Review of Economic Statistics*, XXV (1943) 93–96.
KEIRSTEAD, B. S., Technical advance and economic equilibria, *Canadian Journal of Economics and Political Science*, IX (1943) 55–68.
LANGE, O., A note on innovations, *Review of Economic Statistics*, XXV (1943) 19–25.

VII-B. REINVESTMENT AND DEPRECIATION

BAIN, J. S., Depression pricing and the depreciation function, *Quarterly Journal of Economics*, LI (1936–37) 705–715.
EINARSEN, J., Reinvestment cycles, *Review of Economic Statistics*, XX (1938) 1–10.
BAIN, J. S., The relation of the economic life of equipment to reinvestment cycles, *Review of Economic Statistics*, XXI (1939) 79–88.
BAUER, P. T. and MARRACK, P. R., Depreciation and interest, *Economic Journal*, XLIX (1939) 237–243.
CAPLAN, B., Premature abandonment and the flow of investment, *Quarterly Journal of Economics*, LIV (1939–40) 152–157.
CAPLAN, B., Reinvestment and the rate of interest, *American Economic Review*, XXX (1940) 561–568.

VII-C. INVENTORIES

LACHMANN, L. M., Commodity stocks and equilibrium, *Review of Economic Studies*, III (1935–36) 230–234.
ARTHUR, H. B., Inventory profits in the business cycle, *American Economic Review*, XXVIII (1938) 27–40.
LACHMANN, L. M. and SNAPPER, F., Commodity stocks in the trade cycle, *Economica*, V, new series (1938) 435–454.
SHAW, E. S., Elements of a theory of inventory, *Journal of Political Economy*, XLVIII (1940) 465–485.
METZLER, L. A., The nature and stability of inventory cycles, *Review of Economic Statistics*, XXIII (1941) 113–129.

VIII. WAGES, COSTS AND PRICES IN RELATION TO OUTPUT AND EMPLOYMENT

Includes discussions of wage cuts, cost increases and price rigidity as well as relevant statistical studies of real wages.

Discussions of Pigou's analysis of unemployment are also included.

VIII-A. WAGES AND EMPLOYEE COMPENSATION

HAYES, H. G., The rate of wages and the use of machinery, *American Economic Review*, XIII (1923) 461–465.

HANSEN, A. H., Factors affecting the trend of real wages, *American Economic Review*, XV (1925) 27–42.
MAURETTE, F., Is unemployment insurance a cause of permanent unemployment?, *International Labour Review*, XXIV (1931) 665–684.
HARRIS, S. E., Professor Pigou's theory of unemployment, *Quarterly Journal of Economics*, XLIX (1934–35) 286–324.
HAWTREY, R. G., The "theory of unemployment" by Professor A. C. Pigou, *Economica*, I, new series (1934) 147–166.
HARROD, R. F., Professor Pigou's theory of unemployment, *Economic Journal*, XLIV (1934), 19–32.
SMITHIES, A., Wages policy in the depression, *Economic Record*, XI (1935) 249–268.
MITNITZKY, M., Wage policy to-day and to-morrow, *International Labour Review*, XXXII (1935) 344–373.
KALDOR, N., Wage subsidies as a remedy for unemployment, *Journal of Political Economy*, XLIV (1936) 721–742.
SIGNORELLI, G., Sullo equilibrio fra salari e prezzi nei periodi di depressione economica, *Rivista di Politica Economica*.
WEISS, H., Unemployment prevention through unemployment compensation, *Political Science Quarterly*, LIII (1938) 14–35.
PIGOU, A. C., Real and money wage rates in relation to unemployment, *Economic Journal*, XLVII (1937) 405–422.
KEYNES, J. M., Prof. Pigou on money wages in relation to unemployment, *Economic Journal*, XLVII (1937) 743–745.
KALDOR, N., Prof. Pigou on money wages in relation to unemployment, *Economic Journal*, XLVII (1937) 745–753.
PIGOU, A. C., Money wages in relation to unemployment, *Economic Journal*, XLVIII (1938) 134–138.
SOMERS, H. M., Money wage cuts in relation to unemployment, *Review of Economic Studies*, VI (1939) 161–163.
KALDOR, N., Money wage cuts in relation to unemployment: a reply to Mr. Somers, *Review of Economic Studies*, VI (1939) 232–235.
SOMERS, H. M., Money wage cuts in relation to unemployment: a rejoinder to Mr. Kaldor, *Review of Economic Studies*, VII (1940) 136–137. (With a comment by Mr. Kaldor.)
LERNER, A. P., Ex-ante analysis and wage theory, *Economica*, VI, new series (1939) 436–449.
BANGS, R. B., Wage reduction and employment, *Journal of Political Economy*, L (1942) 251–271.
DUNLOP, J. T., The movement of real and money wage rates, *Economic Journal*, XLVIII (1938) 413–434.
TARSHIS, L., Real wages in the United States and Great Britain, *Canadian Journal of Economics and Political Science*, IV (1938) 362–375.
KEYNES, J. M., Relative movements of real wages and output, *Economic Journal*, XLIX (1939) 34–51.
TARSHIS, L., Changes in real and money wages, *Economic Journal*, XLIX (1939) 150–154.
RICHARDSON, J. H., Real wage movements, *Economic Journal*, XLIX (1939) 425–441.

RUGGLES, R., The relative movements of real and money wage rates, *Quarterly Journal of Economics*, LV (1940–41) 130–149.
DUNLOP, J. T., Real and money wage rates: a reply, *Quarterly Journal of Economics*, LV (1940–41) 683–691.
TARSHIS, L., Real and money wage rates: a further comment, *Quarterly Journal of Economics*, LV (1940–41) 691–697.
RUGGLES, R., Real and money wage rates: rejoinder, *Quarterly Journal of Economics*, LV (1940–41) 697–700.
MARJOLIN, R., Reflections on the Blum experiment, *Economica*, V, new series (1938) 177–191.
KALECKI, M., The lesson of the Blum experiment, *Economic Journal*, XLVIII (1938) 26–41.
TAKATA, Y., Unemployment and wages: a critical review of Mr. Keynes' theory of unemployment, *Kyoto University Economic Review*, XII, No. 2 (1937) 1–18.
WALKER, E. R., Wages policy and business cycles, *International Labour Review*, XXXVIII (1938) 758–793.
DAUGHERTY, C. R., and others, Wages policies, *American Economic Review*, XXVIII (1938, supplement) 155–158.
KING, W. I., Wage rates, wage costs, employment, wage income and the general welfare, *American Economic Review*, XXIX (1939) 34–47.
DUNLOP, J. T., Cyclical variations in wage structure, *Review of Economic Statistics*, XXI (1939) 30–39.
DOUGLAS, P. H., The effect of wage increases upon employment, *American Economic Review*, XXIX (1939, supplement) 138–157.
MOSAK, J. L., Wage increases and employment, *American Economic Review*, XXXI (1941) 330–332.
DOUGLAS, P. H., Wage theory and wage policy, *International Labour Review*, XXXIX (1939) 319–359.
OLIVER, H. M., JR., Wage reductions and employment, *Southern Economic Journal*, V (1939) 302–318.
LERNER, A. P., The relation of wage policies and price policies, *American Economic Review*, XXIX (1939, supplement) 158–169.
LEDERER, E., Industrial fluctuations and wage policy: some unsettled points, *International Labour Review*, XXXIX (1939) 1–33.
DEMARIA, G., Sull' attendibilita di una tesi del Keynes a proposito di variazioni dei salari monetari e reali, *Giornale degli Economisti*, XVII (1939) 681–691.
BERNSTEIN, E. M., Wage rates, investment, and employment, *Journal of Political Economy*, XLVII (1939) 218–231.
OLIVER, H. M. Jr., Does wage reduction aid employment by lowering prices?, *Southern Economic Journal*, VI (1940) 333–343.
BISSELL, R. M. Jr., Price and wage policies and the theory of employment, *Econometrica*, VIII (1940) 199–239.
BROWN, W. M., Some effects of a minimum wage upon the economy as a whole, *American Economic Review*, XXX (1940) 98–107.
MIKESELL, R. F., A note on the effects of minimum wages on the propensity to consume, *American Economic Review*, XXX (1940) 574.

HAGEN, E. E., Elasticity of demand and a minimum wage, *American Economic Review*, XXX (1940) 574–576.
SUFRIN, S. C., The effects of minimum wages, *American Economic Review*, XXX (1940) 576–578.
BROWN, W. M., Some effects of a minimum wage upon the economy as a whole—reply to Messrs. Mikesell, Hagen and Sufrin, *American Economic Review*, XXX (1940) 578–579.
TOBIN, J., Note on the money wage problem, *Quarterly Journal of Economics*, LV (1940–41) 508–516.
SWEEZY, A. R., Wages and investment, *Journal of Political Economy*, L (1942) 117–129.

VIII-B. PRICE RIGIDITY, MONOPOLISTIC FACTORS, COSTS

Wage costs have been discussed in VIII-A and interest costs have been considered in V. This section covers costs as a whole, cost-price relationships and price behavior.

HANSEN, A. H., Prime costs in the business cycle, *Journal of Political Economy*, XXXII (1924) 1–14.
MEANS, G. C., Price inflexibility and the requirements of a stabilizing monetary policy, *Journal of the American Statistical Association*, XXX (1935) 401–413.
EPSTEIN, R. C., and SUMNER, J. D., Effect of the depression upon earnings and prices of regulated and nonregulated industries, *American Economic Review*, XXVI (1936, supplement) 36–45.
WALLACE, D. H., Monopoly prices and depression, *Explorations in Economics*, 346–356 New York and London: McGraw-Hill, 1936.
SMITH, H., Imperfect competition and trade depression, *Manchester School*, VII (1936) 38–49.
MEANS, G. C., Notes on inflexible prices, *American Economic Review*, XXVI (1936, supplement) 23–35.
HARROD, R. F., Imperfect competition and the trade cycle, *Review of Economic Statistics*, XVIII (1936) 84–88.
MCCRACKEN, H. L., Monopolistic competition and business fluctuation, *Southern Economic Journal*, V (1938) 158–178.
LACHMANN, L. M., Investment and costs of production, *American Economic Review*, XLVIII (1938) 469–481.
HINSHAW, R., Rising costs and business cycle crisis, *American Economic Review*, XXVIII (1938) 707–710.
FETTER, F. A., Competition or monopoly, *Proceedings of the Academy of Political Science*, XVIII (1938–40) 100–107.
SINGER, H. W., Price dispersion in periods of change, *Economic Journal*, XLVIII (1938) 658–673.
MASON, E. S., Price inflexibility, *Review of Economic Statistics*, XX (1938) 53–64.
LEDERER, E., Price dislocations versus investments, *Social Research*, V (1938) 149–167.
KING, W. I., Can production of automobiles be stabilized by making their prices flexible?, *Journal of the American Statistical Association*, XXXIV (1939) 641–651.
SUMNER, J. D., Public utility prices and the business cycle: a study in the theory of price rigidity, *Review of Economic Statistics*, XXI (1939) 97–109.

DOBLIN, E., Some aspects of price inflexibility, *Review of Economic Statistics*, XXII (1940) 183–189.
DE SCITOVSZKY, T., Capital accumulation, employment and price rigidity, *Review of Economic Studies*, VIII (1941) 69–88.
BISSELL, R. M., JR., Prices, costs and investment, *American Economic Review*, XXX (1941, supplement) 200–227.
MEANS, G. C., The controversy over the problem of full employment, The Structure of the American Economy, Pt. 2, *Towards Full Use of Resources*, 9–17. Washington: Government Printing Office, 1940.
HANSEN, A. H., Price flexibility and full employment of resources, The Structure of the American Economy, Pt. 2, *Towards Full Use of Resources*, 27–34. Washington: Government Printing Office, 1940.
EZEKIEL, M., Economic policy and the structure of the American economy, The Structure of the American Economy, Pt. 2, *Towards Full Use of Resources*, 35–45. Washington: Government Printing Office, 1940.
MASON, E. S., Price policies, full employment, *Public Policy*, I, 25–58. Cambridge, Mass.: Graduate School of Public Administration, 1940.

IX. SPECIAL INDUSTRY CYCLES: AGRICULTURE AND BUILDING

IX-A. AGRICULTURAL, WEATHER AND COSMIC CYCLES

JEVONS, W. S., The solar period and the price of corn, *Investigations in Currency and Finance*, 175–186. London: Macmillan and Co. Limited, 1909.
JEVONS, H. S., Trade fluctuations and solar activity, *Contemporary Review*, XCVI (1909) 165–189.
GRAUE, E., The relationship of business activity to agriculture, *Journal of Political Economy*, XXXVIII (1930) 472–478.
ANDERSON, M. D., Agricultural theory of business cycles, *American Economic Review*, XXI (1931) 427–449.
HANSEN, A. H., The business cycle in its relation to agriculture, *Journal of Farm Economics*, XIV (1932) 59–67.
JEVONS, H. S., The causes of fluctuations of industrial activity and the price-level, *Journal of the Royal Statistical Society*, XCVI (1933) 545–588. (Discussion, 588–605.)
GARCIA-MATA, C., and F. I. SHAFFNER, Solar and economic relationships: a preliminary report, *Quarterly Journal of Economics*, XLIX (1934–35) 1–51.
COASE, R. H., and R. F. FOWLER, The pig-cycle in Great Britain: an explanation, *Economica*, IV, new series (1937) 55–82.
ALTSCHUL, E. and STRAUSS, F., Technical progress and agricultural depression, *National Bureau of Economic Research, Bulletin* 67 (1937) pp. 32.
*EZEKIEL, M., The cobweb theorem, *Quarterly Journal of Economics*, LII (1937–38) 255–280.
FULMER, J. L., Relationship of the cycle in yields of cotton and apples to solar and sky radiation, *Quarterly Journal of Economics*, LVI (1942) 385–405.

IX-B. BUILDING CYCLES

RIGGELMAN, J. R., Building cycles in the United States, 1875–1932, *Journal of the American Statistical Association*, XXVIII (1933) 174–183.

CONKLIN, W. D., Building costs in the business cycle: with particular reference to building sponsored by governments in the United States, *Journal of Political Economy*, XLIII (1935) 365–392.
BURNS, A. F., Long cycles in residential construction, *Economic Essays* (in Honor of Wesley Clair Mitchell), 63–104. New York: Columbia University Press, 1935.
BOWLEY, M., Fluctuations in house-building and the trade cycle, *Review of Economic Studies*, IV (1936–37) 167–181.
BRAUNTHAL, A., Residential Building in the United States and Great Britain, *Social Research*, IV (1937) 52–73.
BELLMAN, H., Business recovery and the housing program in Great Britain, *Journal of Land and Public Utility Economics*, XIV (1938) 111–119.
LONG, C. D., JR., Long cycles in the building industry, *Quarterly Journal of Economics*, LIII (1938–39) 371–403.
LONG, C. D., JR., The building industry—maker and breaker of booms and depressions, *Dun's Review*, December, 1939, pp. 5.
BOWEN, I., Building output and the trade cycle (U.K., 1924–38), *Oxford Economic Papers*, III (1940) 110–130.
DERKSEN, J. B. D., Long cycles in residential building, an explanation, *Econometrica*, VIII (1940), 97–116.
GREBLER, L., Housing policy and the building cycle, *Review of Economic Statistics*, XXIV (1942) 66–74.
ISARD, W., Transport development and building cycles, *Quarterly Journal of Economics*, LVII (1942) 90–112.
ISARD, W., A neglected cycle: the transport-building cycle, *Review of Economic Statistics*, XXIV (1942) 149–158.

X. SECULAR TENDENCIES: LONG WAVES AND THE STAGNATION THESIS

X-A. LONG WAVES; WARS

This subject is also discussed in some of the "overall" items in I.

KONDRATIEFF, N. D., Die langen Wellen der Konjunktur, *Archiv für Sozialwissenschaft und Sozialpolitik*, LVI (1926) 573–609.
*KONDRATIEFF, N. D., The long waves in economic life, *Review of Economic Statistics*, XVII (1935) 105–115. (Translation of Kondratieff, 1926.)
SPIETHOFF, A., Krisen, *Handwörterbuch der Staatswissenschaften*, VI (1925) 8–91.
MARJOLIN, R., Mouvements de longue durée, des prix et extraction des metaux précieux, *L'Activité Economique*, 2ᵉ année (1937) 119–144.
MACFIE, A. L., The outbreak of war and the trade cycle, *Economic History*, III (1938) 89–97.
MARJOLIN, R., Rationalité ou irrationalité des mouvements économiques de longue durée, *Annales Sociol.* Serie D fasc. 3 (1938).
GLENDAY, R., Long period economic trends, *Journal of the Royal Statistical Society*, Pt. III, CI (1938) 511–552.
GRAS, N. S. B., Secular trends in business, *Quarterly Review of Commerce*, VII (1940) 161–165.

BERNSTEIN, E. M., War and the pattern of business cycles, *American Economic Review*, XXX (1940) 324–335.

DICKINSON, F. G., An aftercost of the World War to the United States, *American Economic Review*, XXX (1940, supplement) 326–339.

ROSE, A., Wars, innovations and long cycles: a brief comment, *American Economic Review*, XXXI (1941) 105–107.

MARJOLIN, R., Long cycles in capital intensity in the French coal mining industry, 1840–1914, *Review of Economic Statistics*, XXIII (1941) 165–175.

X-B. STAGNATION THESIS; POPULATION GROWTH

See also III-D, IV-D and VII-A.

SPENGLER, J. J., Population growth, consumer demand, and business profits, *Harvard Business Review*, XII (1933–34) 204–221.

WOLFE, A. B., The rationalization of production and reproduction, *Carver Essays*, 226–243. Cambridge: Harvard University Press, 1935.

LOESCH, A., Population cycles as a cause of business cycles, *Quarterly Journal of Economics*, LI (1936–37) 649–662.

ÅKERMAN, J., Bevölkerungswellen und Wechsellagen, *Schmollers Jahrbuch*, LXI (1937) Heft 1, 91–98.

LOESCH, A., Noch einmal: Bevölkerungswellen und Wechsellagen, *Schmollers Jahrbuch*, LXI (1937) Heft 4, 71–76.

ÅKERMAN, J., Abschliessende Äusserung, *Schmollers Jahrbuch*, LXI (1937) Heft 4, 76–83.

HOLDEN, T. S., America's capacity to expand, *Conference Board Business Survey*, supplement, July 23, 1938, pp. 4.

STRACHEY, J., J. M. Keynes and the falling rate of profit, *Modern Quarterly*, (1938).

WILLIAMS, J. H., The formation and use of capital, *Proceedings of the Academy of Political Science*, XVIII (1938–40) 57–68.

STAUDINGER, H., Stationary population—stagnant economy?, *Social Research*, VI (1939) 141–153.

LEDERER, E., Is the economic frontier closed?, *Social Research*, VI (1939) 153–162.

*HANSEN, A. H., Economic progress and declining population growth, *American Economic Review*, XXIX (1939) 1–15.

LANGE, O., Is the American economy contracting?, *American Economic Review*, XXIX (1939) 503–513.

KING, W. I., Are we suffering from economic maturity?, *Journal of Political Economy*, XLVII (1939) 609–622.

COLM, G., Comments on W. I. King: Are we suffering from economic maturity?, *Journal of Political Economy*, XLVIII (1940) 114–118.

REED, H. L., Economists on industrial stagnation, *Journal of Political Economy*, XLVIII (1940) 244–250.

HANSEN, A. H., Underlying problems confronting American business, *Conference Board Bulletin*, April 14, 1939, pp. 3.

HANSEN, A. H., Population problems, *American Economic Review*, XXX (1940, supplement) 383–398.

*ELLIS, H. S., Monetary policy and investment, *American Economic Review*, XXX (1940, supplement) 27–38.

Ellis, H. S., Inversiones y politica monetaria, *Revista de Economia*, IV (1941) 281–287.
Sweezy, A. R., Population growth and investment opportunity, *Quarterly Journal of Economics*, LV (1940–41) 64–79.
Hornedo, E., La desocupacion cronica, vista por Keynes, *El Trimestre Economico*, VII (1940) 116–138.
Hansen, A. H., Extensive expansion and population growth, *Journal of Political Economy*, XLVIII (1940) 583–585.
Fellner, W., The technological argument of the stagnation thesis, *Quarterly Journal of Economics*, LV (1940–41) 638–651.
Abramovitz, M., Savings and investment: profits vs. prosperity? *American Economic Review*, XXXII (1942, supplement) 53–88.
Tsiang, S. C., The effect of population growth on the general level of employment and activity, *Economica*, IX (1942) 325–332.
Franzsen, D. G., The secular stagnation thesis and the problem of economic stability, *South African Journal of Economics*, X (1942) 282–294.
Slichter, S. H., The conditions of expansion, *American Economic Review*, XXXII (1942) 1–21.
Rosen, M. M., Population growth, investment, and economic recovery, *American Economic Review*, XXXII (1942) 122–125.
Fellner, W., Monetary policies and hoarding in periods of stagnation, *Journal of Political Economy*, LI (1943) 191–205.
Hildebrand, G. H., Jr., Monopolization and the decline of investment opportunity, *American Economic Review*, XXXIII (1943) 591–601.

XI. INTERNATIONAL ASPECTS

Seligman, E. R. A., International problems in business stability, *The Stabilization of Business*, 283–323. New York: Macmillan, 1923.
Morgenstern, O., International vergleichende Konjunkturforschung, *Zeitschrift für die gesamte Staatswissenschaft*, (1927).
Mühlenfels, A., Internationale Konjunkturzusammenhänge, *Jahrbücher für Nationalökonomie und Statistik*, LXXV, new series (1929) 801–828.
Bullock, C. J. and Micoleau, H. L., Foreign trade and the business cycle, *Review of Economic Statistics*, XIII (1931) 138–159.
Woytinsky, W., International measures to create employment: a remedy for the depression, *International Labour Review*, XXV (1932) 1–22.
Hansen, A. H., International capital movements, *Stabilization of Employment*, 192–205. Bloomington, Indiana: Principia Press, 1933.
Fisher, I., Are booms and depressions transmitted internationally through monetary standards, *Bulletin de l' Institut International de Statistique*, XXVIII (1935) 1–29.
Mitchell, W. C., The international pattern of business cycles, *Bulletin de l' Institut International de Statistique*, XXVIII (1935) 397–403.
Robertson, D. H., Mr. Clark and the foreign trade multiplier, *Economic Journal*, XLIX (1939) 354–358. (Comment by C. Clark.)
Bryce, R. B., The effects on Canada of industrial fluctuations in the United States, *Canadian Journal of Economics and Political Science*, V (1939) 373–386.

Polak, J. J., The international propagation of business cycles, *Review of Economic Studies*, VI (1939) 79–99.
Salant, W. A., Foreign trade policy in the business cycle, *Public Policy*, II, 208–231. Cambridge, Mass.: Graduate School of Public Administration, 1941.
Metzler, L. A., Underemployment equilibrium in international trade, *Econometrica*, X (1942) 97–112.
Metzler, L. A., The transfer problem reconsidered, *Journal of Political Economy*, L (1942) 397–414.
Morgenstern, O., On the international spread of business cycles, *Journal of Political Economy*, LI (1943) 287–309.

XII. DISCUSSIONS OF BUSINESS-CYCLE CONTROL

Fiscal policy has been listed in IV-D, monetary policy in V-C and wage and price policy in VIII. Most other sections also include recommendations for control of business cycles. This section includes overall discussions of business-cycle control, planning and special remedies not elsewhere listed.

Mitchell, W. C., The problem of controlling business cycles, *The Stabilization of Business*, 1–54. New York: Macmillan, 1923.
Mitchell, W. C., The various kinds of remedies proposed, *Business Cycles and Unemployment*, 113–115. New York: McGraw-Hill, 1923.
Röpke, W., Socialism, planning, and the business cycle, *Journal of Political Economy*, XLIV (1936) 318–338.
Feiler, A., The Soviet Union and the business cycle, *Social Research*, III (1936) 282–303.
Viner, J., Business cycle theory—can depressions be tempered or avoided?, *Lectures in Current Economic Problems*, U. S. Department of Agriculture, Graduate School, November, 1936.
Robertson, D. H., The state and economic fluctuations, *Authority and the Individual* 37–47. Cambridge, Mass.: Harvard University Press, 1936. Reprinted as "The Snake and the Worm," in *Essays in Monetary Theory*, 104–113. London: King, 1940.
Robertson, D. H., The trade cycle—An academic view, *Lloyd's Bank Review* (1937). Reprinted in *Essays in Monetary Theory*, 122–132. London, King, 1940.
Ohlin, B., Can world prosperity be maintained?, *Index, Svenska Handelsbanken*, supplement, October, 1937. Pp. 17.
Ohlin, B., Can we control the boom?, *The Day and Hour Series*, No. 20, 3–11 Minneapolis: University of Minnesota Press, 1937.
Machlup, F., Can we control the boom?, *The Day and Hour Series*, No. 20, 11–18. Minneapolis: University of Minnesota Press, 1937.
Marget, A. W., Can we control the boom?, *The Day and Hour Series*, No. 20, 18–22. Minneapolis: University of Minnesota Press, 1937.
Hansen, A. H., Can we control the boom?, *The Day and Hour Series*, No. 20, 25–29. Minneapolis: University of Minnesota Press, 1937.
Mossé, R., L'économie planifiée et les crises, *Revue Economique Internationale*, 29e année I (1937) 323–343.

Sprague, O. M. W., Recovery problem in United States, *American Economic Review*, XXVIII (1938) 1–7.
Tinbergen, J., On the theory of business-cycle control, *Econometrica*, VI (1938) 22–39.
Krout, J. A. (Ed.), Essentials for sustained recovery, *Proceedings of the American Academy of Political Science*, XVIII (1938–39) 1–122.
Kähler, A., Business stabilization in theory and practice, *Social Research*, V (1938) 1–18.
Bratt, E. C., What can we do about depressions?, *Harvard Business Review*, XVI (1938) 273–280.
Putnam, G. E., What shall we do about depressions?, *Journal of Business of the University of Chicago*, XI (1938) 130–147.
Lederer, W., Aspects of the recovery problem, *Social Research*, V (1938) 237–242.
Arthur, H. B., Something business can do about depressions, *Journal of Accountancy*, LXVII (1939) 7–14.
Marschak, J., The task of economic stabilization, *Social Research*, VIII (1941) 361–372.
Langer, H. C., Jr., Maintaining full employment, *American Economic Review*, XXXIII (1943) 888–892.

INDEX OF AUTHORS
CITED IN THE BIBLIOGRAPHY

A

Abramovitz, M., 485
Adams, T. S., 474
Adarkar, B. P., 468, 473
Aftalion, A., 446
Åkerman, J., 448, 449, 484
Albrecht, G., 470
Alexander, S., 455
Altman, O. L., 465
Altschul, E., 449, 482
Ammon, A., 456
Amoroso, L., 449
Anderson, M. D., 451, 453, 459, 482
Anderson, O. N., 450
Andrews, P. W. S., 475
Angell, J. W., 448, 457, 468, 470, 471, 474, 475
Ansiaux, M., 457
Arackie, R., 470
Arthur, H. B., 478, 487

B

Baars, A., 446
Bachmann, H., 457
Bain, J. S., 478
Bangs, R. B., 460, 479
Barger, H., 453, 469
Barnett, P., 448
Bauer, P. T., 478
Beckhart, B. H., 464
Bellman, H., 483
Belz, M. H., 449
Bennion, E. G., 456
Bergson, A., 456
Bernstein, E. M., 480, 484

Berridge, W. A., 457
Bickerdike, C. F., 457, 460
Bielschowsky, G., 462
Bilimovic, A., 467
Bissell, R. M., Jr., 472, 480, 482
Boddy, F. M., 447
Bode, K., 447, 451, 452, 468
Boer, A., 470
Bordin, A., 449
Bouniatian, M., 447, 466, 467, 477
Bowen, I., 483
Bowley, A. L., 454
Bowley, M., 483
Braeutigam, H., 470
Bratt, E. C., 449, 465, 487
Braunthal, A., 483
Bresciani-Turroni, C., 463
Bretherton, R. F., 463
Brissenden, P. F., 453
Brock, F., 467, 470
Bronfenbrenner, M., 453, 471
Brown, A. J., 473
Brown, W. M., 480, 481
Bryce, R. B., 485
Buchanan, N. S., 476
Bullock, C. J., 485
Burchardt, F., 466
Burns, A. F., 483

C

Cadman, P. F., 464
Calkins, R. D., 476
Canning, J. B., 472
Caplan, B., 456, 478
Carell, E., 449
Carver, T. N., 460
Cassel, G., 454, 474

Catchings, W., 457
Chait, B., 450
Chamberlin, E., 457
Champernowne, D. G., 455
Chand, G., 456
Chenault, L. R., 476
Clark, C., 458
Clark, J. M., 446, 447, 448, 453, 455, 457, 458, 459, 460, 461
Clay, H., 446
Coase, R. H., 482
Colm, G., 463, 484
Commons, J. R., 453
Conklin, W. D., 483
Consiglio, V., 473
Coombs, H. C., 458, 464
Copeland, M. A., 453, 464, 465, 466
Cornfield, J., 460
Creedy, F., 449
Crum, W. L., 457
Currie, L., 475
Curtis, M., 452

D

Daly, M. C., 459
Daniels, G. W., 468
Datta, B., 473
Daugherty, C. R., 480
Davidson, D., 455
Delivanis, J., 456
Demaria, G., 449, 480
Dennison, H. S., 475
Derksen, J. B. D., 483
Dickinson, F. G., 462, 484
Dillard, D., 455, 456
Dirks, F. C., 458
Dobb, M., 447
Doblin, E., 482
Douglas, P. H., 457, 480
Dow, J. C. R., 476
Dowdell, E. G., 459
Downing, R. I., 473
D'Souza, V. L., 473
Duncan, A. J., 459
Dunlop, J. T., 479, 480
Durbin, E. F. M., 457

E

Ebersole, J. F., 475
Eccles, M. S., 475
Eddy, G. A., 469
Egle, W., 452, 469, 470
Einarsen, J., 478
Ellis, H. S., 448, 469, 472, 484, 485
Ellsworth, P. T., 472
England, M. T., 477
Epstein, L. A., 460
Epstein, R. C., 481
Espinosa, A. degli, 470
Ezekiel, M., 460, 482

F

Feiler, A., 486
Fellner, W., 452, 466, 473, 485
Fetter, F. A., 481
Ficek, K. F., 468
Firth, G. G., 450
Fisher, A. G. B., 477
Fisher, I., 467, 468, 485
Flamm, I. H., 477
Fleming, J. M., 472
Flood, M., 450
Foa, B., 446
Forbano, J., 450
Forstmann, A., 470
Foster, W. T., 457
Fowler, R. F., 482
Frank, L. K., 460
Frankel, H., 454
Frankel, S. H., 464
Franzsen, D. G., 485
Fraser, L. M., 467
Freund, G., 464
Friend, I., 460
Frisch, R., 449, 450, 460, 461
Fulcher, G. S., 460
Fulmer, J. L., 482

G

Galbraith, J. K., 464
Garcia-Mata, C., 482
Gayer, A. D., 463

INDEX OF AUTHORS

Ghosh, D., 473
Gibson, A. H., 450
Gilbert, D. W., 465
Gilbert, R. V., 451
Gilboy, E. W., 459
Glenday, R., 483
Goodwin, R. M., 474
Gordon, R. A., 464
Gras, N. S. B., 483
Graue, E., 482
Graziani, A., 472
Grebler, L., 483
Gregory, T. E., 477
Greidanus, T., 454

H

Haavelmo, T., 450, 475
Haberler, G., 447, 448, 452, 458, 466, 467, 468, 475
Hagen, E. E., 478, 481
Haig, R. M., 463
Haldane, J. B. S., 449
Halm, G., 471
Hamburger, L., 449
Hammarskjöld, D., 449
Haney, L. H., 447
Hansen, A. H., 447, 452, 454, 457, 461, 463, 467, 468, 475, 477, 479, 481, 482, 484, 485, 486
Hanson, A. C., 460
Haring, A., 461
Hardy, C. O., 452, 455, 465
Harrington, J. L., 462
Harris, S. E., 475, 479
Harrod, R. F., 456, 462, 466, 468, 479, 481
Hart, A. G., 461, 473, 476
Hawtrey, R. G., 448, 452, 455, 461, 462, 463, 466, 467, 468, 470, 471, 472, 479
Hayek, F. A., 451, 452, 467, 468, 469
Hayes, H. G., 478
Heflebower, R. B., 451
Heinig, K., 463
Henderson, H. D., 475
Herring, E. P., 463
Hicks, J. R., 454, 455, 464, 469, 471

Hicks, U. K., 464
Higgins, B., 464, 465, 473
Hildebrand, G. H., Jr., 485
Hill, M., 468
Hinshaw, R., 481
Hobson, J. A., 457
Holden, G. R., 459
Holden, T. S., 484
Holme, H., 449
Hornedo, E., 455, 485
Hubbard, J. C., 462
Humphrey, D. D., 457
Hutchison, T. W., 476

I

Isard, W., 483
Iyengar, S. K., 460

J

Jackson, D. C., 477
James, R. W., 449
Jastram, R. W., 458
Jéramec, P., 449
Jevons, H. S., 467, 482
Jevons, W. S., 482
Jöhr, W. A., 456

K

Kafka, A., 474
Kähler, A., 450, 464, 470, 477, 487
Kahn, R. F., 448, 458, 462
Kaldor, N., 456, 462, 470, 471, 476, 477, 479
Kalecki, M., 449, 473, 476, 477, 480
Kamitz, R., 470
Kazakevich, V. D., 463
Keesing, F. A. G., 450
Keirstead, B. S., 451, 478
Keynes, J. M., 450, 452, 454, 455, 458, 459, 466, 467, 468, 472, 473, 479
Kimball, D. S., 477
King, W. I., 480, 481, 484
Kirty, V. S. R., 471
Klein, L. R., 460

Knight, F. H., 448, 455
Kondratieff, N. D., 483
Koopmans, T., 450
Kreps, T. J., 457
Kroll, G., 470
Krout, J. A., 487
Kuznets, S. S., 448, 453, 461, 465, 466, 477

L

Lachmann, L. M., 470, 471, 472, 476, 478, 481
Landauer, C., 472
Lange, O., 452, 456, 460, 478, 484
Langer, H. C., Jr., 487
Langum, J. K., 447
Lautenbach, W., 472
Lavington, F., 475
Lederer, E., 447, 449, 451, 454, 477, 480, 481, 484
Lederer, W., 470, 487
Lehmann, F., 463
Leontief, W. W., 450, 454, 455
Lerner, A. P., 450, 452, 454, 456, 473, 479, 480
Leser, C. E. V., 474
Lindahl, E., 451
Loesch, A., 484
Lokanathan, P. S., 461, 475
Long, C. D., Jr., 454, 483
Loria, A., 467
Loucks, W. N., 462
Lugli, L., 477
Lusher, D. W., 474
Lutz, F. A., 452, 474
Lutz, H. L., 463

M

MacGibbon, D. A., 465
McCracken, H. L., 457, 477, 481
Macfie, A. L., 483
Machlup, F., 453, 459, 462, 466, 467, 471, 475, 486
Makower, H., 461, 473

Mantoux, E., 455
Marget, A. W., 486
Marjolin, R., 480, 483, 484
Marrack, P. R., 478
Marschak, J., 453, 459, 471, 473, 476, 487
Marx, D., Jr., 474
Mason, E. S., 481, 482
Maurette, F., 479
May, G. C., 454
Meade, J. E., 455, 475
Means, G. C., 454, 481, 482
Mehta, J. K., 447, 473
Melville, L. G., 473, 475, 476
Merwin, C. L., 455
Metzler, L. A., 460, 478, 486
Micoleau, H. L., 485
Mikesell, R. F., 480
Millikan, M. F., 472
Mills, F. C., 446
Mirkowich, N., 457, 477
Mises, L. von, 471
Mitchell, T. W., 476
Mitchell, W. C., 446, 468, 485, 486
Mitchell, W. F., 474
Mitnitzky, M., 458, 479
Monroe, A. E., 451
Morgenstern, O., 451, 485, 486
Morton, W. A., 473
Mosak, J. L., 480
Mossé, R., 486
Moulton, H. G., 474
Mühlenfels, A. von, 456, 485
Mukherjee, B., 448
Muniswamy, M. K., 448
Musgrave, R. A., 464
Myrdal, G., 464, 468

N

Nathan, R. R., 453
Neisser, H., 454, 457, 458, 461, 466, 468, 471, 478
Neuman, A. M., 471
Nicholson, J. L., 475
Nixon, R. A., 454
Nogaro, B., 462
Novogilov, V. V., 457

O

Ohlin, B., 447, 451, 452, 472, 486
O'Leary, J. J., 456
Oliver, H. M., Jr., 480
Olmsted, F. L., 457
Oparin, D. I., 449

P

Palander, I., 471
Pedersen, J., 468, 475
Perlo, V., 451
Peter, H., 448
Pigou, A. C., 454, 466, 479
Plimsoll, J., 456
Plumptre, A. F. W., 459, 475
Poduval, R. N., 462
Polak, J. J., 459, 486
Poole, K. E., 464
Pribram, K., 447
Putnam, G. E., 487

R

Radice, E. A., 450
Reddaway, W. B., 454, 456, 473
Reed, H. L., 469, 484
Reisch, R., 469
Reynaud, P. L., 469
Rhodes, E. C., 460
Richardson, J. H., 479
Richter-Altschaeffer, H., 463
Riggelman, J. R., 482
Riley, R. H., 472
Robbins, L., 467
Robertson, D. H., 446, 452, 455, 457, 461, 466, 467, 468, 469, 470, 471, 472, 474, 475, 485, 486
Robinson, J., 452, 453, 455, 464, 472
Rohtlieb, C., 446
Rombouts, A. L. G. M., 459
Röpke, W., 448, 486
Roos, C. F., 449, 461, 474
Rosa, R. V., 464
Rose, A., 484
Rosen, M. M., 485
Rosenstein-Rodan, P. N., 469

Rostow, W. W., 470
Rübner-Peterson, K., 468
Ruggles, R., 480
Runemark, 463

S

Salant, W. A., 486
Salant, W. S., 464, 473
Samuelson, P. A., 451, 454, 460, 462, 464, 465
Schüller, R., 455
Schumpeter, E. B., 464
Schumpeter, J. A., 446, 447
Schweiter, A., 448
de Scitovszky, T., 473, 482
Scott, H. R., 455
Seligman, E. R. A., 485
Shackle, G. L. S., 459, 468, 476
Shafer, J. E., 466
Shaffner, F. I., 482
Shaw, E. S., 458, 459, 472, 478
Shaw, H. F. R., 463
Shibata, K., 456
Signorelli, G., 479
Silberling, N. J., 461
Simmons, E. C., 468, 469
Simons, H. C., 465
Singer, H. W., 481
Slichter, S. H., 447, 448, 462, 463, 485
Slutzky, E., 450
Smith, D. T., 463, 464
Smith, H., 447, 456, 481
Smithies, A., 451, 458, 465, 471, 474 479
Snapper, F., 478
Snow, E. C., 450
Snyder, C., 469, 474
Somers, H. M., 448, 465, 473, 479
Souter, R. W., 448, 457
Spengler, J. J., 484
Spiethoff, A., 446, 465, 483
Sprague, O. M. W., 446, 474, 487
Sraffa, P., 467
Staehle, H., 458, 459
Stafford, J., 467, 469
Staudinger, H., 484
Stauffacher, C., 464

Steindl, J., 447
Stern, E. H., 465
Sternberg, F., 477
Stolper, W. F., 471
Stone, R., 459
Stone, W. M., 459
Strachey, J., 484
Strauss, F., 482
Strigl, R., 466
Sufrin, S. C., 481
Sumner, J. D., 462, 481
Swan, T. W., 474
Sweezy, A. R., 481, 485
Sweezy, P. M., 476, 478
Szeliski, V. v., 461, 474

T

Takata, Y., 472, 480
Tanaka, K., 470
Tappan, M., 466
Tarshis, L., 479, 480
Taussig, F. W., 453
Theiss, E., 449, 452
Thirlby, G. F., 473
Thomas, B., 469
Thomas, W., 469
Thorp, W. L., 453
Tinbergen, J., 449, 450, 460, 461, 487
Tintner, G., 451
Tippetts, C. S., 461
Tobin, J., 481
Tout, H., 452
Towle, H. L., 462
Tsiang, S. C., 485
Tucker, D. S., 474
Tucker, R. S., 460, 469

V

van der Valk, H. M. H. A., 471
de Vegh, I., 453
Vianelli, S., 450
Villard, H. H., 452, 453, 475
Vinci, F., 446
Viner, J., 455, 486
Vining, R., 455
Vito, F., 452

W

Wagemann, E., 447, 470
Walker, E. R., 452, 463, 480
Wallace, D. H., 481
Wallis, W. A., 460
Warburton, C., 453, 477
Ward, E. E., 455
Warming, J., 462
Wattles, G., 470
Weiss, H., 479
Welinder, C., 461
Wernette, J. P., 447
Wicksell, K., 466
Williams, J. H., 465, 466, 484
Willis, H. P., 474
Wilson, J. D., 447
Wilson, T., 471
Wisniewski, J., 446
Wolfe, A. B., 454, 484
Wolman, L., 463
Wooltson, A. P., 464
Woytinsky, W., 485
Wright, D., 453
Wright, D. McC., 461, 465

Y

Young, A. A., 466